Lecture Notes of the Institute for Computer Sciences, Social Informatics and Telecommunications Engineering   315

More information about this series at http://www.springer.com/series/8197

João L. Afonso · Vítor Monteiro ·
José Gabriel Pinto (Eds.)

Sustainable Energy for Smart Cities

First EAI International Conference, SESC 2019
Braga, Portugal, December 4–6, 2019
Proceedings

 Springer

Editors
João L. Afonso (ID)
Department of Industrial Electronics
University of Minho
Guimaraes, Portugal

Vítor Monteiro (ID)
Department of Industrial Electronics
University of Minho
Guimaraes, Portugal

José Gabriel Pinto (ID)
Department of Industrial Electronics
University of Minho
Guimaraes, Portugal

ISSN 1867-8211   ISSN 1867-822X (electronic)
Lecture Notes of the Institute for Computer Sciences, Social Informatics
and Telecommunications Engineering
ISBN 978-3-030-45693-1   ISBN 978-3-030-45694-8 (eBook)
https://doi.org/10.1007/978-3-030-45694-8

This Springer imprint is published by the registered company Springer Nature Switzerland AG
The registered company address is: Gewerbestrasse 11, 6330 Cham, Switzerland

Preface

We are pleased to present the proceedings of the first edition of the International Conference on Sustainable Energy for Smart Cities (SESC 2019), promoted by the European Alliance for Innovation (EAI) in collaboration with the University of Minho, Portugal. The SESC 2019 conference was part of the 5th annual Smart City 360° Summit Event, held in Braga, Portugal, and stimulated a multidisciplinary scientific meeting contributing answers to complex societal, technological, and economic problems of emergent Smart Cities. As a contributor to reducing the impact of climate change, while maintaining social prosperity as a priority, the broad themes of sustainable energy are vital to ensure a balance between economic growth and environmental sustainability in the scope of Smart Cities. All the topics relevant to these subjects were addressed during SESC 2019.

The SESC 2019 technical program consisted of 24 full papers at the main conference tracks, allowing for 5 oral presentation sessions within 2 days. All the accepted papers were subjected to a double-blind peer-review process, with a minimum of three reviews. Regarding the committees, it was a pleasure to work in collaboration with the excellent organizing team of the EAI, which was absolutely essential for the success of the SESC 2019 conference. In particular, we would like to express our gratitude to Kristina Lappyova and Karolina Marcinova for all the support they provided. We would like also to express our gratitude to all the members of the Technical Program Committee, who helped in the peer-review process of the technical papers, as well as ensured a high-quality technical program. Last but not least, we would like to thank the external reviewers from several areas of expertise and from numerous countries around the world.

The SESC 2019 conference provided a good scientific meeting for all researchers, developers, and practitioners to debate all scientific and technological features pertinent to the Smart City paradigm. With the success of the SESC 2019 conference, as confirmed by the contributions offered in this volume, we are expecting a successful and stimulating future series of SESC conferences.

February 2020

João L. Afonso
Vítor Monteiro
J. G. Pinto

Preface

Organization

Steering Committee

Imrich Chlamtac	University of Trento, Italy
João Luiz Afonso	University of Minho, Portugal
Vítor Monteiro	University of Minho, Portugal
J. G. Pinto	University of Minho, Portugal

Organizing Committee

General Chair

João Luiz Afonso	University of Minho, Portugal

General Co-chairs

Vítor Monteiro	University of Minho, Portugal
J. G. Pinto	University of Minho, Portugal

TPC Chair and Co-chair

Carlos Couto	University of Minho, Portugal
Edson H. Watanabe	Federal University of Rio de Janeiro, Brazil

Sponsorship and Exhibit Chair

João Aparício Fernandes	University of Minho, Portugal

Local Chair

Madalena Araújo	University of Minho, Portugal

Workshops Chair

M. J. Sepúlveda	University of Minho, Portugal

Publicity and Social Media Chair

Paula Ferreira	University of Minho, Portugal

Publications Chair

João C. Ferreira	ISCTE – University Institute of Lisbon, Portugal

Web Chair

Júlio S. Martins	University of Minho, Portugal

Technical Program Committee

João A. Peças Lopes	University of Porto, Portugal
Rune Hylsberg Jacobsen	Aarhus University, Denmark
Carlos Hengeler Antunes	University of Coimbra, Portugal
Adriano Carvalho	University of Porto, Portugal
Marcelo Cabral Cavalcanti	Federal University of Pernambuco, Brazil
João P. S. Catalão	University of Porto, Portugal
José A. Afonso	University of Minho, Portugal
António Pina Martins	University of Porto, Portugal
Hfaiedh Mechergui	University of Tunis, Tunisia
Stanimir Valtchev	NOVA University of Lisbon, Portugal
Rosaldo Rossetti	University of Porto, Portugal
Chunhua Liu	City University of Hong Kong, China
Luís Monteiro	Rio de Janeiro State University, Brazil
Marcin Jarnut	University of Zielona Gora, Poland
João P. P. Carmo	University of São Paulo, Brazil
Luís A. S. B. Martins	University of Minho, Portugal
Marcello Mezaroba	UDESC – Santa Catarina State University, Brazil
João Martins	NOVA University of Lisbon, Portugal
Stefani Carolline Leal de Freitas	Federal University of Tocantins, Brazil
Rui Melicio	University of Evora, Portugal
Paulo Pereirinha	University of Coimbra, Portugal
Orlando Soares	Instituto Politécnico de Bragança, Portugal
José L. Lima	Instituto Politécnico de Bragança, Portugal
Rana Mukherji	ICFAI University, India
Amira Haddouk	University of Tunis, Tunisia
Jelena Loncarski	Polytechnic University of Bari, Italy

Contents

Electric Mobility; Power Electronics; Intelligent Transportation Systems

The Electric Vehicle in Smart Homes: A Review and Future Perspectives . . .   3
    Vitor Monteiro, Jose A. Afonso, Joao C. Ferreira, Tiago J. C. Sousa,
    and Joao L. Afonso

STATCOM Evaluation in Electrified Railway Using V/V and Scott
Power Transformers   18
    Luis A. M. Barros, Mohamed Tanta, António P. Martins, João L. Afonso,
    and J. G. Pinto

Towards Smart Railways: A Charging Strategy for On-Board Energy
Storage Systems   33
    Vítor A. Morais, João L. Afonso, and António P. Martins

A Three-Phase Bidirectional Variable Speed Drive: An Experimental
Validation for a Three-Phase Induction Motor.   47
    Luis Machado, Tiago J. C. Sousa, Delfim Pedrosa, Vitor Monteiro,
    J. G. Pinto, and Joao L. Afonso

Unified Traction and Battery Charging Systems for Electric Vehicles:
A Sustainability Perspective   58
    Tiago J. C. Sousa, Luís Machado, Delfim Pedrosa, Vítor Monteiro,
    and João L. Afonso

Demand Response; Energy; Smart Homes

Smart Auditorium: Development and Analysis of a Power and Environment
Monitoring Platform   73
    Diogo Santos, Bruno Mataloto, João Carlos Ferreira, Vítor Monteiro,
    and João L. Afonso

Modeling and Thermal Energy Management in Smart Homes.   88
    Khaoula Khlifi, Amira Haddouk, Vitor Monteiro, Joao L. Afonso,
    and Hfaiedh Mechergui

Reverse Power Flow Detection Using Optimally Placed μPMUs
in a Distribution System.   98
    Philip Joshua P. Eloja, Niko Avel F. Jorda,
    and Michael Angelo A. Pedrasa

Comparison of Thermal Load Models for MILP-Based Demand
Response Planning   110
    Pedro L. Magalhães and Carlos Henggeler Antunes

Renewable Energy; Smart Grids; Energy and Environment

Development of a Compact and Low-Cost Weather Station
for Renewable Energy Applications.   127
    Jose A. Salgado, Miguel C. Feio, Luis M. Silva, Vitor Monteiro,
    Joao L. Afonso, and Jose A. Afonso

Modelling Interconnected Renewable Electricity Systems   140
    Paula Ferreira and Elizabete Pereira

Integrating PV+Battery Residential Microgrids in Distribution Networks:
How Is the Point of Common Coupling Agreed Upon?   150
    Iolanda Saviuc, Steven Van Passel, and Herbert Peremans

Economic Evaluation of PV Generation Curtailment and Voltage
Regulation Investment in Distribution Networks with High
PV Penetration   165
    Juan Miguel P. Bunagan, Ryan Christopher T. Gonzales,
    and Michael Angelo A. Pedrasa

Increasing Photovoltaic Self-consumption: An Approach with Game
Theory and Blockchain   180
    Matthieu Stephant, Dhaker Abbes, Kahina Hassam-Ouari,
    Antoine Labrunie, and Benoît Robyns

Internet of Things; Monitoring; Network Communications

Development of an Internet of Things System for Smart Home HVAC
Monitoring and Control   197
    Aníbal A. Alves, Vitor Monteiro, J. G. Pinto, Joao L. Afonso,
    and Jose A. Afonso

WaterAMI - Water Automated Metering Infrastructure Based on an Energy
Aware Wireless Mesh Network Communication Protocol   209
    Alexandra Vieira, Carlos Patrão, Tiago Gonçalves, Paulo Monteiro,
    Sylvain Marcelino, Edmundo Filipe, João Damasceno, Hélio Pereira,
    Catarina Sousa, Paulo Oliveira, and João Carvalho

A Versatile High Frequency Electricity Monitoring Framework for Our
Future Connected Home   221
    Benjamin Völker, Marc Pfeifer, Philipp M. Scholl, and Bernd Becker

Construction and Validation of a Low-Cost System for Indoor Air Quality
Measurements in Livestock Facilities. 232
    Leonardo Delgado, Manuel Feliciano, Laercio Frare, Leonardo Furst,
    Paulo Leitão, and Getúlio Igrejas

Acoustic Simultaneous Localization and Mapping Using
a Sensor-Rich Smartphone 246
    Xi Yu Song, Mei Wang, Hong-Bing Qiu, and Xueming Wei

Power Quality; Power Electronics

Advanced Load-Shift System: An Experimental Validation of the ac-dc
Converter as Shunt Active Power Filter 257
    Ana M. C. Rodrigues, Vítor Monteiro, Tiago J. C. Sousa, Tiago Alves,
    J. G. Pinto, and João L. Afonso

A Novel Single-Phase Shunt Active Power Filter Based
on a Current-Source Converter with Reduced Dc-Link. 269
    Catia F. Oliveira, Luis A. M. Barros, Joao L. Afonso, J. G. Pinto,
    Bruno Exposto, and Vitor Monteiro

Three-Phase Smart Energy Meter for Grid-Connected PV Installations. 281
    Manel Hlaili, Amira Haddouk, Khaoula Khlifi, Mechergui Hfaiedh,
    Vítor Monteiro, and João L. Afonso

Towards Green Data Centers 291
    Safae Bourhnane, Mohamed Riduan Abid, Rachid Lghoul,
    Khalid Zine-Dine, Najib Elkamoun, and Driss Benhaddou

Author Index 309

Electric Mobility; Power Electronics; Intelligent Transportation Systems

The Electric Vehicle in Smart Homes: A Review and Future Perspectives

Vitor Monteiro[1]([✉]), Jose A. Afonso[2], Joao C. Ferreira[3], Tiago J. C. Sousa[1], and Joao L. Afonso[1]

[1] ALGORITMI Research Centre, University of Minho, Guimaraes, Portugal
vmonteiro@dei.uminho.pt
[2] CMEMS-UMinho Center, University of Minho, Guimaraes, Portugal
[3] Instituto Universitário de Lisboa (ISCTE-IUL), 1649-026 Lisbon, Portugal

Abstract. The electric mobility dissemination is forcing the adoption of new technologies and operation paradigms, not only focusing on smart grids, but also on smart homes. In fact, the emerging technologies for smart homes are also altering the conventional grids toward smart grids. By combining the key pillars of electric mobility and smart homes, this paper characterizes the paradigms of the electric vehicle (EV) in smart homes, presenting a review about the state-of-the-art and establishing a relation with future perspectives. Since the smart home must be prepared to deal with the necessities of the EV, the analysis of both on-board and off-board battery charging systems are considered in the paper. Moreover, the inclusion of renewable energy sources, energy storage systems, and dc electrical appliances in smart homes towards sustainability is also considered in this paper, but framed in the perspective of an EV off-board battery charging system. As a pertinent contribution, this paper offers future perspectives for the EV in smart homes, including the possibility of ac, dc, and hybrid smart homes. Covering all of these aspects, exemplificative and key results are presented based on numerical simulations and experimental results obtained with a proof-of-concept prototype.

Keywords: Electric vehicle · Smart home · Smart grid · Renewable energy source · Energy storage systems · Power quality

1 Introduction

The electric mobility is increasing its involvement in the transportation sector, where diverse technologies are available as a contribution for sustainability [1, 2]. Among the different technologies, the most emblematic is the plug-in battery electric vehicle, simply designated as electric vehicle (EV) in the scope of this paper. Along the last decades, the number of commercially available EVs is increasing, all of them including on-board EV battery charging systems (EV-BCS) and some of them also including an interface for an off-board EV-BCS [3–6]. Nevertheless, in terms of the EV operation for battery charging, only the possibility of charging directly from the grid is available [7, 8]. This operation mode, common for both on-board and off-board EV-BCS, is denominated as

J. L. Afonso et al. (Eds.): SESC 2019, LNICST 315, pp. 3–17, 2020.
https://doi.org/10.1007/978-3-030-45694-8_1

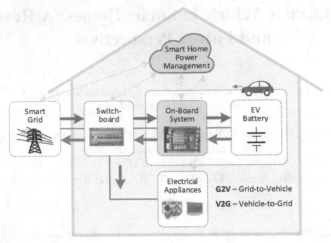

Fig. 1. On-board EV BCS integrated into a smart home, encompassing G2V and V2G (for the smart grid and/or for the smart home) modes.

grid-to-vehicle (G2V), since the power flows from the power grid to the EV. However, from the power grid viewpoint, the EV can be understood not only as an additional load for the system, but also as an energy storage. Therefore, in the perspective of the power grid, the inclusion of the EV will be even more relevant if it can be used as a flexible system capable of three key actions: (a) Absorbing controlled power from the power grid in the place where it is plugged-in; (b) Storing energy and transport it between different places in the power grid; (c) Injecting controlled power into the power grid in the place where it is plugged-in. Thus, alongside the G2V mode, arises the vehicle-to-grid (V2G) mode, where the power flows from the EV to the power grid [9–11]. The different possibilities of interaction between the EV and the power grid through the G2V/V2G modes are the main scope of several studies, as demonstrated in [12–14]. It is important to note that, in a progressive way, the V2G mode is being seen as a new reality; therefore, some manufacturers in the automotive sector have technological solutions for this possibility based on on-board EV-BCS.

Figure 1 illustrates an on-board EV-BCS integrated into a smart home, encompassing the G2V/V2G modes. This is the conventional approach, where the on-board EV-BCS can be controlled by the smart home power management. As illustrated, the EV can consume power from the grid or can deliver power for the smart home or for the smart grid (or even for both).

More recently, new operation paradigms are emerging, not only supported by the controllability of the G2V/V2G modes, as in this figure, but also in the perspective of power quality, for instance, during power outages, during the integration in islanded grids, or during compensation of reactive power [15]. Therefore, the main contributions of this paper are: (a) A more comprehensive review about the state-of-the-art operation modes and technologies for the EV in smart homes and smart grids; (b) A description about future perspectives of operation paradigms; (c) Validation based on numerical simulation and on a proof-of-concept prototype.

2 EV in Smart Homes and Smart Grids: Overview of Operation Modes and Technologies

In the introduction section, the possibility of the EV interacting with the power grid in bidirectional mode was introduced. The G2V/V2G modes are already a reality; however, only for exchanging active power between the EV and the power grid, targeting smart grids in a perspective of an on/off control, without neglecting the grid constraints. This contribution is extremely relevant, allowing to use the plugged-in EVs to overcome problems of efficiency and power quality [16–21]. In this perspective, with the permission and for the benefit of the EV driver (e.g., different tariffs for programs of G2V/V2G), the EV is controlled by an algorithm of power management of the smart grid, which defines the schedules for charging (G2V) and, eventually, for discharging (V2G) [22].

Given the flexibility of the EV to be plugged-in in the power grid (i.e., it can be plugged-in in different places), the controllability offered by the smart grid gains new complexity. Besides, as presented in [23, 24], the flexibility offered by the EV operation is also important in microgrid scenarios. In [25, 26], experimental considerations for the EV in G2V/V2G scenarios are presented, and, in a future perspective, innovative G2V/V2G interactions are offered in [27]. The flexibility offered by these modes is even more applicable as a compensation for the intermittence of the energy obtained from renewable energy sources (RES). In this perspective, the EV can be seen as an energy buffer for the power grid, consuming, storing, or delivering power as a function of the RES intermittence. A perspective of accommodating the EV charging, targeting the RES production as a contribution for mitigating greenhouse gases emissions, is accessible in [28]. Another perspective combining also the EV and RES, targeting to reduce costs and emissions, is considered in [29], and the G2V/V2G operation based on RES for a demand-side management is offered in [30]. Correlating the miscellaneous operation of the EV with RES arises new perspectives, not only for smart grids, but also for smart homes, since, as demonstrated in [31], smart homes have a boost effect for the future innovation in smart grids. In this scenario, technologies and foresights for assimilating the EV in smart homes are discussed in [32], while an optimized EV interaction is presented in [33] from the customer perspective. The aforementioned discussed technologies only involve an on-board EV-BCS in G2V/V2G modes. However, other possibilities of operation are emerging as viable solutions for the EV in smart homes, but prospecting smart grids.

The home-to-vehicle (H2V) is a particular mode of operation for the EV, when it is plugged-in at home. In fact, this mode is comparable to the G2V mode, since the power flows from the power grid to the EV (plugged-in in the home). The differentiating factor resides in the controllability of this mode, more convenient than the on/off G2V mode. With the H2V mode, the charging power can vary dynamically between zero and the maximum power, i.e., it can assume any value of power between the range of operating power.

Similar to the controlled G2V mode, in the H2V mode, the on-board EV-BCS can also be remotely controlled according to the set-points received by the algorithm of power management. This mode is particularly relevant for a smart home management in combination with controlled electrical appliances. In this context, the management algorithm can establish different levels of priority for the EV and for the electrical appliances in accordance with the user preferences (e.g., through a mobile app). From the EV point of view, three main situations can be highlighted: (a) The EV is defined to have maximum priority; therefore, it is charged with maximum power, while the electrical appliances can be turned-off to prevent the circuit breaker trip. This situation corresponds to a critical case when it is fundamental to charge the EV as fast as possible, and the operation of the other electrical appliances is not relevant. (b) The EV is defined to have priority over some specific electrical appliances; therefore, a maximum charging power is defined (e.g., corresponding to 75% of the full power) and the turn-on and turn-off of the electrical appliances is controlled in order to avoid the circuit breaker trip. In this case, the EV is charged with a fixed power and the electrical appliances are controlled avoiding exceeding the maximum power allowed by the circuit breaker. (c) The EV is defined to have minimum priority; therefore, the charging power is defined with a value that corresponds to the difference between the maximum (i.e., allowed by the circuit breaker) and the instantaneous power consumed by the electrical appliances. In this case, the power for the EV charging is directly influenced by the power consumption of the electrical appliances; therefore, the charging process will be extended for a longer period. As mentioned, the H2V is similar to the G2V mode; however, during the discharging process (V2G), the same strategy of controlling the EV operation as a function of the electrical appliances can also be implemented.

3 Future Perspectives of Operation Paradigms

In this section, future perspectives for the EV in smart homes are presented. Therefore, besides the operation paradigms described in the previous section (G2V/V2G/H2V), new challenges in terms of infrastructures are presented, involving the requirements of smart homes.

In Fig. 2 is presented a vision of an on-board EV-BCS in smart homes, contemplating the abovementioned operation modes and a new one related with power quality. As it can be seen, these operation modes are relevant and extremely useful for the smart home, also contributing for new energy policies for smart grids. As an example, in bidirectional mode, three distinct cases can be considered for the on-board EV-BCS: (a) Exchange power with the smart home, where the EV can provide power according to the requirements of the home management system; (b) Exchange power with the smart grid, where the EV can provide power according to the requirements of the smart grid; (c) Exchange power, at the same time, with the smart home and with the smart grid. This example is directly related with the G2V/V2G modes, however, a similar case is for the vehicle-for-grid (V4G) mode, where the on-board EV-BCS can compensate power quality problems, both in the smart home and in the smart grid. It is important to note that, in this case, the on-board EV-BCS can compensate almost all the current harmonics and the power factor of the smart home, but in the smart grid perspective, it only contributes to mitigate part of such problems. In this case, a new perspective for the smart grid arises, which is related with selective harmonic current compensation (where each EV can be controlled to produce a specific harmonic current) and controlled reactive power (where each EV is responsible to produce a small amount of reactive power to compensate a specific value of power factor in the smart grid). Despite the clear benefits of these operation modes for the smart home and for the smart grid, a key

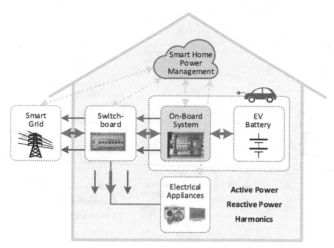

Fig. 2. On-board EV BCS integrated into a smart home, encompassing the G2V and V2G modes, as well as the possibility of compensating power quality problems related with harmonic currents and low power factor (producing reactive power for the smart home or for the smart grid).

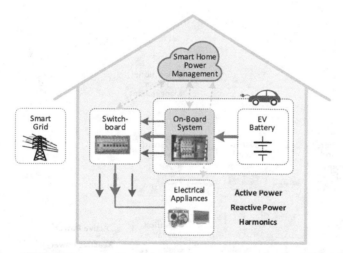

Fig. 3. On-board EV BCS integrated into a smart home, encompassing the G2V and V2G modes, as well as the possibility of compensating power quality problems related to power outages (where the EV is used as power supply with the EV batteries as energy source).

disadvantage is identified: these operation modes are only possible when the on-board EV-BCS is available, i.e., when the EV is parked at the smart home. On the other hand, if analyzed from the power grid point of view, in terms of exchanging power and in terms of controllability, a new key advantage is identified: these operation modes are available in the place where the EV is parked, i.e., the EV is a dynamic system in the smart grid, capable of operating in different modes according to the necessities.

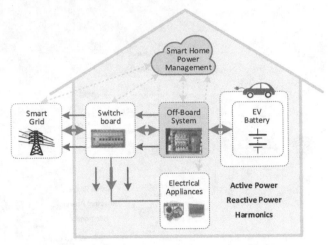

Fig. 4. Off-board EV BCS integrated into a smart home, with a parked EV, encompassing the G2V and V2G modes, as well as the possibility of compensating power quality problems related with harmonic currents and low power factor (producing reactive power for the smart home or for the smart grid).

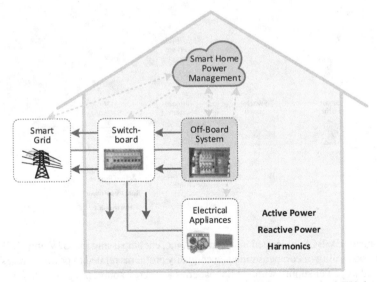

Fig. 5. Off-board EV BCS integrated into a smart home, without a parked EV, but with the possibility of compensating power quality problems related with harmonic currents and low power factor (producing reactive power for the smart home or for the smart grid).

Besides the compensation of power quality problems related with harmonic currents and reactive power, the on-board EV-BCS can also be used during power outages. In this case, illustrated in Fig. 3, the on-board EV-BCS provides power for the smart home, but the current waveform is defined by the electrical appliances (i.e., the on-board EV-BCS

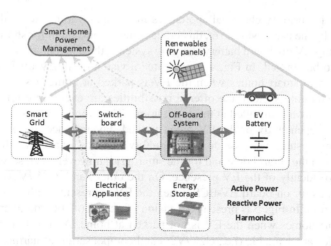

Fig. 6. Off-board EV BCS integrated into a hybrid ac and dc smart home, with a parked EV and interfacing a RES (solar photovoltaic panels) and an ESS (batteries) through a shared dc-link. The electrical appliances are directly connected to the ac grid. The G2V/V2G modes are contemplated, as well as the possibility of compensating power quality problems related with harmonic currents and low power factor (producing reactive power for the smart home or for the smart grid).

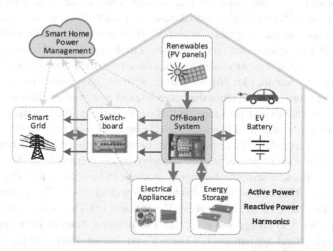

Fig. 7. Off-board EV BCS integrated into a dc smart home, with the EV parked and interfacing a RES (solar photovoltaic panels), an ESS (batteries), and electrical appliances through a shared dc-link. The G2V and V2G operation modes are contemplated, as well as the possibility of compensating power quality problems related with harmonic currents and low power factor (producing reactive power for the smart grid).

can operate with a non-sinusoidal current and low power factor). In this case, the energy source is the EV battery; therefore, it should be used with the convenience of the EV driver. For instance, in this mode, the on-board EV-BCS system can be used only to provide power for priority electrical appliances in the smart home (to be defined and reconfigurable by the user). Moreover, this mode is more convenient for short periods of time. Concerning EV off-board battery charging systems, the abovementioned operation modes can also be applied. In Fig. 4 is presented a vision of an EV off-board battery charging system in smart homes when the EV is parked at home. Using an EV off-board battery charging system, the offered possibilities are even more relevant, since the equipment is always installed at the smart home. Therefore, some operation modes are available independently of the EV being parked. For instance, the EV off-board battery charging system can provide power quality services, exactly as the on-board EV-BCS, for both the smart home and for the smart grid; however, such services can be provided independently of the EV presence. On the other hand, G2V/V2G modes are only available, as for on-board EV-BCS, when the EV is present (with the batteries as the energy source). In Fig. 5 is presented a vision of an EV off-board battery charging system in smart homes when the EV is not parked at home. As illustrated, the same operation modes are available (i.e., G2V/V2G and compensation of harmonic currents and power factor), except the possibility of using the EV battery as power supply during power outages. Nevertheless, the main future perspectives are related with EV off-board battery charging systems and, more precisely, with the possibility of interfacing other technologies for smart homes as RES or as auxiliary energy storage systems (ESS). Thus, the future perspectives are based on the possibility of using the same EV off-board battery charging system to interface, through a shared dc-link, a unidirectional dc-dc converter for RES and a bidirectional dc-dc converter for an auxiliary ESS [34]. It is important to note that the integration of an EV off-board battery charging system with this possibility is a complete solution to encompass in the smart home: electric mobility; RES; ESS. This situation is illustrated in Fig. 6, where the single interface with the power grid is a relevant key feature [35, 36]. Moreover, with the migration from ac grids to dc grids, this is even more relevant, since the necessities of power converters are drastically reduced (it is important to take into account that the majority of the electrical appliances at home level are composed by a front-end ac-dc converter used only to interface the ac grid). Therefore, a complete future perspective of integrating an EV off-board battery charging system in a smart home, mainly focusing in an internal dc grid, is illustrated in Fig. 7. Within this scenario, the following modes can be considered: (a) The power extracted from the RES can be injected into the power grid; (b) The power extracted from the RES can be used to charge the EV batteries; (c) The power extracted from the RES can be used to charge the ESS; (d) The power extracted from the RES can be used by the electrical appliances; (e) The EV can deliver power for the smart home (electrical appliances); (f) The EV can deliver power for the smart grid; (g) The power from the ESS can be delivered to the smart home (electrical appliances); (h) The power from the ESS can be delivered to the smart grid; (i) The power from the grid can be used to charge the EV; (j) The power from the grid can be used to charge the ESS; (k) The power from the grid can be delivered to the smart home (electrical appliances). It is important to note that the EV off-board battery charging system can include a dc-dc converter with a direct interface with the EV battery, or an additional dc-dc converter (within the on-board EV-BCS) can be used between the EV off-board battery charging system and the EV battery.

4 Computational and Experimental Validation

In this section, a comparison between three main cases was considered: (a) A conventional ac smart home with independent power converters for each technology (on-board EV-BCS, RES, ESS, dc electrical appliances, and ac electrical appliances); (b) A hybrid ac/dc smart home with an integrated off-board EV-BCS for a RES and for an ESS, sharing a common dc-link; (c) A dc smart home with an integrated off-board EV-BCS, based on a single interface with the grid and with dc-dc or dc-ac converters for interfacing each technology (on-board EV-BCS, RES, ESS, dc electrical appliances, and ac electrical appliances). These three cases, illustrated in Fig. 8, were simulated using a model developed in PSIM software, where: (a) as RES, a set of photovoltaic (PV) panels was considered; (b) as ESS, a set of lithium batteries was considered; (c) as dc electrical appliances (dcEA), resistive loads were considered; (d) as ac electrical appliances (acEA), an induction motor was considered. In terms of the power converters: (a) for the ac-dc, full-bridge three-level converters were considered; (b) for the dc-dc, unidirectional and bidirectional half-bridge two-level converters were considered; (c) for the dc-ac, full-bridge three-level converters were considered.

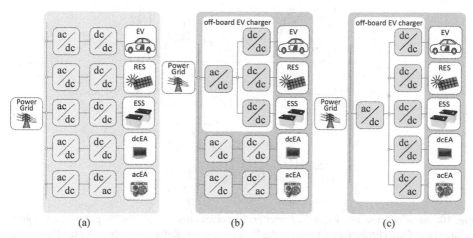

Fig. 8. Considered cases: (a) A conventional ac smart home with independent power converters for each technology; (b) A hybrid ac and dc smart home with an integrated EV off-board battery charging system for interfacing a RES and for an ESS, sharing a common dc-link; (c) A dc smart home with an integrated off-board EV BCS, based on a single interface with the grid and with dc-dc or dc-ac converters for interfacing each technology.

According to the different possibilities of operation modes (cf. Sect. 3 and Fig. 7), the estimated efficiency was determined. These operation modes are: (a) The power extracted from the RES can be injected into the power grid; (b) The power extracted from the RES can be used to charge the EV; (c) The power extracted from the RES can be used to charge the ESS; (d) The power extracted from the RES can be used by the electrical appliances; (e) The EV can deliver power for the smart home (electrical appliances); (f) The EV can deliver power for the smart grid; (g) The power from the

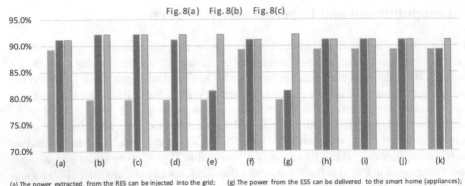

(a) The power extracted from the RES can be injected into the grid;
(b) The power extracted from the RES can be used to charge the EV;
(c) The power extracted from the RES can be used to charge the ESS;
(d) The power extracted from the RES can be used by the appliances;
(e) The EV can deliver power for the smart home (appliances);
(f) The EV can deliver power for the smart grid;

(g) The power from the ESS can be delivered to the smart home (appliances);
(h) The power from the ESS can be delivered to the smart grid;
(i) The power from the grid can be used to charge the EV;
(j) The power from the grid can be used to charge the ESS;
(k) The power from the grid can be delivered to the smart home (appliances).

Fig. 9. Estimated efficiency for each case under study and considering all the possibilities of operation modes.

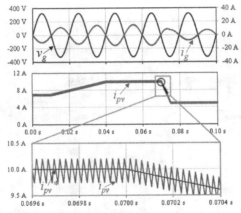

Fig. 10. Simulation results when the power grid receives energy from the PV panels: Power grid voltage (v_g); Grid current (i_g); Current in the PV panels (i_{pv}); Reference current for the PV panels (i_{pv}^*).

ESS can be delivered to the smart home (electrical appliances); (h) The power from the ESS can be delivered to the smart grid; (i) The power from the grid can be used to charge the EV; (j) The power from the grid can be used to charge the ESS; (k) The power from the grid can be delivered to the smart home (electrical appliances).

The estimated efficiency for each mode, considering the three cases under study, is presented in Fig. 9 (for the case #1 the ac-dc with an efficiency of 94% and for the dc-dc with an efficiency of 95%, for the case #2 the ac-dc with an efficiency of 95% and for the dc-dc with an efficiency of 96%, for the case #3 the ac-dc with an efficiency of 95% and for the dc-dc with an efficiency of 96%). As it can be seen, the most efficient solution is obtained with the dc smart home, where a single ac interface with the power

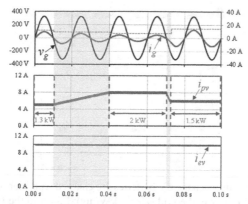

Fig. 11. Simulation results when the EV batteries are charged with energy from the power grid and from the PV panels: Power grid voltage (v_g); Grid current (i_g); Current in the PV panels (i_{pv}); Current in the EV batteries (i_{ev}).

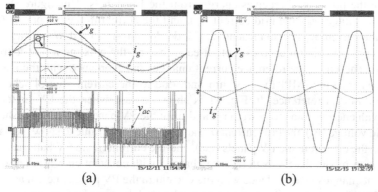

(a)   (b)

Fig. 12. Experimental results when the EV batteries are charged (a) or discharged (b): Power grid voltage (v_g: 100 V/div); Grid current (i_g: 10 A/div); Voltage produced by the ac-dc converter (v_{ac}: 200 V/div).

grid is considered. This is in accordance with the expectable, since the number of power stages is substantially reduced (as well as the required number of power converters). Taking into account that some operation modes are equal for some cases, very similar values of efficiency were obtained. On the other hand, the first case is the worst in terms of efficiency, since several power stages are required, where the power grid is always needed for each operation mode. Concerning the contributions of the future perspective of EV off-board battery charging systems for power quality, some results were obtained, mainly focusing in the ac-dc converter used to interface the power grid. Figure 10 shows the power grid voltage (v_g), the grid current (i_g), and the voltage of the ac-dc converter (v_{ac}) when the EV batteries are charged from the power grid. Besides, a comparative detail of the grid current (i_g) with its reference (i_g^*) is also presented. In this case, a power of 3.6 kW was considered. As expected, the grid current (i_g) is sinusoidal and

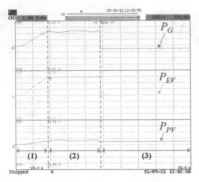

Fig. 13. Experimental results when the EV batteries are charged with energy from the power grid and from the PV panels: Power in the grid (P_G: 1 kW/div); Power in the EV (P_{EV}: 1 kW/div); Power in the PV panels (P_{PV}: 1 kW/div).

the converter operates with unitary power factor. On the other hand, Fig. 10 shows a case when the power grid receives energy from the PV panels. This figure shows the power grid voltage (v_g), the grid current (i_g), and the current in the PV panels (i_{pv}). A detail of the current i_{pv} is also presented. The dc-dc converter used to interface the PV panels is controlled in order to extract, at each instant, the maximum power from the PV panels. Therefore, the reference current changes in accordance with the maximum power point tracking (MPPT) algorithm and, due to the current control scheme, the current follows its reference. In Fig. 11 is shown a case when the EV batteries are charged with energy from the power grid and from the PV panels. This figure shows the power grid voltage (v_g), the grid current (i_g) and its maximum value to show the variation (in green), the current in the PV panels (i_{pv}), and the current in the EV batteries (i_{ev}). In this operation mode, the EV batteries are charged with constant current; therefore, the grid current changes in accordance with the current in the PV panels, i.e., in accordance with the MPPT algorithm. As it can be seen, the grid current changes without sudden variations, allowing to prevent power quality problems. A prototype was considered for experimental results. In Fig. 12(a) are presented some experimental results when the EV batteries are charged with energy from the power grid. As expected, the grid current (i_g) is sinusoidal (THD = 1.4%), even with a power grid voltage (v_g) with harmonic distortion (THD = 3.5%). With this strategy, the integrated topology does not contribute to the harmonic distortion of the power grid voltage. During the injection of power into the grid, Fig. 12(b) shows, in a time interval of 50 ms, the power grid voltage (v_g) and the grid current (i_g) for an operating power of 800 W. As expected, the grid current is in phase opposition with the power grid voltage, meaning that the power grid receives energy from the PV panels. In Fig. 13 is presented a case when the EV batteries are charged with energy from the power grid and from the PV panels. During this case are presented, the power in the grid (P_G), the power in the EV (P_{EV}) and the power in the PV panels (P_{PV}). As it can be seen, the power in the grid (P_G) is the difference between the power in the EV (P_{EV}) and the power in the PV panels (P_{PV}).

5 Conclusions

New technologies for smart homes and smart grids are emerging due to the electric mobility dissemination. Therefore, knowing the relevance of the electric vehicle (EV) as a contribution for smart homes, this paper deals with its characterization in smart homes, where an analysis of the state-of-the-art operation modes is used as a support for establishing a relation with the future perspectives. Aiming to establish an ample study, on-board and off-board battery charging systems are considered, as well as ac smart homes, dc smart homes, and hybrid smart homes. Moreover, the integration of ac and dc electrical appliances, renewable energy sources based on solar photovoltaic panels, and energy storage systems based on batteries is also considered in the perspective of future smart homes. The obtained results are based on three distinct cases of smart homes, where a study of energy efficiency was considered. With the obtained results, it was verified that the first case is the worst in terms of efficiency, since all the equipment are connected to the power grid, therefore, to exchange power between systems the power grid is always used. Some exemplificative experimental results are shown, obtained with a proof-of-concept prototype.

Acknowledgment. This work has been supported by FCT – Fundação para a Ciência e Tecnologia within the Project Scope: UID/CEC/00319/2019. This work has been supported by the FCT Project *newERA4GRIDs* PTDC/EEI-EEE/30283/2017, and by the FCT Project *DAIPESEV* PTDC/EEI-EEE/30382/2017. Tiago Sousa is supported by the doctoral scholarship SFRH/BD/134353/2017 granted by FCT.

References

1. Monteiro, V., Afonso, J.A., Ferreira, J.C., Afonso, J.L.: Vehicle electrification: new challenges and opportunities for smart grids. MDPI Energies **12**(1), 1–20 (2018)
2. Wencong, S., Rahimi-Eichi, H., Zeng, W., Chow, M.-Y.: A survey on the electrification of transportation in a smart grid environment. IEEE Trans. Ind. Electron. **8**(1), 1–10 (2012)
3. Leite, R., Afonso, J.L., Monteiro, V.: A novel multilevel bidirectional topology for on-board ev battery chargers in smart grids. MDPI Energies **11**(12), 1–21 (2018)
4. Monteiro, V., Ferreira, J.C., Nogueiras Meléndez, A.A., Afonso, J.L.: Model predictive control applied to an improved five-level bidirectional converter. IEEE Trans. Industr. Electron. **63**(9), 5879–5890 (2016)
5. Monteiro, V., Ferreira, J.C., Nogueiras Meléndez, A.A., Couto, C., Afonso, J.L.: Experimental validation of a novel architecture based on a dual-stage converter for off-board fast battery chargers of electric vehicles. IEEE Trans. Veh. Technol. **67**(2), 1000–1011 (2018)
6. Monteiro, V., Sousa, T.J.C., Leite, R., Aparício Fernandes, J.C., Couto, C., Afonso, J.L.: Comprehensive analysis and experimental validation of five-level converters for ev battery chargers framed in smart grids. In: YEF-ECE International Young Engineers Forum on Electrical and Computer Engineering, Almada, Portugal, May 2019
7. Gautam, D.S., Musavi, F., Edington, M., Eberle, W., Dunford, W.G.: An automotive onboard 3.3-kW battery charger for PHEV application. IEEE Trans. Veh. Technol. **61**(8), 3466–3474 (2012)
8. Chan, C.C., Bouscayrol, A., Chen, K.: Electric, hybrid, and fuel-cell vehicles: architectures and modeling. IEEE Trans. Veh. Technol. **59**(2), 589–598 (2010)

9. Ferreira, J.C., Monteiro, V., Afonso, J.L.: Vehicle-to-anything application (V2Anything App) for electric vehicles. IEEE Trans. Ind. Informat. **10**(3), 1927–1937 (2014)

10. Monteiro, V., Exposto, B., Ferreira, J.C., Afonso, J.L.: Improved vehicle-to-home (iV2H) operation mode: experimental analysis of the electric vehicle as off-line UPS. IEEE Trans. Smart Grid **8**(6), 2702–2711 (2017)

11. Multin, M., Allerding, F., Schmeck, H.: Integration of electric vehicles in smart homes - an ICT-based solution for V2G scenarios. In: IEEE ISGT PES Innovative Smart Grid Technologies, pp. 1–8, January 2012

12. Ota, Y., Taniguchi, H., Nakajima, T., Liyanage, K.M., Baba, J., Yokoyama, A.: Autonomous distributed V2G (Vehicle-to-Grid) satisfying scheduled charging. IEEE Trans. Smart Grids **3**(1), 559–564 (2012)

13. Yilmaz, M., Krein, P.T.: Review of the Impact of Vehicle-to-Grid Technologies on Distribution Systems and Utility Interfaces. IEEE Trans. Power Electron. **28**(12), 5673–5689 (2013)

14. Rong, Yu., Zhong, W., Xie, S., Yuen, C., Gjessing, S., Zhang, Y.: Balancing power demand through EV mobility in vehicle-to-grid mobile energy networks. IEEE Trans. Ind. Informat. **12**(1), 79–90 (2016)

15. Monteiro, V., Pinto, J.G., Afonso, J.L.: Operation modes for the electric vehicle in smart grids and smart homes: present and proposed modes. IEEE Trans. Veh. Tech. **65**(3), 1007–1020 (2016)

16. Peças Lopes, J.A., Soares, F., Rocha Almeida, P.M.: Integration of electric vehicles in the electric power systems. Proc. IEEE **99**(1), 168–183 (2011)

17. Richardson, P., Flynn, D., Keane, A.: Optimal charging of electric vehicles in low-voltage distribution systems. IEEE Trans. Power Syst. **27**(1), 268–279 (2012)

18. Leou, R.-C.: Optimal charging/discharging control for electric vehicles considering power system constraints and operation costs. IEEE Trans. Power Syst. **31**(3), 1854–1860 (2016)

19. Ferreira, J.C., Monteiro, V., Afonso, J.L.: Electric vehicle assistant based on driver profile. Int. J. Electr. Hybrid Veh. **6**(4), 335–349 (2014)

20. Monteiro, V., Nogueiras Meléndez, A.A., Couto, C., Afonso, J.L.: Model predictive current control of a proposed single-switch three-level active rectifier applied to EV battery chargers. In: IEEE IECON Industrial Electronics Conference, Florence, Italy, pp. 1365–1370, October 2016

21. Luo, A., Xu, Q., Ma, F., Chen, Y.: Overview of power quality analysis and control technology for the smart grid. J. Mod. Power Syst. Clean Energy **4**(1), 1–9 (2016). https://doi.org/10.1007/s40565-016-0185-8

22. Zhang, M., Chen, J.: The energy management and optimized operation of electric vehicles based on microgrid. IEEE Trans. Power Del. **29**(3), 1427–1435 (2014)

23. Gouveia, C., et al.: Experimental validation of smart distribution grids: development of a microgrid and electric mobility laboratory. Electr. Power Energy Syst. **78**, 765–775 (2016)

24. Galus, M.D., Vaya, M.G., Krause, T., Andersson, G.: The role of electric vehicles in smart grids. WIREs Energy Environ. **2**, 384–400 (2013)

25. Monteiro, V., Ferreira, J.C., Afonso, J.L.: Operation modes of battery chargers for electric vehicles in the future smart grids. In: Camarinha-Matos, L.M., Barrento, N.S., Mendonça, R. (eds.) DoCEIS 2014. IAICT, vol. 423, pp. 401–408. Springer, Heidelberg (2014). https://doi.org/10.1007/978-3-642-54734-8_44

26. Monteiro, V., Ferreira, J.C., Meléndez, A.A.N., Afonso, J.L.: Electric vehicles on-board battery charger for the future smart grids. In: Camarinha-Matos, L.M., Tomic, S., Graça, P. (eds.) DoCEIS 2013. IAICT, vol. 394, pp. 351–358. Springer, Heidelberg (2013). https://doi.org/10.1007/978-3-642-37291-9_38

27. Tuttle, D.P., Baldick, R.: The evolution of plug-in electric vehicle-grid interactions. IEEE Trans. Smart Grid **3**(1), 500–505 (2012)

28. Hernandez, J.E., Kreikebaum, F., Divan, D.: Flexible electric vehicle (EV) charging to meet renewable portfolio standard (RPS) mandates and minimize green house gas emissions. In: IEEE ECCE Energy Conversion Congress and Exposition, Atlanta, USA, pp. 4270–4277, September 2010
29. Saber, A.Y., Venayagamoorthy, G.K.: Plug-in vehicles and renewable energy sources for cost and emission reductions. IEEE Trans. Ind. Electron. **58**(4), 1229–1238 (2011)
30. Tushar, M.H.K., Zeineddine, A.W., Assi, C.: Demand-side management by regulating charging and discharging of the EV, ESS, and utilizing renewable energy. IEEE Trans. Ind. Informat. **14**(1), 117–126 (2018)
31. Gungor, V.C., et al.: Smart grid and smart homes - key players and pilot projects. IEEE Ind. Electron. Mag. **6**, 18–34 (2012)
32. Liu, C., Chau, K.T., Wu, D., Gao, S.: Opportunities and challenges of vehicle-to-home, vehicle-to-vehicle, and vehicle-to-grid technologies. Proc. IEEE **101**(11), 2409–2427 (2013)
33. Jin, C., Tang, J., Ghosh, P.: Optimizing electric vehicle charging: a customer's perspective. IEEE Trans. Veh. Technol. **62**(7), 2919–2927 (2013)
34. Monteiro, V., Sousa, T.J.C., Sepúlveda, M.J., Couto, C., Lima, A., Afonso, J.L.: A proposed bidirectional three level dc dc power converter for applications in smart grids: an experimental validation. In: IEEE SEST International Conference on Smart Energy Systems and Technologies, Porto, Portugal, September 2019
35. Monteiro, V., Pinto, J.G., Afonso, J.L.: Experimental validation of a three-port integrated topology to interface electric vehicles and renewables with the electrical grid. IEEE Trans. Industr. Inf. **14**(6), 2364–2374 (2018)
36. Monteiro, V., Sousa, T.J.C., Couto, C., Martins, J.S., Nogueiras Melendez, A.A., Afonso, J.L.: A novel multi-objective off-board EV charging station for smart homes. In: IEEE IECON Industrial Electronics Conference, Washington D.C., United States of America, pp. 1893–1988, October 2018

STATCOM Evaluation in Electrified Railway Using V/V and Scott Power Transformers

Luis A. M. Barros[1]($\boxtimes$), Mohamed Tanta[1], António P. Martins[2], João L. Afonso[1], and J. G. Pinto[1]

[1] Centro ALGORITMI, University of Minho, Guimaraes, Portugal
lbarros@dei.uminho.pt
[2] SYSTEC Research Center, University of Porto, Porto, Portugal

Abstract. Rail transport has always been one of the greatest economic boosters of several world nations, allowing the freight and passenger transport. In addition, it is the most secure and economic land transportation mode. From the energetic perspective, the electric locomotives emerge as one of the most efficient land transportation mode, as well as allow a more sustainable development. However, when an electric locomotive is connected to the three-phase power grid, power quality (PQ) deterioration arise, leading to the distortion and unbalance of the three-phase power grid currents and voltages which imply higher operational costs, raising economic and functional issues. In order to overcome the PQ deterioration phenomena, several solutions based power electronics technology have been studied and developed. These solutions vary in terms of control, functionality, implementation costs and complexity. One of the existing solutions is a static synchronous compensator (STATCOM), which compensates the three-phase currents imbalance and harmonics.

In this paper, a comprehensive review of the electrified railway systems is carried out, identifying the electric PQ phenomena which may appear due to the non-linear dynamic traction loads. Following this topic, a computational simulation of the STATCOM is presented, making analysis of its behavior regarding the PQ improvement in electrified railway systems. Two case studies are presented: (i) a traction power system fed with V/V power transformer; (ii) a traction power system fed with Scott power transformer.

Keywords: Scott power transformer · STATCOM · V/V power transformer

Nomenclature

i_{Comp_A}, i_{Comp_B}, i_{Comp_C}	Instantaneous current compensation value synthesized by STATCOM in phase A, phase B and phase C, respectively
$i_{Comp\_A}{}^*$, $i_{Comp\_B}{}^*$, $i_{Comp\_C}{}^*$	Instantaneous reference value for phase compensation current A, current B and current C, respectively
i_{Rail_A}, i_{Rail_B}, i_{Rail_C}	Instantaneous Phase A, Phase B and Phase C current of the power transformer primary windings (Scott or V/V)

J. L. Afonso et al. (Eds.): SESC 2019, LNICST 315, pp. 18–32, 2020.
https://doi.org/10.1007/978-3-030-45694-8_2

$i_{S\_A}, i_{S\_B}, i_{S\_C}$	Three-phase power grid instantaneous current value of phase A, phase B and phase C
i_x, i_y	Instantaneous current value of catenary x and catenary y
$v_{S\_A}, v_{S\_B}, v_{S\_C}$	Instantaneous voltage value of the phase A, phase B and phase C of the power grid
v_x, v_y	Instantaneous voltage value of catenary x and catenary y, at the secondary windings of the power transformer (Scott or V/V)

1   Introduction

Rail transport is seen as the safer and more economical comparing to other land transportation modes. In addition, it is recognized as one of the main catalysts for the economic growth of nations. For instance, in the European case, railway transportation mode made more than 26.9 billion (26 900 000 000) individual trips in 2012, providing employment to 2.3 million people, reflecting a gross value of 143 billion Euros, more than air and sea transport [1–3]. Despite the strong impact of the rail transport mode on the industrial revolution in the early 18th century, electrification of the railway lines had only occurred almost seventy years later.

In order to cover the railway transport demand, several incentive programs for the technological development of the electric rail system have been created and expanded, such as the AVE (*Alta Velocidad Espanhola*) train in Spain, FRECC (*Frecciarossa Trains*) in Italy, ICE (InterCity Express) in Germany and TGV (*Train à Grande Vitesse*) in France. These programs allowed a rail growth of 17% from 2001 to 2012 in Europe. However, the continuous proliferation of electric locomotives caused a significant power quality (PQ) deterioration in the three-phase electrical power grid.

Nowadays, PQ improvement in the three-phase power grid is one of the major concerns for scholars. The problems of PQ affect not only the costs, but also the functionality of some electronic equipment that are sensitive to power perturbation (e.g., medical and database equipment). In 2006 the Leonard Power Quality Initiative presented a study of PQ impact on the European industry, claiming that this type of problem caused losses of over € 150 billion [4]. Figure 1 presents some of PQ deterioration phenomena existing in the three-phase power grid, highlighting the electric railway system.

Historically, electric railway presents a complex system capable of consuming enormous amount of energy. On the other hand, PQ phenomena could have a more severe impact when several electric locomotives are fed by the same catenary overhead line. Thus, from the electrical point of view, it is necessary to first understand the equivalent electric model of the locomotive as presented in [5] and in Fig. 3. When an electric locomotive is connected into the catenary, different power quality phenomena arise, namely: system unbalance, harmonics, non-unitary power factor and transients. Some of these phenomena are represented in Fig. 2.

Voltage unbalance represented in Fig. 2(a), is the most problematic issue of the electric railway system. Considering the electric locomotives are single-phase loads, they cause currents and voltage unbalance in the three-phase power grid, injecting currents

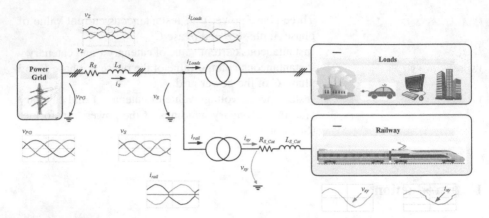

Fig. 1. Example of some PQ deterioration phenomena in the three-phase power grid.

with Negative Sequence Components (NSCs) [6–8]. In this context, and considering the electric model presented in [5], a higher number of locomotives fed by the same catenary line signifies a higher power consumption and consequently, the greater the voltage drop in the power transmission lines represented in Fig. 1.

Harmonic contents represented in Fig. 2(b), is the second most severe PQ phenomenon of electrical railway systems. The electric locomotives use AC/DC/AC power converters to adjust the electric quantities (voltage, current and/or frequency). The first stage of conversion being commonly constituted by an uncontrolled diode bridge rectifier [6]. In turn, there are already solutions that use semi-controlled semiconductors and fully-controlled semiconductors, using for this purpose thyristors, Gate-Turn-OFF

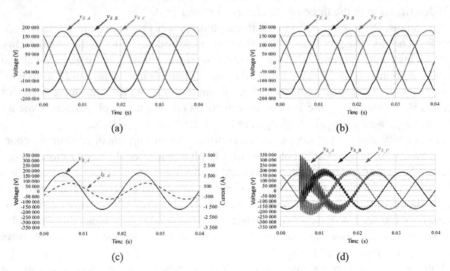

Fig. 2. Examples of power quality phenomena: (a) Voltage unbalance; (b) Voltage harmonics; (c) Low power factor; (d) Voltage transients.

(GTO), and IGBT [9]. Some phenomena associated with this system are identified in [6, 7]. Table 1 presents an example of harmonic components in three-phase electrical power grid, 220 kV line-to-line in this case.

A unitary value of the power factor indicates a low reactive power. In turn, the presence of high reactive power reflects a low power transmission system efficiency [7]. Despite the need for reactive power to the traction system, in the case of an inductive load, its value must be reduced to avoid higher energy losses. This ambiguity can be mitigated by the addition of Active Power Conditioners (APC) capable of locally produce the required reactive power, thus reducing the losses in the power grid and, consequently, the energy costs [6]. An example of a system with non-unitary power factor is represented in Fig. 2(c).

The catenary height, the pantograph wear and the transition between neutral sections (NSs) are some of the intermittent operations of electric locomotive. These momentary operations may originate transients phenomena being able to damage the rail equipment [6, 10], as shown in Fig. 2(d).

Considering the topics mentioned above, this paper presents a study of a STAT-COM compensating PQ phenomena in electrified railway systems powered by V/V and Scott power transformers. In this sense, this work is structured as follows: in Sect. 1, an introduction to the research topic is made, presenting the problems of PQ in the power grid. Section 2 presents the existing solutions to overcome the PQ phenomena, with a higher focusing on the STATCOM topology. Section 3 presents the STATCOM simulation results in V/V and Scott power transformers. Finally, Sect. 4 presents the final conclusion of the work.

Table 1. Example of harmonic components in three-phase electrical power grid (220 kV line-to-line voltage).

Harmonic order	Phase A		Phase B		Phase C	
	(V_{RMS})	$(°)$	(V_{RMS})	$(°)$	(V_{RMS})	$(°)$
1°	126 022	0	126 739	−120	126 960	−240
3°	552	95	828	−257	662	−266
5°	331	135	717.6	−272	828	−155
7°	4 582	44	3 974	−77	3 919	−195
9°	883	−147	828	−160	1 104	−149
11°	2 042	−134	2 153	−12	1987	−249
13°	110	29	110	−292	276	−226
15°	166	−20	221	−20	221	−20
THD%	2.88%		2.64%		2.60%	

2 Railway Power System

In the combustion-engine locomotives, clean and noiseless solutions are required when passing through residential areas and with fewer vibrations for better passenger comfort. The electric railway system presents a viable solution that meets these requirements. In addition, there is a range of potentialities that can be explored, such as the integration of renewable energies and the energy recovering from regenerative braking. However, this system is still complex and needs to be investigated. This chapter discusses the existing solutions to overcome the PQ phenomena.

2.1 Conventional Railway Power Systems

Considering that electric locomotives are single-phase loads, the installation of a single-phase power transformer in a substation would locally intensify the imbalance of the system [11]. For that reason, other power supply schemes are required to reduce the PQ deterioration. One of the most basic, inexpensive and old method is to alternate phase connections of the power transformers with the three-phase power grid, being commonly referred in the literature as a phase-shift method. This method allows to reduce the NSCs and, consequently, the system imbalance [7]. For a better performance, two power transformers, in different phases, are usually installed in a given substation, and the connections in the adjacent substations are alternated.

The catenary may be supplied by electrical power grid with different amplitudes and phases, it is necessary to create NS, in order to avoid short circuits between phases of the power grid. The NS can extend from several meters up to some kilometers [6, 10, 11]. This requirement prevents the power flow of the adjacent substations, as well as causing an interrupted operation when passing through the NS, causing a power perturbation [6, 12]. Despite being a simple solution, it presents high robustness due to the overloading capability and the long-life cycle of the power transformers. However, the currents imbalance is reduced but still remaining.

Considering the rapid growth of railway networks, it is necessary to implement solutions capable of meeting the new requirements. Thus, other configurations using three-phase power transformers are employed, namely the V/V, Scott, Le Blanc, Impedance Matching and Woodbridge power transformers [13]. An example of the integration of these first two solutions into the railway power system is shown in Fig. 3.

V/V power transformer is the most used in railway applications due to its simple construction and the high overloading capability. The transformation ratio is given by $N1{:}N2$, which represents the relation between the three-phase power grid voltages and the catenary voltage [13, 14]. These power transformers are dimensioned to provide all the power required by the single-phase traction loads (e.g., V/V transformer nominal power is comprised between 40 MVA and 60 MVA [1, 7]. On the other side, Scott power transformer is one of the emerging solutions for powering rail systems. Its versatility in balancing operating conditions on the three-phase power grid side contrasts with the complexity at construction level.

However, a dynamic compensation of these PQ phenomena is required, and the integration of APC is important in order to dynamically compensate the PQ phenomena.

From this perspective, APC in conjunction with three-phase transformers present an interesting solution to overcome the power quality phenomena.

2.2 Power Conditioners for Railway Power Systems

With the evolution of technology in power electronics and the introduction of semi-conductors, it was possible to present and implement more flexible solutions in the compensation of PQ phenomena. In this context, APCs present themselves as a very attractive solution to the requirements of the existing electrical system. Some examples of APC are the Static VAr Compensator (SVC), Static Synchronous Compensator (STATCOM), Static Frequency Converter (SFC) and Rail Power Conditioner (RPC). The functionality of the above-mentioned systems is presented with more detail in [6, 7, 10, 15]. STATCOM control algorithm is presented in [16] for the compensation of PQ phenomena. On the other hand, selective control algorithms to be implemented in RPC are presented in [5].

STATCOM will be the main contribution of this study, being shown in Fig. 3 an electric schematic of connection of the STATCOM with the railway power system. In addition, two topologies of power transformers (V/V and Scott) are considered in this study.

The STATCOM, shown in Fig. 3, takes an advantage of the technological evolution of the semiconductors, switching at higher frequencies when compared to the SVC, presenting in this way an attractive solution able to mitigate PQ phenomena related to harmonics, NSC and reactive power [7]. As can be seen, this solution is composed by a DC-bus followed by a voltage source DC-AC power converter. The STATCOM is connected between the three-phase power grid and the railway power system. In addition, the STATCOM is responsible for providing the harmonic contents required by the load, with the power grid being responsible for providing only the active power at the fundamental frequency component (50 Hz). However, because of the low voltage supported by the semiconductors, a power transformer is required to interface between

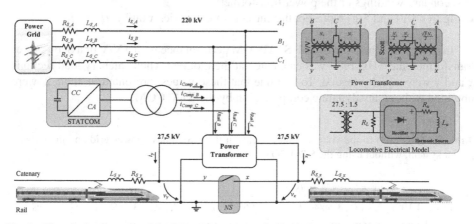

Fig. 3. Electrical schematic of the STATCOM connection with the railway power system powered by V/V or Scott transformers.

the STATCOM and the three-phase power grid, inflating the installation cost [6, 10, 15]. One solution would be the STATCOM based modular and multilevel converters in order to provide the necessary voltage.

3 Simulation Results

For simulation purposes a DC-AC converter with the control theory presented in [16] was implemented. The simulation results are shown in the Fig. 4 for a railway power system powered by a V/V power transformer, and the Fig. 5 shows the simulation results of the system powered by a Scott power transformer. Figure 6 shows an analysis of the THD when a balanced load condition is introduced, with only one locomotive in each catenary.

For the following explanation, it is necessary to refer that were considered different load scenarios, as presented in Figs. 4(a) and 5(a). At the time instant of 0.02 s an electric locomotive is added in the catenary x, and after the time instant of 0.04 s the locomotive is moved to the catenary y. At the time instant of 0.1 s another locomotive is added to the catenary x, thus leaving a locomotive in each catenary. Finally, at the time instant of 0.16 s there are two locomotives in the catenary y and only one in the catenary x, reflecting an unbalance load scenario. These load ratings over the time are reflected in current consumption i_x and i_y, in catenary x and catenary y, respectively. In this context:

- Figures 4(b) and 5(b) represents the three-phase power grid voltages, v_{S_A}, v_{S_B} and v_{S_C};
- Figures 4(c) and 5(c) represents the three-phase power grid currents i_{S_A}, i_{S_B}, i_{S_C};
- Figures 4(d) and 5(d) represents the currents of the power transformer primary windings i_{Rail_A}, i_{Rail_B}, i_{Rail_C};
- Figures 4(e) and 5(e) represents the compensation currents, i_{Comp_A}, i_{Comp_B}, i_{Comp_C}, synthesized by STATCOM;
- Figures 4(f) and 5(f) represents the voltage in the catenaries x and y, v_x and v_y, at the secondary windings of the power transformer;
- Figures 4(g) and 5(g) represent the currents of catenaries x and y, i_x and i_y.

In order to evaluate the overall STATCOM performance with a V/V or a Scott power transformer, the THD ratio was calculated at the moment when catenary load sections x and y were equally loaded. To highline that these values, presented in Table 2, were obtained without any dynamic compensation by the STATCOM.

Table 2. THD ratio in the voltages and currents at the three-phase power grid and the railway power system, without using the STATCOM.

	v_{S_A}	v_{S_B}	v_{S_C}	i_{S_A}	i_{S_B}	i_{S_C}	v_x	v_y	i_x	i_y
V/V	4.10%	3.76%	3.68%	10.6%	10.6%	6.64%	3.75%	3.58%	10.6%	10.6%
Scott	4.07%	3.76%	3.67%	12.7%	10.5%	11.7%	3.83%	3.58%	12.7%	10.6%

It is possible to verify the existence of harmonic contents in the voltages and currents, where the current waveforms contain a higher ratio of THD as presented in Table 2. In addition, almost similar THD ratios were obtained when using the V/V or the Scott power transformer. However, the main difference was in the THD of phase C current i_{S_C}. In general, V/V and Scott power transformers do not totally overcome the PQ phenomena and they cannot follow the dynamic behavior of the non-linear load. With this in mind, a dynamic compensator based on power electronics (e.g., STATCOM) is required.

3.1 Simulation Results of the Railway System Powered by V/V Power Transformer

In relation to the railway power system powered by V/V power transformer, represented in Fig. 4(b) and (f), it is possible to verify that v_{S_A}, $v_{\_B}$, v_{S_C}, v_x and v_y, present harmonic contents caused by non-linear loads connected to the three-phase power grid.

At the time instant of t = 0 s, the railway system is operating without load, being possible to see that v_x lags v_{S_A} by 30°. On the other hand, v_y is 60° behind in relation to v_x, that is, it lags the v_{S_A} by 90°. In addition, it is possible to verify that i_{S_A}, i_{S_B} and i_{S_C} are initially unbalanced and with high THD ratio. When the STATCOM is disabled, the currents i_{Rail_A}, i_{Rail_B} and i_{Rail_C}, are equal to the currents i_{S_A}, i_{S_B} and i_{S_C}. Considering this fact, when a locomotive is added in the catenary x, at the time instant of t = 0.02 s, can be verified the existence of i_x with THD ratio. This phenomenon is reflected in the waveforms of i_{Rail_A} and i_{Rail_C}. After the time instant of 0.04 s, the electric locomotive passes to the catenary y side, replicating the simulation results obtained in the previous instant, being at this time the phase B and C of the three-phase power grid responsible for the power supply. Consequently, the current i_{Rail_B} and i_{Rail_C} present high THD ratio. Additionally, in these two scenarios, it can be seen there is a three-phase high currents imbalance, when only one side of the catenary is loaded.

At the time instant of t = 0.10 s, there are two locomotives in the railway power system, one in the catenary x and the other in the catenary y, consuming a current i_x and i_y, respectively. These two currents are in phase with the respective voltages of the catenary side v_x and v_y. Once again, i_{Rail_A}, i_{Rail_B} and i_{Rail_C} reflect the non-sinusoidal waveform of the catenary side currents, being the current i_{Rail_A} in phase with i_x and i_{Rail_B} in phase with i_y. In addition, summing i_{Rail_A} with i_{Rail_B} results in i_{Rail_C}.

At the time instant of t = 0.16 s, a railway system powered by V/V power transformer, another unbalance scenario was considered in the simulation, in which, catenary x has one locomotive and catenary y has two locomotives. At this moment, it can be verified that the waveforms of i_x and i_y, as well as the currents i_{Rail_A}, i_{Rail_B} and i_{Rail_C}, are distorted. Considering the locomotives are equal and the catenary y has double the load value of catenary x, it can be seen that i_y has twice the amplitude of i_x. Consequently, i_{Rail_B} will also have twice the amplitude of i_{Rail_A}. Once again, by adding these two currents, results in i_{Rail_C}, having a 2.6 times greater amplitude than i_{Rail_A}.

At the moment that STATCOM is activated, at the time instant of t = 0.04 s, it is able to inject the harmonic contents and reactive power, required by the railway system, making i_{S_A}, $i_{\_B}$ and i_{S_C} sinusoidal and balanced. In fact, the railway system continues to consume a highly distorted current, i_{Rail_A}, i_{Rail_B} and i_{Rail_C}, as can be seen in

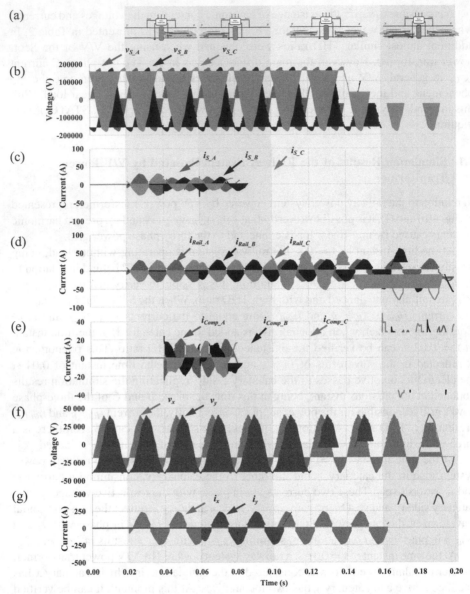

Fig. 4. Simulations results of the STATCOM compensating the power quality problems existing in the railway system powered by a V/V power transformer (a) Case scenarios with different number of locomotives in the catenaries; (b) Three-phase power grid voltages v_{S_A}, v_{S_B} and v_{S_C}; (c) Currents of the power grid i_{S_A}, i_{S_B}, i_{S_C}; (d) currents of the railway system measured at the power grid side, i_{Rail_A}, i_{Rail_B}, i_{Rail_C}; (e) Compensation currents, i_{Comp_A}, i_{Comp_B}, i_{Comp_C}; (f) Voltage in the catenaries, v_x and v_y; (g) Currents of catenaries, i_x and i_y.

Fig. 4(d). To highlight that, the STATCOM was able to dynamically overcome the PQ deterioration, independently of the load variations. At this moment, it is important to highlight that the compensation currents synthetized by the STATCOM have an average peak value of 20 A, reaching a twice of this when two locomotives are connected to the catenary y. By performing a detailed analysis of the obtained results and within the aim of calculating the harmonic distortion, it was possible to verify that the implemented system can reduce the THD of the currents i_{S_A}, $i_{\_B}$ and i_{S_C}, from the values presented in Table 2, for 2.99%, 2.75% and 2.89% respectively. This represent an average reduction of 67% in terms of the THD.

3.2 Simulation Results of the Railway System Powered by Scott Power Transformer

Similarly, to the V/V power transformer, computational simulations were used to study the operation principle of the Scott power transformer with more detail.

At the time instant of t = 0 s, the railway system is operating without load, being possible to see that v_x is in phase with v_{s_A}. On the other hand, v_y is 90° behind in relation to v_x, that is, it lags the v_{S_A} by 90°. In addition, it is possible to verify that i_{S_A}, i_{S_B} and i_{S_C} are initially unbalanced and with high THD ratio.

When the STATCOM is disabled, the currents i_{Rail_A}, i_{Rail_B} and i_{Rail_C}, are equal to the currents i_{S_A}, i_{S_B} and i_{S_C}. Considering this fact, when a locomotive is added in the catenary x, at the time instant of t = 0.02 s, can be verified the existence of i_x with THD ratio. However, it should be noted that on the power grid side, and unlike the V/V power transformer, all phases contribute to supply of the railway system. Although all the phases contribute to the feeding of the system, i_{Rail_A} is double than i_{Rail_B} and i_{Rail_C}.

After the time instant of 0.04 s, the electric locomotive passes to the catenary y side, creating a different phenomenon from the one existed in the previous instant. When only locomotives are found in the catenary y, the unbalance ratio is higher, existing only i_{Rail_B} and i_{Rail_C}.

At the time instant of t = 0.10 s, there are two locomotives in the railway power system, one in the catenary x and the other in the catenary y, consuming a current i_x and i_y, respectively. These two currents are in phase with the respective voltages of the catenary side v_x and v_y. Once again, i_{Rail_A}, i_{Rail_B} and i_{Rail_C} reflect the non-sinusoidal waveform of the catenary side currents, being i_x in phase with i_{Rail_A} and i_y 90° lags the current i_x. However, it should be noted that, in this case, the currents on the power grid side have similar amplitudes, making the system more balanced.

At the time instant of t = 0.16 s, a railway system powered by Scott power transformer, another unbalance scenario was considered in the simulation, in which, catenary x has one locomotive and catenary y has two locomotives. At this moment, it can be verified that the waveforms of i_x and i_y, as well as the currents i_{Rail_A}, i_{Rail_B} and i_{Rail_C}, are distorted. Considering the locomotives are equal and the catenary y has double the load value of catenary x, it can be seen that i_y has twice the amplitude of i_x. On other hand, i_{Rail_A} maintains its previous amplitude and i_{Rail_B} and i_{Rail_C} increase 1.8 times.

At the moment that STATCOM is activated, at the time instant of t = 0.04 s, it is able to inject the harmonic contents and reactive power, required by the railway

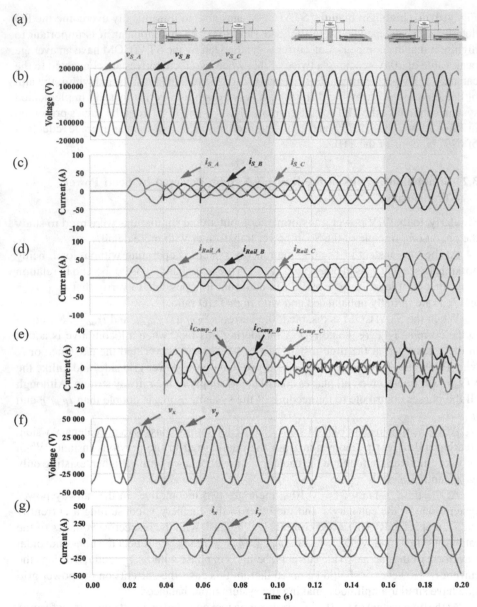

Fig. 5. Simulations results of the STATCOM compensating the power quality problems existing in the railway system powered by a Scott power transformer: (a) Case scenarios with different number of locomotives in the catenaries; (b) Three-phase power grid voltages v_{S_A}, v_{S_B} and v_{S_C}; (c) Currents of the power grid i_{S_A}, i_{S_B}, i_{S_C}; (d) Currents of the railway system measured at the power grid side, i_{Rail_A}, i_{Rail_B}, i_{Rail_C}; (e) Compensation currents, i_{Comp_A}, i_{Comp_B}, i_{Comp_C}; (f) Voltage in the catenaries, v_x and v_y; (g) Currents of catenaries, i_x and i_y.

system, making i_{S_A}, $i_{\_B}$ and i_{S_C} sinusoidal and balanced. In fact, the railway system continues to consume a highly distorted current, i_{Rail_A}, i_{Rail_B} and i_{Rail_C}, as can be seen in Fig. 5(d). To highlight that, the STATCOM was able to dynamically overcome the PQ deterioration, independently of the load variations. At this moment, the biggest differences between this system and the system powered by the V/V is when the railway system has a locomotive in each catenary. As an example, at the time instant between $t = 0.1$ s and $t = 0.16$ s, where STATCOM only has to synthesize a compensation current with 10 A of peak, which represents 1/2 of the value when the same system was to operate with the V/V power transformer. In general, it can be seen that the STATCOM needs to synthesize a much smaller compensation current when the railway system is powered by a Scott power transformer. Continuing with the analysis of the obtained result, it was verified that this system was able to reduce the THD% of the power grid currents, i_{S_A}, $i_{\_B}$ and i_{S_C}, from the values exposed in Table 2, to 2.99%, 2.75%, 2.89% respectively. This represent an average reduction of 75% in terms of the THD.

3.3   Evaluation Performance of the V/V and Scott Power Transformers

In order to evaluate the performance of the STATCOM with different power transformers, the harmonic contents in the three-phase power grid were analyzed. For that purpose, it was only considered the scenario when both of the catenary load. That is, section x and y were equally loaded with one locomotive for each section, as represented in the instant between $t = 0.10$ s and $t = 0.16$ s.

Initially and by considering a railway system powered by a V/V power transformer and without STATCOM, the harmonic spectrum of the i_{S_A}, i_{S_B} and i_{S_C} is shown in Fig. 6(a). At that case, the harmonic contents in i_{S_A} are similar to the ones of i_{S_B}, being i_{S_C} with a higher amplitude. On the contrary, i_{S_C} has a lower value in the 3rd, 9th and 15th harmonic contents. When a dynamic compensation is performed by the STATCOM, it is possible to see in Fig. 6(b) that the APF was able to reduce the harmonic contents in i_{S_A}, i_{S_B} and i_{S_C}. On the other hand, the harmonic contents in i_x and i_y before (Fig. 6(c)) and after (Fig. 6(d)) compensation, does not show a difference.

Considering now the railway power system is powered by a Scott power transformer, it is possible to see the harmonic spectrum of the i_{S_A}, i_{S_B} and i_{S_C} presented in Fig. 6(g). In this case, it can be verified that the harmonic contents of fundamental component is more uniform. When the STATCOM is activated, it is possible to reduce the remaining harmonic contents values, as can be seen in Fig. 6(h). In a similar way to previous system, the harmonic content in i_x and i_y before (Fig. 6(i)) and after (Fig. 6 (j)) compensation does not undergo any alteration in the railway system powered by a Scott.

In terms of voltage harmonics in the catenary, v_x and v_y, both topologies have a similar performance, as can be seen in Fig. 6(e) for the V/V power transformer and in Fig. 6(k) for the Scott power transformer. The major difference is regarding the suppression of the 5th order harmonic at the catenary section x when using the Scott power transformer. However, a dynamic compensation of these PQ phenomena is still required. In this context, STATCOM provides a dynamic compensation that allows to reduce the harmonic distortions in the catenary voltages, as can be seen in Fig. 6(f) for the railway power system powered by V/V power transformer and in Fig. 6(l) for the railway power system powered by Scott power transformer. However, and since the STATCOM

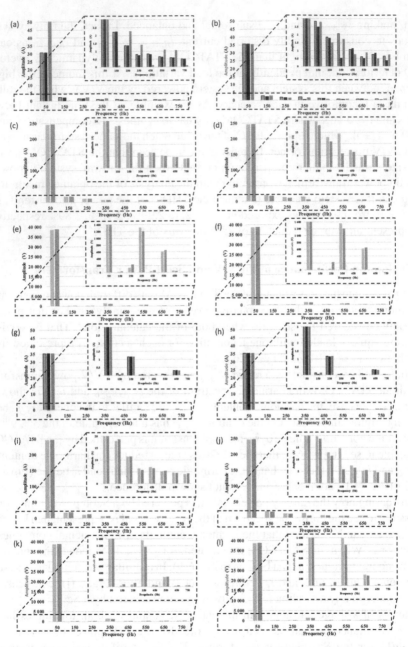

Fig. 6. Harmonic spectrum of the voltages and the currents in the three-phase power grid and in the catenary, before and after STATCOM compensation.

is upstream of the V/V and Scott power transformers, many of the harmonics created by the railway system are induced in the transformers. This causes them to overheat and increase energy losses.

4   Conclusions

This paper showed the importance of a Static Synchronous Compensator (STATCOM) in the electrified railway systems when using V/V or Scott power transformer. Simulation results of STATCOM for a dynamic compensation are presented. For this study it was considered different number of locomotives along the overhead catenary lines.

Results show that Scott power transformer is able to eliminate the 5th harmonic order only in the catenary x, as well as presenting a system more balanced. In fact, the compensation currents of the STATCOM for a railway system powered by a Scott power transformer are much lower than in a system powered by the V/V power transformer. Then, the STATCOM power ratings is lower when using the Scott power transformer. On the other hand, results show that V/V power transformer has less capability to overcome unbalance and harmonic distortions in the three-phase power grid. However, it has a simple structure and lower costs than the Scott power transformer.

The results show that the STATCOM is capable not only to balance the currents in the three-phase power grid, but also to reduce the harmonic contents by 67% and by 75% for a railway system powered by a V/V and Scott power transformer, respectively.

Acknowledgements. This work has been supported by FCT – Fundação para a Ciência e Tecnologia with-in the Project Scope: UID/CEC/00319/2019. This work has been supported by the FCT Project QUALITY4POWER PTDC/EEI-EEE/28813/2017, and by the FCT Project DAIPE-SEV PTDC/EEI-EEE/30382/2017. Mr. Luis A. M. Barros is supported by the doctoral scholarship PD/BD/143006/2018 granted by the Portuguese FCT foundation. Mr. Mohamed Tanta was supported by FCT PhD grant with a reference PD/BD/127815/2016.

References

1. Brenna, M., Foiadelli, F., Zaninelli, D.: Electrical Railway Transportation Systems, vol. 67. Wiley, Piscatawaya (2018). ISBN: 978-1-119-38680-3
2. Frey, S.: Railway Electrification. White Word Publications, Delhi (2012). ISBN:978-81-323-4395-0
3. Mazzino, N., Perez, X., Furio, N., et al.: Rail 2050 Vision: Rail-the Backbone of Europe's Mobility. ERRAC-The European Rail Research Advisory Council, Technical report (2017)
4. Targosz, R., Chapman, D.: Application note-cost of poor power quality, Leonardo Energy (2012)
5. Luo, A., Wu, C., Shen, J., Shuai, Z., Ma, F.: Railway static power conditioners for high-speed train traction power supply systems using three-phase V/V transformers. IEEE Trans. Power Electron. **26**(10), 2844–2856 (2011). https://doi.org/10.1109/TPEL.2011.2128888
6. Tanta, M., Monteiro, V., Sousa, T.J., Martins, A.P., Carvalho, A.S., Afonso, J.L.: Power quality phenomena in electrified railways: conventional and new trends in power quality improvement toward public power systems. In: Young Engineers Forum (YEF-ECE), 2018 International, pp. 25–30 (2018). https://doi.org/10.1109/YEF-ECE.2018.8368934
7. Lao, K.-W., Wong, M.-C., Dai, N.: Co-phase Traction Power Supply with Railway Hybrid Power Quality Conditioner. Springer, Singapore (2019). https://doi.org/10.1007/978-981-13-0438-5. ISBN: 978-981-13-0438-5

8. Lao, K.-W., Wong, M.-C., Dai, N., Lam, C.-S., Wang, L., Wong, C.-K.: Analysis of the effects of operation voltage range in flexible DC control on railway HPQC compensation capability in high-speed co-phase railway power. IEEE Trans. Power Electron. **33**(2), 1760–1774 (2018). https://doi.org/10.1109/TPEL.2017.2684427

9. Steimel, A.: Electric Traction - Motive Power and Energy Supply: Basics and Practical Experience. Oldenbourg Industrieverlag, Munich (2008). ISBN: 978-3-8356-3132-8

10. Gazafrudi, S.M.M., Langerudy, A.T., Fuchs, E.F., Al-Haddad, K.: Power quality issues in railway electrification: a comprehensive perspective. IEEE Trans. Industr. Electron. **62**(5), 3081–3090 (2015). https://doi.org/10.1109/TIE.2014.2386794

11. Abrahamsson, L., Schütte, T., Östlund, S.: Use of converters for feeding of AC railways for all frequencies. Energy. Sustain. Dev. **16**(3), 368–378 (2012). https://doi.org/10.1016/j.esd.2012.05.003

12. Lee, K.: Advances in the application of power electronics to railway traction. In: 2015 6th International Conference on Power Electronics Systems and Applications (PESA), pp. 1–4 (2015). https://doi.org/10.1109/pesa.2015.7398960

13. Serrano-Jiménez, D., Abrahamsson, L., Castaño-Solis, S., Sanz-Feito, J.: Electrical railway power supply systems: Current situation and future trends. Int. J. Electr. Power Energy Syst. **92**, 181–192 (2017). https://doi.org/10.1016/j.ijepes.2017.05.008

14. Xu, Q., et al.: Analysis and comparison of modular railway power conditioner for high-speed railway traction system. IEEE Trans. Power Electron. **32**(8), 6031–6048 (2017). https://doi.org/10.1109/TPEL.2016.2616721

15. Ma, F., et al.: A railway traction power conditioner using modular multilevel converter and its control strategy for high-speed railway system. IEEE Trans. Transp. Electrif. **2**(1), 96–109 (2016). https://doi.org/10.1109/TTE.2016.2515164

16. Pinto, J., Tanta, M., Monteiro, V.D.F., Barros, L.A., Afonso, J.L.: Active power conditioner based on a voltage source converter for harmonics and negative sequence components compensation in electrified railway systems. In: Proceedings of 7th Transport Research Arena TRA 2018 (2018). https://doi.org/10.5281/zenodo.1491309

Towards Smart Railways: A Charging Strategy for On-Board Energy Storage Systems

Vítor A. Morais[1]([✉]) [iD], João L. Afonso[2] [iD], and António P. Martins[1] [iD]

[1] Faculty of Engineering, Systec Research Center, University of Porto, Porto, Portugal
v.morais@fe.up
[2] Centro ALGORITMI, University of Minho, Guimaraes, Portugal

Abstract. The huge power requirements of future railway transportation systems require the usage of energy efficient strategies towards a more intelligent railway system. With the usage of on-board energy storage systems, it is possible to increase the energy efficiency of railways. In this paper, a top-level charging controller for the on-board energy storage system is proposed based on a fuzzy logic controller. As an optimization procedure to increase the energy efficiency of such charging controller, a genetic algorithm meta-heuristic is used to automatically tune the fuzzy rules weight. To validate the proposed controller, two sets of rules were defined, one considering only known rules and the other also considering all possible combinations of rules. As global results, the reduction of regenerated energy reached 30%, and the net energy consumption reduction is near 10%.

Keywords: Railway power systems · On-board energy storage systems · Fuzzy Logic Controllers · Genetic algorithms Meta-heuristics · Energy efficiency

1 Introduction

1.1 Railway Power Systems

The railway system has huge power requirements, which leads the railway operators to focus their efforts to increase the energy efficiency and reduce the energy consumption bill. Modern trains have the possibility to enhance the energy consumption with the usage of power electronic devices, which allows bi-directional power flow and, as ultimate goal, the regeneration of energy due to the braking [1].

From the data from [2], a typical train power consumption has the profile presented in Fig. 1a. In Fig. 1b, it is possible to see a huge dispersion of the power consumption/regeneration, which is caused mostly due to the needs to guarantee a given journey timetable, and in this case, stop in every passenger station. In certain countries, the regenerated energy cannot be "returned" to the Transmission/Distribution System Operator TSO/DSO. Therefore, in these cases, most of the regenerated energy must be burn in the train rheostatic system and the billed energy will not be the blue graph of Fig. 1c, being the red graph. According to [3], in the worst case where the headway between trains is big, almost all of the regenerated energy will not be absorbed by another train,

J. L. Afonso et al. (Eds.): SESC 2019, LNICST 315, pp. 33–46, 2020.
https://doi.org/10.1007/978-3-030-45694-8_3

and it will result in around 60% of energy losses. Therefore, there is a need to minimize the regenerated energy without affecting the train dynamic characteristics. One way to achieve this is with the use of railway Energy Storage Systems (ESS).

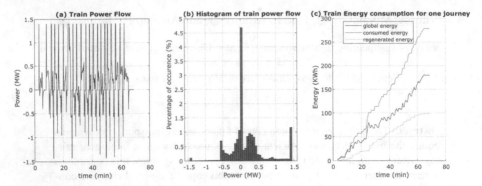

Fig. 1. Details on a train journey power flow: (a) Power consumption/regeneration for a sub-urban train journey; (b) Histogram of train power flow; (c) Train energy consumption.

1.2 Railway Energy Storage Systems

Ideally, the most effective way to increase the global efficiency of traction systems is to use the regenerative braking energy to feed another train in traction mode (and absorbing the totality of the braking energy) [4]. However, this solution requires an excellent synchronism and a small distance between "in traction mode" and "in braking mode" trains. Therefore, in the occurrence of small delays, the regenerative energy cannot be used by another train and can be burned in the train rheostatic system or, if possible, can be returned to the DSO [5].

The usage of regenerative braking energy to charge Energy Storage Systems (ESSs) is one effective way to increase the global efficiency of traction systems [1, 5]. However, due to the high cost of ESSs, alternatives such as reversible Traction Power Substation (TPS) result in a better cost-effective solution [6].

Nevertheless, on-board ESS are the only solution for a catenary-free system [7]. In addition, to the better knowledge of the authors, wayside ESS study only considers the acquisition cost of an infrastructure having the totality of ESS, without considering the possibility of not including batteries (or other storage technology).

In the future, it is possible and needed to have Electric Vehicles (EVs) charging stations located at passenger stations. Therefore, in theory, it is possible to connect the charging stations to the catenary and increase the degree of freedom in the EVs charging strategy. This way, having this possibility, the wayside ESS can now be a cost-effective solution, having multiple charging objectives.

In this paper, an ESS multiple-objective charging strategy is proposed based on Fuzzy Logic Controllers (FLC). This charging controller considers on-board ESS, as a case study, but it can be extended to wayside ESS.

1.3 Optimal Charging Strategy of ESS

The management of ESS charging system is a research topic in smart grids. Usually, the optimal charging strategy is based on scheduling of charging profiles, using the knowledge of a predicted load profile [8].

However, due to the high-variation of the railway energy consumption resulting in a difficult task for energy consumption prediction, the scheduling of the charging profile is not an option. In this work, optimal charging strategies without scheduling are explored to be implemented in a ESS system, where the charging controller decides in real-time the energy flow.

A multi-objective system using a FLC for energy management, as proposed in [9] and extended in [10] and in [11], is a real-time charging strategy, with the rule weights and membership function parameters being the search space of the optimization algorithm.

Since the performance of a fuzzy system is more dependent on rule weights rather than membership function parameters [12], in this work the MF parameters are fixed and were defined upon the authors knowledge of the system. The search space of the Genetic Algorithm is, therefore, the adjustment of the rule weights.

Based on [10], there are two possible objectives for the charging strategy: (i) the financial objective function, purely on the cost of buying/selling energy in different times; and (ii) the battery stress, to represent the physical degradation of the battery. In this work, the financial objective is related to the energy consumption/regenerated, whereas the battery stress is purely on the di/dt of the ESS charging converter (later called converter temperature).

1.4 Structure of the Paper

This paper is structured in five sections. The first section covers the need for ESS. The second section presents the proposed charging optimization strategy, based on FLC. Later in third section, is shown the meta-heuristic strategy to optimize the behavior of FLC, by adjusting the fuzzy rule weights. The case study to illustrate this optimization strategy is presented in Sect. 4, as well as a discussion. In Sect. 5, the conclusions of this work are presented.

2 Proposed Fuzzy-Based Charging Optimization Strategy

In this section, the proposed fuzzy-based charging strategy is presented. The main core of the energy storage control system is a Mamdani Fuzzy Logic Controller (FLC), proposed in [13], having the structure illustrated in the Fig. 2a.

The FLC has multiple inputs (the train power flow value, the ESS SOC and a variable representing the temperature of the ESS) and one output (the set point for the ESS power flow). In Fig. 2b, c, d, e is illustrated the FLC Membership Functions (MF) for the input and output variables.

The first input is the power consumption of the train and it can be categorized as consumption (if the train is in the traction mode and the energy flows from the catenary to the wheels) or categorized as regeneration (if the train is in braking mode and the

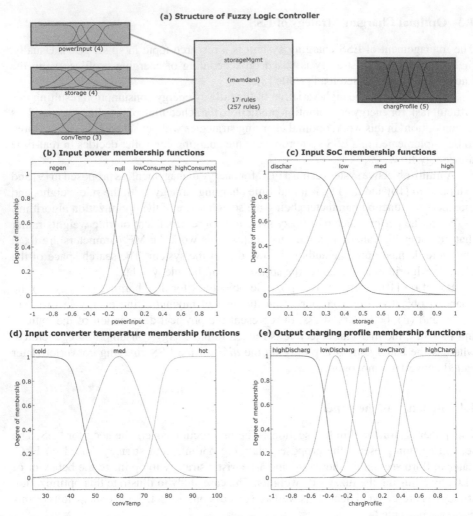

Fig. 2. Implemented Fuzzy Logic Controller (FLC): (a) Structure of controller; (b) Membership Function (MF) of train power consumption input variable; (c) MF of ESS state of charge input variable; (d) MF of converter temperature input variable; (e) MF of charging percentage of the ESS output variable.

regenerated energy from the motors flows back to the catenary). The second input is the on-board ESS State of Charging (SoC) and corresponds to 100% if the system is fully charged or 0% if the system is fully discharged (considering those values the absolute maximum/minimum voltage values, and considering that reaching SoC values above 80% and below 20% should be avoided by the controller). To promote a reasonable usage of the ESS, a third variable is proposed. This variable mimics the semiconductors heating and the battery state of health, and it is a quadratic function of the charging power.

On the FLC output, a variable is proposed to define the ESS charging profile, in an absolute per-unit (p.u.) value. In this work, a hypothetical ESS hardware was arbitrarily chosen. Specifically, the power capabilities of the ESS was set to have 350 kW of charging/discharging maximum power (25% of the train power consumption) and 35 kWh of stored energy (6 min to fully charge the ESS when the charging profile is constant and 1 p.u.).

In this work, the FLC is tested with a test bed in which a near 70-min train journey is considered. The train power consumption presented in Fig. 1a is the independent input of the test bed. The SoC and the converter temperature depends on the previous result of the FLC output variable. Iteratively for each time instant, the stored energy and the ESS temperature variables are calculated from previous values, as follows:

```
REPEAT
      CharProfile[n] = FUZZY(power[n-1], SoC[n-1], ConvTemp[n-1])
      SOC[n] = SOC[n-1] + K_ESS×CharProfile[n]
      ConvTemp[n] = ConvTemp[n-1] + K_temp×(power[n-1])²- K_dissip
UNTIL all time instants [n] are calculated
Compute objective function metrics
```

The K_{ESS} constant defines the storage capacity and the charger design limitations. The K_{temp} and the K_{dissip} represents the temperature increase of the ESS, as quadratic function of the power, and a dissipation factor to promote the temperature reduction. In this work, no effort was made to use a specific ESS system and these values were arbitrary chosen.

To ensure the physical limits, the input variables are limited by its admissible maximum and minimum values and, in the case of the occurrence of over-temperature, over-charge or over-discharge events, the charging profile value is changed to avoid those events.

In this work, two possible sets of rules were defined:

(a)   17 rules were defined, considering the expected behavior of the system, as shown in the Table 1.
(b)   17 + 240 rules, where the first 17 rules were defined based on the expected behavior of the system and the remaining rules corresponds to all possible combinations of rules.

Regarding the fuzzy rule weights, in Sect. 3 of this work is presented an iterative approach to adapt the weights, towards the fulfillment of optimization objectives. As initial values, in the sets of rules presented in (a), all the weights were chosen to be 0.5. In the second set of rules, the "known rules" have an initial value of 0.9 and the remaining 240 rules starts with a weight of 0.1.

Table 1. List of fuzzy rules with the initial weights.

	Rule	Weight
1	If (powerInput is regen) then (chargProfile is highCharg)	0.5
2	If (powerInput is highConsumpt) then (chargProfile is highDischarg)	0.5
3	If (storage is high) then (chargProfile is highDischarg)	0.5
4	If (storage is dischar) then (chargProfile is highCharg)	0.5
5	If (powerInput is null) and (storage is high) then (chargProfile is lowDischarg)	0.5
6	If (powerInput is null) and (storage is med) then (chargProfile is null)	0.5
7	If (powerInput is null) and (storage is low) then (chargProfile is lowCharg)	0.5
8	If (powerInput is lowConsumpt) and (storage is high) then (chargProfile is null)	0.5
9	If (powerInput is lowConsumpt) and (storage is med) then (chargProfile is null)	0.5
10	If (powerInput is lowConsumpt) and (storage is low) then (chargProfile is lowCharg)	0.5
11	If (convTemp is hot) then (chargProfile is null)	0.5
12	If (powerInput is regen) and (convTemp is cold) then (chargProfile is highCharg)	0.5
13	If (powerInput is highConsumpt) and (convTemp is cold) then (chargProfile is highDischarg)	0.5
14	If (storage is high) and (convTemp is cold) then (chargProfile is highDischarg)	0.5
15	If (storage is dischar) and (convTemp is cold) then (chargProfile is lowCharg)	0.5
16	If (convTemp is med) then (chargProfile is lowDischarg)	0.5
17	If (convTemp is med) then (chargProfile is lowCharg)	0.5

3 Meta-heuristic Rule Weight Adjustment

As a way to define the fuzzy rules, the human knowledge is a good starting point to obtain a charging strategy for the FLC. In this section is proposed a genetic algorithm (GA) as a meta-heuristic to define the weights of the fuzzy rules, having an objective function as the optimization criteria.

Therefore, each individual of the GA population will have an array of 17 weights (genes) and a value for its objective function that will be obtained in the FLC for a given test bed. The crossover process considers the best individuals and, a new individual is generated having part of the genetic material from the parent individuals. The mutation considers the random increase/decrease of certain genes. If a gene from previous generation has changed, in the mutation, it has higher probability to increase/decrease accordingly. The algorithm for the implemented GA is presented as follows:

```
START
Generate the initial population
RUN test bed for all individuals
REPEAT
```

```
      Selection
      Crossover
      Mutation
      RUN test bed for all individuals
   UNTIL population has converged OR max generations
   STOP
```

The initial population is generated from five individuals having the weights defined from the human knowledge in the previous section. In addition, 30 new individuals were generated as mutations from those individuals. Then the FLC is tested for all the new rule weights, and the objective function is calculated from the results of the FLC test bed.

In this work, the objective function values were calculated based on four metrics:

(a) The RMS value of the graph of converter temperature;
(b) The RMS value of the resultant charging profile;
(c) The final value of the ESS SoC;
(d) The final value of the regenerated energy.

It is considered, as optimization criteria objective, to avoid peak values in the first two metrics (avoiding high di/dt on the ESS). In the remaining metrics, the optimization objective is to minimize the difference between final and initial values of SoC and to minimize the difference between the regenerated energy without and with the ESS.

In the design of the global objective function metric, all four metrics are considered, having arbitrarily defined weights to better fulfil the expected behavior of the system (in terms of convergence speed, stability of the GA, intuition, etc.). Therefore, to obtain the results presented in Sect. 4, the converter temperature and charging profile metrics, has receive small weights, and the SoC variation and global energy reduction has received a higher weight (with the global energy reduction tuned to rapidly reduce this metric).

4 Results

In this section, two sets of rules were considered to illustrate the evolution of the optimization algorithm. Later, the two cases results are compared and a discussion is presented.

4.1 Preliminary Knowledge of System Behavior

The following results present the testbed evaluated with the 17 known rules. For different generations and the same independent power consumption input (Fig. 3a), in Fig. 3b is illustrated the evolution of stored energy; in Fig. 3c is presented the evolution of the charging profile and in Fig. 3d is visible the evolution of the converter temperature.

At each generation, 40 new individuals are generated from previous population, where 25 of the individuals results of crossing the genetic material (the weight of FLC

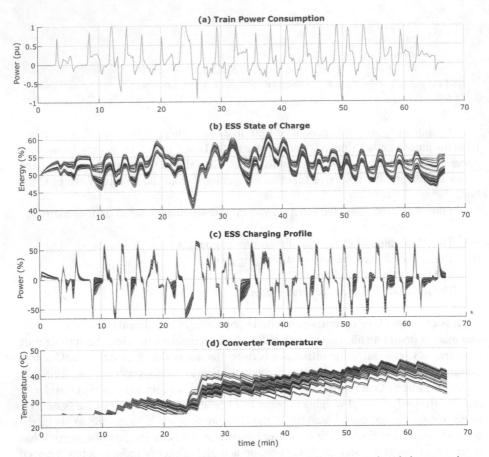

Fig. 3. Evolution of testbed variables, in order of time, for different meta-heuristic generations of fuzzy rule weights: (a) Power consumption for one journey; (b) Stored energy; (c) Charging profile; and (d) Converter temperature.

rules) from previous generation and the other 15 results of mutations on the population. Between generations, only the five best individuals are eligible to pass to the next generation. The evolution of the objective function is presented in Fig. 4.

Figure 4a shows the evolution of individual objective functions. Each of the individual objective functions was adapted to result in a near-unitary value. By providing different weights for each of the metrics, a global objective function is presented in Fig. 4b. Specifically, Fig. 4 illustrates the weights of all individuals of the same generation, plotted with "+" in the graphs, having the best individual of a generation highlighted with a square (in Fig. 4b).

For each rule, the FLC rule weights evolution for 200 generations are presented in the heat map graph of Fig. 5.

From the previous heat map result, certain rules will contribute more to the expected optimality. As example, the heuristic algorithm will increase the weight of rules 1, 3, 6,

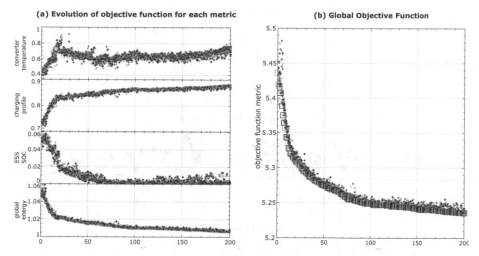

Fig. 4. Evaluation of objective function: (a) Individual evaluation of each metric for all generations; (b) Global objective function as dependent of the generation.

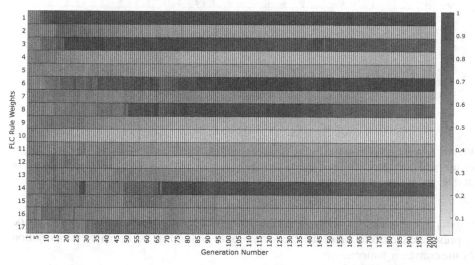

Fig. 5. Heat map of the best FLC rule weights for each generation.

8 and 14, and reduce the weight of remaining rules, in order to achieve lower value of the objective function.

4.2 Extended Optimization of ESS Charging Controller

The following results present the testbed evaluated with the 17 known rules, having an initial weight of 0.9, and the 240 possible combinations for fuzzy rules, with an initial weight of 0.1. For different generations and the same independent power consumption

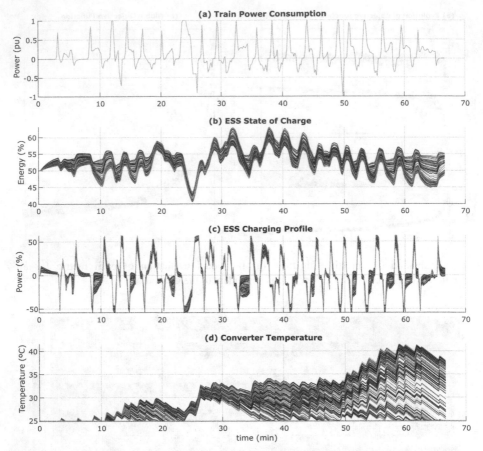

Fig. 6. Evolution of testbed variables, in order of time, for different meta-heuristic generations of fuzzy rule weights: (a) Power consumption for one journey; (b) Stored energy; (c) Charging profile; and (d) Converter temperature.

input, present in Fig. 6a, in Fig. 6b is illustrated the evolution of stored energy; in Fig. 6c is presented the evolution of the charging profile and in Fig. 6d is visible the evolution of the converter temperature.

The metaheuristic algorithm used for this set of rules is the same from the "known-only" rules. The evolution of the objective function for different generations is presented in Fig. 7.

Figure 7a shows similar results from the ones present in Fig. 4, in terms of convergence of the objective function values.

For each rule, the FLC rule weights evolution for 200 generations are presented in the heat map graph of Fig. 8.

From the previous heat map result, the first 17 known rules has a higher prevalence in the final result than the unknown combinations of rules. It is visible that, the unknown rules do not increase inversely proportional to the decrease of the known rules which its

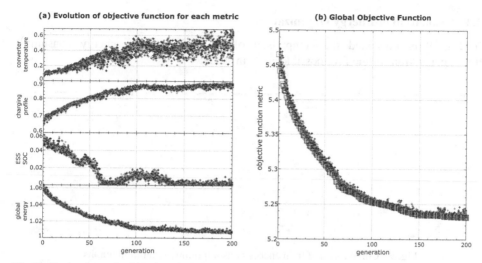

Fig. 7. Evaluation of objective function: (a) Individual evaluation of each metric for all generations; (b) Global objective function as dependent of the generation.

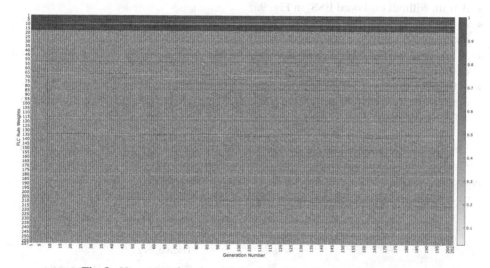

Fig. 8. Heat map of the best FLC rule weights for each generation.

weight is reduced by the GA. Specifically, with this results, it is visible that there is no unknown rule that was "forgotten" in the rule specification stage of the FLC controller design. It is more visible that the known rules are more eligible by the GA to be reduced (or eliminated).

4.3 Evaluation of Energy Optimization

In Fig. 9 is presented the comparison of the train journey energy consumption/regeneration for the four possible cases in study:

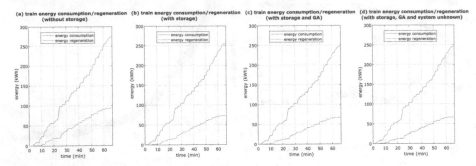

Fig. 9. Comparison of train energy consumption/regeneration graphs.

- A train without on-board ESS, in Fig. 9a;
- A train with ESS, with a FLC charging controller but without fuzzy weights optimization (only with the known rules having the same weights), in Fig. 9b;
- A train with on-board ESS, with the charging controller based on FLC, using the GA optimization criteria over the known rules, in Fig. 9c;
- A train with on-board ESS, with the charging controller based on FLC, using the GA optimization over either the known rules and all possible combinations of unknown rules, in Fig. 9d.

In Table 2 is summarized the comparison of the train energy for the four cases in study: the inclusion or not of the on-board ESS, the inclusion or not of the optimization procedure, and the consideration or not of the unknown rules.

Table 2. Energy optimization results.

	Train energy			
	Consumption		Regeneration	
	kWh	%	kWh	%
Without ESS	273.5	100	93.9	100
With ESS, with known rules, without GA optimization	254.4	93.0	73.0	77.7
With ESS, with GA, only known rules	247.4	90.5	67.0	71.3
With ESS, with GA, with all possible rules	246.1	90.0	66.6	70.9

From the results of the Table 2, a maximum near 30% of reduction on the regenerated energy is achieved, as well as a reduction of 10% of energy consumption. Later, if the on-board charging strategy uses a GA meta-heuristic to increase the energy efficiency, in the case study considered, the reduction of regenerated energy is around 5% and the reduction of the train energy consumption is more than 2%.

4.4 Discussion

The previously presented reduction is of advanced interest since the energy consumption/regeneration reduction is achieved only with the adaptation of the charging strategy and without the adaptation of the ESS hardware. In addition, the FLC is an algorithm with low execution time and, therefore, it can be implemented in to a real-time charging controller for on-board ESS.

The fuzzy rules weights can be adjusted with offline calculation, using the meta-heuristic genetic algorithm presented in this work, or alternative adjustment strategy. By using the knowledge extracted from the operation of other trains and/or from the state of the railway power system, it is possible to better control multiple on-board ESS accordingly.

Therefore, this approach of having a multi-criteria charging strategy is of advanced interest since it has a big level of flexibility in the development of this kind of systems. As example, it is possible that all trains are equipped with ESS, with the FLC structure as the main control strategy and this structure being the same for all the railway ESS. Later, the rule weight adjustment confers each of the trains different behavior towards a better usage of the railway energy, which is essential to have smart railways.

Future research directions of this work will be in the extension of the presented charging strategy to a multi-train simulator system, where each of the trains are supposed to have an on-board ESS. Each of the ESS charging controller complies a FLC with the rule weights being defined by the GA, towards further optimization.

5 Conclusions

The initial approach of a storage charging controller, focused in multiple optimization criteria, and applied to railway transportation systems, is presented here. This optimization strategy combines the knowledge of the expected behavior of the system, by manually defining the rules of a fuzzy logic controller, and later, a meta-heuristic is used to adjust the weight of the fuzzy rules.

The focus of this work is to validate that a feasible charging solution having multiple input variables can be easily implemented with a FLC. This charging solution can result in high reduction of the regenerated energy (near 23%). Later, as an optimization strategy, a meta-heuristic can achieve 5% to 7% of regenerated energy reduction.

Acknowledgments. The research leading to these results has received funding from the FCT – Fundação Ciência e Tecnologia – under grant PD/BD/128051/2016, supported by MCTES national funds and FSE funds through POCH program. This work was supported by UID/EEA/00147/2019 - Research Center for Systems and Technologies funded by national funds through the FCT/MCTES through national funds (PIDDAC).

References

1. Ghaviha, N., Campillo, J., Bohlin, M., Dahlquist, E.: Review of application of energy storage devices in railway transportation. In: Proceedings of the 8th International Conference on Applied Energy, 8–11 October, pp. 4561–4568 (2016)
2. Morais, V.A., Rocha, A.A., Afonso, J.L., Martins, A.P.: Heuristic-based Speed Profile Generation for Multi-Train Simulator. In: Proceedings of the 9th International Conference on Intelligent Systems, 25–27 September, pp. 296–303 (2018)
3. Ortega, J.M., Ibaiondo, H., Romo, A.: Kinetic energy recovery on railway systems with feedback to the grid. In: Proceedings 9th World Congress on Railway Research, 22–26 May, pp. 94–97 (2011)
4. Gelman, V.: Energy storage that may be too good to be true: comparison between wayside storage and reversible thyristor controlled rectifiers for heavy rail. IEEE Veh. Technol. Mag. **8**(4), 70–80 (2013)
5. Arboleya, P., El-Sayed, I., Mohamed, B., Mayet, C.: Modeling, simulation and analysis of on-board hybrid energy storage systems for railway applications. Energies **12**(11), 2199 (2019)
6. Gelman, V.: Braking energy recuperation. IEEE Veh. Technol. Mag. **4**(3), 82–89 (2009)
7. Arboleya, P., Bidaguren, P., Armendariz, U.: Energy is on board: energy storage and other alternatives in modern light railways. IEEE Electrif. Mag. **4**(3), 30–41 (2016)
8. Zheng, Y., et al.: Optimal operation of battery energy storage system considering distribution system uncertainty. IEEE Trans. Sustain. Energy **9**(3), 1051–1060 (2018)
9. De Santis, E., Rizzi, A., Sadeghiany, A., Mascioli, F.M.F.: Genetic optimization of a fuzzy control system for energy flow management in micro-grids. In: Proceedings of Joint IFSA World Congress and NAFIPS Annual Meeting, pp. 418–423 (2013)
10. Leonori, S., De Santis, E., Rizzi, A., Mascioli, F.F.: Multi objective optimization of a fuzzy logic controller for energy management in microgrids. In: Proceedings of IEEE Congress on Evolutionary Computation, pp. 319–326 (2016)
11. Leonori, S., Paschero, M., Rizzi, A., Mascioli, F.M.F.: An optimized microgrid energy management system based on FIS-MO-GA paradigm. In: Proceedings of IEEE International Conference on Fuzzy Systems, pp. 1–6 (2017)
12. Akbarzadeh-T, M.R., Meghdadi, A.H.: Evolutionary fuzzy systems. In: Zilouchian, A., Jamshidi, M. (eds.) Intelligent Control Systems Using Soft Computing Methodologies, pp. 434–461 (2001)
13. Mamdani, E.H., Assilian, S.: An experiment in linguistic synthesis with a fuzzy logic controller. Int. J. Man Mach. Stud. **7**(1), 1–13 (1975)

A Three-Phase Bidirectional Variable Speed Drive: An Experimental Validation for a Three-Phase Induction Motor

Luis Machado, Tiago J. C. Sousa, Delfim Pedrosa, Vitor Monteiro[✉], J. G. Pinto, and Joao L. Afonso

Centro ALGORITMI, University of Minho, Campus de Azurém, Guimarães, Portugal
{lmachado,vmonteiro}@dei.uminho.pt

Abstract. This paper presents the implementation and subsequent experimental verification of an electronic variable speed drive (VSD) for driving an induction motor, which is composed by a three-phase ac-dc converter on the grid-side and by a three-phase dc-ac converter on the motor-side. With the proposed solution, besides driving the motor, it is possible to mitigate power quality problems on the grid-side (e.g., current harmonics and power factor) associated with the use of diode-bridge ac-dc converters in the conventional VSDs. Besides, with the proposed solution, a bidirectional operation is possible, allowing to deliver to the power grid the energy generated in motor braking processes. As demonstrated along the paper, with the proposed VSD, it is possible to control the motor speed (including the rotation direction), and the operation with sinusoidal currents and unitary power factor on the grid-side. A laboratory prototype was developed, permitting to perform an experimental validation and prove the main functionalities of the VSD.

Keywords: Variable speed drive · Active rectifier · Induction motor · Regenerative braking · Power quality

1 Introduction

Nowadays, the three-phase induction motor with squirrel cage rotor represents more than 90% of the electric motors used in industry, contributing to more than 60% of industrial electricity consumption. This situation occurs, not only because the induction motors present low acquisition and maintenance costs and great robustness, but mainly due to constant technological evolution and the development of control techniques that have brought a wider variety of applications [1–3].

Conventionally, variable speed drives (VSDs) for induction motors employ a diode bridge rectifier in order to provide power to the dc-link from the power grid. Although this type of rectifiers is an economical solution, they contribute to the degradation of power quality, since they consume currents with high harmonic content that, in turn, cause distortions in the voltage waveform and low power factor amount of the VSD. Besides,

© ICST Institute for Computer Sciences, Social Informatics and Telecommunications Engineering 2020
Published by Springer Nature Switzerland AG 2020. All Rights Reserved
J. L. Afonso et al. (Eds.): SESC 2019, LNICST 315, pp. 47–57, 2020.
https://doi.org/10.1007/978-3-030-45694-8_4

they do not allow reversing the energy flow, thus rendering the regenerative braking process to the power grid impracticable. For power quality improvement, passive or active filters are frequently installed, meaning additional investment costs [4]. A more recent solution consists in used active rectifiers [4]. Thus, the passive ac-dc converters have been replaced by active ac-dc converters, which present the following advantages as attractive [5, 6]: regulated voltage supply with low ripple to the dc-link; sinusoidal current consumption; maximization of the power factor; and bidirectional power flow, which allows an effective use of the electrical energy generated in braking or decelerating situations of the motor, returning it to the power grid instead of being dissipated in a resistor (braking resistor), or stored in storage elements such as ultracapacitors or batteries [7].

Significant technological advances have emerged in the field of VSDs over the last few years [1]. This growth has been felt in the market of electric motors, especially as regards the sale of induction motors, which has increased, and it is thought that it will continue to increase, not only because of the qualities they have in relation to the dc motors very used in the past, but mainly because of the evolution of VSDs, which has allowed the use of these motors in variable speed applications [1].

The paper is structured as follows: Sect. 2 presents the electrical model of the proposed system under analysis; Sect. 3 presents the implemented control algorithm for each of the power converters; Sect. 4 presents the developed prototype and the obtained experimental results of the VSD and Sect. 5 finalizes the paper with the conclusions.

2 Proposed System

This section presents the electrical model of the proposed system under analysis in this paper. As previously mentioned, a typical topology of a VSD for three-phase induction motors, usually, has a diode bridge rectifier for interfacing with the power grid, also known in the literature as a Graetz bridge [8]. As a disadvantage, this type of converter does not control the input (nor the output) current nor the dc-link voltage (v_{dc}), which is limited to the peak value of the power grid phase voltages. In this way, the proposed system suggests the exchange of the passive semiconductors by active semiconductors, resulting in the electric model of Fig. 1. In this figure, two voltage source converters (active rectifier and inverter) can be seen, both with three legs with two insulate gate bipolar transistors (IGBTs) in each leg. The fact that this topology has only three wires allows to simplify the solution and reduce the costs related with the addition of a fourth IGBT leg for the neutral connection or, if it is connected to the midpoint of the dc-link capacitors, reduce the complexity associated with the voltage regulation in each capacitor terminals.

The converters are connected through a dc-link consisting of a capacitive filter (C_{dc}), whose function is to minimize the ripple of the v_{dc} voltage. At the input of the active rectifier, coupling inductors (L_a, L_b, L_c) are used to smooth the absorbed currents (i_a, i_b, i_c). The stator windings of the induction motor were used to smooth the currents at the output of the inverter (i_{am}, i_{bm}, i_{cm}).

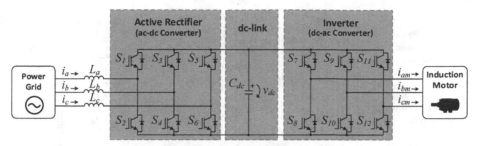

Fig. 1. Proposed system for the VSD.

3   Control Algorithm

This section presents the control algorithm implemented for the proposed solution. For a better understanding, it is divided into two parts: control for the active rectifier and control for the traction system, which involves the inverter and motor.

3.1   Active Rectifier

The block diagram of the strategy used to control the active rectifier can be seen in Fig. 2. In this control strategy, the dc-link voltage (v_{dc}) is measured and compared to the reference value (v_{dc_ref}), from where results the error signal v_{dc_er}, which is submitted to a proportional-integral controller (PI). Posteriorly, the output of this controller is multiplied by each of the sinusoidal references (pll_a, pll_b, pll_c) with unitary amplitude and frequency and phase equal to the fundamental component of the respective power grid voltage. These references are obtained from the ωt angle resulting from the phase locked-loop (PLL) based on the p-q theory [9–13], corresponding to three sinusoidal signals with phase synchronized with the phase of power grid voltage and amplitude i_{pk_ref} dependent of the error and the gains of the PI controller. The currents i_{a_ref}, i_{b_ref} and i_{c_ref} are the reference currents for each input currents (i_a, i_b, i_c). The reference voltages are calculated using a predictive control technique [14–17], which is represented by (1), where ref_x refers to the reference voltage that the converter must produce in phase x, which is calculated based on the simple power grid voltage (v_x), the coupling inductance value per phase (L_x), the sampling time (T_s), the phase current measured at the input of the rectifier (i_x), its reference current (i_{x_ref}) and the current measured at the previous instant ($i_{x\_ref\_pr}$). It should be noted that the voltage drop in the inductor resistive component was not used, since its value can be neglected when compared to the voltage drop in the inductive component.

$$ref_x = v_x - \frac{L_x}{T_s}\left[2i_{x\_ref} - i_{x\_ref\_pr} - i_x\right] \qquad (1)$$

From the reference signals, in order to generate the appropriate duty-cycle of the pulses to be applied to the gates of the IGBTs, the sinusoidal pulse-width modulation (SPWM) method was used.

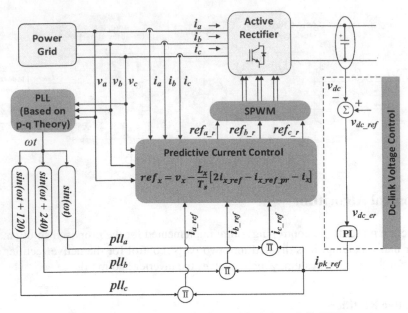

Fig. 2. Control diagram for the rectifier stage of the VSD.

3.2 Motor Control

For the motor control, the closed loop *Volts per Hertz* control was chosen [18–21]. Compared to vector control techniques, it is simpler, more economical and easier to implement [18–21], and is recommended for non-critical applications where good speed and/or torque performances are not relevant [3].

Figure 3 shows the designed block diagram of the control loop implementation for the traction system. As it can be seen, the rotor speed, ω_r, is compared with the reference speed ω_{r_ref} from where, by application of a PI controller, a signal (ω_d) is obtained, which has to be added to the rotor speed in order to obtain the desired synchronous speed (ω_{s_ref}). Once calculated ω_{s_ref}, and, based on this, calculated f_{s_ref} through a pre-established *V/f* ramp, the respective voltage amplitude (v_{s_ref}) that must be applied to each of the stator windings is obtained by (2). A low-frequency compensation part, an offset voltage $V_{0,}$ should be included in the voltage/frequency relation.

$$V_{s\_ref} = \frac{V_s}{f_{nom}} f_{s\_ref} + V_0 \qquad (2)$$

On the other hand, the integration of ω_{s_ref} results in the signal θ_{ref} that defines the frequency of the reference voltages, obtain by (3), that must be synthesized and subsequently applied to a modulation technique. As in the control of the active rectifier, the modulation technique used in the inverter control was SPWM.

$$v_{ref\_x} = V_{s\_ref} sin\left(\theta_{ref} - k_x\right) \qquad (3)$$

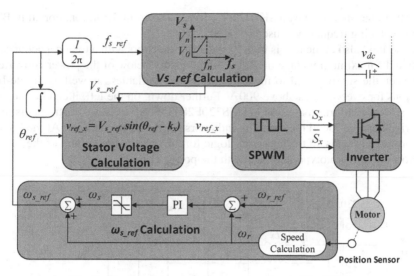

Fig. 3. Control diagram for the inverter stage of the VSD.

4   Experimental Setup and Results

This section presents the obtained experimental results of the developed VSD prototype, which is shown in Fig. 4. At the top of the prototype, the two power converters can be seen, implemented with six SKM400GB12V half-bridge IGBT modules from Semikron.

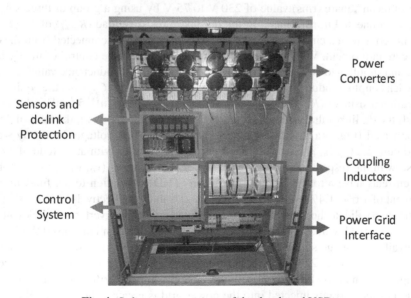

Fig. 4. Laboratory prototype of the developed VSD.

Each half-bridge are driven by a SKHI22AR driver, also from Semikron. For all IGBTs, a 5 kHz switching frequency is used.

The dc-link, also at the top, is built by a set of capacitors with a total capacitance of 5.5 mF and a maximum voltage of 900 V. Immediately below of the power converters, can be seen the sensors used to measure the system variables, as well as the dc-link protections for overvoltages above 900 V. Further down, on the left, it can be seen the control system platform, based on a TMS320F28335 DSP of Texas Instruments, and, on the right, can be found the coupling inductors for the active rectifier. At the bottom of the prototype stands all the necessary logic for the pre-charger system of the dc-link capacitors and the prototype interface with the power grid.

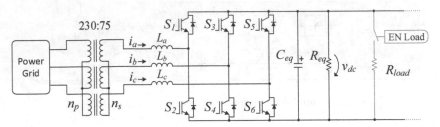

Fig. 5. Power circuit used to obtain the experimental results of the VSD active rectifier.

4.1 Active Rectifier Results

The experimental results concerning the operation of the active rectifier were obtained based on the scheme of Fig. 5. As it can be seen, the power grid voltage is reduced from root mean square (rms) value of 230 V to 75 V by using a group of three single-phase star-connected transformers. In the dc-link, a resistive load (R_{load}) of 25 Ω was placed in series with a circuit breaker, it can be connected or disconnected from the dc-link at certain moment. With this, it was intended to validate the control of the dc-link voltage and simultaneously the predictive current control. The inductance value (L_a, L_b, L_c) of each coupling inductor, the equivalent capacitance value (C_{eq}) and the equivalent equalization resistance (R_{eq}) of the dc-link are, respectively, 3.5 mH, 5.5 mF and 8.4 kΩ.

With the dc-link voltage regulated at 250 V, at a certain moment, the load of 25 Ω was connected (Fig. 6(a)), with an expected drop in dc-link voltage. In steady state, the grid currents (i_a, i_b, i_c) were obtained in the three phases with amplitude of 17 A, in phase with the respective phase-neutral power grid voltages (v_a, v_b, v_c) (Fig. 6(b)). These currents have a total harmonic distortion (THD) in relation to the fundamental component of 1.6%, 1.4% and 1.7% for phases a, b and c, respectively.

In order to validate the operation of the ac-dc converter as an inverter, a dc-link voltage of 120 V was fixed with a voltage source. Due to the modulation index used (85%) and to the available voltage sources, it was necessary to reduce to the power grid voltage, having been changed to 25 V rms. Results were obtained for peak currents reference of 1 A (Fig. 7(a)) and 2 A (Fig. 7(b)). With these results, it was verified that the harmonic distortion of the currents injected into the power grid is greater when the amplitude of the currents is smaller, which is expected, considering that the signal-to-noise ratio is lower in this case.

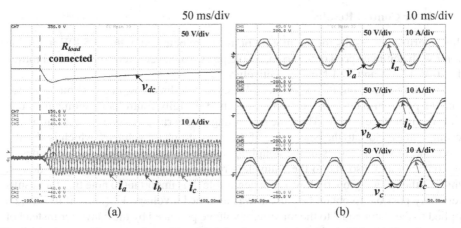

Fig. 6. Active rectifier operation with a 25 Ω load connected to the dc-link: (a) Transient state dc-link voltage and power grid currents; (b) Steady state power grid voltages and currents.

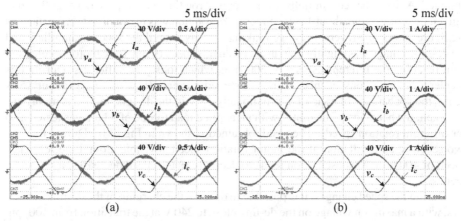

Fig. 7. Power grid voltages and currents for the active rectifier operation for a peak current of: (a) 1 A; (b) 2 A.

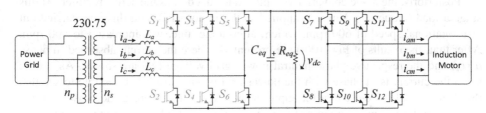

Fig. 8. Power circuit used to obtain the experimental results to VSD.

4.2 Motor Control Results

The experimental results for the motor control were obtained with a 5.5 kW induction motor with nominal speed of 920 rpm, 3 pole pairs, voltage, current and nominal torque of 380 V, 12.3 A and 57.1 Nm, respectively.

In order to carry out the experimental tests, the dc-link was, in a first moment, fed from the power grid through the diodes of each of the fully controllable semiconductors of the rectifier stage (Fig. 8). Thus, the grid voltage (75 V rms) was rectified, resulting in a dc-link voltage close to the peak value of the phase-to-phase voltages, which is slightly lower due to voltage drops in the coupling inductors, voltage drops on the diodes of the converter and also due to the equivalent resistance value of 8.4 kΩ on the dc-link which, although not properly low, is not negligible. It is important to note that the results were only possible to obtain because it was assumed a voltage V_s (present in Eq. (2)) applied to the stator equal to the maximum voltage produced by the converter instead of considering the motor nominal voltage.

In the first test, the induction motor was subjected to a constant load of 3 Nm at different reference speed values (n_{ref}) and the experimental result of Fig. 9(a) was obtained. As it can be seen, initially, the motor was rotating with a speed (n) of 200 rpm in a given direction. After about 1 s the direction of rotation was reversed. At this instant, as the figure shows, the reversal voltage braking was given until the speed is annulled, and the dc-link voltage was slightly increased. From this speed (0 rpm), the motor accelerated until reaching the reference speed of 200 rpm, which took place after 2 s. During this acceleration, as a consequence of the consumed currents (i_{am}, i_{bm}, i_{cm}) (about 15 A peak), the appearance of a sag of approximately 23 V in the dc-link voltage is notorious.

Then, the behavior of the motor with an applied load torque of 5 Nm was tested also for different rotation speeds. The result obtained is shown in Fig. 9(b). During the first two seconds, an oscillation of the motor rotation speed is visible around the reference speed of 400 rpm. This oscillation tends to decrease as the speed decreases, as it can be seen.

During the speed changes, it is possible to observe the charging of the dc-link capacitors, with a maximum voltage on the dc-link close to 240 V at the transition from 400 rpm to 350 rpm. Since in these tests a diode bridge rectifier was used, the current cannot flow to the power grid, so the energy generated by the motor during braking is stored in the dc-link capacitors.

Posteriorly, the ac-dc converter was placed to function as the active rectifier. At this stage a load torque of 5 Nm was applied to the motor shaft, and this was carried out at a rotational speed of 600 rpm, which, after some time, was increased to 800 rpm. After that, the results of Fig. 10(a) are presented, where the current absorbed in phase a (i_a) and the respective phase neutral power grid voltage (v_a) are shown. As can be seen, the current is in phase with the power grid voltage. It is also possible to see that the distortion of the current at the input of the rectifier (i_a) tends to decrease with the increase of the current, as previously verified in the results obtained for the operation of the ac-dc converter as inverter.

Then, in order to analyze the behavior of the system in the event of motor deceleration, the speed of 800 rpm was reduced again to 600 rpm and the results of Fig. 10(b) were obtained. As it can be seen, the current at the input of the rectifier in phase a (i_a) has

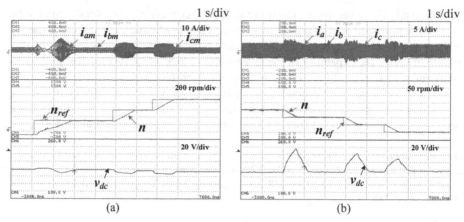

Fig. 9. Results obtained in the operation of the motor for a constant load of: (a) 3 Nm; (b) 5 Nm.

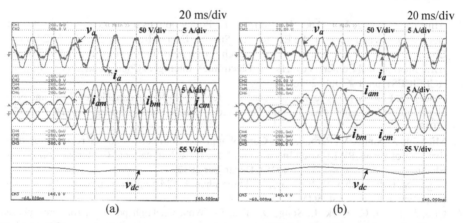

Fig. 10. Results obtained for the motor driving a 5 Nm load during: (a) Acceleration from 600 rpm to 800 rpm; (b) Deceleration from 800 rpm to 600 rpm.

become in phase opposition with the voltage v_a, remaining in this situation for about four power grid cycles. During this time, the current was injected into the power grid, therefore the ac-dc converter was used as an inverter. Also, for this situation, there was an increase of the dc-link voltage by about 14% of the voltage set for regulation (250 V).

5   Conclusions

This paper presents an analysis of a variable speed drive (VSD), which makes use of a three-phase ac-dc power converter to interface with the power grid, and a three-phase dc-ac converter to drive a three-phase induction motor, both converters sharing a capacitive dc-link. An electrical model of the system was developed and, based on it, a laboratory prototype was developed, from which the experimental results presented in this paper

were obtained. These results achieved the objective concerning the experimental validation of the proposed control algorithms, specifically predictive current control (active
rectifier) and closed loop *Volts per Hertz* control (motor speed control). Thus, it was
possible to verify the capability of the system to compensate power quality problems,
in particular, in relation to the currents consumed on the grid side, which presented
sinusoidal waveforms, low harmonic content and unitary power factor. In relation to the
motor control, its operation was validated in the traction mode, as well as in the braking
mode, returning the generated energy to the power grid (regenerative braking).

Acknowledgment. This work has been supported by FCT – Fundação para a Ciência e Tecnologia
within the Project Scope: UID/CEC/00319/2019. This work has been supported by the FCT
Project DAIPESEV PTDC/EEI-EEE/30382/2017, and by the FCT Project QUALITY4POWER
PTDC/EEI-EEE/28813/2017.

References

1. Almeida, A., Fong, J., Falkner, H., Bertoldi, P.: Policy options to promote energy efficient
   electric motors and drives in the EU. Renew. Sustain. Energy Rev. **74**, 1275–1286 (2017)
2. Chavhan, K., Ugale, R.: Automated test bench for an induction motor using LabVIEW. In:
   IEEE International Conference on Power Electronics, Intelligent Control and Energy Systems
   (ICPEICES), pp. 1–6, July 2016
3. Alsofyani, I., Idris, N.: A review on sensorless techniques for sustainable reliablity and efficient variable frequency drives of induction motors. Renew. Sustain. Energy Rev. **24**, 111–121
   (2013)
4. Michalik, J., Smidl, V., Peroutka, Z.: Control approaches of current-source rectifier: predictive control versus PWM-based linear control. In: IEEE International Conference on Power
   Electronics and Drive Systems (PEDS), December 2017
5. Begag, S., Belhaouchet, N., Rahmani, L.: Three-phase PWM rectifier with constant switching
   frequency. J. Electr. Syst. **5**(1), 7–12 (2009)
6. Cho, J., Jeong, C., Baek, J., Song, D., Yoo, D., Won, C.: High power factor three phase
   rectifier for high power density AC/DC conversion applications. In: Applied Power Electronics
   Conference and Exposition, vol. 2, pp. 910–915, March 1999
7. Ekstrom, A., Liss, G.: A refined HVDC control system. IEEE Trans. Power App. Syst. **PAS-
   89**(5), 723–732 (1970)
8. Saidur, R., Mekhilef, S., Ali, M., Safari, A., Mohammed, H.: Applications of variable speed
   drive (VSD) in electrical motors energy savings. Renew. Sustain. Energy Rev. **16**, 543–550
   (2011)
9. Rolim, L., da Costa, D., Aredes, M.: Analysis and software implementation of a robust
   synchronizing PLL circuit based on the pq theory. IEEE Trans. Industr. Electron. **53**(6),
   1919–1926 (2006)
10. Thacker, T., Boroyevich, D., Burgos, R., Wang, F.: Phase-locked loop noise reduction via
    phase detector implementation for single-phase systems. IEEE Trans. Industr. Electron. **58**(6),
    2482–2490 (2011)
11. Golestan, S., Monfared, M., Freijedo, F., Guerrero, J.: Design and tuning of a modified power-
    based PLL for single-phase grid-connected power conditioning systems. IEEE Trans. Power
    Electron. **27**(8), 3639–3650 (2012)
12. Golestan, S., Guerrero, J., Vasquez, J.: Three-phase PLLs: a review of recent advances. IEEE
    Trans. Power Electron. **32**(3), 1894–1907 (2017)

13. Guo, X., Wu, W., Gu, H.: Phase locked loop and synchronization methods for grid-interfaced converters: a review. Przeglad Elektrotechniczny **87**(4), 182–187 (2011)
14. Bosch, S., Staiger, J., Steinhart, H.: Predictive current control for an active power filter with LCL-filter. IEEE Trans. Industr. Electron. **65**, 4943–4952 (2017)
15. Pinto, J.: Nova Topologia de UPQC sem Transformador para Compensação de Problemas de Qualidade de Energia Elétrica. Doctoral thesis, University of Minho, Guimarães (2011)
16. Kumar, K., Michael, P., John, J., Kumar, S.: Simulation and comparison of SPWM and SVPWM control for three phase inverter. ARPN J. Eng. Appl. Sci. **5**(7), 61–74 (2010)
17. Bacon, V., Campanhol, L., Silva, S.: Análise Comparativa das Técnicas SPWM e SVM Aplicadas a um Inversor de Tensão Trifásico. UNOPAR Científica Ciências Exatas e Tecnológicas **10**(1) (2015). http://www.pgsskroton.com.br/seer/index.php/exatas/article/view/508/479. Accessed 28 May 2017
18. Tembhekar, K.: Improvement and analysis of speed control of three phase induction motor drive including two methods. In: 2nd International Conference on Emerging Trends in Engineering and Technology (ICETET), pp. 736–741 (2009)
19. Ross, D., Theys, J., Bowling, S.: Using the dsPIC30F for vector control of an ACIM. Microchip Technologies (2004). http://ww1.microchip.com/downloads/jp/AppNotes/ACIM%20Vector%20Control%2000908a.pdf. Accessed 15 Sept 2017
20. Bodkhe, S., Aware, M.: A variable-speed, sensorless, induction motor drive using DC-link measurements. In: 4th IEEE Conference on Industrial Electronics and Applications, pp. 3591–3596, June 2009
21. Habbi, H.M.D., Ajeel, H.J., Ali, I.I.: Speed control of induction motor using PI and V/F scalar vector controllers. Int. J. Comput. Appl. **151**(7), 36–43 (2016)

Unified Traction and Battery Charging Systems for Electric Vehicles: A Sustainability Perspective

Tiago J. C. Sousa$^{(\boxtimes)}$, Luís Machado, Delfim Pedrosa, Vítor Monteiro, and João L. Afonso

Centro ALGORITMI, University of Minho, Campus de Azurém, Guimarães, Portugal
tsousa@dei.uminho.pt

Abstract. This paper presents an analysis of unified traction and battery charging systems for electric vehicles (EVs), both in terms of operation modes and in terms of implementation cost, when compared to dedicated solutions that perform the same operation modes. Regarding the connection of the EV battery charging system with the power grid, four operation modes are analyzed: (1) Grid–to–Vehicle (G2V); (2) Vehicle–to–Grid (V2G); (3) Vehicle–to–Home (V2H); and (4) Vehicle–for–Grid (V4G). With an EV unified system, each of these operation modes can be used in single–phase and three–phase power grids. Furthermore, a cost estimation is performed for an EV unified system and for dedicated systems that can perform the same functionalities, in order to prove the benefits of the EV unified approach. The cost estimation comprises two power levels, namely 6 kW, single–phase, related to domestic installations, and 50 kW, three–phase, related to industrial installations. The relevance of unified traction and battery charging systems for EVs is proven for single–phase and three–phase power grids.

Keywords: Electric vehicle · Unified system · Smart grids · Cost estimation

1 Introduction

Electric Vehicles (EVs) represent a growing alternative to the conventional fossil fuel powered vehicles towards the reduction of greenhouse emissions at the utilization level, as well as the refraining of fossil resources exploitation [1, 2]. The conjugation of EVs and renewable energy sources represents one major role towards smart grids, with the bidirectional operation for EVs offering new operation modes and grid supporting functionalities [3–5]. Hence, the typical EV battery charging operation (Grid–to–Vehicle – G2V) can be extended to the Vehicle–to–Grid (V2G) operation mode, initially proposed in [6]. Furthermore, other operation modes for the EV have been proposed in the literature, such as Vehicle–to–Home (V2H), where the EV acts as a voltage source for an electrical installation, and Vehicle–for–Grid (V4G), where the EV acts as an active power conditioner, i.e., a Shunt Active Power Filter (SAPF) [7–11].

The referred functionalities are accomplished with an on–board EV battery charger, which is limited to power levels below 19.2 kW in the best–case scenario [12]. However,

J. L. Afonso et al. (Eds.): SESC 2019, LNICST 315, pp. 58–69, 2020.
https://doi.org/10.1007/978-3-030-45694-8_5

with integrated EV battery chargers, i.e., a unified system for traction and battery charging of an EV [13–15], higher power levels are achievable, since the maximum power is dictated by the traction system nominal power, which is typically several dozens or few hundreds of kW for automobiles. This allows the battery charging operation with higher power levels, as well as the other referred operation modes, making it possible to operate in industrial installations, for instance. Moreover, since all the referred operation modes are accomplished with a single system, the use of dedicated equipment for each operation can be discarded, e.g., Load Shift System (LSS) or SAPF.

In this context, this paper presents the advantages of unified traction and battery charging systems for EVs, both in terms of operation modes and in terms of implementation cost, when compared to dedicated solutions that perform the same operation modes. Hence, four operation modes are analyzed: (1) Grid–to–Vehicle (G2V); (2) Vehicle–to–Grid (V2G); (3) Vehicle–to–Home (V2H); and (4) Vehicle–for–Grid (V4G). With a unified system, each of these operation modes can be used in single–phase and three–phase power grids. Furthermore, a cost estimation is performed for a unified system and for dedicated systems that can perform the same functionalities, namely a LSS and a SAPF, in order to prove the benefits of the EV unified approach.

The paper is structured as follows: Sect. 2 presents the operation modes under analysis, as well as simulation results of each one; Sect. 3 presents a cost estimation and comparison with conventional dedicated solutions; finally, Sect. 4 draws the conclusions of this paper.

2   Operation Modes

This section shows the operation modes considered for the EV in the scope of this paper, which are the following: (1) Grid–to–Vehicle (G2V); (2) Vehicle–to–Grid (V2G); (3) Vehicle–to–Home (V2H); and (4) Vehicle–for–Grid (V4G). All the referred operation modes encompass the connection of the EV to an electrical installation, which can be either single–phase or three–phase. Figure 1 shows a block diagram of the general connection of the EV to an electrical installation with the referred operation modes. It should be noted that all the operation modes take in consideration high levels of power quality, which is a relevant feature for smart grids. In the scope of this paper, only the front–end ac–dc converter operation is analyzed.

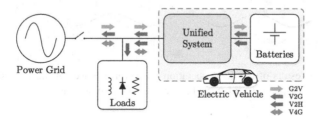

Fig. 1. Block diagram of the EV connection to an ac electrical installation.

2.1 Grid-to-Vehicle (G2V)

The traditional operation of an on–board EV battery charger, i.e., charging the batteries with power provided by the power grid, is commonly referred as G2V. Figure 2 shows a block diagram of this operation mode. The battery charging performed by on–board EV battery chargers is typically classified as slow, since the power level of these systems is limited to 19.2 kW, as previously referred. On the other hand, by using a unified system for traction and battery charging, higher power levels can be used in the battery charging operation, hence equipping the EV with an on–board fast battery charger. With this system, both slow and fast battery charging are possible, which are accomplished by connecting the EV to single–phase and three–phase power grids, respectively.

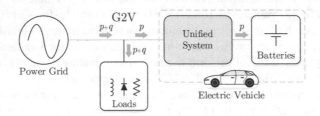

Fig. 2. Block diagram of the Grid–to–Vehicle (G2V) operation mode.

Figure 3 shows a simulation result of this operation mode for an operating power of 3.2 kW (slow battery charging, single–phase), where it can be seen the power grid voltage (v_g) and current (i_g) and the dc–link voltage (v_{dc}). It can be seen that v_g is not sinusoidal, but the system is capable of absorbing a sinusoidal current i_g in phase with v_g, aiming for a practically unitary power factor. Besides, v_{dc} is controlled to the established reference average value of 400 V.

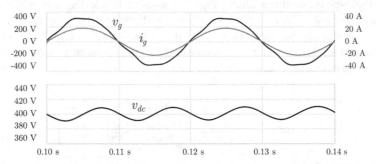

Fig. 3. Simulation results of the G2V operation mode for a power of 3.2 kW (single–phase): Power grid voltage (v_g), power grid current (i_g) and dc–link voltage (v_{dc}).

In order to verify the fast battery charging capability of a unified system, Fig. 4 shows a result of the G2V operation mode for an operating power of 50 kW (fast battery charging, three–phase), where the phase–neutral voltages (v_{ga}, v_{gb}, v_{gc}), the phase currents (i_{ga}, i_{gb}, i_{gc}) and the dc–link voltage (v_{dc}) can be seen. Also, in this case, each phase current is sinusoidal and in phase with the respective phase–neutral voltage, even if the voltage is not sinusoidal. In this case, v_{dc} is controlled to the established reference average value of 800 V.

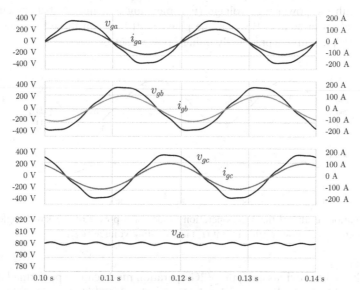

Fig. 4. Simulation results of the G2V operation mode for a power of 50 kW (three–phase): Power grid voltages (v_{gx}), power grid currents (i_{gx}) and dc–link voltage (v_{dc}).

2.2 Vehicle-to-Grid (V2G)

The V2G operation mode consists in delivering energy, previously stored in the EV batteries, back to the power grid. This operation mode, whose block diagram can be seen in Fig. 5, represents a promising benefit for smart grids in the sense that it endows the EV with auxiliary functions to the power grid. Moreover, the combination of G2V and V2G operation modes allows the EV to operate as a LSS. These functions can be accomplished with a conventional bidirectional on–board EV battery charger, with the main difference relatively to a unified system being the admissible power levels for operation. Therefore, the unified system considered in this paper encompasses the V2G

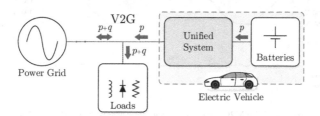

Fig. 5. Block diagram of the Vehicle–to–Grid (V2G) operation mode.

operation mode both in single–phase and three–phase power grids, allowing grid support functionalities, for instance, in domestic and industrial electrical installations.

Figure 6 shows a simulation result of the V2G operation mode for an operating power of 3.2 kW (single–phase), which can be accomplished with almost any bidirectional battery charger. In this case, the power grid current (i_g) is also sinusoidal, but in phase opposition with the power grid voltage (v_g), meaning that the EV battery charger is operating as a power source. Besides, the phase shift between these two quantities is practically 180°, meaning a practically unitary power factor.

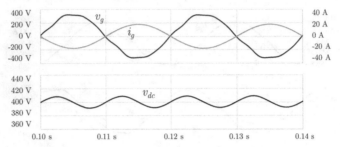

Fig. 6. Simulation results of the V2G operation mode for a power of 3.2 kW (single–phase): Power grid voltage (v_g), power grid current (i_g) and dc–link voltage (v_{dc}).

Similarly to the previous case, the V2G operation mode can be performed in three–phase power grids, for higher power levels. Figure 7 shows this operation with a power of 50 kW (three–phase), where it can be seen the phase–neutral voltages (v_{ga}, v_{gb}, v_{gc}), the phase currents (i_{ga}, i_{gb}, i_{gc}) and the dc–link voltage (v_{dc}). Once again, the injected

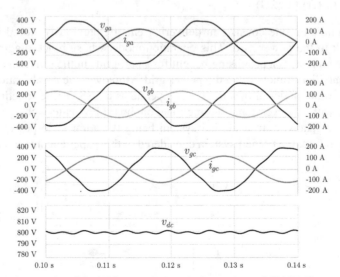

Fig. 7. Simulation results of the V2G operation mode for a power of 50 kW (three–phase): Power grid voltages (v_{gx}), power grid currents (i_{gx}) and dc–link voltage (v_{dc}).

currents are sinusoidal and in phase opposition with the respective voltages, aiming for a unitary power factor.

2.3 Vehicle-to-Home (V2H)

The V2H operation mode, whose block diagram can be seen in Fig. 8, consists in the EV acting as a voltage source for the electrical installation, disconnecting the installation from the upstream grid and supplying the loads with energy stored in the EV batteries. This operation mode can be initiated either in a planned way, such as in LSSs, or triggered by disturbances in the power grid voltage, i.e., overvoltages or undervoltages, similarly to an off–line uninterruptible power supply (UPS). Therefore, by comprising unified systems for traction and battery charging, EVs can act as off–line UPSs in both domestic and industrial installations, which can avoid the use of dedicated UPSs when the EV is parked.

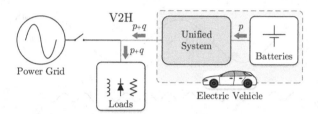

Fig. 8. Block diagram of the Vehicle–to–Home (V2H) operation mode.

Figure 9 shows the V2H operation mode initiated in a planned way, similarly to a LSS when used for self–consumption (single-phase). As it can be seen, the EV battery charger produces a 230 V, 50 Hz ac voltage (v_{ev}) that is practically sinusoidal even with a distorted current consumption (i_{ev}), which is drawn by a linear RL load and a nonlinear diode bridge rectifier with capacitive filter, absorbing a combined power of 5.3 kW. For this operation, due to the increased ripple in the dc–link voltage (v_{dc}) as a consequence of distorted current consumption (approximately 40 V peak–to–peak in this case), its reference value was slightly increased compared to the previous reference value of 400 V, hereby being established the value of 450 V.

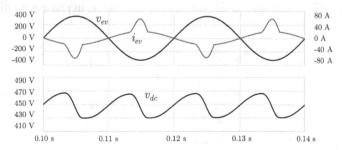

Fig. 9. Simulation results of the V2H operation mode for a power of 5.3 kW (single–phase): Produced ac voltage (v_{ev}), absorbed current (i_{ev}) and dc–link voltage (v_{dc}).

Figure 10 shows the V2H operation mode for three–phase installations, with an operating power of 30 kW drawn by the same two types of load as the previous case. This figure shows the produced ac voltages (v_{eva}, v_{evb}, v_{evc}), the respective consumed currents (i_{eva}, i_{evb}, i_{evc}) and the dc–link voltage (v_{dc}). Similarly to the previous case, the produced voltages are sinusoidal with the desired amplitude even with distorted current consumption.

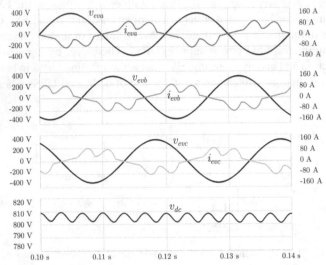

Fig. 10. Simulation results of the V2H operation mode for a power of 30 kW (three–phase): Produced ac voltages (v_{evx}), absorbed currents (i_{evx}) and dc–link voltage (v_{dc}).

2.4   Vehicle-for-Grid (V4G)

The V4G operation mode consists in the compensation of power quality problems to the electrical installation where the vehicle is connected to. This operation mode can be performed simultaneously with either the operation modes G2V or V2G, as the bidirectional arrows of Fig. 11 suggest. The main difference between the V4G and the regular G2V or V2G operation modes resides in the current, absorbed or injected from the power grid. The current is sinusoidal in G2V and V2G operation modes, while in V4G the purpose is to guarantee a sinusoidal grid current and in phase with the voltage,

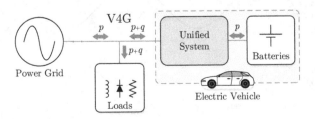

Fig. 11. Block diagram of the Vehicle–for–Grid (V4G) operation mode.

i.e., with the EV acting as a SAPF. Once again, with a unified system, this operation mode can be accomplished in single–phase and three–phase installations, allowing power conditioning functionalities in both domestic and industrial facilities.

Figure 12 shows the V4G operation mode in single–phase installations for two different scenarios, with Fig. 12 (a) showing the combination of V4G and G2V and Fig. 12 (b) showing the combination of V4G and V2G. In both cases, the connected loads (a linear RL and a nonlinear diode bridge rectifier with capacitive filter) present a power consumption of 1.5 kW. Both figures show the power grid voltage (v_g), the load current (i_{ld}), the current produced by the EV battery charger (i_{ev}), the resulting grid current (i_g) and the dc–link voltage (v_{dc}).

In Fig. 12 (a), the EV batteries are being charged with a power of 3 kW. In order to perform the V4G operation, the current absorbed by the EV battery charger is not sinusoidal, but contains the necessary harmonic distortion to obtain a sinusoidal current from the power grid point of view. As it can be seen, the current i_g is sinusoidal and in phase with the voltage v_g.

In Fig. 12 (b), the EV batteries are being discharged with a power of 3 kW. Once again, the current injected by the EV battery charger is not sinusoidal in order to perform the V4G operation. As it can be seen, the current i_g is sinusoidal and in phase opposition with v_g, meaning that energy is being delivered into the power grid with unitary power factor. This happens because the power delivered by the EV battery charger is higher than the power consumed by the loads, otherwise the resulting current i_g would be in phase with v_g, i.e., the power grid would have to provide the power difference to supply the loads. Hence, the power grid is absorbing 1.5 kW.

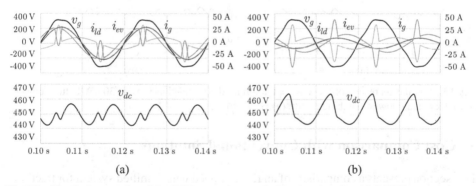

Fig. 12. Simulation results of the V4G operation mode (single–phase), with 3 kW battery power and 1.5 kW load power, combined with: (a) G2V; (b) V2G.

Figure 13 shows the same operation mode in a three–phase power grid, where it can be seen the power grid voltages (v_{ga}, v_{gb}, v_{gc}), the load currents (i_{lda}, i_{ldb}, i_{ldc}), the currents produced by the EV battery charger (i_{eva}, i_{evb}, i_{evc}), the resulting grid currents (i_{ga}, i_{gb}, i_{gc}) and the dc–link voltage (v_{dc}). In both cases, the loads absorb a power of 10 kW.

Figure 13 (a) shows the combination of V4G and G2V operation modes, where the EV batteries are being charged with 30 kW. As it can be seen, the EV battery charger consumes distorted currents so that the power grid currents are sinusoidal and in phase with the respective voltages.

Figure 13 (b) shows the combination of V4G and V2G operation modes, where the EV batteries are being discharged with 30 kW. Once again, the currents produced by the EV battery charger are distorted, turning the power grid currents sinusoidal and in phase opposition with the respective voltages. Since the EV battery charger delivers 30 kW and the loads absorb 10 kW, the power grid is receiving 20 kW, therefore its currents are in phase opposition with the corresponding voltages.

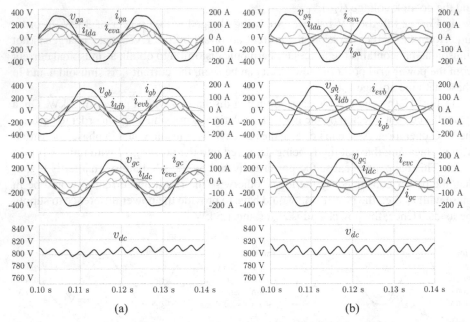

(a)   (b)

Fig. 13. Simulation results of the V4G operation mode (three–phase), with 30 kW battery power and 10 kW load power, combined with: (a) G2V; (b) V2G.

3   Cost Comparison with Conventional Solutions

This section presents a comparison of an EV equipped with a unified system for traction and battery charging with the conventional dedicated systems for performing the above-mentioned functionalities. Hence, an average cost estimation of a LSS and a SAPF is performed for two power ratings, namely 6 kW (single–phase) and 50 kW (three–phase), in order to compare with the slow and fast EV battery charging operation, respectively.

In terms of power electronics converters, a SAPF basically comprises an ac–dc converter. On the other hand, a LSS comprises the same structure, plus a dc–dc converter and the energy storage elements that are indispensable in a LSS, mostly based on lead acid or li–ion batteries [16–19]. However, the storage elements were discarded from the cost estimation, since that would require a more detailed and complex analysis regarding EVs.

There upon, Fig. 14 depicts a cost estimation of the power converters necessary to implement a SAPF (red) and a LSS (blue) for a 6 kW power rating (Fig. 14 (a)) and for a 50 kW power rating (Fig. 14 (b)). It should be referred that the presented cost values are average values of a wide value range, since a power converter cost can depend on the topology of implementation, semiconductor approach, type of sensors, capacitor technology, among others. Besides, the prices vary with the retailer and with the quantity, with small quantities being considered in this case. As it can be seen, the LSS power stage has a slightly higher cost due to the additional dc–dc converter to interface the ac–dc converter dc–link with the energy storage system. The cost estimation of the power converters for a 50 kW LSS is also valid for an EV unified system, since the structure is the same.

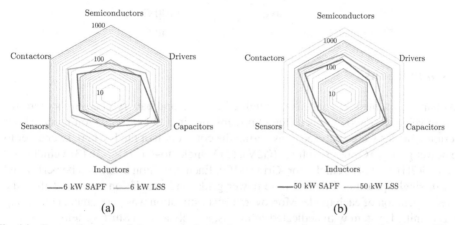

(a)   (b)

Fig. 14. Cost estimation of the power electronics converters for a Shunt Active Power Filter (SAPF) (red) and for a Load Shift System (LSS) (blue) considering a power rating of: (a) 6 kW (single–phase); (b) 50 kW (three–phase). (Color figure online)

The total cost estimation of the power electronics converters for a SAPF, LSS and EV unified system can be seen in Table 1, both for 6 kW and 50 kW. As previously referred, the LSS and the EV unified system present the same average cost, which is the higher cost in the Table (3 040 €). However, the EV can perform the same functionalities of the SAPF for the same power, without adding extra 1 870 €, besides being able to operate as a UPS. Moreover, the EV unified system can be seen as a mobile power electronics system, for instance, operating at home during the night and operating in a higher power installation during the day (i.e., at work), being able to perform the functionalities of two separate systems.

From this, it can be seen that the EV has an important role in power grids, being able to concentrate several operation modes in a single equipment, and it has even more relevance when a unified traction and battery charging system is used. It should be noted that this analysis only concerns the acquisition costs of the power electronics converters, not considering the battery costs. Besides, the analysis does not consider the investment payback that can be attained (e.g., with load shift operation), neither considers battery aging, which is a relevant issue in EVs. Nevertheless, the investment of an EV is already advantageous, both economically, environmentally and for the power grid, as long as its battery charger is capable of operating with good characteristics (i.e., sinusoidal current and bidirectional operation), and it can be even more advantageous when renewable energy sources are integrated. Accordingly, the advantages of the EV can be extended from households to industrial facilities if its EV battery charger is able to operate with higher power levels, i.e., by using a unified traction and battery charging system.

Table 1. Total cost estimation of the SAPF, LSS and EV unified system.

	Single-phase (6 kW)	Three-phase (50 kW)
SAPF	650 €	1 870 €
LSS	900 €	3 040 €
EV Unified System	–	3 040 €

4 Conclusions

This paper presented an analysis of a unified traction and battery charging system for electric vehicles (EVs) and its different possibilities in terms of operation modes. Four operation modes were analyzed considering the connection of the EV battery charger to the power grid: (1) Grid–to–Vehicle (G2V); (2) Vehicle–to–Grid (V2G); (3) Vehicle–to–Home (V2H); and (4) Vehicle–for–Grid (V4G). Each operation mode can be performed both in single–phase and three–phase power grids, and simulation results verified the correct operation of each mode. Moreover, a cost estimation was performed, comparing the EV unified system with dedicated solutions, namely a Load Shift System (LSS) and a Shunt Active Power Filter (SAPF) for two power levels: 6 kW – related to domestic installations and slow battery charging operation; and 50 kW – related to industrial installations and fast battery charging operation. The cost estimation and the different possible operation modes prove that an EV with a unified system can play a relevant role in single–phase and three–phase power grids, and it can be even more relevant considering the paradigm of smart grids.

Acknowledgments. This work has been supported by FCT – Fundação para a Ciência e Tecnologia within the Project Scope: UID/CEC/00319/2019. This work has been supported by the FCT Project DAIPESEV PTDC/EEI-EEE/30382/2017, and by the FCT Project new ERA4GRIDs PTDC/EEI-EEE/30283/2017.

References

1. Chan, C.C., Wong, Y.S.: Electric vehicles charge forward. IEEE Power Energ. Mag. **2**(6), 24–33 (2004)
2. Milberg, J., Schlenker, A.: Plug into the future. IEEE Power Energ. Mag. **9**(1), 56–65 (2011)
3. Ansari, J., Gholami, A., Kazemi, A., Jamei, M.: Environmental/economic dispatch incorporating renewable energy sources and plug-in vehicles. IET Gener. Transm. Distrib. **8**(12), 2183–2198 (2014)

4. Knezovic, K., Martinenas, S., Andersen, P.B., Zecchino, A., Marinelli, M.: Enhancing the role of electric vehicles in the power grid: field validation of multiple ancillary services. IEEE Transactions on Transportation Electrification 3(1), 201–209 (2017)
5. Nguyen, H.N.T., Zhang, C., Zhang, J.: Dynamic demand control of electric vehicles to support power grid with high penetration level of renewable energy. IEEE Transactions on Transportation Electrification 2(1), 66–75 (2016)
6. Kempton, W., Tomić, J.: Vehicle-to-grid power implementation: From stabilizing the grid to supporting large-scale renewable energy. J. Power Sources 144(1), 280–294 (2005)
7. Monteiro, V., Pinto, J.G., Afonso, J.L.: Operation modes for the electric vehicle in smart grids and smart homes: present and proposed modes. IEEE Trans. Veh. Technol. 65(3), 1007–1020 (2016)
8. Monteiro, V., Exposto, B., Ferreira, J.C., Afonso, J.L.: Improved Vehicle-to-Home (iV2H) operation mode: experimental analysis of the electric vehicle as off-line UPS. IEEE Transactions on Smart Grid 8(6), 2702–2711 (2017)
9. Su, S., et al.: Reactive power compensation using electric vehicles considering drivers' reasons. IET Gener. Transm. Distrib. 12(20), 4407–4418 (2018)
10. Kesler, M., Kisacikoglu, M.C., Tolbert, L.M.: Vehicle-to-Grid reactive power operation using plug-in electric vehicle bidirectional offboard charger. IEEE Trans. Industr. Electron. 61(12), 6778–6784 (2014)
11. Hou, R., Emadi, A.: Applied integrated active filter auxiliary power module for electrified vehicles with single-phase onboard chargers. IEEE Trans. Power Electron. 32(3), 1860–1871 (2017)
12. Yilmaz, M., Krein, P.T.: Review of battery charger topologies, charging power levels, and infrastructure for plug-in electric and hybrid vehicles. IEEE Trans. Power Electron. 28(5), 2151–2169 (2013)
13. Rippel, W.: Integrated traction inverter and battery charger apparatus, US4920475A (1990)
14. Rippel, W., Cocconi, A.: Integrated motor drive and recharge system, US5099186A (1992)
15. Cocconi, A.: Combined motor drive and battery charger system, US5341075A (1994)
16. Albright, G., Edie, J., Al-Hallaj, S.: A comparison of lead acid to lithium-ion in stationary storage applications. AllCell Technologies White Paper, no. March, p. 14 (2012)
17. McKeon, B.B., Furukawa, J., Fenstermacher, S.: Advanced lead-acid batteries and the development of grid-scale energy storage systems. Proc. IEEE 102(6), 951–963 (2014)
18. May, G.J., Davidson, A., Monahov, B.: Lead batteries for utility energy storage: a review. J. Energy Storage 15, 145–157 (2018)
19. Jinlei, S., Lei, P., Ruihang, L., Qian, M., Chuanyu, T., Tianru, W.: Economic Operation Optimization for 2nd Use Batteries in Battery Energy Storage Systems. IEEE Access 7, 41852–41859 (2019)

Demand Response; Energy; Smart Homes

Smart Auditorium: Development and Analysis of a Power and Environment Monitoring Platform

Diogo Santos[1]([✉]), Bruno Mataloto[1], João Carlos Ferreira[2], Vítor Monteiro[3],
and João L. Afonso[3]

[1] Instituto Universitário de Lisboa (ISCTE-IUL), 1649-026 Lisbon, Portugal
{dalss,Bruno_Mataloto}@iscte-iul.pt
[2] Instituto Universitário de Lisboa (ISCTE-IUL) and INOV INESC Inovação – Instituto de
Novas Tecnologias, 1649-026 Lisbon, Portugal
Joao.Carlos.Ferreira@iscte-iul.pt
[3] Dei, University of Minho (UMinho), 4710-057 Braga, Portugal
{vmonteiro,jla}@dei.uminho.pt

Abstract. The Internet of Things (IoT) is applied to many cases on the topic of smart cities. In the scope of this paper, we apply a flexible IoT-Developed platform, using LoRa communication, applied to university auditoriums in order to try and find patterns and/or anomalies in energy consumption and in the interior temperature. This platform enables the interested parties to monitor the energy consumption of lighting, of HVAC (Heating, Ventilation, and Air Conditioning) and if electrical plugs alongside the monitoring of temperatures, aiming to create a report about the efficient, the thermal insulation and the HVAC behavior. Based on the acquired information, a management strategy is applied to find that the lack of certain systems leads to an extreme waste of energy and the lack of proper cleaning procedures can lead to decreasing the efficiency of the HVAC.

Keywords: IoT · Power consumption sensors · LoRa · Sensors · Temperature sensor · Classroom monitoring · Smart cities

1 Introduction

With an increase in the world's population, resource wasting follows closely. Waste of resources originates from a different number of factors including, but not only, the lack of regulations, the misuse of existing regulations and in more extreme cases the complete disregard for those regulations, in both household and enterprise environments. One of many approaches used to tackle the problems related to resource wasting was the production and improvement of sensorial devices, the means to communicate between them and the analytical information obtained from using these devices, thus giving birth to the Internet of Things (IoT).

J. L. Afonso et al. (Eds.): SESC 2019, LNICST 315, pp. 73–87, 2020.
https://doi.org/10.1007/978-3-030-45694-8_6

These sensors are able to act both independently and with ease of use due to their mostly plug and play features.

Obviously, with the increasing search for IoT devices, the market is already flooded with devices like this, and by 2025 this market will be valued at $6.3 trillion according to McKinsey Global and, in line with this, International Data Corporation (IDC) specified that, by 2025, data load will increase all the way up to 163 zetabytes thus reaching 10 times the value from 2016 [1].

More than 80 million LoRa connected devices are working in tandem between more than 100 countries and with a CAGR for 100% or double each year [2]. This type of device can work as emergency alerts or automation controls with the lowest latency on the downlink.

Considering this scenario, and based on our previous works, we developed a low-cost LoRa sensorial solutions and the respective web server capable of monitoring power consumption and the environment in classrooms with the objective that smart classrooms and campuses may be able to improve learning experiences for students, while also improving operational efficiency. The reason for choosing LoRa was due to the poor Wi-Fi connection in certain environments, as well as the authentication factor that required more than a simple password in order to connect. In this paper, in order to evaluate our work, we also detail the assessment of an auditorium that was described as a heavy consumer of electricity and the interested party wanted to find out why, alongside an evaluation of the HVAC to find out possible improvements.

2 State of the Art

Energy efficiency and energy consumption saving are one of the most popular problems in the world of IoT research. To this end the European Union not only has created several sustainability programs with focus on reducing carbon emissions by 40% and increasing the use of renewable energy by 32% [3], but also created directives with measures that focus on the achieving of 1.5% energy efficiency increase per year by energy distributors and promote energy-efficient renovations by government-owned buildings to an extent of at least 3% of the floor area [4]. Within these initiatives, GAIA (Green Awareness in Action) [5] is one of the main contexts of this paper. It's main objectives focuses on the creation of Information and Communications Technologies (ICT) ecosystems specifically for educational buildings that motivate and support citizens' behavioral change to achieve greater energy efficiency in over 24 educational sector buildings in 3 countries covering North, Central and South Europe leading up to reductions of over 15% on the energy that could be influenced by the end-users.

Stricter regulations lead to an increase in demand for the creation of efficient energy management inside buildings, therefore, leading to the creation of more IoT projects and infrastructures. The work in [6] presents an example of both the positives and negatives of the increasing demand for efficiency measuring platforms for HVACs. It presents an example of how the lack of proper network infrastructure that can be an impediment for efficient measuring. Yet another issue faced by researchers is the lack of standardization for data generated by energy monitoring solutions. Brick [7] proposes uniform schemas that define a concrete ontology for end-devices, subsystems, and relationships among themselves, which would enable portable applications. Edge Computing [8] is also another problem-solver whose main objective is to bring the computer processing as close to the data source as possible, as in, some cases, the end-device itself. This way we're saving finite resources such as bandwidth, server resources and the costs caused by cloud processing while increasing the solution's "awareness" and reducing latency between the time the events occur and when the user is notified.

In [9], the authors presented the design and evaluation of the system PTEC, a thermal and energy control prediction system in a data centre. The focus of the study was to verify if the PTEC could efficiently perform monitoring of the data centre with a low cost in the use of power. The system collects data from both the server fans and the air conditioner and checks whether the information on both temperature and consumption are within a margin of safety for the data centre. The evaluation of the system is carried out by means of simulation to verify the efficiency and lability of the PTEC. The PTEC evaluation has shown that it can reduce cooling and circulation energy consumption by up to 34% and 30%.

In [10] a low-cost solution is developed with its main objective being, in a similar manner to ours, the power monitoring in educational buildings with the use of an open-source IoT infrastructure and XBee Devices. This solutional experiment has provided insights based on the data obtained for several power consumers, thus managing descriptive analytics of those consumers. A different approach used in power consumption research mentioned in the article [11] is the use of occupancy sensors in large commercial buildings. These occupancy sensors determine the occupancy in the selected areas and generate patterns that can create a more efficient HVAC schedule patter. This could bring reducing energy consumption up to 38% without reducing thermal comfort.

Aside from research solutions, there are also several commercial devices available in the market, in this paper we present three of the most common: (1) Smart Energy by Develco Products [12], focused on the overall building energy monitoring in an intrusive way, it also allows for the measurement of energy generation created, for example, by photovoltaics, using communication standards such as Zigbee, Z-Wave, WLAN, Wireless M-Bus, and Bluetooth Low Energy. (2) Sense: Home Energy [13], like this work, makes use of amperage clamps or current transformers to measure power consumption, therefore making it a non-intrusive solution. (3) Engage: Efergy [14] is yet another home energy consumption monitoring solution that uses Current Transformer (CT) Sensors to measure energy with the possibility to mix with future energy electrical plugs thus allowing for both intrusive and non-intrusive experience.

In this paper, a similar solution is described. CT sensors will connect to an Arduino MKR1300 and sent power consumption per interval data to an open-sourced web server which will place all data on a MySQL database. The users will then be able to analyze the data using PowerBI.

Table 1 presents the mentioned devices studied.

Table 1. Related works table

System	Source	Sensor type	Communication	Main use	Commercial
This paper	Open	**Non-invasive:** CT sensor	LoRa	Any power source	No
PTEC [9]	Closed	**Invasive:** Power meter **Non-invasive:** Temperature sensor	IEEE 802.15.4 Ethernet	Data center cooling	No
[10]	Open	**Non-invasive:** CT sensor	IEEE 802.15.4	Educational buildings/any power source	No
[11]	Closed	**Non-invasive:** Occupancy sensor	Not specified	HVAC	No
Smart Energy by Develco Products [12]	Closed	**Invasive:** Plugs, meter interface	Zigbee, Z-Wave, WLAN, Wireless M-Bus, BLE	Any power source	Yes
Sense: Home Energy [13]	Closed	**Non-invasive:** CT sensor	Wi-Fi	Any power source	Yes
Engage: Efergy [14]	Closed	**Non-Invasive:** CT sensor **Invasive:** Power plug (future)	Not specified	Any power source	Yes

WLAN: Wireless Lan, BLE: Bluetooth Low Energy, HVAC: Heating, Ventilation and Air Conditioning.

All of the devices above have at least one form of communication protocol. In order to enumerate some of the key differences between several communication standards used by IoT and the LoRaWAN we are using, the following Table 2 is also presented:

Table 2. - Overview of Common IoT Communication Standards

Wireless technology	Data rate	Max payload length	Comm. range	Security	Strengths	Ref
LoRaWAN (This paper)	50 kb/s	243 bytes	~5 km urban ~15 km–20 km rural	128 bit AES	(1) Low power consumption (2) Long communication range (3) Low cost (4) Secure (5) Easily available	[15] [16] [17]

(continued)

Table 2. (*continued*)

Wireless technology	Data rate	Max payload length	Comm. range	Security	Strengths	Ref
Sigfox	100 b/s	12 bytes	~10 km urban ~40 km rural	No encryption	(1) Long communication range (2) Low power consumption	[17]
NB-IoT	200 kb/s	1600 bytes	~1 km urban ~10 km rural	LTE encryption	(1) Large maximum payload length (2) Low power consumption (3) Secure	[17]
Wi-Fi	Top 1 Gb/s - IEEE 802.11ac	2034 bytes	1–100 m	WPA/WPA2	(1) High speed (2) Advanced/mature standard	[18] [16]
ZigBee	250 kb/s@2.4Ghz 40 kb/s@915 MHz 20 kb/s@868 MHz	255 bytes	10-300 m direct line sight 75–100 m indoor	128 bit AES	(1) Low cost (2) Low power consumption (3) Large number of nodes (up to 65000 nodes) (4) Secure	[19] [20] [21]
Bluetooth 5	2 Mb/s 500 kb/s (long range S = 2) 125 kb/s (long range S = 7	255 bytes	Up to 200 m +200 m (BLE)	L1 – No security L2 – AES 128 L3 – AES and pairing L4 – ECDHE	(1) Ease of access and setup (2) Simple Hardware (3) Secure (4) Low power consumption (BLE)	[22]
NFC	424 kb/s	$2^{32} - 1$ byte	<20 cm	Short range	(1) Continuous evolution (2) Stable technology for short range devices	[23]

AES: Advanced Encryption Standard, WPA: Wi-Fi Protected Access, BLE: Bluetooth Low Energy,
ECDHE: Elliptic-curve Diffie–Hellman Exchange, LTE: Long Term Evolution

3 System Architecture

In short, our system consists of three main layers as shown in Fig. 1.

Sensor Layer: End Devices consist of the Environment Sensor integrated with a LoRa Seeduino board and the Power Consumption Sensors integrated into the Arduino MKR WAN 1300 that enables data to be sent through a LoRa network into the closest gateway. End devices are also able to receive messages from the gateway, therefore, communication is bidirectional. These devices are powered by a lithium battery, in the environment sensor's case, or directly by the power plug, such as the power consumption sensor, and their only way of communication is through a LoRa network. Temperature sensors are used for the HVAC evaluation and Power Consumption Sensors are used for the HVAC, Lighting, and Room Electrical Plugs.

Network Layer: Consists of a LoRa Gateway connected to a Cisco's Router that receives Uplinks from several end devices and sends them to the Actility networks management service. This management service routes messages, through an Internet Protocol, to one or more application servers depending on the application they were defined to be sent to, while, also, forwarding messages from those application servers to the respective End Devices, in case there is a need to send a command, or correct the sensor's internal clock.

Knowledge Layer: The Flask web servers/application servers, a scalable solution, receives the data from the gateway and provides the treatment and processing of that data while also sending messages to defined sensors to calibrate their internal clock or provide commands, the MariaDB databases provide the data storage and backup, all while PowerBI provides the dashboard that analyzes and displays the data which is then used to make conclusions.

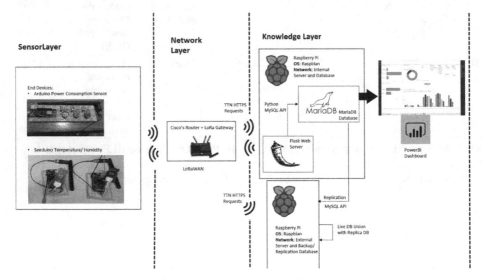

Fig. 1. Developed system architecture

3.1 Sensor Layer

Power Consumption Sensor. Power consumption sensors (See Fig. 2) were placed in auditoriums in phases corresponding to the Lighting, HVAC and Electrical Plugs, each of them formed by 3-phased power distribution. These prototypes use an Arduino MKR 1300 connected to a set of Current Transformer (CT) sensors with accuracies that will vary depending on the power consumption passing through the main cable at the time:

- With values close to the expected rating of the CT Sensor we can expect $\mp 3\%$ error [24].
- When measuring values that are very close to zero we can see errors up to 10% [24].
- However, if we go above the expected maximum rating by a large factor we risk obtaining error results up to 70% due to saturation [24].

Each sensor is able to connect to three-phases simultaneously, read each phase individually, and sum the values (kWh per reading interval) received from the phases. The sensor sums the value with each read and resets that sum every time it sends the data (as long as the data was received by the server), while also waiting to receive any message from the server. The LoRa limitation comes from the fact that it can only receive messages right after sending data to the server due to the way the device is defined. The type of message this sensor can receive can come in two forms:

- A single command, to change a variety of settings such as the interval of power reading or data sending.
- A corrective message sent automatically by the Application server. This message has the single purpose of correcting the end-device's Real-Time Clock (RTC) when it gets out of sync with real-time.

Environment Sensor. The environment sensor, see Fig. 3, used to analyze the HVAC alongside the CT sensor, uses LoRa32u4 II cards based on the Atmega32u4 microcontroller connected to a temperature and humidity sensor SHT31, which has an accuracy of ± 0.3 °C. As these sensors are designed to be portable and easy to place anywhere

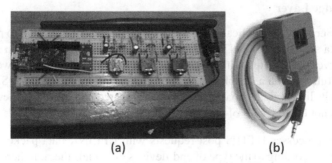

(a)   (b)

Fig. 2. Developed power consumption sensor board (a) and the CT sensor (b) that is connected to the jacks.

Fig. 3. Developed environment sensor

in the Auditoriums, they are powered by 2400 mAh lithium batteries, the durability of which is extended by code optimization and sleeps between submissions.

3.2 Network Layer

The entire system depends on 2 wireless communications protocols:

- The LoRaWAN protocol. Establishes a connection between the end-devices and the LoRa.
- HTTPS connects the LoRa gateway to the WebServer/Application Server.

As a co-founder of the LoRa Alliance, Actility is a worldwide project with over 30000 gateways interconnected, with a focus on the creation of a secure IoT network based on LoRa technology and LoRaWAN protocol. Each end-device is inserted into the network using the Actility console that provides an interface to enable flexible device management. It also allows the integration of a variety of services such as HTTP, MQTT, and cloud services such as Azure or AWS, however, the Application server used connects directly to Actility using HTTPS.

LoRa communication allows the device to work in a different variety of environments even when Wi-Fi is not available due to its low frequency. Low frequency also means that obstacles such as sturdy walls in building basements are also not an issue.

3.3 Knowledge Layer

Application Server. The application server has one main responsibility, to receive data from the LoRa server through HTTPS and then save it onto a database. In order to do this a web server was created with Flask, a python web framework. This web server is kept running full-time on a Raspberry PI configured with the Raspbian OS. Flask was chosen due to its lightweight capability. It is an un-bloated and simple framework which means it does not occupy a lot of computational resources to run.

The server processes HTTPS post requests with UPLINK data packets. It creates specific objects according to the type of end-devices that sends them. It then sends those objects unto a database running on the local IP. As mentioned above the server will also send corrective messages to the end-devices when their RTCs get out of sync with real-time.

The data collected is inserted into individual tables in a SQL database so that they can be further analyzed, consulted and, in case there is a need, exported.

While power consumption sensors provide consumed kWh per time interval, the environment sensor will provide temperature data. In the database temporal information is inserted alongside data such as the location of the sensors, auditorium occupancy, etc.

Dashboard. To create the dashboard PowerBI was used. It's a Windows OS only tool. Based on well the database is prepared for business intelligence it will provide a simple way to create interactive visualizations with pre-defined filters created by the developer. PowerBI, however, is mostly used for non-real-time business indicates, but even then the developer can achieve near-real-time updates while also connecting to different APIs and web services. It also allows the capability of using scripts from common programming languages such as R or Python.

PowerBI connects locally to a MySQL database. Temperature, power consumption and other variables for each auditorium are acquired and stored on the same device. This allows for data extraction alongside the displaying of gathered information using gauges, bar, line, and circular charts.

In Fig. 4 we can see an example of the monthly report (a), that can be filtered for each month, Type of consumption (Lights, HVAC, Plugs), Room, Weekday, Period of Time and even hour of the day, enabling, for example, to find anomalies such as computers that are left ON overnight leading to power waste.

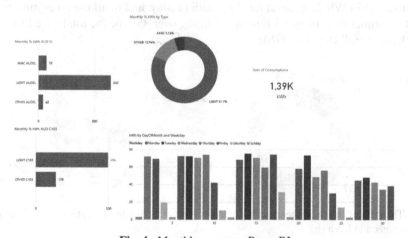

Fig. 4. Monthly report on PowerBI

In Fig. 5 is presented an example of the reporting for the Auditorium C103, alongside this image, while not visible, we can also filter by the several devices in the room including an interval of dates.

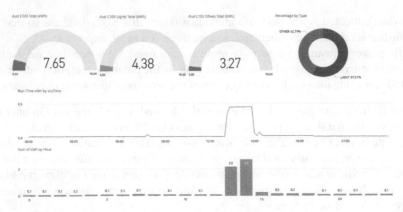

Fig. 5. Daily auditorium C103 report

4 Results

In order to evaluate our work, we ran our solution in several auditoriums, but one particular was chosen for analysis because of its particular high power consumption. The solutions ran for 3 months and we decided to pick May as our main evaluation month since it was the month with no school holidays. Overall the total energy consumption for the 3 months in this evaluated auditorium was 1710 kWh with May consuming 44% of that total, 755 kWh. In general for the month of May, and in all the other months the biggest consumer was, in fact, Lighting, reaching over 85% of the total (See Fig. 6(a)) or 642 kWh overall (See Fig. 6(b)).

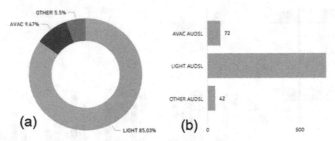

Fig. 6. The ratio of the total energy consumed per type of device in percentage (a) and the total value consumed in kWh (b)

The main reason for these values is an issue where light switches are in a hard-to-reach location within the auditorium, therefore the only people allowed to turn that switch on or off are the security guards for the building. This, in turn, leads to heavy power consumption since the security guards won't bother turning the lights off when no classes are occurring in the auditorium/between classes. The automated scheduled classes also have partial blame, since security guards are to be told that classes were going to occur in the auditorium but then no one would show up. In this auditorium, out of those 642 kWh used for lighting, approximately 248 kWh were wasted, which corresponds to 38% of the total lighting consumption and 32% of the overall power consumption in the month of May. The best solution for this issue would be to add a new light switch accessible to all users which would make sure they would be able to turn the lights on and off when they please. Figure 7 shows the difference between wasted power consumption in an auditorium with a normal light switch (b) and this auditorium (a). The residual daily consumption we see in the second auditorium is related to cleaning schedules that happen every day except Sundays.

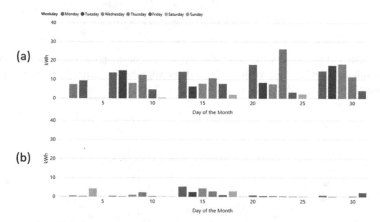

Fig. 7. The daily difference in wasted power between the evaluated auditorium with out-of-reach light switches (a) and one with user-moderated switches (b).

Still on this same topic and already within the values above, we also can see that lights are turned on too early, by which we mean that between 7 AM to 8 AM we have lighting consumptions values of 43.96 kWh in the evaluated auditorium while in the normal auditorium those values barely reach 8 kWh, which is used for cleaning duties (See Fig. 8, highlighted square). In this figure we also note the difference in hourly variation; while in the evaluated auditorium (a) the values tend to be higher and more close together between each hour with slight variations, the normal auditorium (b) seems to have bigger variations between each hour, which can clearly be seen between lunch hours (12 AM block).

As for the auditorium's environment first, we decided to compare the daily maximum and minimum temperatures inside the auditorium with the outside temperature (See Fig. 9). The auditorium temperature was measured starting in April and it's still running to this day.

In Figs. 9 and 10 we see that, while the outside temperature tends to vary quite a bit, the temperature inside the auditoriums is always relatively constant, never below 18 °C but also never above 25 °C, whereas temperatures outside reached less than 13 °C and went over 34 °C. In order to analyze how the people feel inside the auditorium we tried to correlate the temperature inside and when the AC is turned on and how long does it run for, the results can be seen in Fig. 11.

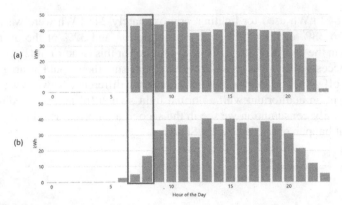

Fig. 8. The hourly difference in the sum of daily power consumption between the evaluated auditorium with out-of-reach light switches (a) and one with user-moderated switches (b). Power consumption within hours 6 AM to 8 AM exclusive marked.

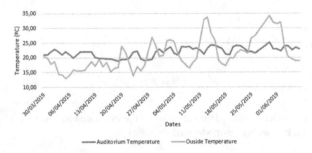

Fig. 9. The difference in daily maximum temperatures and daily minimum temperatures

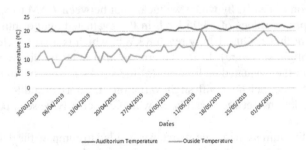

Fig. 10. The difference in daily maximum temperatures between the outside temperature and the temperature inside the auditorium.

The first thing we noticed is that the AC is never started up with temperatures below the 20.5 °C (although after being turned on for a while it does reaches temperatures below that level) and while we clearly see that temperatures below 22.5 °C tend to warrantless AC time (Fig. 11 red outline), we also see that most of the times where the AC is on for over 20 min the temperatures tend to be above that value, 22.5 °C (Fig. 11 Green

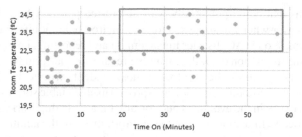

Fig. 11. The relation between the temperature inside the auditorium and how much time the Air Conditioning (AC) is turned on. (Color figure online)

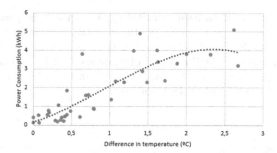

Fig. 12. The relation between the decrease in room temperature and the power consumption while the AC is turned on.

Outline). The number of times the AC was started up over the course of 2 months is also pretty low, only reaching 38 times overall, so it's pretty safe to say that the auditorium has a good thermal insulation that helps keep the room cool when the outside is hot and vice versa which means, as also presented in Fig. 6, that the HVAC's power consumption isn't really an issue. In Fig. 12 we see how efficient the AC is, the results tell us that in most cases a slight consumption will lead to very small reductions. In order to reduce the temperature by at least 1 °C, normally, it will require at least a total consumption of 1 kWh over a continuous time period. Overall we think that the AC efficiency could be improved by a proper condenser and vents cleaning since it takes quite a lot of electrical power to receive a small decrease in temperatures for the auditorium. However, this data does not account for the number of people in the room, which can increase the consumption required to reduce the temperature.

5 Conclusions

In this work, we applied a developed IoT solution with a dashboard to a classroom monitoring system, which can have effects on factors such as energy waste management, comfort levels, and operating costs. With the developed system, it is possible to determine not only anomalies but also to create clean dashboards that can help on reporting how each classroom/auditorium is being used and who are the biggest offenders when it comes to power consumption. With the use of the server, it is also possible to apply alarm applications that could potentially warn interested parties when classrooms are using more/any power when not supposed to. The environment monitoring can also find issues when it comes to HVAC disaster management and reporting, i.e., usage of power without temperature reduction overall, or simply prepare the auditoriums to receive more students without leaving aside the comfort of those students with technologies such as HVAC automation. LoRa communication also proved itself a viable solution to the lack of a proper Wi-Fi network in the evaluated auditorium. Finally, in this work, a management strategy was applied to find anomalies in the auditorium. With the auditorium measured we managed to find out that the lack of proper light switches leads to a considerable waste of energy every month, and the HVAC seems to require quite the electricity consumption in order to properly control the environment inside the auditorium.

Acknowledgments. This work has been supported by FCT – Fundação para a Ciência e Tecnologia within the Project Scope: UID/CEC/00319/2019. This work is financed by the ERDF – European Regional Development Fund through the Operational Programme for Competitiveness and Internationalisation – COMPETE 2020 Programme, and by National Funds through the Portuguese funding agency, FCT – Fundação para a Ciência e a Tecnologia, within project SAICTPAC/0004/2015 – POCI – 01–0145–FEDER–016434.

References

1. Reinsel, D., Gantz, J., Rydning, J.: Data age 2025: the evolution of data to life-critical (2017)
2. Verma, U.: Smart building device-maker integrates LoRa for in-building connectivity (2019)
3. European Commission: Europe leads the global clean energy transition: commission welcomes ambitious agreement on further renewable energy development in the EU (2018). http://europa.eu/rapid/press-release_STATEMENT-18-4155_en.htm
4. European Commission: Energy Efficiency Directive
5. European Commission: GAIA. http://gaia-project.eu/index.php/en/gaia-objectives/. Accessed 17 May 2019
6. Brunelli, D., Minakov, I., Passerone, R., Rossi, M.: Smart monitoring for sustainable and energy-efficient buildings: a case study, pp. 186–191 (2015)
7. Balaji, B., et al.: Brick: towards a unified metadata schema for buildings. In: Proceedings of the 3rd ACM International Conference on Systems for Energy-Efficient Built Environments, pp. 41–50 (2016)
8. Hamilton, E.: What Is Edge Computing? (2018). https://www.cloudwards.net/what-is-edge-computing//. Accessed 17 May 2019
9. Chen, J., Tan, R., Xing, G., Wang, X.: PTEC: a system for predictive thermal and energy control in data centers. In: 2014 IEEE Real-Time Systems Symposium, pp. 218–227 (2014)
10. Pocero, L., Amaxilatis, D., Mylonas, G., Chatzigiannakis, I.: Open source IoT meter devices for smart and energy-efficient school buildings. HardwareX 1, 54–67 (2017)
11. Ardakanian, O., Bhattacharya, A., Culler, D.: Non-intrusive techniques for establishing occupancy related energy savings in commercial buildings. In: Proceedings of the 3rd ACM International Conference on Systems for Energy-Efficient Built Environments, pp. 21–30 (2016)
12. Develco Products Smart Energy. https://www.develcoproducts.com/business-areas/smart-energy/. Accessed 25 Apr 2019
13. Sense: Home Monitor. https://sense.com/product. Accessed 25 Apr 2018

14. Engage: Engage: Efergy. https://engage.efergy.com/. Accessed 17 May 2019
15. Adelantado, F., Vilajosana, X., Tuset-Peiro, P., Martinez, B., Melia-Segui, J., Watteyne, T.: Understanding the limits of LoRaWAN. IEEE Commun. Mag. **55**(9), 34–40 (2017)
16. Gloria, A., Cercas, F., Souto, N.: Comparison of communication protocols for low cost Internet of Things devices, pp. 1–6 (2017)
17. Mekki, K., Bajic, E., Chaxel, F., Meyer, F.: Overview of cellular LPWAN technologies for IoT deployment: Sigfox, LoRaWAN, and NB-IoT. In: 2018 IEEE International Conference on Pervasive Computing and Communications Workshops (PerCom Workshops), pp. 197–202 (2018)
18. Kassner, M.: Cheat sheet: what you need to know about 802.11ac (2013). https://www.techrepublic.com/blog/data-center/cheat-sheet-what-you-need-to-know-about-80211ac/. Accessed 27 May 2019
19. Kasar, A.R., Tiwari, S.: ZigBee on Wireless Sensor Network (2018)
20. Rapiński, J.: The application of ZigBee phase shift measurement in ranging. Acta Geodyn. Geomater. **12**(291780) (2015)
21. Alliance, Z.: ZigBee 3.0. https://www.zigbee.org/zigbee-for-developers/zigbee-3-0/. Accessed 27 May 2019
22. Collotta, M., Pau, G., Talty, T., Tonguz, O.K.: Bluetooth 5: a concrete step forward toward the IoT. IEEE Commun. Mag. **56**(7), 125–131 (2018)
23. Remédios, D., Sousa, L., Barata, M., Osório, L.: NFC technologies in mobile phones and emerging applications. BASYS 2006. IIFIP, vol. 220, pp. 425–434. Springer, Boston, MA (2006). https://doi.org/10.1007/978-0-387-36594-7_45
24. Wall, R.: YHDC SCT-013-000 Current Transformer Report. https://learn.openenergymonitor.org/electricity-monitoring/ct-sensors/yhdc-sct-013-000-ct-sensor-report. Accessed 01 Feb 2019

Modeling and Thermal Energy Management in Smart Homes

Khaoula Khlifi[1](✉), Amira Haddouk[1], Vitor Monteiro[2], Joao L. Afonso[2], and Hfaiedh Mechergui[1]

[1] University of Tunis, ENSIT, Research Laboratory: LISIER,
Ecole Nationale Supérieure Des Ingénieurs de Tunis, Tunis, Tunisia
Khlifi.kh@hotmail.com,
{amira.haddouk,hfaiedh.mechergui}@ensit.rnu.tn
[2] ALGORITMI Research Centre-University of Minho Guimarães, Guimarães, Portugal
{vitor.monteiro,joao.l.afonso}@algoritmi.uminho.pt

Abstract. In this paper, it is demonstrated the importance of the information concerning the power flow and the state of a building's thermal system for the management and control of electricity consumption. The proposed approach is evaluated simulating the heating exchange behavior of a configurable base model for an isolated and non-thermally insulated habitat in order to determine the influence of the energy losses on the control system. Based on the results obtained with this study, some improvements were carried-out for the management system of the heating flow by introducing appropriated parameters into the control algorithm.

Keywords: Thermal energy management · Smart home · Load control · Modeling

1 Introduction

Nowadays, heating consumption is considered the first lever for energy saving in residential buildings. As particular case, in Tunisia, the abundance of electricity consumption comes mainly from heating and domestic hot water uses whose final demand is 65% of total consumption. Otherwise, due to economic crisis and ecological concerns, it is always interesting to consume less for paying less. The loads of type thermal comfort, which are heating, ventilation and cooling, represent between 30% and 50% of residential and service electric energy consumption. This type of loads offers interesting load control possibilities [1]. In fact, the use of buildings thermal inertia allows to relieving these loads for a while without altering occupant comfort. Buildings can also be preheated or precooled in anticipation of constraints on the grid or during periods when the energy price is low [2]. Information on energy flows and system states are necessary for management, exploitation and the distribution of energy resources, where the main information is measured [3]. Another requirement related to the control of loads is the metering and statements transmission. It is also recalled that data collected must be specific with standardized and secure communications [4]. The controllability of a load

J. L. Afonso et al. (Eds.): SESC 2019, LNICST 315, pp. 88–97, 2020.
https://doi.org/10.1007/978-3-030-45694-8_7

is defined as his ability to be underpowered, in energy saving mode or turned off for a while in response to an outside call. This signal can be linked to a security or an economic aspect. Therefore, the modeling of a thermal system is necessary to understand his behavior by setting up a set of equations describing relationship between its inputs and outputs so [5]; it becomes possible to simulate its impact on the electricity consumption of heating with a rather fine temporal resolution. We also note that we can check the response of the load subjected to several solicitations such as climate change or thermal losses [6]. This approach can then be defined as a behavioral diagnostic describing the relationship between energy requirement and the total consumption cost. The aim of this work is the simulation of an energy system model based on the state representation to descried its behavior and establish a measurement report. Indeed, we are interested in considering the building as a system that dynamically interacts with a set of climate data while being conditioned by the need of the consumer [7]. To achieve such management, we must first start by structuring the model behavior. The simulation software that will serve is Matlab Simulink, Simscape and Power system.

2 Modeling and Mathematical Representation of the Components Involved in the Buildings Thermal Exchange

The modeling methods are numerous. The main classification takes place between static and dynamic ones [8]. There is also physical modeling based on fundamental knowledge and physical phenomena that affect the system. There is also the empirical modeling method called «black box» , based on the mathematical relations inputs and outputs of the system [9]. In this work, the model will initially have a simple basic structure that will be modified and parameterized as and when required. The goal is to simulate the heat exchange evolution of an insulated or non-insulated room using or not an electric heating.

The overall system state representation is obtained from the combination of the following linear thermal equations. These last allow defining the elements that make up the room in terms of heat transfer and thermal mass.

2.1 Model of a Wall Without Insulation

The linear thermal Eq. (1) represents the modeling of an ordinary wall [10]:

$$\frac{dT_\omega}{dt} = \frac{A_\omega}{C_\omega}[U_{\omega i}(T_{ai} - T_\omega) + U_{\omega o}(T_{ao} - T_\omega)] \tag{1}$$

With $\frac{dT_\omega}{dt}$ is the thermal flow into the wall ($^\circ C/s$), T_ω is the wall temperature ($^\circ C$), A_ω wall surface (m^2), C_ω wall thermal capacity (J/K), T_{ai} indoor air temperature ($^\circ C$), $U_{\omega i}$ coefficient of thermal transfer inside the wall ($W/m^2.K$), $U_{\omega}0$ coefficient of thermal transfer outside the wall ($W/m^2.K$), and T_{ao} outside air temperature ($^\circ C$).

Where $U_w = \frac{\lambda_w}{e} = \frac{1}{R_{th}}$ with λ_w is the conductivity of the wall, e is the thickness of the wall and R_{th} is the wall thermal resistance.

2.2 Model of a Ceiling Without Insulation

The ceiling model of a room is given by the following equation:

$$\frac{dT_c}{dt} = \frac{A_c}{C_c}[U_{ci}(T_{ai} - T_c) + U_{co}(T_{ao} - T_c)] \qquad (2)$$

Where T_c is the ceiling temperature $(°C)$, A_c ceiling surface (m^2), C_c ceiling thermal capacity (J/K), U_{ci} coefficient of thermal transfer inside the ceiling $(W/m^2.K)$ and U_{co} coefficient of thermal transfer outside the ceiling $(W/m^2.K)$.

2.3 Model of a Door Without Insulation

In general case, the model of a door takes into account the heat exchange between the temperatures of the two parts that it separates. In our case, the room is considered the simulation house so the heat exchange takes place between that room and the outside air.

$$\frac{dT_d}{dt} = \frac{A_d}{C_d}[U_{di}(T_{ai} - T_d) + U_{do}(T_{ao} - T_d)] \qquad (3)$$

With T_d the door temperature $(°C)$, A_d door surface (m^2), C_d door thermal capacity (J/K), U_{di} and U_{do} are respectively the coefficient of thermal transfer inside and outside the door $(W/m^2.K)$.

2.4 Model of a Window Without Insulation (Single Glazing)

$$Q_{g-air} = \frac{dT_{g-air}}{dt} = \frac{A_g}{C_g}[U_g(T_{ao} - T_{ai})] \qquad (4)$$

The ordinary differential Eq. (4) represents the model of the window where Q_{g-air} is the thermal flow of the window towards inside the house $(°C/s)$, A_g the window surface (m^2) and U_g the coefficient of window thermal transfer $(W/m^2.K)$.

2.5 Indoor Air Model (Room Temperature)

$$\frac{dT_{ai}}{dt} = \frac{1}{C_a}[Q_e + A_\omega U_{\omega i}(T_\omega - T_{ai}) + A_c U_{ci}(T_c - T_{ai}) + A_d U_{di}(T_d - T_{ai}) + A_g U_g(T_{ao} - T_{ai})] \qquad (5)$$

Where C_a is the thermal air capacity (J/K) and Q_e the thermal flow of indoor equipment (W).

The first objective is to give a global vision on the physical aspect of the heat exchange behavior and the impact of insulation on the losses before installing the heater. The mentioned components are characterized by their heat flow and capacity, which will make it possible to determine the heat exchange in the house depending on its surface.

2.6 Input Parameters

We consider a surface room of 3 m^2 without heating and thermal insulation, which contains a single glazed window. The input parameters are the dimensions of this room, shown in Table 1. The outside temperature is fixed at 10 °C and the initial inside temperature, considered as the starting limit condition, is 20 °C.

Table 1. Model room dimensions.

	Width (m)	Length (m)	Height (m)	Surface (m^2)	Thickness (cm)
Room	3	3	2.5	9	–
Wall	–	3	2.5	7.5	10
Ceiling	3	3	2.5	9	10
Door	0.9	–	2.15	1.935	5
Window	0.6	–	1	0.6	0.4[a]

[a]thickness of a window glass

3 Simulations and Results

3.1 Simulation Model 1

The purpose of this first simulation is to determine how long the outside temperature is reached for two identical houses: house 1 without thermal insulation and house 2 with thermal insulation (Fig. 1).

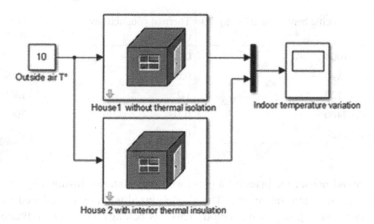

Fig. 1. Thermal system without heating.

Only the heat exchange through the window, the walls and the ceiling is taken into account. The slab and the walls orientations of the house are not considered.

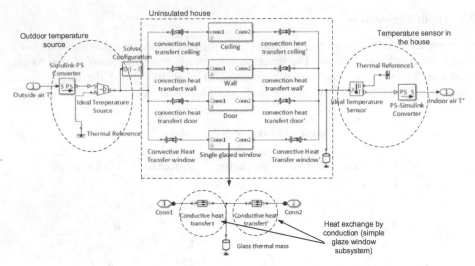

Fig. 2. Subsystems and blocks content.

The global model of house 1, without insulation, is illustrated in Fig. 2. Referring to Eqs. (1) to (5), the wall, ceiling, door and window blocks, each contain the conduction heat transfer subsystem for transferring heat flow through the house walls. These last are subsequently connected to the convective heat transfer blocks that transfer the heat amount from the outside to the surface materials of the house that we represent their characteristics in Table 2. A temperature sensor is placed inside the room.

Table 2. Thermal properties of the house materials.

	Specific heat capacity (J/kg.K)	Thermal conductivity λ (W/m.K)	Density ρ (kg/m^3)
Air	1004	0.2	1.2
Brick	840	0.84	1500
Glass	720	1.2	1530
Oak wood	2400	0.16	700
Pain wood	2227	0.15	1

In the second house, we inserted a glass wool type interior insulation at the levels of the walls surfaces and the ceiling. The single glazed window is replaced by a double glazed one with argon gas insulation. This gas belongs to the constituents of the earth's atmosphere and to the noble gases family. The choice of these insulators are fixed according to their characteristics in the following Table 3.

Table 3. Thermal properties of insulation materials.

	Thickness (cm)	Specific heat capacity (J/kg.K)	Thermal conductivity λ (W/m.K)	Density ρ (kg/m^3)
Glass wool (wall and ceiling insulation)	10	839	0.033	25
Argon (window insulation)	1.2	320	0.01772	1.783

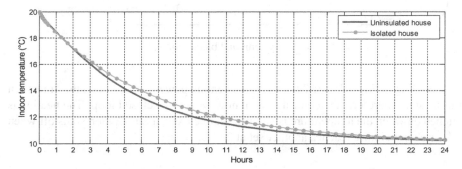

Fig. 3. Simulation results 1 (24 h). (Color figure online)

The comparison of simulation results is represented in Fig. 3. The green curve shows that the room 2, with thermal insulation, reaches the outside temperature set at 10 °C in over 24 h illustrating the decrease of the initial temperature. However, the heat is clearly lost faster in the house 1 (blue curve) due to the absence of insulation so losses are obviously much more important. It must then heat in both cases.

3.2 Simulation Model 2: Insulated House with Heating/Insulated House with Heating and Regulation

The thermal inertia of a house depends on the materials that make up its interior, so most houses are insulated from inside. Let us consider now that the house 1, (Table 2), is inside thermally insulated and heated by inserting a heat source representing the electric heating power of 200 W. This model is shown in Fig. 4 with the insulating blocks and the heating connected directly to the house thermal mass.

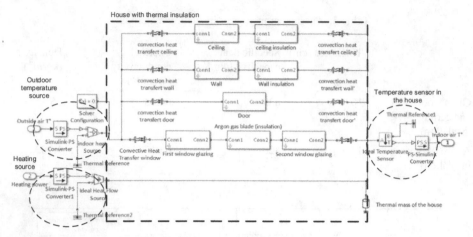

Fig. 4. Subsystems and blocks content.

According to Fig. 5, house 2 has the same heating power but equipped this time with a thermostat. Therefore, the control system now works in a closed loop. The heating is switched on when the temperature is below a set one fixed at 20 °C, then shuts off when the house temperature reaches another set at 22 °C.

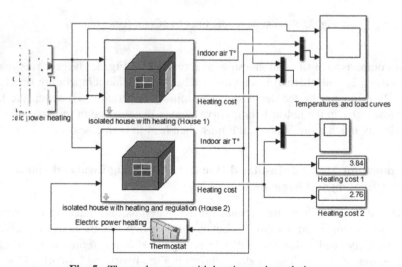

Fig. 5. Thermal system with heating and regulation.

In order to better understand the studied system and to consider the environmental demands, it is proposed to use the weather data temperature recorded, hour by hour, during the dates 01-01-2019 and 02-01-2019 (Fig. 7).

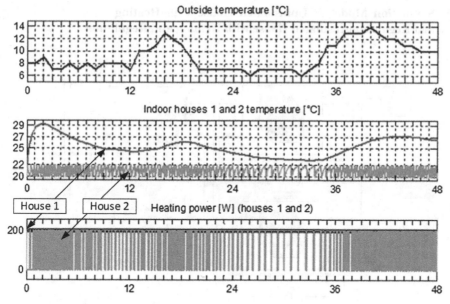

Outside temperature [°C]

Indoor houses 1 and 2 temperature [°C]

House 1   House 2   Heating power [W] (houses 1 and 2)

Fig. 6. Simulation results 2 (48 h). (Color figure online)

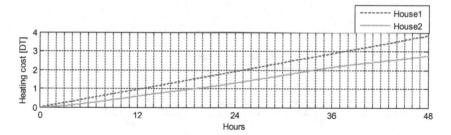

Fig. 7. Power consumption cost curves.

Minimum and maximum outdoor temperatures recorded during these 48 h are respectively 6 and 14 °C. The heating without regulation of the house 1 operates continuously since it is heating period. The power is then maximum throughout the simulation and it is noted from the red curve of Fig. 6, illustrating the indoor temperatures, that the comfort is missing. Indeed, after two hours of the startup, temperatures reached are very high at about 30 °C then, vary between 23 and 27 °C. On the other hand, in the case of the house 2, with heating regulation, the ambient temperature is comfortable and maintained between 20 and 22 °C. We also calculated the cost of heating consumption during these two days for the both houses and we deduct that house 1 records a higher consumption that house 2 with regulation (Fig. 8).

3.3 Simulation Model 3: Uninsulated House with Heating and Regulation/Insulated House with Heating and Regulation

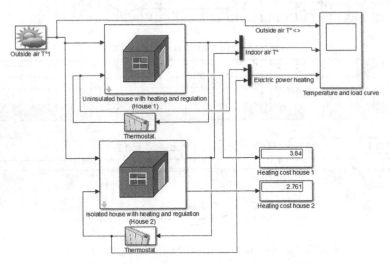

Fig. 8. Thermal system with heating and regulation.

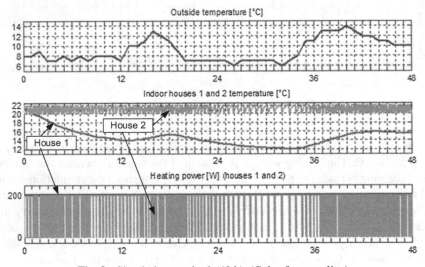

Fig. 9. Simulation results 3 (48 h). (Color figure online)

In this last case, the importance of insulation is put again to the test. Both houses are now equipped with regulated heating. According to the indoor temperature variation curves of Fig. 9, we note that without thermal insulation (red curve), the average house temperature for 48 h is 16 °C. The heating starts but control stops because there are many losses and the ambient temperature does not reach the thermostat set point one while heating remains in permanent operation at full power during all the simulation period. This leads to a consumption cost increase up to 3.84TND for only two days and this amount to the same billing of house 1 in the simulation model 2 without regulation.

4 Conclusion

With the work proposed in this paper, it was possible to conclude that without thermal insulation we lose comfort occupant and economy, despite the regulation of heating at ambient temperatures. Based on the obtained results, it is also noted that the heating method without isolating the building does not limit the consumption wastage even if we put the heating regulation according to predetermined set temperatures. Indeed, this study shows that the building heating economy is based on, first of all, a priority step which the thermal insulation then the regulation by various means including the intelligent thermostat and the remote control to ensure an efficient load control and realize electric energy economy.

References

1. Boëda, D.: Etude de la contribution du pilotage de charges à la fourniture de services aux réseaux électriques. Thesis, Polytechnic institute of Grenoble (2009)
2. Leclercq, F., Leclercq, T.: Le système de chauffage et la production d'eau chaude sanitaire.: MATRIciel sa, Energy engineering, Environment and Special thechniques, University square, 25 – 1348 Louvain-la-Neuve, Bruxelles environment, IBGE –Brussels Institute for environmental Management (2017)
3. EUDEEP project: Keynote paper, WP3-S9. Automation and control issue for DER and technologies involving LTS (2004)
4. CRISP project: Distributed Intelligence in Critical Infrastructures for Sustainable Power, ENK8-CT-2002-00673, deliverable D1.2, Market-oriented online supply-demand matching (2004)
5. Dang, H.A.: Modélisation en vue de la simulation énergétique des bâtiments: Application au prototypage virtuel et à la gestion optimale de PREDIS MHI, Thesis (2013)
6. Saker, N., Petit, M., Vannier, J.-C., Coullon, J.-L.: Demand side management of electrical water heaters and evaluation of the cold load pick-up characteristics (CLPU). In: IEEE PES Trondheim PowerTech, pp. 1–8 (2011)
7. Richalet, V.: Caractérisation énergétique des bâtiments sur site. Identification de modèles dynamiques. Méthodes de signature Energétique, Thesis, INPG (1991)
8. Gevers, M., Bazanella, A.S., Bombois, X., Miskovic, L.: Identification and the information matrix: how to get just sufficiently rich. IEEE Trans. Autom. Control **54**, 2828–2840 (2009)
9. Ruellan, M., Park, H., Bennacer, R.: Residential building energy demand and thermal comfort: thermal dynamics of electrical appliances and their impact (2016). https://doi.org/10.1016/j.enbuild.2016.07.029
10. Abarkan, M., Kouider, M.N.: Modélisation et Analyse du comportement d'un Bâtiment équipé d'un Système Multi Sources d'énergie, Thesis (2014)

Reverse Power Flow Detection Using Optimally Placed μPMUs in a Distribution System

Philip Joshua P. Eloja, Niko Avel F. Jorda, and Michael Angelo A. Pedrasa[✉]

Electrical and Electronics Engineering Institute, University of the Philippines Diliman, 1101 Quezon City, Philippines
philip.eloja@eee.upd.edu.ph, {nfjorda,mapedrasa}@up.edu.ph

Abstract. The rise in the accessibility of photovoltaic (PV) generators to consumers increases the possibility of reverse power flow (RPF) in the electric distribution system. RPF occurs when power flows to the design of the system. Overvoltage, power losses and protection system coordination are among the problems that could occur due to the presence of RPF. This paper describes an algorithm to detect the presence of RPF using optimally-placed micro-phasor measurement units (μPMUs) in the IEEE 34-Bus System with 5 PV generators. A machine learning algorithm based on a feedforward artificial neural network (ANN) was developed. The algorithm was able to detect the presence of RPF using (1) voltage and current and (2) polar- and (3) rectangular-impedance methods for training. The algorithm was also able to detect RPF under scenarios that were not used during the training process. Sensitivity analyses were performed for cases such as PV outage, PV relocation, PV addition, PV expansion and load increase. The susceptibility of the algorithm to true value errors (TVEs) was tested by adding error vectors on the μPMU measurements for both the training and testing populations.

Keywords: Reverse power flow (RPF) · μPMU · Machine learning

1 Introduction

Photovoltaic (PV) generators have been a great addition to the electric power system (EPS) in terms of its supply of sustainable energy. The sun is a renewable energy source that can be placed anywhere in the power system. As a solar farm, it can deliver bulk amounts of power to the grid. As an additional source of power for commercial and residential units, it can lower monthly electricity bills and export power to the network when it produces excess energy.

But with PV generators installed more and more in distribution systems as price drops, reverse power flow (RPF) becomes a problem. RPF occurs when power flows opposite where the system designed for it to flow which could be a huge risk for the distribution network as most of these systems are only designed to absorb power and not deliver power. Problems associated with RPF include, overvoltage, distribution protection coordination and power quality. [1] has claimed that RPF is the major cause of overvoltage in the distribution system. [2] has suggested that DGs could change short

© ICST Institute for Computer Sciences, Social Informatics and Telecommunications Engineering 2020
Published by Springer Nature Switzerland AG 2020. All Rights Reserved
J. L. Afonso et al. (Eds.): SESC 2019, LNICST 315, pp. 98–109, 2020.
https://doi.org/10.1007/978-3-030-45694-8_8

circuit levels in the system compromising the coordination of protection devices. According to [3], DGs may increase the power loss of the system depending on its network configuration.

2   Related Works

2.1   Micro-Phasor Measurement Unit (μPMU)

Growth in DGs in distribution network presents variability and uncertainty. As such, a more fast and precise measurement device needs to be developed to accurately assess the state of the system. The researchers in [4] addressed the issues faced by traditional supervisory control and data acquisition monitoring systems by developing a phasor measurement unit (PMU) that provides real-time and synchronized measurements. PMUs are more commonly used in transmission systems. In [5], the researchers further improved PMUs into micro-synchrophasors which can be used even in distribution systems. A micro-phasor measurement unit (μPMU) is a high-precision measurement unit that uses synchrophasor technology to observe the state of electric power systems. It can estimate the magnitude and phase angle of voltages and currents in the distribution system.

Optimal μPMU Placement (OPP) Problem. Installing μPMU in each node of the system would be ideal but not economical. But with the assumption that line data are available an optimal number of μPMU can be used to observe the system while reducing the cost. The fitness function that represents the OPP problem for an n-bus system is: [6]

$$\sum_{i}^{n} w_i x_i \tag{1}$$

where w_i is the cost and x_i is the binary decision variable of installing a PMU at bus i. A significant number of studies [6–9] have solved the OPP problem in various bus systems using different optimization algorithms.

2.2   Reverse Power Flow Detection

Directional relays have been in used to detect RPF in synchronous generators [10]. In [11] a directional power relay was employed to protect a distribution system from RPF caused by DG. The directional relays, however, are generally used to automate trippings due to faults.

[12] used an electronics-based transformer called a smart transformer to control the reverse power flows in the system. While this is a novel solution, the production of power can be more economical when the energy source is generous thus limiting its production is not the best option. With a proper analysis tool using the reverse power flow to the advantage of the system could be better by diverting where power is needed. But in order for such a tool to be used, an analysis to determine whether RPF is present in the system or not is needed.

Voltage Angle Difference Method. Consider two adjacent buses bus j and k. It can be seen in Eq. 2 that the sign of P_k and therefore its direction is related by the value of the angle inside the sine function. When θ_j is greater than θ_k the quantity inside the sine function is negative making the value of P_k negative since sine is an odd function. For the Reactive power on the other hand the direction of power of Q_k is dictated by V_k and V_j. When V_j is greater than V_k, the reactive power is negative.

$$P_k = \frac{|V_k||V_j|}{X} \sin(\theta_k - \theta_j) \tag{2}$$

$$Q_k = \frac{|V_k|}{X}[|V_k| - |V_j|\cos(\theta_k - \theta_j)] \tag{3}$$

P_k: real power injection through bus k
Q_k: reactive power injection through bus k
V_k: voltage magnitude at bus k
V_j: voltage magnitude at bus j
θ_k: voltage angle at bus k
θ_j: voltage angle at bus j
X: line impedance from bus k to j

In this paper, only the fundamental frequency was considered due to the high sampling rate of μPMUs.

Impedance Method. A relationship between power and impedance can also be drawn, [1] uses this method to determine at what impedance level the reverse power flow occurs from PV injections. Impedance as seen by bus k can be expressed as:

$$Z_k = \frac{V_k}{I_k} \tag{4}$$

$$Z_k = \frac{V_k}{\left(\frac{P_k + Q_k}{V_k}\right)^*} \tag{5}$$

$$Z_k = \left(\frac{P_k + jQ_k}{P_k^2 + Q_k^2}\right)|V_k|^2 \tag{6}$$

I_k: current going through bus k to bus j

Equation 6 can be further decomposed to its resistance (R_k) and reactance (X_k) components.

$$R_k = \left(\frac{P_k}{P_k^2 + Q_k^2}\right)|V_k|^2 \tag{7}$$

$$X_k = \left(\frac{Q_k}{P_k^2 + Q_k^2} \right) |V_k|^2 \tag{8}$$

As P_k flows to the opposite direction, the value of R_k and X_k will be negative.

2.3 Classification Algorithms in Machine Learning

There are several techniques in tackling classification problems such as support vector machines (SVM), random tree and neural networks among others. For the purposes of this study, the proponents will be focusing on neural networks.

Neural Networks. Neural Network or also known as artificial neural networks (ANN) is a problem-solving technique developed to tackle non-linear and complex problems [13]. For [14], ANN is one of the best techniques for data classification.

Primarily, the ANN is composed of two major components, the neurons and connections [15]. To put it simply, neurons are the data processing units of the algorithm. It analyzes inputs and its relation to the output in order to create a relationship between the two. Connections, on the other hand, are the one that delivers this data from neuron to neuron. It is the carrier of information.

While there are a number of topologies in the ANN architecture, the most popular is the feedforward network [15] shown in Fig. 1. This topology consists of three or more layers. The first layer is called the input layer, the next layers are called the hidden layer, while the last layer is called the output layer. In this setup, data travels from one layer to another without reversing. The bulk of the processing happens in the hidden layer.

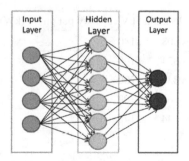

Fig. 1. Feedforward topology

3 Methodology

3.1 Testbed Creation

To develop an algorithm that can detect the presence of RPF, a testbed is needed in order to train and test it. This testbed was created using OpenDSS.

Bus System Modelling. The proponents adapted the bus network used in [10] as shown in the Fig. 2 while modifying the placement of μPMU in node 836 to node 860. μPMU will be placed on primary lines just before buses 814, 852 and 860 to measure voltages and currents of the lines and not the buses itself. A μPMU is also placed just after reference bus 800. The system will have 5 3-phase PVs attached to buses, 808, 824, 830, 844 and 860. Capacities of these PVs can be seen in Table 1.

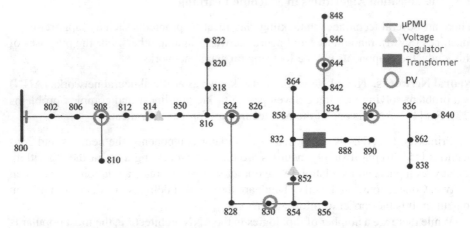

Fig. 2. Modified IEEE-34 bus network with optimally placed μPMUs

Table 1. 3-phase PV locations and capacities

PV location	PV capacity per phase (kW)
Bus 808	180
Bus 824	100
Bus 830	200
Bus 860	100
Bus 844	140

Bus System Modeling. There were 3 different types of samples that were generated: (1) average loading, (2) variable loading and (3) PV outage with variable loading.

For the first type of samples shown in Fig. 3, the percent loading of each bus will be varied from each other while maintaining a mean percent loading for the whole system. The mean percent loading will be swept from 20% to 100% with a 2% increment. With this, percent loading for each bus will deviate by around 5% from the suggested mean percent loading across the system. For each increment of the mean percent loading, the 5 PVs will be injecting real power to the system from 0% capacity to 100% capacity incremented uniformly by 1%. 4100 samples will be generated from this method.

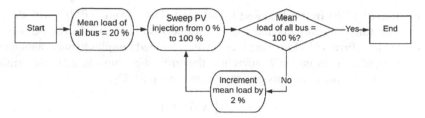

Fig. 3. Process of generating the samples with average loading

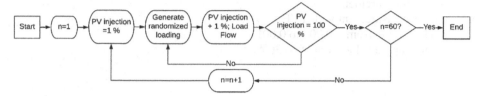

Fig. 4. Process of generating the sample with variable loading

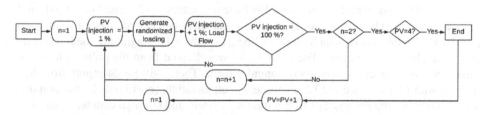

Fig. 5. Process of generating the samples for PV outage with variable loading

For the second type of samples, as shown in Fig. 4, percent loading for each bus in the system will be varied from each other. This method will ensure that as the 5 PVs injects power from 0% to 100%, each 1% increment of power injection will have a different set of percent loading for each bus that will be varied from 20% to 100%. This method will generate a batch of samples that will be as varied from each other as possible. 6000 samples will be generated from this method.

For the third type of samples shown in Fig. 5, PV Outage will be simulated. Percent loading of each bus will be acquired using the method for acquiring percent loading in the second type of samples. PVs in operation will be decreased from 5 PVs up to 1 PV while considering all 30 possible combinations for PV operation. For each combination 200 samples were generated which amounted to 6000 samples.

Each sample generated have a tag of 0 if RPF is not present in the system and 1 if RPF is present. Impedance method was used to tag each sample. Since RPF will first occur on buses where generators are present, impedances as seen on the buses where PVs are placed were computed. Where resistance was seen as negative in a bus, there is RPF in the system.

Introduction of TVEs in the Training Population. Data from μPMU will deviate from the true values of currents and voltages in the system by 0.1%. The proponents added True Value Errors (TVEs) to the previously generated samples to make another set of training population. Equation 9 shows how the errors were introduced to the original voltage and current measurements gathered from the 4 μPMUs.

$$A^* = A + \left[e(|A|\angle\delta) \right] \tag{9}$$

Where,

A: phasor measurement
A*:   phasor measurement with TVE
E: random value from −0.001 to 0.001
Δ: random angle value from 0° to 360°

3.2 Machine Learning Implementation

Algorithm Training and Testing. Three models for the RPF detection were used. One model had 48 inputs which consists of 12 voltage magnitudes, 12 current magnitude and 18 phasor angles. The second model used the impedances calculated, in polar form, from μPMU measurements of which there will be 24 inputs - 12 magnitude measurements and 12 angles measurements. The third model was derived from the polar form of the impedance by converting it to its rectangular form. There will be 24 inputs from this method with 12 resistance and 12 reactance. For all model there will only be two outputs, 1 which denotes the presence of RPF within the system and 0 which denotes otherwise. The MATLAB's Deep Learning Toolbox was used in training the algorithm with a feedforward topology and 10 hidden nodes in the ANN architecture. 80% of the 16,100 samples were used for the training of the algorithm while the remaining 20% were used for testing.

Performance Evaluation. The algorithms developed were subjected to another round of testing using 1000 samples that were generated outside of the 16100 samples of the training population. The results of the testing using these samples will serve as the base case.

Sensitivity Analysis. The trained algorithms were tested using test samples that were not included in the training population. Five scenarios were established to test the robustness of the algorithm. For each case 1000 test samples were generated.

PV Outage. The system simulated events wherein 1 or more PVs are offline. The number of functioning PVs was reduced decrementally from 5 to 1. PVs were relocated to the adjacent 3-phase bus one at a time. Each of the 5 PVs, while retaining their capacity output, were relocated twice, as there were two adjacent buses for each of the PVs.

PV Relocation. The PVs were relocated to their adjacent 3-phase bus one at a time. Each of the 5 PVs were relocated twice, as there were two adjacent buses for each of the PVs. The capacities of the PVS were retained.

PV Addition. Another 3-phase PV Generator was added to a random bus in the IEEE-34 bus system, making the total number of PVs to 6. The addition of 3-phase PV to the system will be repeated 10 times amounting to 1000 test samples (Table 2).

Table 2. Sizing and placement of additional PV

Bus	Capacity per phase (kW)	Voltage (kV)
840	10	14.376
890	70	2.401
848	20	14.376
858	80	14.376
816	50	14.376
802	100	14.376
854	50	14.376
850	75	14.376
832	80	14.376
828	75	14.376

PV Expansion. The capacities of the 5 existing 3-phase PVs were increased while maintaining the per-unit voltage of the system to 1.1 p.u. A total of 100 kW was added to the total PV power output (Table 3).

Table 3. New PV capacity after expansion

PV location	New PV capacity per phase (kW)
Bus 808	180
Bus 824	100
Bus 830	200
Bus 860	100
Bus 844	140

Load Increase. An increase in power consumption was simulated for this test case. The base loads of each bus were increased to up to 150% while still retaining the old capacities of the 5 PVs.

Introduction of TVEs in the Testing Population. TVEs were also introduced to the 5000 test samples generated for the sensitivity analysis. This will test the susceptibility of the algorithms trained to errors in the measurements. All of the testing mentioned above were repeated after adding TVEs.

4   Results and Analysis

Algorithms developed have significantly high accuracies and are close to each other whether trained using the standard training population set or the modified training population with accuracies up to 99.7%. Upon evaluating the performance of the algorithms, the accuracies scored near the 99% mark (Tables 4 and 5).

Table 4. Accuracy results of the algorithm training and testing

Algorithm method	Algorithm accuracy with standard training population	Algorithm accuracy with modified training population
Voltage and current	99.7	99.7
Polar impedance	98.7	98.9
Rectangular impedance	98.5	98.6

Table 5. Accuracy results of the algorithm performance evaluation

Algorithm method	Algorithm accuracy with standard training population	Algorithm accuracy with modified training population
Voltage and current	98.7	98.8
Polar impedance	99.2	98.9
Rectangular impedance	98.2	98.3

For the sensitivity analysis of the algorithms developed using the standard training population using test samples with no TVE, accuracies are above 90%. PV outage, PV relocation and PV expansion are the only scenarios where the algorithm only got almost 93% as the rest scored above 95%. Upon the introduction of TVE in test samples however, for the voltage and current method, accuracies are down to almost 50%. Both the algorithms using impedance method scored the same accuracies as their counterpart algorithm (Tables 6 and 7).

Table 6. Accuracy results for the sensitivity analysis of algorithms for standard training population without TVE

Test case	Voltage and current method	Polar impedance method	Rectangular impedance method
Base case	98.7	99.2	98.2
PV outage	93.9	93.6	93.3
PV relocation	93.6	93.1	92.4
PV addition	98.5	98.8	98
PV expansion	98.6	99.1	98.5
Load increase	92.8	95.4	92.5

Table 7. Accuracy results for the sensitivity analysis of algorithms for standard training population with TVE

Test case	Voltage and current method	Polar impedance method	Rectangular impedance method
Base case	53.4	99.2	98.2
PV outage	52.3	93.6	93.3
PV relocation	52.6	93.1	92.4
PV addition	53.6	98.9	98
PV expansion	53.7	99.1	98.5
Load increase	54	95.4	92.5

The algorithms with a modified training population on the other hand had high accuracy results for the sensitivity analysis. The voltage and current method had also significantly improved accuracies for all test cases where test samples have been introduced with TVE (Tables 8 and 9).

Table 8. Accuracy results for the sensitivity analysis of algorithms for modified training population without TVE

Test case	Voltage and current method	Polar impedance method	Rectangular impedance method
Base case	98.8	98.9	98.3
PV outage	93.8	93.8	94.4
PV relocation	93.1	93.5	92.4
PV addition	98.7	98.7	97.6
PV expansion	98.7	98.7	98.8
Load increase	96.8	93.4	97.8

Table 9. Accuracy results for the sensitivity analysis of algorithms for modified training population with TVE

Test case	Voltage and current method	Polar impedance method	Rectangular impedance method
Base case	98.6	98.9	98.4
PV outage	94.1	93.8	94.3
PV relocation	93	93.6	92.4
PV addition	98.8	98.7	97.6
PV expansion	98.7	98.7	98.8
Load increase	97.4	93.4	97.8

5 Conclusion

This paper describes machine learning algorithms based on ANN that can detect reverse power flow in distribution networks with PV generators. The algorithm uses measurements gathered by optimally placed μPMU along the network and another μPMU in the substation bus. Several algorithms were developed: one using the raw phasor voltage and current measurements as inputs and two using the apparent downstream impedance as inputs (first has the impedance in rectangular form, and other in polar form).

The IEEE 34-bus system with 5 PV generators and 3 optimally placed μPMUs was used to demonstrate the performance of the system. The robustness of the algorithm was also investigated by adding noise to the measurements and using the algorithm to detect RPF on a network that is slightly different from the network where training data was gathered. The algorithms were able to detect RPF with high accuracy except on cases where the testing data contained measurement errors while the training population did not. The performance improved when the algorithm was trained using measurements that contained noise.

References

1. Mortazavi, H., Mehrjerdi, H., Saad, M., Lefebvre, S., Asber, D., Lenoir, L.: A monitoring technique for reversed power flow detection with high PV penetration level. IEEE Trans. Smart Grid **6**, 2221–2232 (2015)
2. Antonova, G., Nardi, M., Scott, A., Pesin, M.: Distributed generation and its impact on power grids and microgrids protection. In: 2012 65th Annual Conference for Protective Relay Engineers, pp. 152–161 (2012)
3. Sarabia, A.: Impact of distributed generation on distribution system. Master's thesis, Department of Energy Technology Aalborg University, Pontoppidanstraede 101, 9220 Aalborg East Denmark (2011)
4. Phadke, A.G., Thorp, J.S., Karimi, K.J.: State estimlatjon with phasor measurements. IEEE Trans. Power Syst. **1**, 233–238 (1986)
5. von Meier, A., Culler, D., McEachern, A., Arghandeh, R.: Micro-synchrophasors for distribution systems. In: ISGT 2014, pp. 1–5 (2014)
6. Mabaning, A.A.G., Orillaza, J.R.C., von Meier, A.: Optimal PMU placement for distribution networks. In: 2017 IEEE Innovative Smart Grid Technologies - Asia (ISGT-Asia), pp. 1–6 (2017)
7. Tahabilder, A., Ghosh, P.K., Chatterjee, S., Rahman, N.: Distribution system monitoring by using micro-PMU in graph-theoretic way. In: 2017 4th International Conference on Advances in Electrical Engineering (ICAEE), pp. 159–163 (2017)
8. Al Rammal, Z., Abou Daher, N., Kanaan, H., Mougharbel, I., Saad, M.: Optimal PMU placement for reverse power flow detection, pp. 1–5 (2018)
9. Jamei, M., et al.: Anomaly detection using optimally placed μPMU sensors in distribution grids. IEEE Trans. Power Syst. **33**, 3611–3623 (2018)
10. Yaghobi, H.: Fast predictive technique for reverse power detection in synchronous generator. IET Electr. Power Appl. **12**(4), 508–517 (2018)
11. Sudhakar, P., Malaji, S., Sarvesh, B.: Reducing the impact of dg on distribution networks protection with reverse power relay. In: International Conference on Processing of Materials, Minerals and Energy. Materials Today: Proceedings, Ongole, Andhra Pradesh, India, 29th–30th July, vol. 5, no. 1, Part 1, pp. 51– 57 (2016)

12. De Carne, G., Buticchi, G., Zou, Z., Liserre, M.: Reverse power flow control in a st-fed distribution grid. IEEE Trans. Smart Grid **9**, 3811–3819 (2018)
13. Lari, N.S., Abadeh, M.S.: Training artificial neural network by krill-herd algorithm. In: 2014 IEEE 7th Joint International Information Technology and Artificial Intelligence Conference, pp. 63–67 (2014)
14. Hong, Z.: A preliminary study on artificial neural network. In: 2011 6th IEEE Joint International Information Technology and Artificial Intelligence Conference, vol. 2, pp. 336–338 (2011)
15. Kriesel, D.: A brief introduction to neural networks (2007)

Comparison of Thermal Load Models for MILP-Based Demand Response Planning

Pedro L. Magalhães$^{(\boxtimes)}$ and Carlos Henggeler Antunes

INESC Coimbra, Departamento de Engenharia Electrotécnica e de Computadores,
Universidade de Coimbra, Rua Sílvio Lima, 3030-290 Coimbra, Portugal
{pmlpm,ch}@deec.uc.pt

Abstract. Demand response has the potential to reduce end-users electricity costs by promoting judicious use of existing power system infrastructure. This is most often assumed to require the adoption of time-varying electricity prices which can make load scheduling and energy resource management difficult to carry out in a time-effective and comfortable way without computational assistance and automated control. Automated home energy management systems can facilitate this process including by providing users with optimised plans. Creating these plans requires optimisation tools operating on mathematical models of the underlying problem. Mixed-integer linear programming (MILP) has been used extensively for this purpose though increasing complexity and time resolution can render this approach impractical. In this paper, we describe and compare MILP formulations of the same demand response problems using alternative thermal load models. The results, obtained using a state-of-the-art solver, can be summarised as follows: (1) the elimination of continuous temperature variables in one thermal load submodel increased the computation time in 99% of cases and by 981% on average; (2) two new discrete control formulations leading to a 40% reduction in the number of binary variables relative to the standard formulation were found to decrease the computation time in approximately 63% of cases and by 38–40% on average. Efforts are ongoing to evaluate these techniques under more diverse scenarios.

Keywords: Demand response · Thermal load model · Mixed-integer linear programming

1 Introduction

1.1 Context and Motivation

Demand response (DR) programs are often advanced as a way to ensure the existing power system infrastructure is used rationally and efficiently, and also to integrate increasing shares of variable renewable energy resources into power grids [1,2]. This potential implies the dissemination of intelligible information

© ICST Institute for Computer Sciences, Social Informatics and Telecommunications Engineering 2020
Published by Springer Nature Switzerland AG 2020. All Rights Reserved
J. L. Afonso et al. (Eds.): SESC 2019, LNICST 315, pp. 110–124, 2020.
https://doi.org/10.1007/978-3-030-45694-8_9

about the power system for a given period – most often in the form of time-differentiated electricity prices and ad-hoc demand reduction requests – so as to indirectly influence end-users' aggregate electricity consumption. Once in possession of this information, end-users are expected to decide when and how to adjust their actions to meet their objectives. For residential end-users, this implies scheduling and configuring domestic appliances as well managing local energy resources, particularly storage units, if there are any. However, for end-users to minimise their electricity bill under these circumstances while meeting their needs requires a level of effort most if not all end-users will want to avoid without computer assistance and control, arguably due to the task's participative, repetitive, schedule-constraining and computationally-demanding nature [3,4]. As such, automated home energy management systems have been proposed to not only carry out part of these actions but also to support the decision-making process by providing users with optimised reference plans [5].

Generating these plans requires the use of optimisation tools operating on mathematical models of the underlying DR problem and should be sufficiently time-effective to avoid protracted interactions with end-users. One common approach is to model DR problems using mixed-integer linear programming (MILP) and produce optimised solutions via MILP solvers. A wide range of DR problems have been modelled using MILP including those featuring thermal loads with significant DR potential, such as domestic hot water (DHW) vessels and air-conditioned spaces, since these allow loads to be deferred to an extent that allows for significant flexibility and possibly lower costs. Modelling thermal loads and respective actuators using MILP can thus be ascribed some importance. This paper describes a study comparing the computational performance of MILP formulations of DR problems using different yet equivalent thermal load models.

1.2 Literature Review

The thermal load MILP models surveyed in the literature cover loads such as hot water vessels, air-conditioned spaces, radiators and refrigerated compartments, and are mostly physical phenomena-inspired as opposed to physics-agnostic models. Most commonly, thermal loads are modelled as single-node temperature models that can be derived from first order ordinary linear differential equations, and often rely on continuous decision variables to hold temperature values [3,6–12]. One-dimensional multi-node models can also be found in the literature, particularly to model thermal stratification in storage vessels [13,14] and heat transfer across building envelopes [15,16]. In a few cases, thermal loads have also been modelled as time-shiftable or interruptible loads [17,18].

The models reviewed encompass combinations of temperature, power, and control constraints. Temperature constraints have generally been used to ensure safety and comfort standards [3,8,12], either constant or changing over time due to occupancy or demand, rather than the model's own accuracy (e.g., due to phase changes). Power constraints have been used to comply with individual equipment's power ratings [8,9,11,19] or those defined by fuses or the utility grid [3,17,20]. Control constraints have been used to implement discrete part-load operation, 2 level hysteresis control and minimum operation and inactivity cycle durations [20,21], and to ensure some modes are mutually-exclusive (e.g., heating or cooling) [8,22]. Accommodating these features may be a necessity but these also increase the computational burden, particularly for short time steps, due to the additional binary variables needed. Ultimately, models of a strongly-combinatorial nature (due to the number of binary variables) can be too difficult to solve within an acceptable time-frame (e.g., close to real-time) using affordable and low power computational resources [6,8,12,18–22], which limits the attractiveness of MILP models for in-house residential DR planning.

1.3 Objectives and Approach

The study described here set out to explore the effect of two modelling techniques on the ability to efficiently solve MILP-formulated residential demand response problems featuring thermal loads. The techniques evaluated sought to reduce the number of continuous and binary variables necessary to reproduce the same DR problem. The first technique concerns the elimination of continuous load temperature variables. The second technique relates to modelling multi-level discrete control of appliances interacting with thermal loads: three equivalent formulations were compared, namely the traditional one relying on one binary variable per level and time interval plus constraints to ensure that only one can be used at any given time interval, and two others potentially relying on a reduced set of binary variables and constraints. The main thrust was thus to understand how these techniques influence the computational performance of MILP-formulated DR problems involving thermal loads and under time-differentiated electricity prices. For this purpose, a state-of-the-art solver was used to produce optimised solutions to the same DR problem formulated differently and the computation times compared. A diverse set of case studies was defined and employed to reduce the possibility of bias influencing the conclusions. This effort is presented over 5 additional sections: Sect. 2 describes the DR problem under consideration; Sect. 3 details the models used to reproduce the problem; Sect. 4 defines the case studies considered; Sect. 5 presents and analyses the optimisation results; Sect. 6 summarises this endeavour's main conclusions.

2   Problem Description

The DR problem addressed in this study is centred around a grid-connected single-family household where the end-users' electricity consumption during a 36-hour period is charged according to a discretely-increasing (power) demand rate and time-differentiated energy prices. The automated home energy management system is tasked with preparing optimised plans and managing the operation of domestic appliances and energy resources to maximize profits while maintaining safety and comfort standards, and without interfering with the non-controllable demand (NCD). The other demand component is due to an electric water heater (EWH), a refrigerator (REF), a reversible speed-controlled heat pump (HP) as well as single dishwasher (DW), laundry machine (LM) and tumble dryer (TD) cycles observing user-designated appliance-specific comfort periods. Temperatures limits have to be observed in the refrigerated compartments, the air-conditioned room, and the water vessel. A photovoltaics-based behind-the-meter local electricity generation system is also present to allow for reduced energy costs via load matching and/or revenue by selling excess electricity to the utility grid as long as utility-specified power limits are observed.

3   Mathematical Model

A customisable MILP formulation of the single-household DR problem described in the previous chapter was developed to carry out this study. The MILP model relies on generic submodels for time-shiftable and single-node thermal loads, which were instantiated three times each to accommodate all appliances under consideration: the dishwasher, laundry machine, tumble dryer cycles were modelled as time-shiftable loads while the EWH, the refrigerator and the heat pump were assumed to interact with uniform temperature thermal loads using three different controls: on/off, proportional and multi-level discrete controls, respectively. A demand rate submodel is also used to relate power needs into costs and feed-in constraints. More information about the model is provided next.

3.1   Objective Function

The objective for this model is to maximise profits over the entire planning period duration (PPD) by simultaneously minimising energy and power costs and maximising revenue while meeting safety and comfort standards. Revenue is obtained by selling locally-generated excess electricity to the utility whereas costs are due to the NCD and L additional electrical loads, consisting of N_{SL} time-shiftable loads and N_{TL} thermal load-related electrical loads, and cost penalties prompted by excessive temperatures in selected thermal loads. Loads are identified through the set $S_L = \{1, ..., L\}$ and subsets $S_{SL} \subseteq S_L$ and $S_{TL} \subseteq S_L$ for time-shiftable and thermal load-related electrical loads, respectively, such that: $S_{SL} \cap S_{TL} = \emptyset; S_{SL} \cup S_{TL} = S_L$. Additional subsets include $S_{TL,\Delta t} \subseteq S_{TL}$ and $S_{TL,PPD} \subseteq S_{TL}$ to identify thermal loads capable of inducing costs due to excessive temperatures during each time interval and temperature reductions between planning periods, respectively. The objective function is thus given by (1), where $P_{IMP,k}^{ELEC}$ and $P_{EXP,k}^{ELEC}$ stand for the mean power drawn from and fed to the utility grid, respectively, during time interval k of the planning period (out of $K \in \mathbb{N}$, Δt-long intervals: $K = PPD/\Delta t$), $y_{U,p}$ indicates whether the nonnegative power level $P_{U,p}$ was exceeded during the planning period ($P_{U,0} = 0$ W, for islanded operation), $\Delta\theta_{l,PPD}$ is thermal load l's ($\forall l \in S_{TL,PPD}$) temperature decrease, if any, between planning periods, and $\Delta\theta_{l,k}^{UPPER}$ represents thermal load l's ($\forall l \in S_{TL,\Delta t}$) temperature increase, if any, above the reference temperature ($\theta_{l,REF}^{UPPER}$) during time interval k. With regard to the objective function coefficients, $p_{IMP,k}^{ELEC}$ and $p_{EXP,k}^{ELEC}$ are respectively the prices charged and offered to the end-user for electricity consumed from and delivered to the grid during time interval k, $c_{U,p}$ is the cost of exceeding the power level $P_{U,p}$, $c_{l,PPD}$ is the cost of increasing load l's ($\forall l \in S_{TL,PPD}$) temperature by one degree after the planning period, and $c_{l,k}^{UPPER}$ is the cost of load l's ($\forall l \in S_{TL,\Delta t}$) temperature exceeding $\theta_{l,REF}^{UPPER}$ by one degree during time step k.

$$\min \sum_{l \in S_{TL,\Delta t}} \sum_{k=1}^{K} c_{l,k}^{UPPER} \Delta\theta_{l,k}^{UPPER} + \sum_{l \in S_{TL,PPD}} c_{l,PPD} \Delta\theta_{l,PPD} + \sum_{p=0}^{P-1} c_{U,p} y_{U,p}$$

$$+ \Delta t \sum_{k=1}^{K} (p_{IMP,k}^{ELEC} P_{IMP,k}^{ELEC} - p_{EXP,k}^{ELEC} P_{EXP,k}^{ELEC}) \quad (1)$$

$$P_{IMP,k}^{ELEC} \geq 0, \quad k = 1, ..., K; \quad P_{EXP,k}^{ELEC} \geq 0, \quad k = 1, ..., K \quad (2)$$

$$y_{U,p} \in \{0,1\}, \quad p = 0, ..., P-1 \quad (3)$$

$$\Delta\theta_{l,PPD} \geq 0, \quad l \in S_{TL,PPD} \quad (4)$$

$$\Delta\theta_{l,k}^{UPPER} \geq 0, \quad k = 1, ..., K; \quad l \in S_{TL,\Delta t} \quad (5)$$

3.2   Power Balances

Both $P_{IMP,k}^{ELEC}$ and $P_{EXP,k}^{ELEC}$ are defined using the power balance equations in (6), where $P_{l,k}$ is the mean power demand due to load l ($\forall l \in S_L$) during time interval k in accordance with (7), $P_{NCD,k}$ is the mean power for the NCD during time interval k, and $P_{LEG,k}$ is the mean power supplied by the local electricity generation system during time interval k.

$$\sum_{l \in S_L} P_{l,k} + P_{NCD,k} - P_{LEG,k} = P_{IMP,k}^{ELEC} - P_{EXP,k}^{ELEC}, \quad k = 1, ..., K \quad (6)$$

$$P_{l,k} \geq 0, \quad l \in S_L, \quad k = 1, ..., K \quad (7)$$

3.3   Demand Rate

The demand rate submodel consists of (8)–(11). The peak mean net power demanded from the utility grid during the planning period (P_{PEAK}) is constrained by (8) and (9), and used to determine which power levels have been exceeded in (10), where $P_{U,p}$ is the peak power afforded by the demand rate level p (for P positive levels: $p = 0, ..., P$). Simultaneously, (11) ensures compliance between $P_{EXP,k}^{ELEC}$ and the maximum power the system is allowed to deliver to the grid, defined as a fixed percentage (λ_{EXP}) of the demand rate-defined peak power.

$$P_{IMP,k}^{ELEC} - P_{EXP,k}^{ELEC} - P_{PEAK} \leq 0, \quad k = 1, ..., K \quad (8)$$

$$0 \leq P_{PEAK} \leq P_{U,P} \quad (9)$$

$$P_{PEAK} - P_{U,P}y_{U,p} \leq P_{U,p}, \quad p = 0, ..., P - 1 \tag{10}$$

$$P_{EXP,k}^{ELEC} - \lambda_{EXP} \sum_{p=0}^{P-1} y_{U,p}(P_{U,p+1} - P_{U,p}) \leq 0, \quad k = 1, ..., K \tag{11}$$

3.4 Time-shiftable Loads

The behaviour of time-shiftable loads was reproduced using the model proposed in [21,23]. This model assumes such loads are characterised by non-interruptible cycles, each defined by an ordered sequence of stages with specific power demand levels, whose scheduling must conform to predefined comfort periods.

3.5 Thermal Loads

Thermal loads were generically modelled after uniform temperature bodies controlled through appliances in accordance with (12), where $\theta_l(t)$ is the effective temperature for load l ($\forall l \in S_{TL}$) at time $t \in \mathbb{R}$, $x_{l,m}(t)$ is the actuator control signal component m ($\forall m \in S_{M,l} = \{1, ..., M_l\}$) at time t, while $a_l(t)$, $b_l(t)$, $c_l(t)$ and $d_{l,m}(t)$ are potentially time-varying load- and context-specific coefficients.

$$a_l(t) \cdot \theta_l'(t) = b_l(t) \cdot \theta_l(t) + c_l(t) + \sum_{m \in S_{M,l}} d_{l,m}(t)x_{l,m}(t), \quad l \in S_{TL} \tag{12}$$

The solution to (12) was approximated by assuming the coefficients are constant during one time step (zero-order hold). In doing so, a closed-form solution can be produced and the process repeated for multiple time steps. The corresponding MILP formulation is given in (13) for a given load l ($\forall l \in S_{TL}$) and time interval k, where $\theta_{l,k}$ is its temperature at the start of time interval k, $x_{l,m,k}$ is the decision variable for mode m, and $a_{l,k}$, $b_{l,k}$, $c_{l,k}$ and $d_{l,m,k}$ are coefficients.

$$\theta_{l,k+1} - \theta_{l,k} \exp(\frac{b_{l,k}}{a_{l,k}}\Delta t) - b_{l,k}^{-1}(c_{l,k} + \sum_{m \in S_{M,l}} d_{l,m,k}x_{l,m,k})(\exp(\frac{b_{l,k}}{a_{l,k}}\Delta t) - 1) = 0,$$
$$\tag{13}$$
$$k = 1, ..., K, \quad l \in S_{TL}$$

The load temperatures determined by (13) have to comply with minimum ($\theta_{MIN,l,k}$) and maximum ($\theta_{MAX,l,k}$) temperature limits during each time interval in accordance with (14)–(15) while separate ones constrain $\Delta\theta_{l,\Delta t}$ and $\Delta\theta_{l,k}^{UPPER}$ using (16) and (17), where $\theta_{l,1}$ is the initial load temperature.

$$\theta_{l,k} \geq \theta_{MIN,l,k}, \quad k = 2, ..., K + 1, \quad l \in S_{TL} \tag{14}$$

$$\theta_{l,k} \leq \theta_{MAX,l,k}, \quad k = 2, ..., K+1, \quad l \in S_{TL} \tag{15}$$

$$\theta_{l,K+1} - \theta_{l,1} \geq -\Delta\theta_{l,PPD}, \quad l \in S_{TL,PPD} \tag{16}$$

$$\theta_{l,k} - \theta_{l,REF}^{UPPER} \leq \Delta\theta_{l,k}^{UPPER}, \quad k = 2, ..., K+1, \quad l \in S_{TL,\Delta t} \tag{17}$$

Appliance Control. One of three actuator control types was considered for each thermal load: on/off, proportional and multi-level discrete controls. Thermal loads modelled using these controls can be respectively identified through the subsets $S_{TL,ON-OFF}$, $S_{TL,PROP}$ and $S_{TL,MULTI}$ ($\subseteq S_{TL}$) such that:

$$S_{TL,ON-OFF} \cap S_{TL,PROP} \cap S_{TL,MULTI} = \emptyset \tag{18}$$

$$S_{TL,ON-OFF} \cup S_{TL,PROP} \cup S_{TL,MULTI} = S_{TL} \tag{19}$$

The choice of actuator control ultimately defines the number of signal components (M_l) needed for each load, which can include one or two active heat transfer directions (i.e., heating and cooling). Consequently, it also defines the decision variable ($x_{l,m,k}$) types and associated constraints. Among the choices, on/off control is the simplest and requires one binary variable per time interval and heat transfer direction ($M_l = 1$ or 2) in accordance with (20).

$$x_{l,m,k} \in \{0,1\}, \quad k = 1, ..., K, \quad m \in S_{M,l}, \quad l \in S_{TL,ON-OFF} \tag{20}$$

Proportional control, defined as a semi-continuous monotonically-increasing piecewise linear function above a minimum positive level, requires two control signal components per time interval and heat transfer direction ($M_l = 2$ or 4) in accordance with (21) and (22): one binary variable sets the minimum actuator level and a continuous variable sets the actuator level above the mininum level.

$$x_{l,2n-1,k} \in \{0,1\}, \quad x_{l,2n,k} \in [0,1], \quad l \in S_{TL,PROP} \tag{21}$$
$$k = 1, ..., K, \quad n = 1, ..., M_l/2$$

$$x_{l,2n-1,k} \geq x_{l,2n,k}, \quad k = 1, ..., K, \quad l \in S_{TL,PROP}, \tag{22}$$
$$n = 1, ..., M_l/2$$

Multi-level discrete control is primarily intended to reproduce full- and part-load operation of appliances controlling thermal load temperatures and can be formulated in three alternative ways, all of which exclusively rely on binary variables in accordance with (23). The standard one (STD) uses one binary variable per positive load level and time interval for each heat transfer direction and prevents more than one of those corresponding to the same time interval (k) from being positive in accordance with (24).

$$x_{l,m,k} \in \{0,1\}, \quad k = 1, ..., K, \quad m \in S_{M,l}, \quad l \in S_{TL,MULTI} \tag{23}$$

$$\sum_{m \in S_{M,l}} x_{l,m,k} \leq 1, \quad k = 1, ..., K, \quad l \in S_{TL,MULTI} \tag{24}$$

If the appliances can be assumed to operate with power-invariant COPs and the normalised load levels are separated at regular steps between 0 (no load) and 1 (full load), then two other formulations can be used. Both reproduce a specified set of load levels ($T_l = \{1, ..., N_l\}$) using combinations of those levels to achieve the same outcome using a subset of the original levels ($T_l' \subseteq T_l$), in accordance with (25), where $e_{l,m,k}$ and $e_{l,n,k}$ are the surrogates for $d_{l,m,k}$ needed to employ T_l and T_l', respectively, as surrogates for $S_{M,l}$. In doing so, these formulations have the potential to dispense with all the constraints and a part of the variables needed using the standard formulation, depending on the number of levels and heat transfer directions. For example, no reduction of binary variables is possible if 2 levels per heat transfer direction are considered but at 3, 5 and 10 levels, reductions of 33, 40 and 60% are possible. Additional constraints are not necessary if only one heat transfer direction is considered – otherwise (24) is necessary to prevent simultaneous heating and cooling modes – and if any potential combination only reproduces the original levels.

$$e_{l,m,k} = \sum_{n \in T_l'} e_{l,n,k} w_{l,n,k}, \quad w_{l,n,k} \in \{0,1\}, \quad k = 1, ..., K, \quad m \in T_l, \quad l \in S_{TL,MULTI}$$
$$\tag{25}$$

The differences between the two non-standard formulations concern the approach by which to rule out solutions reproducing load levels not found in the original set, specifically those that exceed load ratings – since intermediate levels are implicitly excluded. The first of these more specific formulations (SPC1) does this by enforcing upper and lower load level limits for heating and cooling modes, respectively, in accordance with (26)–(27), if applicable.

$$\sum_{n \in T_l'} d_{l,n,k} x_{l,n,k} \leq \max_{m \in T_l} d_{l,m,k}, \quad k = 1, ..., K, \quad l \in S_{TL,MULTI} \tag{26}$$

$$\sum_{n \in T_l'} d_{l,n,k} x_{l,n,k} \geq \min_{m \in T_l} d_{l,m,k}, \quad k = 1, ..., K, \quad l \in S_{TL,MULTI} \tag{27}$$

The second formulation (SPC2) uses the linearised 0–1 polynomial constraints given in (28)–(29) to rule out any binary decision variable combinations that allow those limits to be exceeded, where V is the number of binary combinations to exclude and $S_{l,0,v}$ and $S_{l,1,v}$ are sets ($\forall v = 1, ..., V$; $S_{l,0,v}, S_{l,1,v} \subseteq S_{M,l}$; $S_{l,0,v} \cap S_{l,1,v} = \emptyset$) containing the indexes for the decision variables that equal nought and one, respectively, in the binary combination v.

$$\sum_{r \in S_{l,1,v}} x_{l,r,k} - \sum_{s \in S_{l,0,v}} x_{l,s,k} \le |S_{l,1,v}| - 1, \quad k = 1, ..., K, \quad v = 1, ..., V, \quad l \in S_{TL,MULTI}$$

$$(28)$$

$$- \sum_{r \in S_{l,1,v}} x_{l,r,k} + \sum_{s \in S_{l,0,v}} x_{l,s,k} \le |S_{l,0,v}|, \quad k = 1, ..., K, \quad v = 1, ..., V, \quad l \in S_{TL,MULTI}$$

$$(29)$$

Elimination of Load Temperature Variables. Employing continuous load temperature variables $\theta_l = [\theta_{l,2}, ..., \theta_{l,K+1}]$ in the thermal load submodel is not strictly required since their use can be replaced by equivalent functions of actuator variables, specifically (30), where x_l is given by (31). To do this, a constraint i ($\forall i \in \{1, ..., I\}$) whose left- and right-hand sides can be represented by $[\phi_i, \psi_i] [\theta_l, x_l]^T$ and ξ_i would have to be converted into one with $f_i \cdot x_l^T$ and g_i, respectively, which can be shown to require adopting (32) and (33), where $f_{i,j}$ is the element at column j of the vector f_i and similarly for $\alpha_{l,k,j}$, $\phi_{i,k}$ and $\psi_{i,j}$.

$$\theta_{l,k+1} = \alpha_{l,k} \cdot x_l^T - \beta_{l,k}, \quad k = 1, ..., K, \quad l \in S_{TL} \tag{30}$$

$$x_l = [x_{l,1}, ..., x_{l,M_l}], \quad x_{l,m} = [x_{l,m,1}, ..., x_{l,m,K}], \quad m \in S_{M,l}, \quad l \in S_{TL} \tag{31}$$

$$f_{i,j} = \psi_{i,j} + \sum_{k=1}^{K} \phi_{i,k} \alpha_{l,k,j}, \quad i = 1, ..., I, \quad j = 1, ..., J = M_l \cdot K, \quad l \in S_{TL} \tag{32}$$

$$g_i = \xi_i + \sum_{k=1}^{K} \phi_{i,k} \beta_{l,k}, \quad i = 1, ..., I, \quad l \in S_{TL} \tag{33}$$

4   Case Studies

The modelling techniques addressed in this study were evaluated using a set of case studies. These consist of 108 DR problems defined by different data and time interval duration combinations. Time interval durations of 300, 600, 900 and 1800 s were considered as well as 3 indoor heat gain profiles, 3 DHW demand profiles and 3 NCD profiles – each of which resampled using the appropriate time interval duration. For each of these case studies, one problem was created per combination of the two modelling techniques considered: multi-level discrete control formulation and load temperature variable elimination. In total, 648 problems were created and optimised to provide 324 and 216 sets of comparisons to explore the effect of variable elimination and the different control formulations, respectively.

The two modelling techniques under consideration were applied solely to the thermal load submodel for the air-conditioned room. This model assumes a heat pump can be off or cooling the room using 20, 40, 60, 80 or 100% of its rated power capacity. These 5 levels were reproduced using the various discrete control formulations. In the case of the SPC1 and SPC2 formulations, 3 levels, namely 20, 40 and 60%, were used to reproduce the 5 original ones thus enabling a 40% reduction in the number of binary variables. On the other hand, the SPC1 and SPC2 formulations required additional constraints to prevent the heat pump's rated capacity from being exceeded. The two remaining thermal loads, namely the EWH and the refrigerator, were modelled as using on/off and proportional control, respectively. In the latter case, the type of control selected was meant to represent on/off operation during less than one full time step to facilitate obtaining feasible solutions to problems defined using a comparatively-long Δt.

4.1 Problem Data

The case studies were defined primarily using data from [24]. This included the shiftable load operation cycles and comfort periods, the demand rates and respective power levels, the electricity prices, the local electricity generation profile, the indoor heat gain profile, the NCD profile, the outdoor temperature profile, the indoor temperature profile (for the EWH and refrigerator models), the utility water temperature profile, and most thermal load data. The exceptions concerned: the air-conditioned room's lumped capacity, which was doubled; the heat pump's specifications [25]; the refrigerator's COP temperature dependence [26]; the EWH lower and upper reference temperatures (60 and 70 °C); $c_{l,k}^{UPPER}$, defined as the ratio between the maximum cost prompted by not shifting the EWH load and the difference between the maximum and upper reference temperatures; the refrigerator's minimum cycle duration (3 min); the daily DHW volume (200 L at 45 °C); the DHW profile, instead based on the RAND profile [27]; the occupancy vector, defined as the sign function of the DHW profile. Finally, the indoor heat gain, DHW demand and NCD profiles were created using stochastic functions of the reference ones.

4.2 Computational Resources and Solver Settings

The MILP problems were optimised using IBM's CPLEX 12.8.0.0 which ran on a shared machine featuring an Intel Xeon Gold 6138 CPU and 320 GB of RAM. The solver was invoked from MATLAB using the official CPLEX class API. Standard solver settings were used except the termination criteria which included optimality, a 1% relative gap and a 15-min computational budget.

4.3 Methodology

The methodology adopted relied on comparisons between the optimisation results obtained for the same problem but formulated using different models.

As such, investigating the effect of load temperature variables required comparing solutions to problems whose models differ only on whether those variables are used or not. The same holds for the effect of different multi-level discrete control formulations but in that case three comparisons are possible per problem: SPC1 vs STD; SPC2 vs STD; SCP1 vs SCP2. For reasons of brevity, this study mainly focuses on performance variations relative to the standard formulation. Finally, computational performance was measured via the deterministic computation time, as returned by CPLEX, which is a repeatable measure of effort involved in solving each problem rather than the actual time to obtain a solution.

5   Results and Analysis

Optimised solutions and best bounds were determined for the 648 MILP problems created. The optimised solution to one of these is represented in Fig. 1.

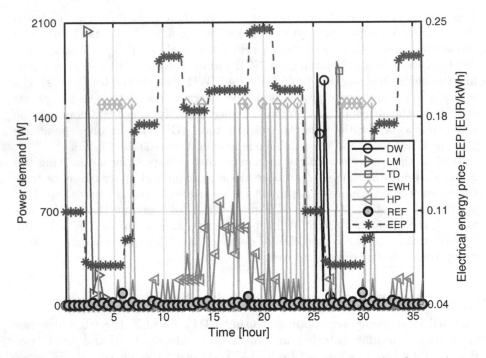

Fig. 1. Optimisation results for one DR problem (900 s time interval; reference input data) using load temperature variables and the STD formulation: power demand from scheduled loads and electrical energy price (EEP) versus planning period time.

5.1   Model Equivalence

Objective function differences were used to examine whether the formulations can be regarded as equivalent or not. In general, the differences due to the effect of load temperature variables and the multi-level discrete control formulations were lower than 0.075 €, relative to objective function values in the range of 4.6–5.3 € (<1.5%). More importantly, the best bound differences obtained do not exceed 0.025 € (<0.5%) and the objective function differences reached with the best solutions do not exceed 0.029 € (<0.7%). In light of the errors observed and the potential for improvement (via a higher computational budget and a lower relative MIP gap), the formulations compared can be regarded as equivalent.

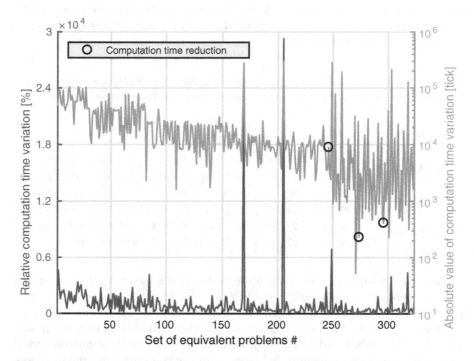

Fig. 2. Absolute value of and relative deterministic computation time variation (positive for increases) caused by the elimination of load temperature variables, for each set of equivalent problems. The circles point to the cases of computation time decreases.

5.2 Effect of Eliminating Load Temperature Variables

The comparisons undertaken show that eliminating the continuous load temperature variables led to computation time increases in almost all cases. More precisely, computation time increases were detected in 321 out of 324 cases (99%) and by as much as 29,292% (about 294 times higher) and 981% (11 times higher) on average, as illustrated in Fig. 2. In turn, the computation time decreased by as much as 32% (and 22% on average) in three cases – highlighted in Fig. 2 – none of which for the two shortest time intervals. These results show that inessential continuous variables can reduce the time needed to obtain practical solutions though a different inquiry is necessary to understand why this happens.

5.3   Effect of the Multi-level Discrete Control Formulation

The effect of the multi-level discrete control formulations on the computation time is summarised in Table 1. According to the results, in most cases (63%) the SPC1 and SPC2-based models required less time to be solved than the STD-based model. This advantage was also observed when considering each time interval duration separately, and found to be inversely correlated – to some extent. On the other hand, the differences between the SPC1- and SPC2-based models were far less significant, with the former outperforming the latter in 52% of cases though not for each time interval duration separately. The other factors (i.e., input data) did not produce recognisable patterns on the results.

Table 1. Number of times a formulation (SPC1, SPC2 or STD) was solved in less (deterministic computation) time by formulation pair and time interval duration.

Comparison	Formulation	Time interval duration				Total
		300	600	900	1800	
SPC1 vs STD	SPC1	40 (74%)	34 (63%)	29 (54%)	33 (61%)	136 (63%)
	STD	14 (26%)	20 (37%)	25 (46%)	21 (39%)	80 (37%)
SPC2 vs STD	SPC2	36 (67%)	33 (61%)	33 (61%)	35 (65%)	137 (63%)
	STD	18 (33%)	21 (39%)	21 (39%)	19 (35%)	79 (37%)
SPC1 vs SPC2	SPC1	27 (50%)	31 (57%)	25 (46%)	30 (56%)	113 (52%)
	SPC2	27 (50%)	23 (43%)	29 (54%)	24 (44%)	103 (48%)

Magnitude-wise, no formulation appears to have a meaningful or consistent advantage. On average, the SPC1 and SPC2 formulations were unable to reduce the computation time by more than half or increase it by more than twice (38–40% reductions vs 80–97% increases). However, the computation time reductions afforded by the SPC1 and SPC2 formulations over the STD formulation were, on average, one order of magnitude higher than the computation time increases. These results can be partially explained by the correlation between time interval duration and computation time (i.e., finer time-discretisation contributes to a more strongly-combinatorial model) and the fact that SPC1- and SPC2-based models tended to fare better at lower time interval durations – cf. Table 1.

6   Conclusions

The efforts described in this paper concern an investigation into the effect of two modelling techniques on the computational performance of MILP-formulated residential DR problems. The techniques concern new multi-level discrete control formulations and the elimination of continuous load temperature decision variables. These techniques were compared using a state-of-the-art solver to optimise a set of equivalent single-household DR problems.

This endeavour's main conclusions can be summarised as follows: (1) the elimination of load temperature variables was found to increase the computation time in 99% of cases and by 981% on average; (2) the new multi-level discrete control formulations required less time to be solved than the standard formulation in most cases (63%), achieving computation time reductions of 38–40% on average for a 40% reduction in the number of binary variables. These results indicate that additional continuous decision variables can be desirable to reduce computation times whereas using less binary variables does not necessarily lower the computation time. Future work will focus on causality, namely by reproducing more diverse conditions and examining the formulation strength and size [28].

Acknowledgements. This work was partially supported by projects UID/MULTI/ 00308/2013 and by the European Regional Development Fund through the COMPETE 2020 Programme, FCT - Portuguese Foundation for Science and Technology and Regional Operational Program of the Center Region (CENTRO2020) within projects ESGRIDS (POCI-01-0145-FEDER-016434) and MAnAGER (POCI-01-0145-FEDER-028040).

References

1. Strbac, B.: Demand side management: benefits and challenges. Energy Policy **36**(12), 4419–4426 (2008)
2. Siano, P.: Demand response and smart grids—a survey. Renew. Sustain. Energy Rev. **30**, 461–478 (2014)
3. Hubert, T., Grijalva, S.: Modeling for residential electricity optimization in dynamic pricing environments. IEEE Trans. Smart Grid **3**(4), 2224–2231 (2012)
4. Good, N., Ellis, K.A., Mancarella, P.: Review and classification of barriers and enablers of demand response in the smart grid. Renew. Sustain. Energy Rev. **72**, 57–72 (2017)
5. Shareef, H., Ahmed, M.S., Mohamed, A., Al Hassan, E.: Review on home energy management system considering demand responses, smart technologies, and intelligent controllers. IEEE Access **6**, 24498–24509 (2018)
6. Du, P., Lu, N.: Appliance commitment for household load scheduling. IEEE Trans. Smart Grid **2**, 411–419 (2011)
7. Fux, S.F., Benz, M.J., Guzzella, L.: Economic and environmental aspects of the component sizing for a stand-alone building energy system: a case study. Renew. Energy **55**, 438–447 (2013)
8. Patteeuw, D., Helsen, L.: Residential buildings with heat pumps, a verified bottom-up model for demand side management studies. In: International Conference on System Simulation in Buildings, Liège, Belgium, 10–12 October (2014)
9. Althaher, S., Mancarella, P., Mutale, J.: Automated demand response from home energy management system under dynamic pricing and power and comfort constraints. IEEE Trans. Smart Grid **6**(4), 1874–1883 (2015)
10. Arteconi, A., Patteeuw, D., Bruninx, K., Delarue, E., Dhaeseleer, W., Helsen, L.: Active demand response with electric heating systems: impact of market penetration. Appl. Energy **177**, 636–648 (2016)
11. Renaldi, R., Kiprakis, A., Friedrich, D.: An optimisation framework for thermal energy storage integration in a residential heat pump heating system. Appl. Energy **186**, 520–529 (2017)

12. Iria, J.P., Soares, F.J., Matos, M.A.: Trading small prosumers flexibility in the energy and tertiary reserve markets. IEEE Trans. Smart Grid **10**(3), 2371–2382 (2019)
13. Schütz, T., Streblow, R., Müller, D.: A comparison of thermal energy storage models for building energy system optimization. Energy Build. **93**, 23–31 (2015)
14. Steen, D., Stadler, M., Cardoso, G., Groissböck, M., DeForest, N., Marnay, C.: Modeling of thermal storage systems in MILP distributed energy resource models. Appl. Energy **137**, 782–792 (2015)
15. Wang, H., et al.: Demand response through smart home energy management using thermal inertia. In: 2013 Australasian Universities Power Engineering Conference (AUPEC), pp. 1–6. IEEE (2013)
16. Wang, H., Meng, K., Dong, Z.Y., Xu, Z., Luo, F., Wong, K.P.: A MILP approach to accommodate more building integrated photovoltaic system in distribution network. In: 2015 IEEE Power & Energy Society General Meeting, pp. 1–5. IEEE (2015)
17. Bradac, Z., Kaczmarczyk, V., Fiedler, P.: Optimal scheduling of domestic appliances via MILP. Energies **8**, 217–232 (2015)
18. Antunes, C.H., Rasouli, V., Alves, M.J., Gomes, Á.: A mixed-integer linear programming model for optimal management of residential electrical loads under dynamic tariffs. In: 2018 International Conference on Smart Energy Systems and Technologies (SEST), Sevilla, 2018, pp. 1–6 (2018)
19. Baeten, B., Rogiers, F., Patteeuw, D., Helsen, L.: Comparison of optimal control formulations for stratified sensible thermal energy storage in space heating applications. In: The 13th International Conference on Energy Storage (2015)
20. Bapat, T., Sengupta, N., Ghai, S.K., Arya, V., Shrinivasan, Y.B., Seetharam, D.: User-sensitive scheduling of home appliances. In: Proceedings of the 2nd ACM SIGCOMM Workshop on Green Networking, pp. 43–48. ACM (2011)
21. Antunes, C.H., Rasouli, V., Alves, M.J., Gomes, Á., Costa, J.J., Gaspar, A.: A discussion of mixed integer linear programming models of thermostatic loads in demand response. In: 2nd International Symposium on Energy System Optimization, Karlsruhe, Germany, 10–11 October 2018 (2018)
22. Bozchalui, M.C., Hashmi, S.A., Hassen, H., Canizares, C.A., Bhattacharya, K.: Optimal operation of residential energy hubs in smart grids. IEEE Trans. Smart Grid **3**(4), 1755–1766 (2012)
23. Alves, M.J., Antunes, C.H., Carrasqueira, P.: A hybrid genetic algorithm for the interaction of electricity retailers with demand response. In: Squillero, G., Burelli, P. (eds.) EvoApplications 2016. LNCS, vol. 9597, pp. 459–474. Springer, Cham (2016). https://doi.org/10.1007/978-3-319-31204-0_30
24. Gonçalves, I., Gomes, Á., Antunes, C.H.: Optimizing the management of smart home energy resources under different power cost scenarios. Appl. Energy **242**, 351–363 (2019)
25. Gomes, Á., Antunes, C.H., Martinho, J.: A physically-based model for simulating inverter type air conditioners/heat pumps. Energy **50**, 110–119 (2013)
26. Harrington, L., Aye, L., Fuller, B.: Impact of room temperature on energy consumption of household refrigerators: lessons from analysis of field and laboratory data. Appl. Energy **211**, 346–357 (2018)
27. Mutch, J.: Residential water heating: fuel conservation, economics, and public policy. R-1498-NSF. RAND Corporation (1974)
28. Vielma, J.P.: Mixed integer linear programming formulation techniques. SIAM Rev. **57**(1), 3–57 (2015)

Renewable Energy; Smart Grids; Energy and Environment

Development of a Compact and Low-Cost Weather Station for Renewable Energy Applications

Jose A. Salgado[1], Miguel C. Feio[2], Luis M. Silva[2], Vitor Monteiro[2], Joao L. Afonso[2], and Jose A. Afonso[1(✉)]

[1] CMEMS-UMinho Center, University of Minho, Guimarães, Portugal
jose.afonso@dei.uminho.pt
[2] ALGORITMI Research Centre, University of Minho, Guimarães, Portugal

Abstract. This paper describes the development of a weather station integrating several sensors which allows the measurement and data storage of the following environmental parameters: solar irradiance, temperature, humidity, wind speed, and wind direction. The collected data is later transferred to a mobile device, where it is stored in a database and processed in order to be visualized and analyzed by the user. For such purpose, a dedicated mobile app was developed and presented along the paper. The weather station also integrates small solar photovoltaic modules of three different technologies: polycrystalline, monocrystalline and amorphous silicon. Based on that, the weather station also collects information that may be employed to help the user in determining the most suitable solar photovoltaic technology for installation in a particular location. The developed system uses a Bluetooth Low Energy (BLE) wireless network to transfer the data to the mobile device when the user approaches the weather station. The system operation was validated through experimental tests that encompass all the main developed features, from the data acquisition in the weather station, to the visualization in the mobile device.

Keywords: Weather station · Solar photovoltaic modules · Bluetooth Low Energy · Mobile app

1 Introduction

As the world population increases, the demand for energy grows with it. Fossil fuels like coal, oil and natural gas still supply 80% of the energy demand. However, the environmental effects are a major problem associated with these sources of energy, due to the CO_2 emissions [1]. Therefore, there is a need to focus on energy sources as optimal long-term solutions.

In this context, solar energy is one of main renewable energy sources that has been considered to tackle this problem. A total of 1.8×10^{11} MW of solar power is received by the Earth at instant [2]. Despite not covering all energy consumption needs, solar

J. L. Afonso et al. (Eds.): SESC 2019, LNICST 315, pp. 127–139, 2020.
https://doi.org/10.1007/978-3-030-45694-8_10

energy has the potential to cover a significant share of it. Photovoltaics (PV) is one of the methods to convert solar energy into electricity, and this technology has had a significantly improvement in the last years in terms of efficiency. It is based on semiconductors materials that exhibit the photovoltaic effect to convert the sunlight into electrical energy. These semiconductors are mainly made of silicon, which has a large availability in the Earth's crust. In terms of environmental effects, PV generates no pollution and its greenhouse gas emissions are non-existent. It also provides great scalability, meaning that its applications can range from few milliwatts to several hundreds of megawatts. However, the main disadvantage is that the production of energy is restricted to a range of hours during the day, which many times does not match the peak energy demand hours [3].

Concerning solar photovoltaic technologies, there is a variety of options. The most suitable choice will depend on the location and the scale of application. Crystalline silicon is the most prevalent material for solar photovoltaic modules. Its working principle is based on the concept of the p-n junction. Various sub-types of crystalline silicon materials can be used to develop solar photovoltaic modules. The most popular ones are monocrystalline silicon and polycrystalline silicon. Monocrystalline silicon is more efficient, but generally more expansive than other types. Polycrystalline are less efficient, but less expensive than the monocrystalline silicon ones, so they are the most common type used. Thin-film technologies are also commonly used to develop solar photovoltaic modules. Currently, the most used thin-film technology is the amorphous silicon. Despite producing less energy when comparing to crystalline technologies, it has the advantage of being flexible, which can be useful in some applications [4].

To determine the best solar photovoltaic technology to be used in a given location, the information about the weather conditions in that place is very important. The local temperature, solar irradiance, and even wind speed and direction, are some factors that have impact on the energy produced by solar photovoltaic modules, and that impact can be different for different technologies [5].

Concerning related work, in [6] a system to monitor the performance of solar panels using a low-cost Wireless Sensor Network (WSN) is proposed. Solar irradiance, and temperature, as well as the current and voltage from the solar panels were the measured variables. In this case, the collected data was continuously transmitted to a nearby personal computer using ZigBee. In [7] a remote data logger for weather forecasting based in a GPRS (General Packet Radio Service) connection was developed. The data gathered was stored locally in a SD (Secure Digital) card. The File Transfer Protocol (FTP) was used to transmit the collected data to a remote server. Every time the data logger receives a report with the measured parameters, it creates a new text file in the SD card and sends the file to the remote server. The GPRS connection requires a cellular device with a SIM (Subscriber Identification Module) card, meaning associated costs with the data transmission. In contrast, this paper proposes an innovative solution, where the data is stored locally and transferred to user device using a short-range wireless network when he approaches the weather station, which avoids the costs associated with data transfer.

As main contribution, this work presents the development of a compact and low-cost weather station to measure multiple environmental parameters. The collected data is later transferred to a smartphone, where it is stored and displayed to the user through a developed mobile app, specially dedicated for such purposes. The developed weather

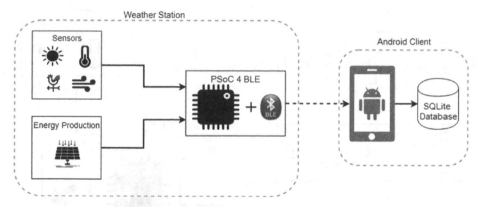

Fig. 1. Architecture of the developed system.

station prototype also integrates small solar photovoltaic modules of three different technologies: polycrystalline, monocrystalline and amorphous silicon. The aim is to allow correlating the collected environmental data to the power production of the three different solar photovoltaic technologies, in order to determine which technology is the most suitable for use in a particular location.

For convenience and easiness of access, the data is transferred to the user's mobile device using a wireless connection instead of cables, since the weather station may be installed in a hard-to-reach location. The developed system uses Bluetooth Low Energy (BLE) for the wireless data transfer due to native integration in mobile devices as well as its low energy consumption [8]. An alternative would be the use of an IEEE 802.11/Wi-Fi wireless network [9], which provides higher data rates, but with higher energy consumption. Other wireless network alternatives, like LoRa [10] and ZigBee [11], were excluded due to their lack of native support in smartphones and lower data rates.

2 Developed System

This section describes the development of the different components of the proposed weather station. Multiple sensors were used to allow the measurement of the following local weather parameters: solar irradiance, temperature, humidity, wind speed, and wind direction. The developed system is also able to measure the energy generated by three different solar photovoltaic technologies, in order to correlate their power production with the measurements of the weather sensors.

The architecture of the developed system, represented in Fig. 1, is composed by two main parts: a weather station and an Android client. The data collected by the weather station is processed and stored locally in a SD memory card. When requested by the Android mobile app, the data is transferred to the mobile device using BLE, where it is stored in a local SQLite database and may be visualized by the user.

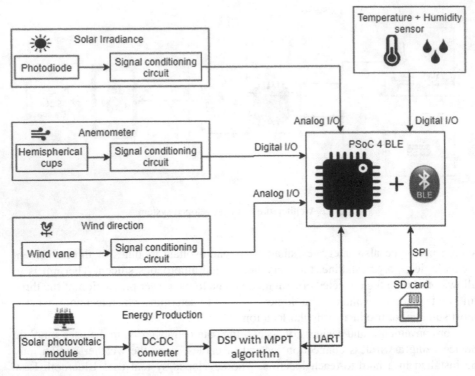

Fig. 2. Block diagram of the hardware used in the data acquisition process.

2.1 Data Acquisition and Storage

The block diagram of the data acquisition hardware implemented in the weather station is presented in Fig. 2. The data acquisition and processing (as well as the wireless communication with the Android client) is performed by a PSoC 4 BLE module [12], from Cypress Semiconductor. This module, used in the developed system, includes an ARM Cortex-M0 32-bit microcontroller with integrated Bluetooth 4.2 protocol stack. It contains blocks for serial communication via UART (Universal asynchronous receiver/transmitter), SPI (Serial Peripheral Interface), or I2C (Inter Integrated Circuit). It also provides an ADC (Analog to Digital Converter) with a maximum resolution of 12-bits, four programmable operational amplifiers and four TCPWM (Timer Counter Pulse Width Modulator) blocks, which can be used for timers, counters or PWM generators.

The firmware of the PSoC 4 BLE microcontroller was programmed in C using the PSoC Creator IDE (Integrated Development Environment), which is also provided by Cypress. During the development phase, the PSoC 4 BLE module was attached to a development board for programming and debugging. Both of these boards are supplied in the CY8CKIT-042-BLE-A kit [12].

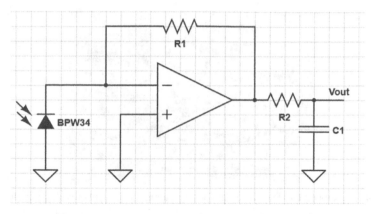

Fig. 3. Circuit used for measuring the solar irradiance.

The photodiode BPW34 [13] was used to measure the solar irradiance. This sensor was chosen taking into consideration the minimum and maximum values for the solar spectral radiation wavelengths, the cost and availability. The signal produced by the photodiode is fed into a signal conditioning circuit to convert the current produced into a voltage that can be read by the ADC of the microcontroller. This circuit was implemented using a transimpedance amplifier, as shown in Fig. 3. For this purpose, one of the programmable operational amplifiers integrated inside the PSoC 4 BLE module was used in the circuit. For this purpose, the inputs and output of the operational amplifier were programmed to be connected to pins of the microcontroller using the PSoC Creator IDE. A low-pass filter was placed at the output of the operational amplifier to filter ambient noise. A precision pyranometer was used to correlate the output to provide a solar irradiation measurement in W/m^2.

The DHT22/AM2302 sensor was used to measure both the temperature and the humidity [14]. This sensor can measure temperatures from –40 °C to 80 °C and relative humidity from 0 to 100%. The output of this sensor is a 1-wire bus digital signal that can be read in a digital pin of the microcontroller. The data packet is composed of 40 bits, with 16 bits for the relative humidity data, 16 bits for the temperature data and 8 bits for checksum.

An anemometer is used to measure the wind speed. For this purpose, a magnet was attached to the rotational axis of the anemometer. The magnetic field created by this magnet is then detected by a Hall effect sensor [15], allowing to convert the mechanical movement into an electric signal. The output of this sensor is connected to a digital pin of the microcontroller, where it is processed in order to produce wind speed measurements in Rotations Per Minute (RPM).

An electronic wind vane was used to measure the wind direction. For this purpose, a magnet is attached to the rotational axis, and the magnetic field is then detected by a reed switch. A total of 8 reed switches are used for 8 different wind directions. Each reed switch is connected in series with a resistor of different value. Depending on the wind direction, a single reed switch will be closed. Another resistor at the end of the circuit forms a voltage divider with the resistor associated with the activated reed switch, which

Fig. 4. Developed DC-DC converter for interfacing the solar photovoltaic modules.

means that for each wind direction, a different voltage value is obtained. The resulting voltage is then measured with the ADC of the microcontroller.

A DC-DC converter in a step-up topology was also developed, as shown in Fig. 4, to work in conjunction with the solar photovoltaic modules. Varying the value of the duty-cycle applied in the semiconductor S, it is possible to adjust the operating power (sampling and switching frequency of 40 kHz and 20 kHz were considered, respectively). The converter is controlled by a MPPT (Maximum Power Point Tracking) algorithm implemented in a Digital Signal Processor (DSP) [16]. The objective is to measure the power produced by the three technologies of solar photovoltaic modules installed in the weather station, where the MPPT algorithm is responsible to guarantee that the solar photovoltaic modules are operating at the maximum power. A power resistor was used as load of the DC-DC converter. On the DC-DC converter input, a voltage and a current sensor were installed, and supported by a developed signal conditioning circuit, the current and voltage values are acquired by the ADC of the DSP (where is implemented the MPPT algorithm). The MPPT algorithm was digitally implemented in the development board LAUNCHXL-F28027F from Texas Instruments. It is important to note that in our approach, a single DC-DC converter was developed, but, based on an external circuit, it is connected sequentially to each solar photovoltaic module. The values obtained by this board are then saved and transferred to the PSoC board using the UART interface when required.

The Perturb and Observe (P&O) MPPT algorithm was used, which is a trial and error algorithm, where the controller adjusts the duty-cycle while measuring the output power. This process is continuously performed until there is no more power increase. This method is the easiest to implement, but has the disadvantage to cause some oscillations in the power output; however, it is not critical for the purpose of the weather station presented in this paper.

To acquire the data from all the sensors, various peripherals were programmed in the PSoC module. A timer was programmed to establish the polling rate at which the data from the sensors are acquired. This value is set by the user in the Android mobile app. This timer functions in interrupt mode, activating a flag inside the ISR (Interrupt Service Routine). This flag is then verified in the main loop and, in case of being activated, the

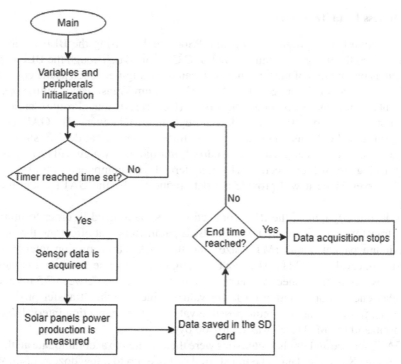

Fig. 5. Flowchart of the main function used for the data acquisition.

values are acquired from the sensors. To measure the solar irradiation and wind direction, the ADC of the microcontroller was programmed with the maximum resolution of 12 bits, a sample frequency of 4 kHz and a voltage reference of 5 V. For measurement the wind speed, a counter was programmed in interrupt mode to count the amount of time for a rotation to be completed and then the value is converted to RPM.

The data from all the sensors is saved periodically in a text file corresponding to the day of acquisition. This process is done until it reaches the end time, defined by the user. Figure 5 presents a flowchart about the main function for the data acquisition process.

An SD card is used to store the measured data locally in the weather station. For this purpose, a module to interface the SD card to the microcontroller was used. This module communicates with the microcontroller using the SPI protocol. A communication block in the microcontroller was programmed as SPI master, whereas the SD card module works as SPI slave. The open source file system FatFs is used to read and write the text files in the SD card. A new text file is created to store all the data acquired on each day. Another text file, called *dates.txt*, is used to store the starting and end times of acquisition for all the days, as well as the sampling rate. Every time there is new data to save in the SD card, it checks if it is a new day or is it still the same day and acts accordingly.

2.2 Wireless Data Transfer

The BLE network was programmed in the PSoC module using the BLE component, where is placed the design diagram of the PSoC Creator IDE. Though the BLE component, various parameters of the BLE network can be configured, such as the connection interval, the advertising interval and the MTU (Maximum Transmission Unit) size. This component also allows the creation of the GATT (Generic Attribute Profile) services and characteristics that used to transfer the data through the BLE network. The GAP (Generic Access Profile) role of this component was defined as peripheral device, since it will advertise its presence to central device (Android smartphone), which will be responsible for establishing the BLE connection. The peripheral device component was also defined as GATT server, since it will provide the data requested by the GATT client (central device).

The data throughput of the BLE connection was maximized in order to minimize the data transfer time. There are two main BLE parameters that affect the throughput: the maximum packet length (MTU size) and the packet transmission interval (BLE connection interval). The MTU size can be configured to a value between 23 bytes and 512 bytes, whereas the connection interval can be set to a value between 7.5 ms and 4 s, with higher energy consumption for lower values. Since the data transfer process will not be much frequent, the minimum possible value for the connection interval (7.5 ms) was chosen, and the MTU size was set to 500 bytes.

A GATT service and its characteristics were then created to accommodate all the data transfer needs. Since the data to be transferred can take up to a few dozens of kilobytes per text file, a characteristic called *DataArray*, with a type of 16-bit integer array and a length of 250 bytes, was created. With a maximum of 500 bytes to be transferred per packet, this characteristic needs to be read several times. For that, an algorithm to transfer the data was created, as shown in Fig. 6. After reading the data from the text file, it is saved in a buffer in the RAM (Random Access Memory). It was also created a characteristic called *NumBytes*, used to notify the Android device of the amount of data about to be received per packet. Another characteristic, called *Next*, was also created to inform the GATT server (PSoC device) when the *DataArray* characteristic was read. After receiving each 500-byte data segment form the buffer, the Android device writes the value '1' in the *Next* characteristic, meaning that it is ready to receive the next 500 bytes from the buffer (or up to 500 bytes, in the case of the last data packet). This process is done multiple times until the end of the buffer.

2.3 Mobile App

An Android mobile app was developed in order to handle the BLE data transfer and to allow the storage and visualization of the data received from the weather station. The mobile app also allows the configuration of some parameters related to the data acquisition performed by the weather station. The mobile app was developed using the Android Studio IDE.

To use the Bluetooth hardware of the Android device, it was necessary to require some permissions in the Android manifest. It was developed an activity to scan for BLE devices, which displays their names or addresses, as well as their RSSI (Received Signal

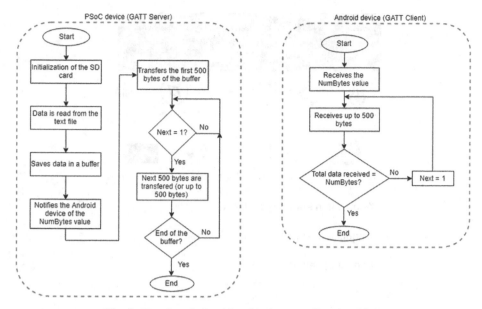

Fig. 6. Developed algorithm for data transfer using BLE.

Strength Indication). After selecting the weather station device from the presented list of BLE devices, the user is asked for the password to access the other features of the app. A service was created to accommodate all the processes related to BLE, including connecting to the GATT server, discovering services, as well as handling the data transfer process.

The mobile app design is then divided into two main fragments. A fragment called *HomeFragment* is used to display the current values of the data acquired by the weather station in real-time. This screen also allows the configuration of the daily starting and ending data acquisition times, as well as the sampling period for the data acquisition. The other fragment, called *DataFragment*, is used to transfer the data stored in the weather station. In this screen, the user can select the day from the available dates. It is also possible to enable an option that transfers the data gathered from all the days so far. After transferring the data, it is saved locally in a SQLite database using two tables for this purpose. A ListView is then updated in the screen with the available dates. To visualize the collected data, the user can choose a date from the list, and another activity dedicated to presenting graphs is opened, where the user can select the parameters that he wishes to visualize. This activity was developed using the MPAndroidChart library.

3   Experimental Results

This section presents the main results obtained from experimental tests, which are used to validate the implementation of the whole system, ranging from the data acquisition in the weather station to the visualization in a smartphone . The developed mobile app has

Fig. 7. Home screen of the developed mobile app.

a bottom navigation menu that allows the user to transition between its screens. After connecting to the weather station, the default screen is the home screen, as shown in Fig. 7.

This screen allows the user to set the start and ending times of the acquisition, as well as the sampling period (in this case, a fragment dedicated to choosing the hours and minutes will pop up). It is also possible to change the value of the sampling period (the default value is 30 s). When the data acquisition starts, the TextView elements that present the last acquired values, from all the weather station sensors, are continuously updated in real-time (top of the screen). The user can also change the start and end times of acquisition, as well as the sampling period, even if there is data being acquired (the new values will be updated for the next day).

The second screen, shown in Fig. 8, is dedicated to download and visualize the weather station data. Here, the user can choose a day to download the respective acquired

Fig. 8. Data visualization screen of the developed mobile app.

data, or enable an option that will download the data acquired from all the available days. A progress bar is updated as the data is transferred. The data is stored in a SQLite database, and, after finishing the download, a list is updated in the screen with the dates and the respective starting and ending times.

To visualize the data, the user can tap on one of the elements of the list. This will retrieve the data from the SQLite database and open the activity that allows the user to view the data in charts, as shown in Fig. 9. In this screen, the user can choose which information to visualize, by selecting one of the checkboxes. The axes scales with the maximum and minimum values for the chart will automatically change according to the data values. The example shown in Fig. 9 presents the temperature values collected by the weather station, obtained between 10 am and 14 pm of July 12, 2019.

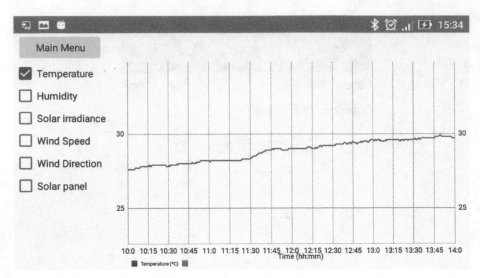

Fig. 9. Screen of the developed mobile app, showing the chart activity that allows the user to visualize the collected data.

4 Conclusions

This paper presents the development of a weather station dedicated to renewable energies applications, which also includes a mobile app that provides a user interface and allows data transfer, storage and visualization. The developed system is composed by various sensors used to measure the state of the weather, as well as the power production from the three different technologies of solar photovoltaic modules, installed in the weather station (a module of each type: polycrystalline, monocrystalline and amorphous silicon). The key purpose of using these different solar photovoltaic modules is measuring the produced power for each one of them in order to gauge which technology would be me more suitable for the specific location where the weather location is installed.

All the data acquired is processed and stored locally in the weather station. When necessary, the user can download the data to an Android mobile device through a BLE wireless network connection using the developed mobile app, presented in this paper. This transferred data is stored in a SQLite database and allows the user to visualize it, with the help of dedicated charts for the measured variables.

The system was validated through experimental tests, by acquiring data using all the sensors, storing the information locally in the weather station, transferring the data to an Android smartphone via BLE, storing it in the smartphone, and presenting the data to the user. The starting and ending times of acquisition, as well as the sampling period, can be defined by the user with the developed mobile app.

References

1. Pazheri, F.R., Othman, M.F., Malik, N.H.: A review on global renewable electricity scenario. Renew. Sustain. Energy Rev. **31**, 835–845 (2014)
2. Raza, M.Q., Nadarajah, M., Ekanayake, C.: On recent advances in PV output power forecast. Sol. Energy **136**, 125–144 (2016)
3. Lo Piano, S., Mayumi, K.: Toward an integrated assessment of the performance of photovoltaic power stations for electricity generation. Appl. Energy **186**, 167–174 (2017)
4. Nayak, P.K., Mahesh, S., Snaith, H.J., Cahen, D.: Photovoltaic solar cell technologies: analysing the state of the art. Nat. Rev. Mater. **4**(4), 269–285 (2019)
5. Perraki, V., Kounavis, P.: Effect of temperature and radiation on the parameters of photovoltaic modules. J. Renew. Sustain. **8**(2016), 013102 (2017)
6. Ranhotigamage, C., Mukhopadhyay, S.C.: Field trials and performance monitoring of distributed solar panels using a low-cost wireless sensors network for domestic applications. IEEE Sens. J. **11**(10), 2583–2590 (2011)
7. Kovacs, A., Nicolcioiu, A., Arhip, J., Caşu, G.: Design and implementation of a GPRS remote data logger for weather forecasting. In: IEEE International Conference on Communication (2014)
8. Hortelano, D., Olivares, T., Ruiz, M.C., Garrido-Hidalgo, C., López, V.: From sensor networks to internet of things. Bluetooth low energy, a standard for this evolution. Sensors (Switzerland) **17**(2), 1–31 (2017)
9. Hiertz, G.R., Denteneer, D., Stibor, L., Zang, Y., Costa, X.P., Walke, B.: The IEEE 802.11 universe. IEEE Commun. Mag. **48**(1), 62–70 (2010)
10. Raza, U., Kulkarni, P., Sooriyabandara, M.: Low power wide area networks: an overview. IEEE Commun. Surv. Tutor. **19**(2), 855–873 (2017)
11. Baronti, P., Pillai, P., Chook, V.W.C., Chessa, S., Gotta, A., Hu, Y.F.: Wireless sensor networks: a survey on the state of the art and the 802.15.4 and ZigBee standards. Comput. Commun. **30**(7), 1655–1695 (2007)
12. Cypress Semiconductor: CY8CKIT-042-BLE-A Bluetooth Low Energy 4.2 Compliant Pioneer Kit. https://www.cypress.com/documentation/development-kitsboards/cy8ckit-042-ble-bluetooth-low-energy-42-compliant-pioneer-kit. Accessed 09 July 2019
13. Vishay Semiconductors: bpw34.pdf. https://www.vishay.com/docs/81521/bpw34.pdf. Accessed 09 July 2019
14. WaveShare: DHT22 Temperature-Humidity Sensor. https://www.waveshare.com/wiki/DHT22_Temperature-Humidity_Sensor
15. Ramsden, E.: Hall-Effect Sensors Theory and Application. Newnes, Oxford (2006)
16. Subudhi, B., Pradhan, R.: A comparative study on maximum power point tracking techniques for photovoltaic power systems. IEEE Trans. Sustain. Energy **4**(1), 89–98 (2013)

Modelling Interconnected Renewable Electricity Systems

Paula Ferreira[1]([⊠]) [iD] and Elizabete Pereira[2]

[1] Centro ALGORITMI, University of Minho, Campus Azurém, 4800-058 Guimarães, Portugal
paulaf@dps.uminho.pt
[2] School of Engineering, University of Minho, Campus Azurém, 4800-058 Guimarães, Portugal

Abstract. This paper addresses the long-term power planning in interconnected system with high renewable share. A case close to the Portuguese electricity system was modeled to assess the relevance of the interconnection with Spain in future scenarios. The results show that the increase on the renewable energy share will lead to a higher total cost of the system mainly due to investment costs. On the other hand, CO_2 emissions will be significantly reduced for each scenario in question. Another significant result is that the increase on renewable power, will lead to an excess of electricity production mainly during winter. For a 100% renewable scenario, the importance of interconnection is demonstrated, in particular, for the summer months for which importation can compensate the reduction of wind and hydropower output.

Keywords: Electricity planning · Renewables · Importations

1 Introduction

The sustainable use of energy and production of electricity are essential for the reduction of carbon dioxide (CO_2) emissions. Different energy strategies have been emerging and amongst which the development of renewable energy sources can be highlighted. The gradual integration of renewable energies leads to changes in the operation of the electricity grid as production tends to be seasonal and variable, but the security of supply remains essential. Electricity planning using optimization models has proven to be an effective tool in recognizing the level of impact that renewable technologies have on the electricity sector and for the definition of future strategies.

According to Pina et al. [1] modeling of energy systems has become more complex and realistic as new opportunities in the energy market have emerged, allowing the combination of two or more models. The complexity of optimization problems results from the diversity of existing production technologies, the temporal and/or spatial evolution of the parameters included in the model and the social and environmental arguments integrated in the model. In short, with the increasing contribution and integration of renewable energy sources (RES) in the grid, the complexity in idealizing an electric planning becomes bigger and for that reason, the optimization models are essential

J. L. Afonso et al. (Eds.): SESC 2019, LNICST 315, pp. 140–149, 2020.
https://doi.org/10.1007/978-3-030-45694-8_11

tools for the decision making, since they can include technical restrictions, economic, environmental and system ones [2].

This paper aims to contribute for the modeling and analysis of electricity system with a high RES share. The study will outline a long-term planning model for possible 100% renewable electricity system in Portugal, either isolated or interconnected with Spain. A model previously developed for long-term sustainable electricity planning was adjusted and applied to the Portuguese power system to include different renewable technologies, with the aim of minimizing the cost and also allowing to assess the impact on CO_2 emissions, throughout a planning period of 20 years.

2 Modelling and Electricity Planning

The modeling of energy systems operates as a tool to transform a complex reality into a simpler reality, making it possible to understand and analyze a problem. There is a wide variety of models in which the mathematical formulas allow to simulate or optimize a system [3]. Mathematical optimization models have been used for planning, operation and control problems of the power system and may have as their main objective to minimize, for example cost, operational errors and energy losses, or to maximize, for example, quality and efficiency of the system [4]. According to [5], models can guide the search for electricity and energy systems by comparing different modeled scenarios in order to apply the lower cost scenario and account for the efficiency and safety of the system.

Ringkjob et al. [6] reviewed 75 tools commonly used to analyze energy systems. The authors, with the help of the creators of the tools presented in the article, updated them in key points so that most of the current challenges related to electrical planning could be assessed. According to [2], optimization models remain as essential tools to aid in energy decision-making, but constraints and impacts must be integrated into these models reflecting the market conditions and specificities of each system under analysis. The case of the increasing integration of RES in the systems are gaining a remarkable importance, as the transition from fossil energy sources to RES has several impacts on the energy system. In addition, energy systems can also be analyzed as isolated systems (islands) or as systems interconnected to other areas. The interconnection between distinct systems allows for the import/export of electricity increase the complexity of the models, but represent also an important aspect to be taken into account.

The increasing importance of RES gave rise to several studies including the projection of a 100% renewable energy system with a great mix of energy sources but its implementation remains a challenge [7]. In addition to economic issues, the technical problems can challenge an energy system to become 100% renewable. These problems are frequently related to the variability of some renewable (wind and solar) which are not necessarily correlated to demand. On the other hand, if some RES present greater intra-daily variability, RES such as hydro and biomass can be more variable at a seasonal level [7].

According to Santos et al. [8], a number of studies have been conducted to assess the potential of a 100% renewable system in terms of climate change mitigation and resource efficiency, or to gain an understanding of the expected technical challenges. Despite all the information available and studies on 100% renewable system, this subject is still not absolutely consensual. In energy systems with high integration of renewable energy in order to obtain the maximum use of these sources of production, the electric system must somehow balance the intrinsic variability of its energy production [9]. According to Deason [9], flexibility options for the efficient integration of variable RES to reach a 100% renewable scenario can be added in different ways to the electricity system through energy production (e.g. hydroelectricity, biofuels and solar thermal energy concentrated storage), interconnected power grids, energy storage (e.g. thermal storage, compressed air, pumped storage, or batteries) and flexible demand. Thus, the extent of the real cost of integrating variable sources depends on the flexibility of the specific energy system, i.e., to what extent the supply side and demand side can deal with this variability.

In conclusion, Heard et al. [10] pointed out that strong empirical evidence must be demonstrated for any study attempting to construct or model a future low-carbon system by combining renewable technologies. For the authors, the desire to promote the 100% renewable ideal, without critical evaluation, delayed the identification and implementation of efficient ways of decarbonising. In contrast, Brown et al. [11] argued that energy systems 100% based on renewables are not only feasible, but also already economically viable and decreasing in cost every year.

For the case of Portugal, the results obtained by Krajacic et al. [7] found a solution for a 100% renewable system, which would be theoretically possible to achieve if there is an additional expansion of the grid to allow for a greater exchange of renewable electric energy (import-export). In addition, the authors emphasized that the incorporation of storage systems such as batteries and hydrogen, together with the existing pumping hydraulics, would allow the combination of these with the transport system and would contribute for the implementation of the electric vehicles. In Fernandes and Ferreira [12], the results also showed that it is theoretically possible to implement a 100% renewable system. Hydro and wind energy would have a dominant role in the system but the authors underline the need to complement it with other technologies (such as biomass, solar and wave), due to the seasonality and in order to reduce the required installed capacity. Santos et al. [8], investigated the economic component of the implementation of a 100% renewable system with energy interconnection and storage. The results showed that both the export and the storage by hydro pumping could be two viable solutions for dealing with the excess of electricity production from RES. According to the authors, the interconnection capacity would allow to save costs and improve production efficiency.

3 The Portuguese Electricity System

In Portugal, the RES power has been gradually increasing and represented in 2017, close to 70% of the total installed power. Figure 1 shows the evolution of the installed RES power in Portugal between 2005 and 2017. Figure 2 represents the contribution of each renewable and non-renewable technology to the production of electricity in 2017.

The figures clearly show a remarkable increase on RES in particular in what concerns wind. This strategy allowed to increase RES power output and make the system less dependent on the hydropower. Nevertheless, the importance of hydropower remains unquestionable as for example RES share in reached 2016 about 57% of the total electricity production against the 42% for 2017. This difference was mainly driven by the rain conditions, as 2016 was a wet year (well above the average) and 2017 was a dry year (well below the average).

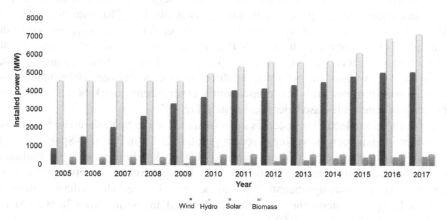

Fig. 1. Installed RES power in Portugal (source: data from [13, 14])

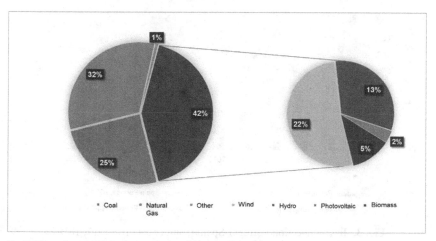

Fig. 2. RES and non-RES share of electricity production in Portugal, 2017 (source: data from [14])

Future projections for Portugal point to further investment on RES, with high focus on solar technologies. According to the Monitoring Report on the Security of Supply of the National Electric System 2017–2030 [15], the trajectories traced to 2025 and expanded for 2030, indicate that RES output will represent about 80% of the total electricity use in Portugal. More recently, the Roadmap for Carbon Neutrality in Portugal (RNCP) for 2050 was presented with the objective of reducing greenhouse gas emissions, i.e. the balance between emissions and their removal from the atmosphere should be zero. This Roadmap [16] presents ambitious goals for the power system since it has a fundamental role to carbon neutrality. The objectives of this document reinforce the predominant use of renewable endogenous resources that will significantly reduce energy dependence, as well as allowing for more than 80% of primary energy consumption by 2050. As for the final energy consumption, the Roadmap states that by 2050, more than 65% of final energy consumption will be electricity, which reinforces the sharp reduction in consumption of petroleum products [16]. The scenario outlined for 2050 assumes that electricity will be exclusively obtained from RES, including decentralized production, namely solar, as well as an investment in different storage options. Interconnections with neighboring power grids and consequently other electric markets will allow the transition to a renewable-based electrical system [16].

The Portuguese electricity system is interconnected to the Spanish territory and this interconnection has been increasing in recent years. In 2017, in Portugal-Spain (export) direction, the interconnection capacity reached 2600 MW, while in the Spain-Portugal (import) direction, this limit was 2000 MW [17]. Energy exchanges between Portugal and Spain have increased significantly through the years. Figure 3 shows the evolution of energy exchanges by interconnection between Portugal and Spain, from 2008 to 2018, as well as the average price (€/MWh).

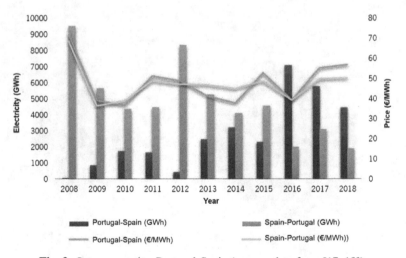

Fig. 3. Interconnection Portugal-Spain (source: data from [17, 18]).

4 Modelling Approach

The model implemented departed from a previous version from Pereira et al. [2], also developed for long-term power planning in Portugal using a cost minimization approach. The model was adapted for this particular study, with the inclusion of additional technologies, the extension of the planning period and the inclusion of the interconnection possibility. This resulted in a Mixed Integer Linear Problem (MILP), which was programmed in GAMS (General Algebric Modeling System) language. The solver CPLEX was used to obtain the numerical results of the cost minimization problem.

Besides the cost equation (objective function), a set of equations was included to reflect the constraints of the model. These constraints are imposed conditions in the formulation of the model and allow defining viable values of the decision variables for the specific case of the Portuguese electricity system. As such, the input information for the problem includes the mathematical formulation of the objectives and constraints. These constraints addressed:

- Demand, ensuring that the demand for electricity is always met over the planning horizon.
- Renewables, representing the minimum renewable shares for each scenario.
- System, which take into account the technical characteristics of the system and of the power plants (capacity, reserve, hydro and natural gas).

The input data describe the technical and economic characteristics of the existing and candidate power plants and the expected load (demand) pattern. The proposed model includes the following data modules:

- Information on all the generating units in the system at the start of the study and a list of retirements and fixed additions to the system.
- Information on the various generating units to be considered as candidates for expanding the generating system.
- Information on monthly demand, peak load for the planning period and the previously committed production (non-modelled).

The model does not deal with individual power plants but with technologies. Average values for the efficiency, CO_2 emission factors and specific fuel consumption are considered for each technology based on the average operating conditions occurred in previous years (for existing power plants) and on the expected performance of future power plants. It should be also underlined that the model does not foresee compensation payments for plants that although not producing or producing very little during the planning period would still be available as reserve. The model assumes that the fixed O&M will always be incurred even for these non-operational power plants.

The assumptions used as well as the source of data collection were presented, and according to the state of the Portuguese electricity system in 2017, three scenarios are established for further analysis:

- Scenario 1: "Base", assumed the minimum 80% share of renewable according to the "Monitoring Report on the Security of the National Electric System Supply 2017–2030", set as a restriction to the model.
- Scenario 2: "Maximum Renewable" (MAX-REN), is based on the year 2017 and provides for the maximum integration of renewable energy supply (100% renewable system), with no interconnection. This 100% RES share was also set as a restriction to the model.

– Scenario 3: "Interconnection System" (S-INT), 100% renewable system with the possibility of interconnection with Spain. The 100% RES was set as a restriction and the interconnection possibility was included on the cost objective as virtual generator with no investment or fixed costs.

5 Results

The optimization results for the three different scenarios in terms of total cost and CO_2 emissions for a 20-year planning period are shown in Table 1.

For the "BASE" scenario and for the "MAX-REN" scenario, the total cost assumes different parameters such as the cost of new units, i.e. new investments in renewable technology, fixed and variable cost of operation and maintenance (O&M), the fuel cost used in each production unit and the license cost for CO2 emissions.

Table 1. Characterization of the 3 scenarios

Scenario	Cost (€/MWh)	Emissions (t/MWh)	RES share (%)
Base	6.41	0.031	80
MAX-REN	9.03	0.019	100
S-INT	7.87	0	100

In the "S-INT" scenario, in addition to the previously mentioned parameters, the importation costs are also included in the objective function. A low importation cost of around € 9/MWh was assumed, which, despite being lower than the average value observed in the Iberian Market (MIBEL) will ensure that importations will be included in the model, albeit with optimistic costs. In fact, given the investments already made and the constraints imposed by the minimum share of renewables, it appears that with higher cost values the model would tend to reduce imports or even avoid them. This result comes

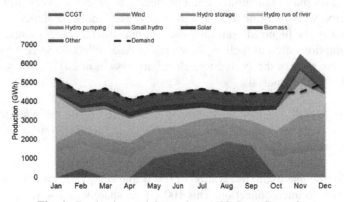

Fig. 4. Production and demand, year 20, Base Scenario

mainly from the use of monthly average values which do not allow for capturing strategic decisions and short-term needs, which are often related to import/export decisions.

Figure 4 illustrates the evolution of monthly energy production and consumption forecast in the "Base" scenario in year 20 of the planning period.

The analysis of electricity production per month allows observing the seasonality of each technology in production, in particular for hydro and wind power. The production highly relies on RES with the exception of the summer months for which combined cycle gas turbines (CCGT) would be called to operate and compensate the low hydropower production. As for winter months (November and December), some excess production may be observed given the more favorable wind and hydro conditions.

Figure 5 shows the evolution of energy production and consumption for the "MAX-REN" scenario in year 20 of the planning period.

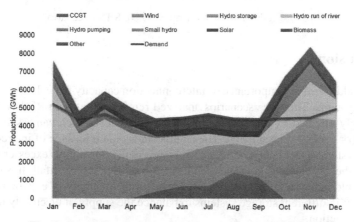

Fig. 5. Production and demand, year 20, MAX-REN scenario

The results are quite similar to the ones presented in the previous scenario, although with the seasonality being even more evident, which leads to higher installed capacity of RES and consequently to higher excess production during the winter. Given that the restriction imposing a 100% RES share was set on an annual basis as ratio between production and demand, the model tends to use CCGT during the summer which would be compensated by the excess of electricity production in the winter. As such, the yearly demand equals RES production but the system does reach the full decarbonization.

As for the "S-INT" scenario, it represents also a 100% RES system but now with the possibility of trading with Spain. Imports would occur in months of lower RES production, such as May, June, July, August and September, which reflect the lower hydro availability. The importation of electricity allows the consumption to be satisfied in these months, without recourse to the gas technologies as verified in the previous scenarios and allowing also for a reduction of installed power of new wind power plants, as presented in Fig. 6. The system would then be fully decarbonized.

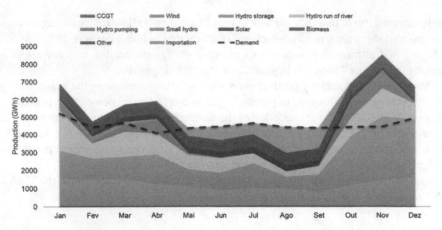

Fig. 6. Production and demand, year 20, S-INT scenario

6 Conclusions

This paper addressed the importance of interconnection capacity to deal with renewable electricity systems. The three scenarios analyzed reinforce that high RES system tend to be strongly affected by the seasonality of the resources, which can result in either curtailment or excess of production. The results shows the relevance of interconnected electricity system to tackle this problem. The interconnection allows excesses not to be wasted and the system does not fail when there is a production shortfall. It is clear that imports should be considered as a strategy for security of supply of electricity as well as investment in different storage systems to balance the supply of electricity in months of lower production.

Although a simplified approach was used in this study, it became evident that the interconnection can have a positive impact is what concerns costs, emissions and security of supply. However, the cost impact of this strategy is yet to be properly assessed as the proposed approach relied on a simplification of the market assuming only the possibility of importations and at a very low price. In fact, when considering exportations as well, the model would tend to converge to solutions of profit maximization through the increase on production of electricity. This solution, although mathematically sound would not reflect the restrictions associated to the market operation. It also would not take into account the strategic options of market agents Thus, the cost function can reflect the costs of importation, but not the possible revenues of the possible exports that would always be dependent on strategic decisions and the interest of the Spanish market in this excess of electricity produced in Portugal. This open avenues for important research for the inclusion of the short-term market operating model in the long term generation expansion problems and for the assessment of the best options for the decarbonization of the electricity system.

Acknowledgement. This work has been supported by FCT – Fundação para a Ciência e Tecnologia within the R&D Units Project Scope: UIDB/00319/2020.

References

1. Pina, A., Silva, C.A., Ferrão, P.: High-resolution modeling framework for planning electricity systems with high penetration of renewables. Appl. Energy **112**, 215–223 (2013)
2. Pereira, S., Ferreira, P., Vaz, A.I.F.: Optimization modeling to support renewables integration in power systems. Renew. Sustain. Energy Rev. **55**, 316–325 (2016)
3. NEP - Nordic Energy Perspectives: Coordinated use of energy system models in energy and climate policy analysis - lessons learned from the Nordic Energy Perspectives project. PR-Offset, Mölndal (2010). ISBN 978-91-978585-9-5
4. Bansal, R.C.: Optimization methods for electric power systems: an overview. Int. J. Emerging Electr. Power Syst. **2**(1) (2005)
5. Foley, A.M., Ó Gallachóir, B., Hur, P., Baldick, R., McKeogh, E.J.: A strategic review of electricity systems models. Energy **35**(12), 4522–4530 (2010)
6. Ringkjøb, H., Haugan, P.M., Solbrekke, I.M., Zürich, E.T.H., Pfenninger, S.: A review of modelling tools for energy and electricity systems with large shares of variable renewables. Renew. Sustain. Energy Rev. **96**, 440–459 (2018)
7. Krajačić, G., Duić, N., da Graça Carvalho, M.: How to achieve a 100% RES electricity supply for Portugal? Appl. Energy **88**(2), 508–517 (2011)
8. Santos, M.J., Ferreira, P., Araujo, M.: Least-cost 100% renewable electricity scenarios. In: International Conference on the European Energy Market, EEM, Porto, Portugal (2016)
9. Deason, W.: Comparison of 100% renewable energy system scenarios with a focus on flexibility and cost. Renew. Sustain. Energy Rev. **82**, 3168–3178 (2018)
10. Heard, B.P., Brook, B.W., Wigley, T.M.L., Bradshaw, C.J.A.: Burden of proof: a comprehensive review of the feasibility of 100% renewable-electricity systems. Renew. Sustain. Energy Rev. **76**, 1122–1133 (2017)
11. Brown, T.W., Bischof-niemz, T., Blok, K., Breyer, C., Lund, H., Mathiesen, B.V.: Response to 'Burden of proof: a comprehensive review of the feasibility of 100% renewable-electricity systems'. Renew. Sustain. Energy Rev. **92**, 834–847 (2018)
12. Fernandes, L., Ferreira, P.: Renewable energy scenarios in the portuguese electricity system. Energy **69**, 51–57 (2014)
13. REN – Rede Elétrica Nacional: Dados Técnicos 2005. www.centrodeinformacao.ren.pt. Accessed 24 Sept 2018
14. REN – Rede Elétrica Nacional: Dados Técnicos 2017. www.centrodeinformacao.ren.pt. Accessed 24 Sept 2018
15. DGGE- Direção Geral de Geologia e Energia: RMSA-E – Relatório de Monitorização da Segurança de Abastecimento do Sistema Elétrico Nacional 2017–2030. www.dgge.pt. Accessed 29 Oct 2018
16. Republica Portuguesa: RNC – Roteiro para a Neutralidade Carbónica 2050. https://descarbonizar2050.pt. Accessed 20 Jan 2019
17. REN – Rede Elétrica Nacional: Mercado de Eletricidade: Síntese Anual 2014–2018. www.centrodeinformacao.ren.pt. Accessed 01 Nov 2018
18. REN – Rede Elétrica Nacional: Mercado de Eletricidade: Síntese Anual 2008–2012. www.centrodeinformacao.ren.pt. Accessed 01 Nov 2018

Integrating PV+Battery Residential Microgrids in Distribution Networks: How Is the Point of Common Coupling Agreed Upon?

Iolanda Saviuc[1]([✉]) [iD], Steven Van Passel[1,2] [iD], and Herbert Peremans[1] [iD]

[1] Department of Engineering Management, Faculty of Business and Economics, University of Antwerp, Antwerp, Belgium
iolanda.saviuc@uantwerpen.be
[2] Centre for Environmental Sciences, Hasselt University, Hasselt, Belgium

Abstract. The anticipated development of decentralized electricity generation is expected to strengthen the opportunities of prosumers in the residential areas of cities, in line with the predicted establishment of renewable energy generation and storage. Based on academic research and on successful case studies, the opportunity for residential prosumers to organize in microgrids emerges as a viable and promising solution. This paper focuses on microgrids that are planned to generate electricity with a PV unit and use a shared storage system, and that opt to have a connection with the main grid. However, the point of common coupling needs to be agreed first between the microgrid operator and the network operator, and this agreement is determined by several factors and conditions beyond the basic technical and regulatory requirements. A survey of academic literature on the determinant factors for such an agreement exposes the fact that current research either focuses on the integration of individual prosumers in the main grid, or regards the point of common coupling as a given component of microgrids. We argue that neither of the two approaches is helpful in the case of microgrids vs. main grid, seeing as the agreement is not self-evident under just any circumstances, nor can the microgrid be equated to a single, large prosumer. Therefore this short paper compiles a set of determinant factors for the microgrid integration, as they emerge from academic literature, with the aim to document further research needs and support the discussion on microgrid integration.

Keywords: Decentralization · Microgrids · Point of common coupling · Residential prosumers

© ICST Institute for Computer Sciences, Social Informatics and Telecommunications Engineering 2020
Published by Springer Nature Switzerland AG 2020. All Rights Reserved
J. L. Afonso et al. (Eds.): SESC 2019, LNICST 315, pp. 150–164, 2020.
https://doi.org/10.1007/978-3-030-45694-8_12

Nomenclature

DG	Distributed Generation
DNO	Distribution Network Operator
DSM	Demand Side Management
ESS	Electricity Storage System
EV	Electric Vehicle
HC	Hosting Capacity
LV	Low Voltage
MG	Microgrid
PCC	Point of Common Coupling
RES	Renewable Energy Sources
TSO	Transmission Service Operator

1   Introduction

Advantages of distributed generation (DG) are documented by both academic literature and successful case studies, and they range from decongestion of the main grid to improvements in reliability and power quality [45,62]. Solutions such as microgrids (MGs) can in fact include any energy sources, but they are found to be a promising vehicle for the integration of renewable energy sources (RES) [75], featuring in roadmaps for the development of energy network towards climate change mitigation [27], especially in cities [9,15].

In fact, the current EU projections and policies regard the retail electricity market and individual consumers as having a fundamental role in the energy transition, with a special attention to the ways in which consumers can become 'prosumers' with RES such as PV panels and electricity storage systems (ESS) [19]. ESS such as batteries complement photovoltaic electricity generation [24] by making the PV units controllable, supporting peak shaving and helping mitigate the so-called 'duck curve' at the level of residential prosumers. Pooling a shared ESS in MGs has been found to be especially beneficial in terms of resilience and power quality [4,39,49], and for economic viability [43].

The technological development along with the lower prices of ESS and PV panels [30] on the one hand, and the favourable social and political context on the other hand, outline a scenario for the future in which microgrids interconnecting residential prosumers with rooftop PV panels and batteries become widespread in European cities.

Problem Identification and Research Question. An urban residential MG matching the scenario outlined above would feature, apart from the PV unit and the ESS, a connection to the main grid, realized through one point of common coupling (PCC). The underlying assumption of this set-up is that the PCC is regarded as a given, whereas in reality it only exists if both sides of the PCC, the MG operator and the district network operator (DNO), reach an agreement. This oversight can be attributed to the straightforward nature and clear scope of the interconnection standard IEEE 1547 [29]: a comprehensive list of technical requirements that, if fulfilled, guarantee a functioning PCC. An additional legal aspect is addressed usually at the country- or state level.

We argue that after complying with all technical and regulatory requirements, there are further factors and conditions affecting the agreement between the DNO and the MG party.

However, a review of relevant literature reveals that the factors and conditions governing the PCC are not being addressed together as such, but instead separately and rather indirectly. The major research gap that we identify consists in the fact that the individual prosumers are being investigated in their relation with the DNO (DG as single households), while communities of prosumers (DG as integrated MGs) – less so. However communities of prosumers – such as, in our case, MGs – cannot be regarded as one single large prosumer, mainly due to their robust control capabilities, smoothened load curve and resilience [63], which can constitute a service offered to the DNO.

In this context, our work addresses the research gap by compiling an overview of the factors and conditions governing the PCC. The resulting paper seeks to provide clarity and facilitate further discussion on urban residential MGs.

2   Method

For this survey 42 academic papers have been reviewed, published between 2005 and 1 Jun 2019. The search and selection process has been carried out by first using a dedicated software (Publish or Perish) with the following keywords: "microgrid DNO", "point of common coupling", "distribution network microgrids", "microgrid integration". A twofold sorting of the results was carried out: the first, by number of citations; the second, by publication date. Review articles were preferred. The selection process was then augmented by following references from the resulting papers, whenever necessary.

The 42 papers consulted come from academic journals (37) and conference proceedings (5). The most academic journals from which the consulted articles originate are the following: Applied Energy (7), International Journal of Electric Power and Energy Systems (5), Renewable and Sustainable Energy Reviews (4), Energy Policy (4).

Players and Roles. The residential MG is a community (e.g. an apartment building, a street of houses, a real estate development) having one common PV unit or several PV units pooled together for common use. The ESS (e.g. Li-Ion battery) is, similarly, either a common purchase or several units pooled together for shared use. On the other side, the DNO is an intermediary between the transmission service operator (TSO) and the consumers, in charge of transforming the electricity to low voltage (LV) at substations, providing the connection between the substations and clients, balancing the power flow and charging the customers for consumption.

By seeking a connection to the main grid, the MG is in fact looking for a backup electricity source, a possibility to sell excess electricity, and support in frequency stabilization. In exchange, it offers peak shaving, resilience, and benefits to the power quality. Both parties would agree to connect if the costs are compensated by benefits.

Assumptions. We acknowledge that the challenges of coupling one single prosumer at a substation are lower than connecting and balancing several consumers. Therefore this research case assumes the perspective of connecting the nth MG, where $n + 1 \leq HC$, the maximum Hosting Capacity of the substation (see [53]). The distribution network is considered at LV and radial. It is assumed that the distribution of costs, obligations, benefits and roles within the MG is already settled, and that the remaining last step is the connection of the main grid with a PCC. In the interaction between the MG and the DNO, the DNO regards the MG as a single unit represented by a cooperative, an aggregator business, or similar.

3 Literature Review

There is a significant body of research regarding DG integration, identifying the shortcomings and solutions for improvement. While acknowledging that the current electricity networks are not prepared for the future system requirements [7], it is clear that DG cannot be regarded as a 'negative load' [42]. Engineering research addresses the negative effects of high penetration of PV such as voltage issues, power issues, frequency issues, unintentional islanding [31,35,53,66]. The intermittency of the PV source can be compensated by the ESS [8], which is why the PV+Battery combination is particularly attractive, both technically [12] and economically [40]. However, as mentioned before, current research is largely focused on the integration of single prosumers.

For this review we have focused on DG as integrated MGs and found that the realization of a PCC needs first to be feasible, and second to be attractive, both technically and economically. On the level of feasibility there are technical requirements, rules and obligations clearly laid out in national guidelines (e.g. the Small Generator Interconnection Agreement in the US, [57]) which are based on the IEEE 1547 interconnection standard and make the PCC contract possible under the conditions in each country.

In the following subsection we briefly address the requirements that make the PCC feasible (technical and regulatory criteria) and after that we elaborate on the further factors and their implications.

3.1 Factors Which Make the PCC Feasible

The main factors that ensure interconnection feasibility can be found directly in the pro-forma agreements developed under the supervision of the energy regulatory bodies (e.g. [57] in the US, [70] in Germany). They document the requirements governing the PCC agreement such as the interconnection procedures, obligations of insurance and cost allocation methodologies [51].

In order to fulfill said requirements, the main concern from the point of view of the DNO when integrating DG regards harmonics, for which there are technical standards in place (e.g. IEEE 519 [28]). The perturbations at the PCC are subject to extensive research in technical literature (see [14, 16, 74]).

From the point of view of the MG the two great challenges of MGs are control and protection [34, 44, 76], as well as the issues of power flow stabilization [47]. It is worth noting at this point that the technical requirements constitute the category of factors where research seems to be most advanced and with the most clear results.

3.2   Factors Which Make the PCC Attractive

Technical: While the technical requirements for the existence of a PCC are found to have a clear scope, the range of improvements suggested by academic research is broad. Among the main identified factors were found: optimal MG position and distance to the substation; sizing of the battery at the MG; the energy scheduling and management within the MG with existence of demand side management (DSM); the use of DC current by the MG; the existence of electric vehicles (EV).

One of the main features of MGs in relation to the DNO, as mentioned above, is to help enhance resilience. That is mainly achieved by the MG being able to quickly disconnect and go into island mode [25, 35, 68] and help restore power supply in case of extreme weather conditions [73].

However, the sizing and controllability of the battery emerges as the one factor that can markedly improve the technical performance of PV+Battery systems in terms of stability [5, 10, 11, 37]. In fact, higher ESS capacities coupled with appropriate management strategy mitigate net load variance and avoid costs for the DNO [18].

The storage power optimal scheduling is a well-documented area, with a consistent body of research investigating various optimization methods [59]. In addition to that, the existence of demand side management (DSM) control capabilities avoids power losses and reduces peak demand [71].

In order to mitigate the risk of overvoltage when there is bidirectional power flow, the distance between the PV units and the distribution substation should be minimized [32, 69, 72]. In the planning of a PCC, another determinant factor has been found to be whether electric vehicles (EV) should be taken into account, as their batteries require significantly higher charging power [22, 26]. If the MG operators decides to use DC current in the MG, the overall system efficiency is improved [13].

The DNO can, in turn, improve the technical attractivity of the main grid with voltage regulators and improved grid planning measures [6].

Non-technical: A wealth of research is being carried out regarding the energy management within the MG, closely mirroring the technical features of DSM and battery control capabilities. Both stochastic and robust optimization models are being examined [52,64]. In turn, the DNO also has the possibility to optimize the coordination of multiple MGs, thus making the integration of MGs more economically sound [2,46,61].

A further major aspect that ensures fair transactions at the PCC is the electricity pricing. By including RES in MGs, the prosumers will inevitably be subjected to local regulation aimed at supporting PV production and/ or self-consumption. From the most widespread pricing mechanisms, the net-metering has been shown to actively disincentivize the use of batteries [60], the feed-in tariff promotes exchange with the grid over self-consumption [36], whereas the time-of-use tariffs have been found to best support DSM [65] but strain the substations with peak demand [54]. However, it is worth noting that volumetric pricing schemes might be unsuitable for PV+Battery MGs, as is has been found that energy-based tariffs neglecting the impact of prosumers aggravates the regional distributional disparities [23]. The discussion on pricing is not settled yet at this point, due to the pricing policies designed to support residential PV production through an encouraged exchange with the grid. This puts the PV generation in conflict with the desirable integration of ESS in the system, as the ESS do not benefit from policies that would support energy saving.

However, the key aspect in reaching the agreement between the MG and the DNO seems to be a fair allocation of costs. As research points out, the representation of fairness appears different in the two respective views. It is shown for example that "with the current grid tariff schemes, operators of PV installation and storage can reduce their grid fees without reducing the costs they cause to the grid", especially under the net-metering scheme [33]. When it comes to benefits, it is possible that the generators capture more benefits than the DNOs and than the society [67]. Furthermore there is a danger that passive consumers (non-prosumers) would find themselves contributing to the cost recovery of the DNO or to the newly necessary network upgrades, without having incurred any costs to begin with [2,61]. Solutions proposed in order to even this out include charging for smart connections [3] or simple stand-by charges [1].

From the MG perspective, the benefits are still not allocated fairly, but the reason is that some externalities are not monetized – such as the flexibility provided by the resources in a MG [20]. A solution is proposed in form of contract deferral schemes [21,55] or simply the formalization of grid balancing services [39]. In fact, the flexibility feature can be further captured by allowing for peer-to-peer trading [41,78,79], and make the case for a new business entity that coordinates the behind-the-meter assets [50].

4 Summary and Discussion

Our literature survey has summarized the factors that constitute minimum requirements for the feasibility of a PCC, and revealed an additional number of factors that, while not strictly addressed by the PCC contract, can increase or decrease the attractiveness of a PCC between a MG and a DNO.

Figure 1 provides an overview of the factors and assigns them to the party which can do something about them. For example in the case of minimum requirements, technical aspects have to be agreed upon by both sides. However, among those technical factors, there are aspects of control and protection which are in the scope of the MG operator, whereas the DNO can (and is required to) address the concerns regarding harmonics and perturbations. In the lower half of 1, which summarizes those factors outside of the bare-minimum, the non-technical aspects can regard addressing energy management solutions from the point of view of the MG operator, whereas the DNO can improve the attractiveness of the PCC by improving their energy pricing system.

In a further step of our analysis we look at list of factors identified in Fig. 1 and trace them back to the academic literature from which we have drawn them, in light of the question 'Is it based on MG-specific literature? Or is the insight based on DG-literature?'. In this case we refer to literature about integrating individual prosumers as 'DG-literature'. The background of this question is that the factors identified from DG-literature have to be reassessed in the context of a MG (as shown in the introduction, a MG is different than a sum of individual prosumers).

Table 1 summarizes the factors found in our literature survey and further structures them based on the following criteria:

- Whether the factors are technical (Tech.) or non-technical (nTech.);
- Identifies the agent who can initiate the identified influence, between the MG operator (MG) and the distribution network operator (DNO);
- Whether the article(s) cited address the case of DG as individual prosumer (DG-lit) or indeed the integration of a microgrid as such (MG-lit)

Table 1. Summary of factors

Factor	Tech	non-Tech	Agent	DG-lit	MG-lit	References
Emergency response	✓		MG		✓	[25,35,68,73]
MG siting and sizing	✓		MG		✓	[32,69,72]
ESS sizing	✓		MG	✓	✓	[5,10,11,18,37]
EV vehicles	✓		MG		✓	[22,26]
Energy scheduling	✓		MG	✓		[38,59,77]
DSM capabilities	✓		MG	✓		[17,71]
Use of DC in the MG	✓		MG		✓	[13]
Voltage regulators	✓		DNO	✓		[6,48]
Grid planning	✓		DNO	✓		[6,56]
Energy management in MG		✓	MG		✓	[52,64]
Optimized MG coordination		✓	DNO		✓	[2,46,61]
Electricity pricing		✓	DNO	✓	✓	[23,36,54,60,65]
Smart/standby charges		✓	DNO	✓	✓	[1,3]
Deferral schemes		✓	MG	✓		[21,55]
Grid balancing services		✓	MG		✓	[20,39]
Peer-to-peer trade		✓	MG		✓	[41,78,79]

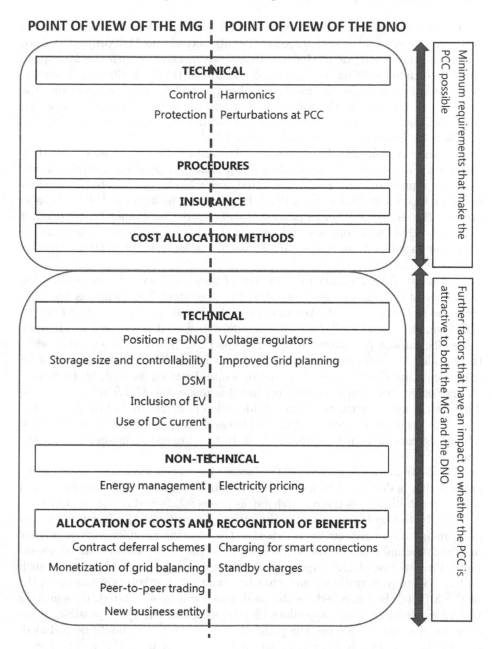

Fig. 1. Summary of factors identified in literature to impact feasibility and attractivity of the PCC, from both the point of view of the MG and of the DNO

For example in the case of "ESS sizing": it is a factor that has been found to have an impact on how advantageous (i.e. attractive) the MG project is, since the appropriate sizing of the battery brings advantages to both the MG (peak shaving, demand shifting, cost savings) and to the DNO (flexibility). However, it is a technical measure that has to be taken by the MG planner/operator – the "Agent", in this case is the MG. The five references [5, 10, 11, 18, 37] on which the identification of this factor is based are addressing both research of DG as individual consumers, and DG as integrated MGs.

On the other hand, the measure of incurring smart charges or stand-by charges is a non-technical factor (does not primarily depend on installing a new device or reprogramming a controller) that surely has to be accepted by the MG operator before agreeing upon a PCC. In this case the agent is the DNO, who imposes the charges (although possibilities of negotiation cannot be excluded, it is still the DNO who imposes and collects the charges). The two references on which we have based our finding are researching microgrid integration, what we have labeled as MG-literature.

A look at Table 1 points to a number of insights. First, the factors labeled as primarily technical mostly correspond to the agent MG, whereas the non-technical factors are mixed. We can explain this imbalance with the fact that the MG is smaller and more flexible, able to adopt new solutions in order to become more efficient and persuasive in favour of the PCC. Second, the fact that while the options MG operator are mostly towards improving the perspective of an agreement, the DNO can work in the opposite direction as well, by increasing charges or by providing electricity pricing that makes the MG function at a loss. This insight agrees with the mismatch identified in literature in how distributed energy projects are financially evaluated between the private sector and utilities, which suggests in turn that the DNO is in fact interested in maintaining the status-quo [58].

Third, we notice that some of the factors have been identified based on literature that is dedicated to individual prosumers, and not to DG as integrated MGs – which illustrates the research gap as it was mentioned in the introduction.

Finally, the table points to the limitation of our study: the fact that is does not provide an assessment as to whether the identified factors have a *positive* or a *negative* influence on the attractiveness of the PCC. This is due to several facts. First, the academic papers which argue in favour of novel solutions such as the peer-to-peer trade suggest that by adopting that solution the strengths of the MG will be improved, or the weaknesses will be alleviated, thus making the interconnection more appealing to the DNO and the PCC possible. However, for the sake of balance, the point of view of the DNO should be included, but to the best of our knowledge so far the research from the point of view of the utilities does not mirror closely the findings of novel solutions. Second, the implementation of a novel measure – e.g. installation of voltage regulators by the DNO at relevant substations to sustain reliable PCCs – can be considered to have a positive impact on the perspective of the interconnection. However, most of the studies do not provide a cost-benefit analysis of the proposed solutions, therefore it is not clear whether the voltage regulators, while having a positive impact on MG integration, might in fact be too expensive and hence not a realistic proposal.

The factors listed in Table 1 have been labelled as 'technical' or 'non-technical', but it is understood that a) they can be translated into economic benefits or savings (e.g. the appropriate ESS sizing at the MG can save grid upgrading costs at the DNO), and b) they can interact (e.g. offering grid balancing services influences the ESS sizing, and in part the MG siting). A closer examination and mapping of the interactions is an avenue for further research within the current discussion on burden sharing between MGs and DNOs.

5   Conclusion

The integration of microgrids in distribution networks takes place by connecting the MG to the main grid via one point of common coupling. We have found that in academic literature the PCC is either regarded as a given, or equated to a connection point between the main grid and an individual prosumer. While the MG cannot be equated to a large prosumer, we argued that the PCC cannot be a formality either. In this paper we have briefly reviewed the factors which amount to basic requirements that make the PCC possible: compliance with IEEE standards and protection measures important for the MG. Having established that, we surveyed the academic literature and compiled a list of factors which are not obligatory requirements for the existence of the PCC, but they can determine how appealing the interconnection is for both parties.

The resulting list of factors proposes a starting point for further additions and discussions, and offers right from the beginning a clear illustration of the imbalance between the agency power of the MG operator and the one of the DNO. It also suggests that the main strength of MGs consists in its small size and flexibility, making it capable to quickly include improvements in technical equipment and operation.

At this stage of our research we can conclude that an agreement on a PCC between the MG and the DNO can be influenced by the MG mainly through technical measures, whereas the DNO tends to have stronger non-technical instruments at its disposal.

References

1. Abdelmotteleb, I., Gómez, T., Chaves Ávila, J.P., Reneses, J.: Designing efficient distribution network charges in the context of active customers. Appl. Energy **210**, 815–826 (2018)
2. Anaya, K.L., Pollitt, M.G.: Integrating distributed generation: regulation and trends in three leading countries. Energy Policy **85**, 475–486 (2015)
3. Anaya, K.L., Pollitt, M.G.: Going smarter in the connection of distributed generation. Energy Policy **105**, 608–617 (2017)
4. Barbour, E., Parra, D., Awwad, Z., González, M.C.: Community energy storage: a smart choice for the smart grid? Appl. Energy **212**, 489–497 (2018)

5. Bashir, A.A., Pourakbari-Kasmaei, M., Contreras, J., Lehtonen, M.: A novel energy scheduling framework for reliable and economic operation of islanded and grid-connected microgrids. Electr. Pow. Syst. Res. **171**, 85–96 (2019)
6. Bayer, B., Matschoss, P., Thomas, H., Marian, A.: The German experience with integrating photovoltaic systems into the low-voltage grids. Renewable Energy **119**, 129–141 (2018)
7. Blokhuis, E., Brouwers, B., van der Putten, E., Schaefer, W.: Peak loads and network investments in sustainable energy transitions. Energy Policy **39**(10), 6220–6233 (2011)
8. Canizes, B., Soares, J., Lezama, F., Silva, C., Vale, Z., Corchado, J.M.: Optimal expansion planning considering storage investment and seasonal effect of demand and renewable generation. Renewable Energy **138**, 937–954 (2019)
9. Clarke, T., Lambert, E., Deavis-Marks, M., Ceccarelli, A.: Improving the robustness of urban electricity networks. Technical report, IRENE (2015). http://ireneproject.eu/wp-content/uploads/2016/01/IRENE-D1.1r2-.pdf. Accessed 30 June 2019
10. Crossland, A.F., Jones, D., Wade, N.S.: Planning the location and rating of distributed energy storage in LV networks using a genetic algorithm with simulated annealing. Int. J. Elec. Power Energy Syst. **59**, 103–110 (2014)
11. Das, C.K., Bass, O., Kothapalli, G., Mahmoud, T.S., Habibi, D.: Overview of energy storage systems in distribution networks: placement, sizing, operation, and power quality. Renew. Sustain. Energy Rev. **91**, 1205–1230 (2018)
12. Elbasuony, G.S., Abdel Aleem, S.H., Ibrahim, A.M., Sharaf, A.M.: A unified index for power quality evaluation in distributed generation systems. Energy **149**, 607–622 (2018)
13. Elsayed, A.T., Mohamed, A.A., Mohammed, O.A.: DC microgrids and distribution systems: an overview. Electr. Pow. Syst. Res. **119**, 407–417 (2015)
14. Eltigani, D., Masri, S.: Challenges of integrating renewable energy sources to smart grids: a review. Renew. Sustain. Energy Rev. **52**, 770–780 (2015)
15. European Commission: Energy roadmap 2050. Technical report, April 2012. http://www.roadmap2050.eu. Accessed 30 June 2019
16. Fernandez, F.M., Nair, P.S.C.: Method for separation of customer and utility contributions of harmonics at point of common coupling. IET Gener. Transm. Dis. **7**(4), 374–381 (2013)
17. Ferruzzi, G., Graditi, G., Rossi, F., Russo, A.: Optimal operation of a residential microgrid: the role of demand side management. Intell. Ind. Syst. **1**(1), 61–82 (2015)
18. Freitas, S., Reinhart, C., Brito, M.C.: Minimizing storage needs for large scale photovoltaics in the urban environment. Sol. Energy **159**, 375–389 (2018)
19. GfK Belgium: Study on "Residential Prosumers in the European Energy Union". Technical report, May, European Commission, Brussels (2017). https://ec.europa.eu/commission/sites/beta-political/files/study-residential-prosumers-energy-union_en.pdf. Accessed 30 June 2019
20. Goutte, S., Vassilopoulos, P.: The value of flexibility in power markets. Energy Policy **125**, 347–357 (2019)
21. Haesen, E., Alarcon-Rodriguez, A.D., Driesen, J., Belmans, R., Ault, G.: Opportunities for active DER management in deferral of distribution system reinforcements. In: 2009 IEEE/PES Power Systems Conference and Exposition, pp. 1–8, March 2009

22. Heymann, F., Silva, J., Miranda, V., Melo, J., Soares, F.J., Padilha-Feltrin, A.: Distribution network planning considering technology diffusion dynamics and spatial net-load behavior. Int. J. Elec. Power Energy Syst. **106**, 254–265 (2019)
23. Hinz, F., Schmidt, M., Möst, D.: Regional distribution effects of different electricity network tariff designs with a distributed generation structure: the case of Germany. Energy Policy **113**, 97–111 (2018)
24. Home-Ortiz, J.M., Pourakbari-Kasmaei, M., Lehtonen, M., Sanches Mantovani, J.R.: Optimal location-allocation of storage devices and renewable-based DG in distribution systems. Electr. Pow. Syst. Res. **172**, 11–21 (2019)
25. Hussain, A., Bui, V.H., Kim, H.M.: Microgrids as a resilience resource and strategies used by microgrids for enhancing resilience. Appl. Energy **240**, 56–72 (2019)
26. Iacobucci, R., McLellan, B., Tezuka, T.: The synergies of shared autonomous electric vehicles with renewable energy in a virtual power plant and microgrid. Energies **11**(8), 2016 (2018)
27. IEA: Smart Grids in Distribution Networks: Roadmap Development and Implementation. Technical report, IEA, Paris (2015). https://www.iea.org/publications/freepublications/publication/TechnologyRoad-mapHow2GuideforSmartGridsin DistributionNetworks.pdf. Accessed 30 June 2019
28. Li, C., Xu, W.: On defining harmonic contributions at the point of common coupling. IEEE Power Eng. Rev. **22**(7), 44–45 (2002)
29. IEEE Standard Association: IEEE Std. 1547–2018 (Revision of IEEE Std 1547–2003) Standard for Interconnection and Interoperability of Distributed Energy Resources with Associated Electric Power Systems Interfaces (2018). https://standards.ieee.org/standard/1547-2018.html. Accessed 30 June 2019
30. IRENA: IRENA cost and competitiveness indicators rooftop solar PV. Technical report, December 2017. http://www.irena.org/publications. Accessed 30 June 2019
31. Janda, K., Málek, J., Rečka, L.: Influence of renewable energy sources on transmission networks in Central Europe. Energy Policy **108**, 524–537 (2017)
32. Jannesar, M.R., Sedighi, A., Savaghebi, M., Guerrero, J.M.: Optimal placement, sizing, and daily charge/discharge of battery energy storage in low voltage distribution network with high photovoltaic penetration. Appl. Energy **226**, 957–966 (2018)
33. Jargstorf, J., De Jonghe, C., Belmans, R.: Assessing the reflectivity of residential grid tariffs for a user reaction through photovoltaics and battery storage. Sustain. Energy Grids Netw. **1**, 85–98 (2015)
34. Kai-Hui, Z., Ming-Chao, X.: Impacts of microgrid on protection of distribution networks and protection strategy of microgrid. In: 2011 International Conference on Advanced Power System Automation and Protection, vol. 1, pp. 356–359, October 2011
35. Karimi, M., Mokhlis, H., Naidu, K., Uddin, S., Bakar, A.H.: Photovoltaic penetration issues and impacts in distribution network - a review. Renew. Sustain. Energy Rev. **53**, 594–605 (2016)
36. Khalilpour, K.R., Vassallo, A.: Technoeconomic parametric analysis of PV-battery systems. Renewable Energy **97**, 757–768 (2016)
37. Khodadoost Arani, A.A., Gharehpetian, G.B., Abedi, M.: Review on energy storage systems control methods in microgrids. Int. J. Elec. Power Energy Syst. **107**, 745–757 (2019)
38. Khodaei, A.: Resiliency-oriented microgrid optimal scheduling. IEEE Trans. Smart Grid **5**(4), 1584–1591 (2014)

39. Koirala, B.P., van Oost, E., van der Windt, H.: Community energy storage: a responsible innovation towards a sustainable energy system? Appl. Energy **231**, 570–585 (2018)

40. Liu, X., Yan, Z., Wu, J.: Optimal coordinated operation of a multi-energy community considering interactions between energy storage and conversion devices. Appl. Energy **248**, 256–273 (2019)

41. Long, C., Wu, J., Zhang, C., Cheng, M., Al-Wakeel, A.: Feasibility of peer-to-peer energy trading in low voltage electrical distribution networks. Energy Procedia **105**, 2227–2232 (2017)

42. Lopes, J.A.P., Hatziargyriou, N., Mutale, J., Djapic, P., Jenkins, N.: Integrating distributed generation into electric power systems: a review of drivers, challenges and opportunities. Electr. Pow. Syst. Res. **77**(9), 1189–1203 (2007)

43. Luthander, R., Widén, J., Munkhammar, J., Lingfors, D.: Self-consumption enhancement and peak shaving of residential photovoltaics using storage and curtailment. Energy **112**, 221–231 (2016)

44. Meliopoulos, S.: Microgrids Architectures and Control, 1st edn. Wiley, Hoboken (2014)

45. Mohammed, Y.S., Mustafa, M.W., Bashir, N.: Hybrid renewable energy systems for off-grid electric power: review of substantial issues. Renew. Sustain. Energy Rev. **35**, 527–539 (2014)

46. Mohiti, M., Monsef, H., Anvari-moghaddam, A., Guerrero, J., Lesani, H.: A decentralized robust model for optimal operation of distribution companies with private microgrids. Int. J. Elect. Power Energy Syst. **106**, 105–123 (2019)

47. Molina, M.G., Mercado, P.E.: Power flow stabilization and control of microgrid with wind generation by superconducting magnetic energy storage. IEEE Trans. Power Electron. **26**(3), 910–922 (2011)

48. Muttaqi, K.M., Le, A.D.T., Negnevitsky, M., Ledwich, G.: A coordinated voltage control approach for coordination of OLTC, voltage regulator, and DG to regulate voltage in a distribution feeder. IEEE Trans. Ind. Appl. **51**(2), 1239–1248 (2015)

49. NREL: Distributed solar PV for electricity system resiliency: policy and regulatory considerations. Technical report (2014). https://www.nrel.gov/docs/fy15osti/62631.pdf. Accessed 30 June 2019

50. Ossenbrink, J.: How feed-in remuneration design shapes residential PV prosumer paradigms. Energy Policy **108**, 239–255 (2017)

51. Oueid, R.K.: Microgrid finance, revenue, and regulation considerations. Electr. J. **32**(5), 2–9 (2019)

52. Pandžić, H.: Optimal battery energy storage investment in buildings. Energ. Buildings **175**, 189–198 (2018)

53. Passey, R., Spooner, T., MacGill, I., Watt, M., Syngellakis, K.: The potential impacts of grid-connected distributed generation and how to address them: a review of technical and non-technical factors. Energy Policy **39**(10), 6280–6290 (2011)

54. Pimm, A.J., Cockerill, T.T., Taylor, P.G.: Time-of-use and time-of-export tariffs for home batteries: effects on low voltage distribution networks. J. Energy Storage **18**, 447–458 (2018)

55. Poudineh, R., Jamasb, T.: Distributed generation, storage, demand response and energy efficiency as alternatives to grid capacity enhancement. Energy Policy **67**, 222–231 (2014)

56. Preda, T., Uhlen, K., Nordgård, D.E.: An overview of the present grid codes for integration of distributed generation. In: CIRED 2012 Workshop: Integration of Renewables into the Distribution Grid, pp. 1–4, May 2012

57. Public Service Company of Colorado: Small Generator Interconnection Agreement (2018). https://www.xcelenergy.com/staticfiles/xe-responsive/WorkingWithUs/RenewableDevelopers/SmallGeneratorInterconnectionAgreement_Customer-Owned_9.24.2018_SAMPLE.pdf. Accessed 30 June 2019

58. Pullins, S.: Why microgrids are becoming an important part of the energy infrastructure. Electr. J. **32**, 17–21 (2019)

59. Saboori, H., Hemmati, R., Ghiasi, S.M.S., Dehghan, S.: Energy storage planning in electric power distribution networks - a state-of-the-art review. Renew. Sustain. Energy Rev. **79**, 1108–1121 (2017)

60. Saviuc, I., Peremans, H., Van Passel, S., Milis, K.: Economic performance of using batteries in European residential microgrids under the net-metering scheme. Energies **12**(1), 165 (2019)

61. Schittekatte, T., Momber, I., Meeus, L.: Future-proof tariff design: recovering sunk grid costs in a world where consumers are pushing back. Energy Econ. **70**, 484–498 (2018)

62. Schwaegerl, C., Tao, L.: Quantification of technical, economic, environmental and social benefits of microgrid operation. In: Hatziargyriou, N. (ed.) Microgrids - Architecture and Control, chap. 7, 1st edn., pp. 275–312. Wiley, Hoboken (2014)

63. Schwaegerl, C., Tao, L.: The concept of microgrids. In: Hatziargyriou, N.D. (ed.) Microgrids - Architecture and Control, chap. 1, 1st edn., pp. 1–24. Wiley, Hoboken (2014)

64. Sedighizadeh, M., Esmaili, M., Jamshidi, A., Ghaderi, M.H.: Stochastic multi-objective economic-environmental energy and reserve scheduling of microgrids considering battery energy storage system. Int. J. Elec. Power Energy Syst. **106**, 1–16 (2019)

65. Sedighizadeh, M., Mohammadpour, A.H., Alavi, S.M.M.: A two-stage optimal energy management by using ADP and HBB-BC algorithms for microgrids with renewable energy sources and storages. J. Energy Storage **21**, 460–480 (2019)

66. Silva, E.N., Rodrigues, A.B., Da Silva, M.D.G.: Stochastic assessment of the impact of photovoltaic distributed generation on the power quality indices of distribution networks. Elect. Pow. Syst. Res. **135**, 59–67 (2016)

67. Sioshansi, R.: When energy storage reduces social welfare. Energy Econ. **41**, 106–116 (2014)

68. Syrri, A.L., Martinez Cesena, E.A., Mancarella, P.: Contribution of Microgrids to distribution network reliability. In: 2015 IEEE Eindhoven PowerTech (2015)

69. Vallem, M.R., Mitra, J.: Siting and sizing of distributed generation for optimal microgrid architecture. In: Proceedings of the 37th Annual North American Power Symposium, pp. 611–616, October 2005

70. VDEW: Eigenerzeugungsanlagen am Niederspannungsnetz. Richtlinie für Anschluß und Parallelbetrieb von Eiegnerzeugungsanlagen am Niederspannungsnetz (2005). http://www.sw-netz.de/wp-content/uploads/tv-n_eigen-nsvdn_2005-09-nl.pdf. Accessed 30 June 2019

71. Viana, M.S., Manassero, G., Udaeta, M.E.: Analysis of demand response and photovoltaic distributed generation as resources for power utility planning. Appl. Energy **217**, 456–466 (2018)

72. Wang, C., Song, G., Li, P., Ji, H., Zhao, J., Wu, J.: Optimal siting and sizing of soft open points in active electrical distribution networks. Appl. Energy **189**, 301–309 (2017)

73. Wang, J., Xie, N., Wu, W., Han, D., Wang, C., Zhu, B.: Resilience enhancement strategy using microgrids in distribution network. Global Energy Interconnection **1**(5), 537–543 (2018)

74. Xu, W., Liu, Y.: A method for determining customer and utility harmonic contributions at the point of common coupling. IEEE Trans. Power Delivery **15**(2), 804–811 (2000)
75. Yan, J., Zhai, Y., Wijayatunga, P., Mohamed, A.M., Campana, P.E.: Renewable energy integration with mini/micro-grids. Appl. Energy **201**, 241–244 (2017)
76. Zaidi, A.A., Kupzog, F.: Microgrid automation - a self-configuring approach. In: 2008 IEEE International Multitopic Conference, pp. 565–570, December 2008
77. Zakariazadeh, A., Jadid, S., Siano, P.: Smart microgrid energy and reserve scheduling with demand response using stochastic optimization. Int. J. Elec. Power Energy Syst. **63**, 523–533 (2014)
78. Zepter, J.M., Lüth, A., del Granado, P.C., Egging, R.: Prosumer integration in wholesale electricity markets: synergies of peer-to-peer trade and residential storage. Energ. Buildings **184**, 163–176 (2019)
79. Zhang, C., Wu, J., Zhou, Y., Cheng, M., Long, C.: Peer-to-Peer energy trading in a Microgrid. Appl. Energy **220**, 1–12 (2018)

Economic Evaluation of PV Generation Curtailment and Voltage Regulation Investment in Distribution Networks with High PV Penetration

Juan Miguel P. Bunagan, Ryan Christopher T. Gonzales,
and Michael Angelo A. Pedrasa[⊠]

Electrical and Electronics Engineering Institute,
University of the Philippines - Diliman, Quezon City, Philippines
{juan.miguel.bunagan,ryan.gonzales}@eee.upd.edu.ph, mapedrasa@up.edu.ph

Abstract. The continuing increase of photovoltaic (PV) generation in distribution systems comes with difficulties in keeping voltages within acceptable limits, especially during peak generation. Two conventional alternatives exist to solve these overvoltage issues: to install voltage regulation equipment (AVR) or curtail PV generation, but there is no existing procedure to aid distribution system operators (DSO) in choosing either solution from an economical perspective. This project presents a methodology to evaluate the two aforementioned alternatives. The equivalent annual cost of installing automatic voltage regulator systems in the network was compared to the annual compensation awarded to curtailed PV generator owners. Several case studies were explored and show that in some situations, curtailment can be more cost-effective depending on the curtailment compensation scheme used, amount of PV penetration, location of PV in the network, and demand profiles. Additionally, the researchers explored the economic viability of using curtailment in conjunction with existing AVR installations instead of installing additional AVRs.

Keywords: Photovoltaics · Renewable generation · Distribution networks · Voltage regulators · Curtailment

1 Introduction

In a move towards a future independent of fossil fuels, countries worldwide have adopted renewable energy systems. The use of renewable resources in distribution networks is steadily increasing, especially photovoltaic (PV) systems. It is predicted to further increase in the future because of the incentives provided by governments to prosumers and the adverse impacts of using conventional sources of power generation in the environment. The increase in connected renewable resources comes with its drawbacks. It may threaten the power quality in

© ICST Institute for Computer Sciences, Social Informatics and Telecommunications Engineering 2020
Published by Springer Nature Switzerland AG 2020. All Rights Reserved
J. L. Afonso et al. (Eds.): SESC 2019, LNICST 315, pp. 165–179, 2020.
https://doi.org/10.1007/978-3-030-45694-8_13

distribution networks and cause issues like voltage swell and voltage sag. These can cause detrimental effects on existing protection schemes and increase wear on utility equipment [1].

Voltage level is one of the crucial parameters of the grid that a distribution system operator (DSO) must always maintain within limits so that the load side of the network will have an acceptable range of voltage supply. An option for DSOs is to invest in additional voltage regulation equipment to maintain voltages within these required limits. Traditionally, DSOs upgrade their networks by adding conventional on-load tap changer transformers (OLTC) coupled with automatic voltage regulator (AVR) relays to regulate transformer output voltages within the set voltage limits [2]. The OLTC is an automatic relay-controlled transformer component where it changes the voltage at the system using the tap settings of transformers [3]. Meanwhile, the AVR determines the load-side voltages and currents of the transformer, and eventually differentiates the measured voltage and reference voltage. If the difference surpasses the AVR's tolerance setting, then the tap setting will be automatically adjusted to normalize the transformer voltage at load side [4]. The AVR relay helps to control the local or remotely-located voltages in the system to keep them within set limits [5].

Since installing voltage regulation equipment may require a considerable investment in time and money for DSOs, an alternative is to curtail the output of generation. Curtailment today typically occurs because of constraints in the network or as a precaution against a foreseen instability in the system. However, curtailing renewable generation is seen negatively by the general public as "green" energy is lost. Generation from renewable sources has nearly zero marginal costs and so, it can be an economic loss as well. That said, curtailment can be a viable solution to problems when integrating this generation into the grid. Full integration of all generation can lead to excessive investment in equipment upgrades, infrastructure extension and deter further investment into renewable generation.

There are four main categories of curtailment situations, which can be both voluntary and involuntary: (1) network constraints, (2) security, (3) excess generation and (4) strategic bidding. Curtailment for security, excess generation, and strategic bidding is mainly used with the goal of minimizing market-related costs. For network constraints, the goal is to avoid over-investment in capacity and/or to delay investing in increasing capacity. It is suggested that compensation, in the case of network constraints or network extension delays, can be shouldered by the DSO using market prices or a fraction thereof [6].

A DSO is concerned not only with keeping system operations stable but also economical, so some cost analysis and comparison is required when considering if delaying network upgrades through curtailment is still profitable. Currently, no procedure or platform exists to make it easier for the DSO to choose between curtailment or investment in voltage regulation equipment.

This paper presents a procedure to assist DSOs in the economic evaluation of two alternatives to solve overvoltage problems caused by high PV penetration in their networks: (1) installing voltage regulation equipment or (2) curtailment of

PV generation. In particular, the equivalent annual cost for voltage regulation installation will be compared to the total annual compensation to generator owners.

2   Methodology

To build the test system, data regarding load and generation profiles and cost analysis were acquired. After building the base test system, a baseline scenario was applied and simulated. Using the results of the baseline scenario, economic analysis for the AVR installation and curtailment was performed. Lastly, several case studies were observed.

2.1   Test System Building

Building the test system required hourly residential and commercial load profiles, as well as hourly irradiation data which were acquired from [7,8] respectively.

The IEEE 34 node test feeder without AVRs was used for the test network. The IEEE 34-bus system is a standard test network that was designed to evaluate and benchmark algorithms in solving unbalanced radial distribution systems, and is also suited for use in systems with distributed generation. This test network is an actual radial distribution feeder operating at 60 Hz, 24.9 kV and 12 MVA, depicted in Fig. 1. In order to manage the undervoltage in the system at peak load, specifically at bus 890, the capacitor bank is removed, and the spot load at bus 890 is decreased.

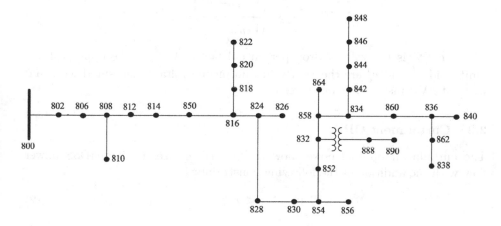

Fig. 1. Modified IEEE 34-bus system

Each PV system connected to the network is modeled as a 60 kW capacity generator operating at unity power factor.

The power flow is conducted using the EPRI distribution simulation tool, OpenDSS. OpenDSS is used for its full multiphase model, built-in IEEE 34 feeder test case code, and relatively easy data exchange interface with MATLAB.

2.2   Optimal AVR Positioning

The method in [9] is used for the initial placement of AVR in the test system based on technical criteria. The method is started by using load flow to compute the bus voltages. From the results of the load flow, critical paths are identified. A critical path is the path from a bus with the highest overvoltage to the substation. In each critical path, an AVR is positioned at the end node. After that, a load flow is run to check the overvoltage in the system. Then, an objective function considering technical aspects, the voltage drop percentual factor $F_{at_v}\%$, is computed using the configuration. The $F_{at_v}\%$ is used to show the quality of a certain placement of AVR in terms of voltages, shown in 1. Next, the AVR is moved upstream to the next bus of the critical path and the steps are repeated until the substation bus is reached. The AVR is positioned at the bus which produced the smallest $F_{at_v}\%$ and did not contain overvoltages throughout the system. The method is tested using the load and PV generation data of the average hour in the month where the highest overvoltage for the whole year occurred, which in this case is at hour 13 of May. A flowchart of the algorithm is presented in Fig. 2.

$$F_{at_v}\% = \frac{\sum_{i=1}^{N}\left(V_{nom} - v_i^f\right)^2}{\sum_{i=1}^{N}\left(V_{nom} - v_i^0\right)^2} \cdot 100 \tag{1}$$

where $F_{at_v}\%$ is the voltage drop percentual factor, V_{nom} is the upper voltage limit, and v_i^f and v_i^0 are the hourly instantaneous voltages measured with and without AVR installed at bus i, respectively.

2.3   Curtailment OPF

The curtailment optimal power flow (OPF) still utilizes the OpenDSS power flow with the addition of the following constraints:

$$0 \leq P_{gi} \leq P_{gi}^{max} \tag{2}$$

$$0.9pu \leq v_i \leq 1.10pu \tag{3}$$

where P_{gi} is the active power generation dispatched at bus i for the specified hour, P_{gi}^{max} is the maximum active power generation for bus i and v_i is the instantaneous voltage measured at bus i for the specified hour.

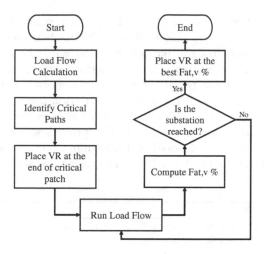

Fig. 2. AVR positioning method

Curtailment priority is modeled as an optimal dispatch problem, shown in 4, with a linear cost function Ω_{gi} shown in 5.

$$min \left(\sum_{i=1}^{N} \Omega_{gi} \left(P_{gi} \right) + \sum_{i=1}^{N} W_i \right) \tag{4}$$

$$\Omega_{gi} \left(P_{gi} \right) = P_{gi}^{max} - P_{gi} \tag{5}$$

$$W_i = \begin{cases} S_i \left(v_i - V_{max} \right)^2 & V_{max} \\ S_i \left(v_i - V_{min} \right)^2 & V_{min} \end{cases} \tag{6}$$

The constrained optimization problem is expressed as an unconstrained optimization problem by expressing the voltage constraint 3 as a penalty function W_i, shown in 6. S_i is the penalty factor which is set at an arbitrarily large number. V_{min} and V_{max} are the lower and upper voltage limits, respectively.

Constriction Factor Particle Swarm Optimization (CF-PSO) is then used for the optimization, described in [10]. The CF-PSO algorithm is initialized by generating a random population, referred to as a swarm. Each swarm is composed of individual solutions called particles, initialized with random positions in the solution space with random velocities (update rate). At each iteration, the positions and velocities are updated based on the swarm and particle behavior. Each particle position and velocity is updated using 7 and 8 respectively, and this facilitates the optimization process.

$$x_i^{t+1} = x_i^t + u_i^{t+1} \tag{7}$$

$$u_i^{t+1} = k \left[u_i^t + r_1 c_1 \left(p_i - x_i^t \right) + r_2 c_2 \left(p_g - x_i^t \right) \right] \tag{8}$$

t represents the iteration count, x_i is the particle position, u_i is the velocity, $(p_i - x_i^t)$ compares the particle position with its best performance (particle best), $(p_g - x_i^t)$ compares the particle position with the swarm's best performance (global best), c_1 and c_2 are coefficients that represent the trade-off between the influence of the particle best and the global best, r_1 and r_2 are random numbers between 0 and 1, k is the constriction factor. The values of c_1, c_2 and k are set to $c_1 = c_2 = 2.05$ and $k = 0.7298$ to ensure convergence and efficiency in the optimization process [11]. The process was repeated until the difference between the values of global best functions in 50 consecutive iterations are between a tolerance value of 1×10^{-6}. The process is shown in Fig. 3.

Algorithm 1:

    input: Objective function C_{tobj}, swarm size M,
            CF-PSO parameters

1 **for** *each particle* $i = 1, ..., M$ **do**
2   Initialize particle's position $\mathbf{x}_i$;
3   Initialize particle's velocity $\mathbf{v}_i$;
4 **end**
5 Solve DLF to calculate C_{tobj};
6 Initialize particle's best known position $\mathbf{P}_i$;
7 Initialize swarm's best known position $\mathbf{P}_g$;
8 **while** *stopping criterion is false* **do**
9   **for** *each particle* $i = 1, ..., M$ **do**
10   Update particle's velocity $\mathbf{v}_i$;
11   Update particle's position $\mathbf{x}_i$;
12   Solve DLF to calculate C_{tobj};
13   **if** $C_{tobj}(\mathbf{x}_i) < C_{tobj}(\mathbf{P}_i)$ **then**
14   Update particle's best known position $\mathbf{P}_i$;
15   **if** $C_{tobj}(\mathbf{P}_i) < C_{tobj}(\mathbf{P}_g)$ **then**
16   Update swarm's best known position $\mathbf{P}_g$;
17   **end**
18   **end**
19   **end**
20 **end**

Fig. 3. CF-PSO algorithm

The CF-PSO algorithm was implemented using MATLAB and interfaced with OpenDSS using the provided Component Object Model (COM) server Dynamic Link Library (DLL) as illustrated in Fig. 4.

2.4 Baseline Simulation

An initial load flow was conducted without PV systems to ensure that the base test system did not contain any voltage violations.

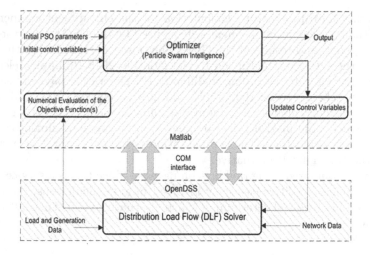

Fig. 4. Platform for CF-PSO MATLAB and OpenDSS loadflow

The PV systems were then connected for the baseline scenario. The PV penetration level is defined as the maximum generation of an individual PV system based on the percentage of total peak load of the system. All 34 nodes have a PV system connected, and the penetration level for the whole system was set at 140% of the total peak load or 60 kW per PV generator. This served as the basis of the power computations for the sizing of the AVR installation and amount of curtailment. AVR installation consists of one AVR based on the result of the method used in optimal AVR positioning. The curtailment scheme implemented is pro rata (equal cost function coefficient π_{gi}).

2.5 Economic Analysis

AVR Installation. Several types of costs were considered when calculating for the equivalent annual cost (EAC) for the AVR over its useful life:

- First cost (investment plus installation cost)
- Annual operation and maintenance costs
- Annual system loss

The EAC for the AVR installation alternative was computed using

$$EAC = FC(A/P, i\%, N) + O + S \tag{9}$$

$$(A/P, i\%, N) = \frac{i(1+i)^N}{(1+i)^N - 1} \tag{10}$$

where FC is the first cost, O is the annual operation and maintenance cost, S is the annual system loss. The system loss is computed from DSO system loss rates and network losses from OpenDSS load flow simulations.

Curtailment Compensation. Calculation for the curtailment compensation considers the PV generation payment scheme used by the DSO to pay the owner of the PV system and results of the OPF. The power curtailed from the generators using the OPF was multiplied to the monthly 2018 Philippine electricity blended generation rates according to different PV generation payment schemes. The payment schemes were: 100%, 50% and 25% of market price, and 3% and 10% maximum curtailment. Maximum curtailment means that the generator owner will receive full market price compensation for any curtailment that goes above a certain percentage. The compensation to be paid over 1 year was the EAC for the curtailment alternative.

Both were compared using ranking comparison. Since this is a service project with no revenue or positive cash flow involved in any calculations, the ranking comparisons only involved determining which alternative yielded a smaller equivalent annual cost.

3   Results

3.1   Initial Load Flow

The initial load flow was carried out for 24 1-h intervals for an average day in each month for 2018.

Shown in red in Fig. 5 are the results of the initial load flow at the month with the highest overvoltage (May at hour 13), without an AVR installed in the system or curtailment applied. On average, the month of May has the highest difference in PV generation and demand at hour 13 or 1:00 PM, so all the AVR sizing and placement is based on the load flow results of this month and hour.

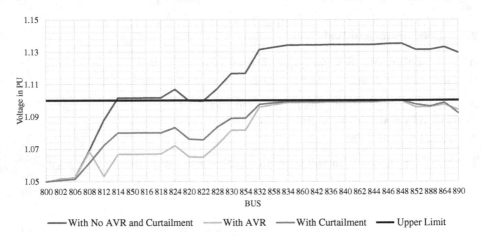

Fig. 5. Voltage profile of buses (phase A) at May Hour 13 (Color figure online)

3.2   Baseline Simulation

Installed AVR. The results of the initial load flow show that the first occurrence of overvoltage in the system is at bus 814. To find the optimal position of the AVR, the first placement of the AVR is between buses 812 and 814. Following the procedure and moving upstream to the substation bus, the optimal location of the AVR is found to be between buses 808 and 812 because it has the lowest voltage drop percentual factor, F_{at_v}% at 76.24% and it does not have overvoltage throughout the system.

Curtailment of PV Generation. Pro rata or equal curtailment among all PV generators was applied to the system using the objective function $min\,(60 - P_{gi})$ in the CF-PSO algorithm. This type of curtailment yields a generation profile that is the same shape but scaled down from the original. The effect of curtailment on the voltage profile is shown at the hour and month with the worst overvoltage levels in Fig. 5. In total, the amount curtailed for the test system over the year for the baseline simulation was 403 MW.

Table 1. Cost comparison between AVR installation and curtailment compensation for baseline simulation

Compensation scheme	Compensation	AVR installation cost
Full price	$39,810	$26,710
0.5 price	$19,905	
0.25 price	$9,953	
3% max curtailment	$32,000	
10% max curtailment	$17,835	

3.3   Economic Analysis

As presented in Table 1, at the base case or 140% PV penetration, AVR installation is more economical compared to pro rata curtailment at full market price and 3% maximum curtailment compensation. Pro rata curtailment with compensation at 50% and 25% market price, and 10% maximum curtailment are significantly more cost-effective compared to AVR installation.

3.4   Case Studies

Case Study I - Increasing PV Penetration Level. The percentage of the PV penetration is increased by increments of 5% of total peak load starting with the baseline 140% of total peak load.

As shown in Fig. 6, AVR installation is more economical than curtailment compensation at full price and 3% maximum curtailment for all penetration levels. At 50% of full price and 10% maximum curtailment, curtailment is more economical but only up to between 145% and 150%. Curtailment is more economical for penetration levels up to 170% at 25% of full price.

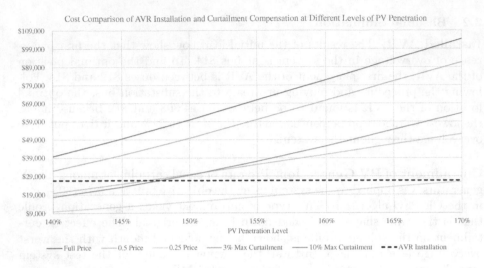

Fig. 6. Cost comparison of AVR installation and curtailment compensation at different levels of PV penetration

Case Study II - Different PV Positioning. Three different placement patterns are tested on the network to see how it affects the overvoltage levels. The PVs are placed at every other node, near the substation, and far from the substation, and compared to the baseline scenario of PVs place at every node.

As presented in Table 2, in the cases where the PVs are positioned at every node (baseline) and at every other node, the cost of AVR installation was cheaper than compensating curtailment at full price and 3% max curtailment, and less economical for the other compensation methods. In the case that the PVs are placed far from the substation, it was more economical to install two AVRs than compensating curtailment for any compensation scheme other than 25% of market price. That being the case, it is more economical to curtail if the majority of PVs in the network are situated near the substation.

Table 2. Cost comparison of AVR installation and curtailment compensation at different positions of PVs in the system

Compensation scheme	Every node	Every other node	Near S/S	Far from S/S
Full price	$39,810	$43,610	$0	$159,094
0.5 price	$19,905	$21,805	$0	$79,547
0.25 price	$9,953	$10,903	$0	$39,773
3% max curtailment	$32,000	$35,398	$0	$146,414
10% max curtailment	$17,835	$19,944	$0	$117,679

Case Study III - Variation of Load Type. Several different percentages of commercial load is mixed in with the baseline scenario of purely residential load: 5% commercial and 95% residential load, 10% commercial and 90% residential load, and 25% commercial and 95% residential load.

At 100% residential and the combination of 5% commercial and 95% residential load, it is less expensive to install an AVR compared to only the full price curtailment compensation scheme as shown in Fig. 7. While at the combination of 10% commercial and 90% residential load, and at the combination of 25% commercial and 75% residential load, all the curtailment compensation schemes are more cost-efficient compared to AVR installation. Generally, as the amount of commercial load mixed in with residential load increases, the more economical it is to curtail PV generation.

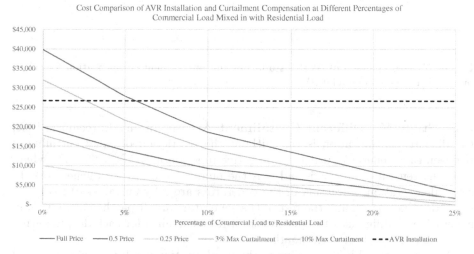

Fig. 7. Cost comparison of AVR installation and curtailment compensation at different percentages of commercial load mixed in with residential load

Case Study IV - Impact of Installing a Large Commercial PV System. This case study aims to find the effect of a sudden large power injection due to installing a large PV generator at one node in a system with only small residential PV systems. Initially, every bus has a 10 kW PV generator, and a single 1.7 MW PV generator is added at one bus.

When the large commercial PV was connected to the buses near the substation it barely caused overvoltage in the system. Conversely, when the large commercial PV was connected to the buses far from the substation, large overvoltages occured at several buses. If we only look at the buses where placement of a large commercial PV causes overvoltage, curtailment compensation (at all schemes) is more economical than AVR installation only when placed at buses 814 and 816. It can be observed that if larger PV capacities are installed nearer to the substation, curtailment is generally more economical than AVR installation, shown in Fig. 8.

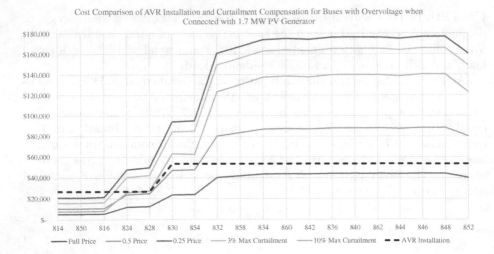

Fig. 8. Cost comparison of AVR installation and curtailment compensation for select buses with large commercial PV

Case Study V - Different Curtailment Arrangement. In technical best, the dispatch optimization is run without the restriction of equal curtailment between each generator, using the objective function $min(\sum_{i=1}^{N}(60 - P_i))$ where P_i is the generation at bus i, and N is the number of buses with generators. In scheduled rotation, a fraction of the generators are fully curtailed (0 kW) at a given day and month and the rest of the generators are dispatched at maximum generation. A different set of generators will be curtailed for each day, following a rotation assigned for each month.

As seen from Table 3, assigning a scheduled rotation yields the highest annual cost out of the three arrangements due to the requirement that any curtailed generator has to be at 0 kW dispatch. This makes curtailed generators near the substation be inefficiently curtailed as they are generally insensitive to power injections, as demonstrated in Case Study IV. It is recommended in this case to compensate the curtailed generators at 50% or 20% of full market price or 10% maximum compensation. Curtailing according to technical best is a more economical curtailment method with dispatch at full price marginally smaller than the baseline AVR annual cost.

Table 3. Cost comparison of AVR installation and curtailment compensation for different curtailment arrangements

Compensation scheme	Pro rata	Tech best	Sched rota
Full price	$39,810	$26,477	$66,484
0.5 price	$19,905	$13,239	$33,242
0.25 price	$9,953	$6,619	$16,621
3% max curtailment	$32,000	$25,056	$64,490
10% max curtailment	$17,835	$22,029	$59,836

Case Study VI - Additional AVR Installation Due to Generation and Load Growth. It may be essential to add AVRs to stabilize the voltage in the system when it increases due to annual generation growth.

As the generation and load is annually increased, there is a need to add AVRs in the network every 3 years so that it can withstand the resulting increase in voltage, as shown in Table 4.

Table 4. Cost analysis of additional AVR installation due to generation and load growth

Case	AVR position	Tap changes	Total annual cost
3 years	808-812; 828-830	20; 31	$53,438
6 years	808-812; 812-814; 828-830; 854-852	26; 28; 54; 89	$107,371
9 years	806-808; 808-812; 812-814; 828-830; 854-852; 852-832	11; 27; 50; 92; 223; 11	$167,261

Case Study VII - Combining Curtailment with AVR Installation/s Versus Additional AVR Installations. Curtailment is applied in conjunction with AVR installations as an alternative to purely curtailing generation or additional AVR installations. Since Case Study VI already tackled additional AVR installations, the results of that case study was the basis for the methodology of this case study.

Table 5 shows the economically best combination of each scenario along with the results of Case Study VI. At 3 years of generation and load growth, curtailment in combination with one AVR is more economical than installing an additional AVR for all compensation methods, but only marginally cheaper at full market price compensation. At 6 years of generation and load growth, curtailment in combination with two AVRs is more economical than installing two additional AVRs for all compensation methods. At 9 years of generation and load growth, curtailment in combination with 5 AVRs (one additional AVR) is more economical than installing an additional AVR for all compensation methods.

Table 5. Cost comparison of additional AVR installations and the combination of curtailment with AVR installation

Case	No. of AVRs (Total cost)	Curtailment + AVRs	Compensation scheme	Compensation
3 years	2 AVRs 808-812; 828-830 ($53,438)	Curtailment + 1 AVR 808-812	Full price	$51,003
			0.5 price	$38,857
			0.25 price	$32,783
			3% max curtailment	$44,316
			10% max curtailment	$33,857
6 years	4 AVRs 808-812; 812-814; 828-830; 854-852 ($107,371)	Curtailment + 2 AVRs 808-812; 828-830	Full price	$70,693
			0.5 price	$62,066
			0.25 price	$57,752
			3% max curtailment	$64,252
			10% max curtailment	$54,959
9 years	6 AVRs 806-808; 808-812; 812-814; 828-830; 854-852; 852-832 ($167,261)	Curtailment + 5 AVRs 808-812; 812-814; 828-830; 854-852; 852-832	Full price	$136,719
			0.5 price	$135,935
			0.25 price	$135,542
			3% max curtailment	$135,150
			10% max curtailment	$135,150

4   Conclusion

This research provides a procedure to evaluate between the cost of installing AVRs and the cost of curtailment compensation in a distribution network that is heavily integrated with grid-injecting PV systems. The method makes use of power flow to find the AVR placement and optimal curtailment for a given baseline network, and computing the associated costs for each alternative. The resulting cost computations are projected across the lifetime of the AVR and compared. Upon applying and testing the baseline simulation and several case studies, the researchers found that the procedure can be easily implemented for existing and possible future grid scenarios. It is flexible, as the program used in the IEEE-34 bus system can be easily applied to different radial configurations and use different optimization methods due to the use of OpenDSS and MATLAB. The procedure can be a helpful tool in network planning for DSOs, for example, in the placement of future renewable generation in the network and/or appraisal of non-firm connections. It can also be a useful aid for regulatory bodies and legislators in determining pricing regulations for curtailment compensation. Future work may extend to feasibility studies involving investment in power electronics solutions capable of simultaneously maximizing PV generation and minimizing power quality issues.

References

1. Schoene, J., Zheglov, V., Houseman, D., Smith, J.C., Ellis, A.: Photovoltaics in distribution systems – integration issues and simulation challenges. In: 2013 IEEE Power & Energy Society General Meeting, pp. 1–5. IEEE, Vancouver (2013). https://doi.org/10.1109/PESMG.2013.6672879. Accessed 12 Mar 2019
2. Kenneth, A.P., Folly, K.: Voltage rise issue with high penetration of grid connected PV. IFAC Proc. Vol. **47**(3), 4959–4966 (2014). https://doi.org/10.3182/20140824-6-ZA-1003.01989. Accessed 24 Feb 2019
3. Hashim, T.J.T., Mohamed, A., Shareef, H.: A review on voltage control methods for active distribution networks. Wydawnictwo SIGMA - N O T Sp. z o.o. **88**, 304–312 (2012). Accessed 2 Apr 2019
4. Hiscock, N., Hazel, T.G., Hiscock, J.: Voltage regulation at sites with distributed generation. IEEE Trans. Ind. Appl. **44**(2), 445–454 (2008). https://doi.org/10.1109/TIA.2008.916749. Accessed 13 Apr 2019
5. Madzonga, L., Munda, J., Jimoh, A.: Analysis of bus voltage regulation and OLTC performance on mismatched parallel-connected transformers. In: AFRICON 2009, pp. 1–5. IEEE, Nairobi, September 2009. https://doi.org/10.1109/AFRCON.2009.5308082. Accessed 7 Mar 2019
6. Klinge Jacobsen, H., Schröder, S.T.: Curtailment of renewable generation: economic optimality and incentives. Energy Policy **49**, 663–675 (2012). https://doi.org/10.1016/j.enpol.2012.07.004. Accessed 16 Feb 2019
7. OpenEI and US Department of Energy: Commercial and Residential Hourly Load Profiles for all TMY3 Locations in the United States - OpenEI DOE Open Data. https://openei.org/doe-opendata/dataset/. Accessed 12 Mar 2019
8. Copernicus Atmosphere Monitoring Service: CAMS McClear Service for estimating irradiation under clear-sky. http://www.soda-pro.com/web-services/radiation/cams-mcclear. Accessed 29 Apr 2019
9. Pereira, C.A.N., Castro, C.A.: Optimal placement of voltage regulators in distribution systems. In: 2009 IEEE Bucharest PowerTech. IEEE, June 2009. https://doi.org/10.1109/PTC.2009.5282031. Accessed 14 Mar 2019
10. Anwar, A., Mahmood, A.N.: Swarm intelligence based multi-phase OPF for peak power loss reduction in a smart grid. In: 2014 IEEE PES General Meeting — Conference & Exposition, pp. 1–5. IEEE, National Harbor, July 2014. https://doi.org/10.1109/PESGM.2014.6939824. Accessed 26 Mar 2019
11. Clerc, M., Kennedy, J.: The particle swarm - explosion, stability, and convergence in a multidimensional complex space. IEEE Trans. Evol. Comput. **6**(1), 58–73 (2002). https://doi.org/10.1109/4235.985692. Accessed 15 Mar 2019

Increasing Photovoltaic Self-consumption: An Approach with Game Theory and Blockchain

Matthieu Stephant[1]([✉]), Dhaker Abbes[1], Kahina Hassam-Ouari[2],
Antoine Labrunie[3], and Benoît Robyns[1]

[1] L2EP, Univ. Lille, Centrale Lille, Arts et Metiers Paris Tech, HEI, EA 2697, L2EP,
Laboratory of Electrical Engineering and Power Electronics, 59000 Lille, France
{matthieu.stephant,dhaker.abbes,benoit.robyns}@yncrea.fr
[2] HEI, Yncrea-Hauts-De France, 13 Rue de Toul, 59000 Lille, France
kahina.hassam@yncrea.fr
[3] Greenbirdie, 13 rue Raymond Losserand, 75014 Paris, France
antoine.labrunie@gb-solar.fr

Abstract. In this paper, we present a distributed approach to optimise self-consumption on a university campus grid. The grid contains photovoltaic generators, electric vehicles, loads and a battery. We propose to solve the optimisation problem with a distributed method using game theory, where each element of the grid tries to reach its own objectives. In addition to this optimisation framework, we develop a physical model of the grid. This model uses real consumption and production data. We use it to simulate the production and consumption profiles obtained from the optimisation problem in order to check if these solutions respect the grid constraints. Finally, we propose to implement concretely this distributed approach using a private blockchain, which stores production and consumption data. In addition, a smart contract is deployed on the blockchain to transcribe the game theory framework. The smart contract collects the preferences of each element of the grid and launches the optimisation process. Then the blockchain gathers the results and replaces the role of a central optimisation supervisor. We present some preliminary results to illustrate our method.

Keywords: Photovoltaic self-consumption · Game theory · Blockchain

1 Introduction

Due to environmental concerns, many countries have promoted the development of photovoltaic (PV) generators through diverse financial incentives, leading to an increase of the worldwide PV capacity from about more than 10 GWp in 2008 to more than 500 GWp at the end of 2018 [1]. PV generators differ from

Supported by the European city of Lille (MEL) and Greenbirdie under the Smart Buildings as nodes of Smart Grid (SBnodesSG) Chair.

traditional power plants like nuclear or coal power plants: their capacity is much lower so they are spread on large geographical areas and often connected to low or medium voltage grid. For example, small PV generators of less than 4 kWp counted for 21% of the total PV capacity installed in the UK in 2016 [2]. As a result, new uses of electricity networks appear with the development of PV generators. The continuous decrease of PV installation costs encourages consumers to produce their own electricity from rooftop solar panels. This situation corresponds to self-consumption. The overall electrical grid can benefit from self-consumption behaviour with a decrease of energy flows on the lines, leading to a decrease of investments costs [3].

We define the self-consumption rate as the part of the electricity produced by the PV generators that is locally consumed over the total local consumption [4]. Increasing this self-consumption rate requires adapting the consumption to the PV production, which is highly intermittent. Generally, we consider two main options to reach this aim. First, the use of a storage system, such as electrochemical batteries, can store the PV generation during the day and deliver power to the consumer at night. Second, demand-side management (DSM) system adapts the consumption so that it fits the period of high PV production [4].

France, Sweden and the Netherlands now also allow collective self-consumption, in which a group of consumers shares the local PV production on the low voltage grid over a small area, creating a local energy community [5]. The idea is to benefit from the differences between the consumption profiles of all the consumers in order to maximise the self-consumption rate. Consumers and producers exchange the local energy production. However, collective self-consumption projects are still at an early stage and we believe that a large-scale development requires a new framework to optimise the self-consumption rate and thus to make collective self-consumption attractive for all participants.

The question this article deals with is: how to optimise energy exchanges on a local energy community in a distributed way? Indeed, to support decentralisation of the grid, we believe that a distributed method is more relevant and enables to get rid of a central agent.

In this perspective, we propose a new approach to improve the self-consumption rate between several tertiary buildings. We base our study on the grid of Lille Catholic University, France, which combines PV generators, a battery, charging stations for electric vehicles and tertiary buildings. We define a global optimisation problem to increase the self-consumption rate. In order to take into account the preferences of each participant, we decompose this global problem in several smaller local problems. Thus, we build a decentralised framework using game theory, in which each participant acts freely in order to reach its individual objectives. Game theory is gaining popularity in the literature as a distributed optimisation method for smart grid, as it reflects its distributed and heterogeneous nature [6]. In [7], the authors introduce a bargaining game to manage a micro-grid both in connected or islanded mode. Nguyen et al. use game theory for demand side management in a system containing storage devices [8].

The results show a decrease of energy costs for energy consumers and a peak power reduction of the overall system.

In our case, we define a specific non-cooperative game so that the self-consumption rate increases when each player tends to meet its own objectives by adjusting its consumption or production profile. We introduce parameters so that each element is able to adjust its objective function (called utility function) according to its own preferences. These preferences can represent the cost paid (or earned) for electricity consumption (or production), the users' comfort, or the will to consume the local PV production. The benefit of such an approach is that it only requires that the participants optimise locally their behaviour, without any cooperation. Thus, it does not require a central agent to coordinate all the participants.

To verify the relevance of our work, we aim to test the results of the proposed optimisation framework on a physical model of the grid, including real production and consumption data. We test the results with the model in order to guarantee that the real grid can support the energy flows between the different elements.

In addition, in order to implement concretely this framework, we propose to use blockchain technology. Blockchain consists in a distributed and secured database, supporting the execution of algorithms called smart contracts [9]. It shows promising features for collective self-consumption and energy sharing and interest for this topic is growing. One of the main applications observed in the literature is the implementation of energy markets between consumers and producers. Mengelkamp *et al.* propose to improve energy sharing by creating local markets supported by blockchain [10]. In [11] and [12] authors use blockchain to implement local markets with an auction scheme, where producers and consumers publish demand offers and sell offers with smart contracts, and blockchain automatically matches the offers. In [13], the authors present a method to solve an optimal power flow in micro-grid networks. The global problem is first divided in local problems and then blockchain aggregates all the local solutions to provide the overall optimum.

In our vision, we suggest using this technology to store in a secure way the production and consumption data. Moreover, a specific smart contract will collect each user's preferences and launches the optimisation process. Thus, blockchain is a promising tool to implement concretely the distributed optimisation framework that we introduced.

The novelty of our work consists in proposing a concrete and fully distributed method to increase self-consumption rate in a local energy community by the combination of different tools (game theory and blockchain). We exploit the distributed nature of the grid and of the blockchain to get rid of a central optimisation agent. Moreover, the test of our approach on a physical model of a real grid, provided with real production and consumption data, shows the feasibility of such an approach.

This paper is divided as follows. In the second part, we introduce the optimisation problem and the game theory framework used to solve it. In the third part, we detail how we combine the three tools (optimisation algorithm, physical model of the grid, blockchain) to implement this framework. Then, we show and analyse some preliminary results on simple scenarios.

2   Optimisation Framework Using Game Theory

In our problem, we consider a local university grid that contains loads (buildings), a storage system (an electrochemical battery), rooftop PV generators and several charging station for electric vehicles. There is a connection point to the distribution grid. We aim to increase the self-consumption rate of the local grid, by adjusting the charge and discharge schedule of the battery and the electric vehicles, and eventually by delaying the consumption of the buildings. Thus we define an optimisation problem.

Two main approaches exist for solving optimisation problems: centralised or distributed methods. In centralised methods, a supervisor agent knows the entire characteristics of the system, computes the solution of the optimisation problem with a specific algorithm and then sends the results to each element of the grid. Thus, the central agent imposes the actions to take to the entire system. However, in distributed methods, the global optimisation problem is divided in local sub-problems so that finding the local solutions for all sub-problems provides the overall solution. Distributed methods benefit from several advantages. First, the local sub-problems are simpler and therefore easier to solve than the global problem. Second, to solve a local problem, we do not need to know the situation of the entire system. Thus, they are often more robust because they are not impacted by the failure of one element [14].

Regarding electrical networks, a distributed approach is interesting because it reflects the real structure of the grid. Indeed, a grid contains many different elements (loads, generators...) connected between them, but each one has very limited information about its neighbouring environment. Moreover, each element tries to optimise individually its situation, for example the payoffs or the comfort, without considering the global situation of the grid. To reflect this reality, we choose to apply a distributed method to our optimisation problem. More specifically, we choose to use game theory, that defines a mathematical framework for distributed optimisation in which each element of the system aims to optimise its own individual situation.

Game theory is a relevant method in our case for several reasons. First, it models a situation where players are in competition. This reflect the case of a local energy community where players are in competition to reach their consumption/production objectives. Second, game theory enables to take into account not only cost objectives, but also other considerations like comfort [15]. Finally, game theory is interesting because each agent has to solve a simpler problem, in comparison to the global optimisation problem.

2.1   Problem Formulation

We define a non-cooperative game in which each element tries to reach its personal objectives, without any coordination with the other elements. As we mentioned previously, this situation reflects the reality of a local grid where participants have limited knowledge about the structure of the grid and do not necessary communicate between them to meet their goals. Thus, we consider a game with N players, which are the N elements of the grid (loads, PV generators, battery, electric vehicles charging stations). The game is defined by the set $G = \{N, (S_i)_{i \in N}, (U_i)_{i \in N}\}$, where S_i is the strategy set of the player i and U_i its utility function. Here, the strategy set is defined as $S_i = \{x_i\}$, where x_i is the energy consumption or production profile of the player.

The utility function, or objective function, mathematically translates the goals of the player and measures user's satisfaction. The players tend to maximise their utility function by adjusting their strategy, here their energy consumption or production profile. The next paragraph details the objectives and the utility function of each player. In the following, we note $c(t)$ the price function of the electrical energy in the local grid over time.

Utility Functions

EV User. For an EV user connected to the charging station, we propose the following function (we write $x_{PV}^{forecast}$ for the forecast local PV production):

$$U_{EV}(x_{EV}(t)) = \alpha_1 \ln(1 + x_{EV}(t)) - \alpha_2\, c(t)\, x_{EV}(t) - \alpha_3 \ln(1 + \frac{x_{PV}^{forecast}(t)}{x_{EV}(t)}) \quad (1)$$

The term $\alpha_1 \ln(1 + x_{EV}(t))$ represents the objective to charge the vehicle. With the term $\alpha_2 c(t) x_{EV}(t)$, the user aims to minimise the cost to pay. Then we introduce the term $\alpha_3 \ln(1 + \frac{x_{PV}^{forecast}(t)}{x_{EV}(t)})$ to represent the objective to use preferentially the local PV production. The natural logarithm function is classically used for energy buyers as it models the satiety of the users [11]. We introduce the weight coefficients α_1, α_2 and α_3 so that each user can adjust its preferences. These coefficients are commonly used in the literature for multi-objective optimisation to combine different objectives into a unique objective function. We impose $\alpha_1 + \alpha_2 + \alpha_3 = 1$ [16].

For each EV, we have to consider some constraints. We authorize only charge and the charging power is limited by the maximum power of the charging station:

$$0 \leq P_{EV}(t) \leq P_{max}^{EV} \quad (2)$$

Moreover, the state of charge (SOC) has upper and lower bounds, which are characteristics of the vehicle battery:

$$SOC_{EV}^{min} \leq SOC_{EV}(t) \leq SOC_{EV}^{max} \quad (3)$$

Battery. We consider that the battery has three objectives: first to maximise its availability, which means to keep a median SOC in order to be able to charge or discharge at any time, second to optimise its payoffs, and third to charge using local PV production. Thus, we propose the following utility function:

$$U_b(x_b(t)) = \beta_1 D(t) - \beta_2\, c(t)\, x_b(t) - \beta_3(x_{PV}^{forecast}(t) - x_b(t))^2 \qquad (4)$$

Here also we use the coefficients β_1, β_2 and β_3 to detail the player's preferences, and we impose the sum to be equal to one. The term $D(t)$ represents the availability of the battery, and models the fact that the battery aims to keep a median SOC, written SOC_{median}. This function is equal to 0 when the SOC is equal to SOC_b^{min} and SOC_b^{max}, and 1 for SOC_b^{median}.

The charging power and discharging power of the battery are limited:

$$0 \leq P_b(t) \leq P_b^{charge,max} \qquad (5)$$

$$0 \geq P_b(t) \geq P_b^{discharge,max} \qquad (6)$$

Moreover, similarly to the EV, the SOC has boundaries:

$$SOC_b^{min} \leq SOC_b(t) \leq SOC_b^{max} \qquad (7)$$

PV Generators. PV generators simply tend to maximise their production, because their marginal production cost is equal to zero [13]. So their goals are to optimise their payoff, and to limit the production curtailment. Therefore, we write the following utility function with the two respective terms:

$$U_{PV}(x_{PV}(t)) = \gamma_1\, c(t)\, x_{PV}(t) - \gamma_2(x_{PV}^{forecast}(t) - x_{PV}(t))^2 \qquad (8)$$

The coefficients γ_1 and γ_2 model the user's choice, and we impose $\gamma_1 + \gamma_2 = 1$.

Loads. We consider that the loads have some flexibility, which means that they can decrease their consumption compared to their expected consumption $x_{load}^{expected}$. However, we impose that the total energy consumed at the end of the day is equal to the expected consumption for the entire day. In other words, loads can delay their consumption but do not globally decrease it. Then the objectives are to minimise the cost paid for electricity, to minimise the decrease of consumption, that represents a loss of comfort for the user, and to consume the local PV production. Therefore, following [7], we write the following utility equation:

$$U_l(x_l(t)) = -\delta_1\, c(t)\, x_l(t) - \delta_2(x_l^{expected}(t) - x_l(t))^2 - \delta_3 \ln(1 + \frac{x_{PV}^{forecast}(t)}{x_l(t)}) \qquad (9)$$

Each user can specify its preferences by adjusting δ_1, δ_2 and δ_3 (with $\delta_1 + \delta_2 + \delta_3 = 1$). The constraint on the flexibility f imposes:

$$x_l^{expected}(t)(1 - f) \leq x_l(t) \leq x_l^{expected}(t)(1 + f) \qquad (10)$$

Nash Equilibrium. One important concept in game theory is the Nash equilibrium, a situation in which no player can increase its utility by being the only to change its strategy [6]. Mathematically, if we write $X^* = \{x_1^*, ..., x_N^*\}$ the strategy of the players at the Nash equilibrium and x_{-i} the strategy of all players except player i, the Nash equilibrium corresponds to:

$$U_i(x_i^*, x_{-i}^*) \geq U_i(x_i, x_{-i}^*), \forall x_i \in S_i \tag{11}$$

This Nash equilibrium is important as it guarantees that when all players maximise individually their utility function, the global system reaches an equilibrium point.

All the utility functions U_i specified in this article are concave and continuous in x_i. Moreover, all the constraints (on the power limits and the SOC) impose that for each player, the strategy set is a segment: $\forall i \in N, S_i = \{x_i | x_i \in [x_i^{min}, x_i^{max}]\}$, so it is a convex set. This guarantees the existence of at least one Nash equilibrium for our problem [17].

If we consider in a first approach a cost function that does not depend on the consumption and production profiles of the players but that it imposed by the distribution grid, for example a peak and off-peak hours price function, then [18] ensures the unicity of the Nash equilibrium.

3 Optimisation Implementation

In this section we present how we concretely tend to deploy the proposed optimisation process, and more specifically how we connect the physical model of the grid and the blockchain to the theoretical game theory framework. The combination of these three parts form a new tool which gives a concrete distributed framework for optimising self-consumption on real local grids, as illustrated on Fig. 1.

3.1 Role of Blockchain

Blockchain is a distributed and secured database divided in blocks. A block contains data and some additional information related to the previous block. Thus, all blocks form a chain [9]. Each user holds a copy of the database. Adding a new block to the existing chain requires a consensus between all users, so the blockchain works without any central supervisor nor trusted third-party.

In addition, blockchain supports the execution of specific algorithms, called smart contracts, that enable to automatically proceed to previously defined tasks, such as triggering a transaction between two users [19]. Practically, a smart contract is a piece of code defining some functions that is deployed over the blockchain and interacts with every node of the network. Thanks to its distributed architecture, blockchain and smart contracts are interesting tools to support smart grids decentralisation and we intend to use them in order to deploy the distributed optimisation process.

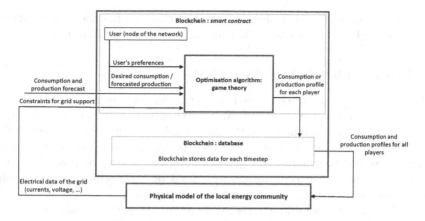

Fig. 1. Overview of the overall optimisation process

In our system, blockchain serves as the communication layer between the players and aggregates the results. It replaces the role of a central optimisation agent. More precisely, we deploy a private blockchain between all the elements of the grid. Thus, each player of the game represents one node of a peer-to-peer communication network. A smart contract deployed on the blockchain implements the game theory framework presented in the previous section. More precisely, the smart contract contains different functions to perform the following tasks: (1) collect the preferences coefficients of all users (coefficients α_i for EV, β_i for the battery, γ_i for the PV generators and δ_i for the loads); (2) trigger the optimisation process (optimising locally each user's utility); (3) gather the results; (4) send the results to the physical modal of the grid. Thus, we see blockchain as a tool to concretely implement our game theory framework in a real grid.

The main interest of this implementation is that, through the smart contract, blockchain gets rid of the need for a central optimisation supervisor that would know the production and consumption details and the preferences of all the grid elements. Moreover, blockchain has the benefit to have a distributed structure, so it guarantees security and trust between the elements of the grid. Blockchain is also more resilient to changes than a unique central agent: new element can simply be added to or deleted from the blockchain without any consequence on the overall framework.

3.2   Game Theory Algorithm

As we mentioned in the previous paragraph, each player of the game constitutes one node of the blockchain. This node locally optimises the user's utility for a defined time period. We make the assumption that the local PV forecast is available through the smart contract for all elements and that each load knows its desired consumption. Moreover, the smart contract provides the preferences coefficients in input for each player. The algorithm returns the consumption or production profile of each player that maximises its utility function.

3.3   Physical Model of the Real Grid

In the theoretical framework defined in Sect. 2, we have not taken into account the constraints related to the grid. More precisely, the proposed game theory framework implicitly assumes that the grid is able to transfer all the power flows according to the optimisation results. However, the grid elements are connected through lines that have a limited capacity. Therefore, it may be possible that the consumption and production profiles processed by the optimisation algorithms lead to some over-currents or over-voltages on the lines.

For this reason, we build a physical model of the grid at stake in which we model the physical properties of the lines (see Fig. 2). We use PowerFactory, a software used by grid operators for grid modelling and analysis [20]. The local network contains 4 buildings considered to be loads, 2 PV generators, one battery and 6 EV charging stations (Fig. 2).

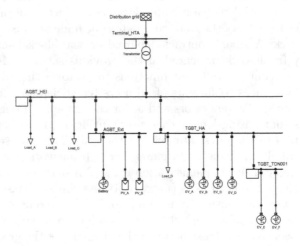

Fig. 2. Physical model of the grid

We aim to test the consumption and production profiles of all the players provided by the optimisation process on the grid model in order to check if they create line congestion or over-voltages. In this case, we can identify precisely the problems that occur on the physical model. Then we can impose additional constraints to the optimisation process (for example curtail the PV production) in order to obtain profiles that will respect the grid constraints.

The combination of the theoretical optimisation framework with the simulations on the physical model ensures that our solutions are realistic and will not damage the grid.

4 Results

To illustrate our approach, we present in this section some preliminary results. We consider the grid of Lille Catholic University (represented on Fig. 2), with only one electric vehicle connected between 13:40 and 20:10. We use consumption and production data for one day. We present two cases: in the first one, the elements want to consume the local PV production (scenario (a)); in the second one, they do not have a preference to consume local PV production (scenario (b)). Tables 1 and 2 show the preferences coefficients and the parameters of the different grid elements used for the simulations, respectively for scenario (a) and scenario (b). These first results were obtained with MATLAB.

Table 1. Parameters of grid elements for scenario (a)

Element	Coefficients			Parameters
EV	$\alpha_1 = 0.2$	$\alpha_2 = 0.1$	$\alpha_3 = 0.7$	Initial SOC = 40%
Battery	$\beta_1 = 0.1$	$\beta_2 = 0.1$	$\beta_3 = 0.8$	Initial SOC = 25%
PV generator$_a$	$\gamma_1 = 0.8$	$\gamma_2 = 0.2$	–	–
PV generator$_b$	$\gamma_1 = 0.6$	$\gamma_2 = 0.4$	–	–
Load$_a$	$\delta_1 = 0.1$	$\delta_2 = 0.1$	$\delta_3 = 0.8$	Flexibility = 10%
Load$_b$	$\delta_1 = 0.2$	$\delta_2 = 0.2$	$\delta_3 = 0.6$	Flexibility = 20%
Load$_c$	$\delta_1 = 0.2$	$\delta_2 = 0.2$	$\delta_3 = 0.5$	Flexibility = 10%
Load$_d$	$\delta_1 = 0.3$	$\delta_2 = 0.1$	$\delta_3 = 0.6$	Flexibility = 15%

Table 2. Parameters of grid elements for scenario (b)

Element	Coefficients			Parameters
EV	$\alpha_1 = 0.8$	$\alpha_2 = 0.2$	$\alpha_3 = 0$	Initial SOC = 40%
Battery	$\beta_1 = 0.3$	$\beta_2 = 0.7$	$\beta_3 = 0$	Initial SOC = 25%
PV generator$_a$	$\gamma_1 = 0.8$	$\gamma_2 = 0.2$	–	–
PV generator$_b$	$\gamma_1 = 0.6$	$\gamma_2 = 0.4$	–	–
Load$_a$	$\delta_1 = 0.3$	$\delta_2 = 0.7$	$\delta_3 = 0$	Flexibility = 10%
Load$_b$	$\delta_1 = 0.5$	$\delta_2 = 0.5$	$\delta_3 = 0$	Flexibility = 20%
Load$_c$	$\delta_1 = 0.1$	$\delta_2 = 0.9$	$\delta_3 = 0$	Flexibility = 10%
Load$_d$	$\delta_1 = 0.4$	$\delta_2 = 0.6$	$\delta_3 = 0$	Flexibility = 15%

Figures 3 and 4 illustrate the results obtained respectively for scenarios (a) and (b).

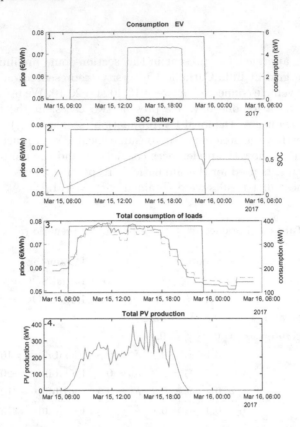

Fig. 3. Results for scenario (a), for: (1) the EV, (2) the battery, (3) the aggregated load (the green line shows the desired consumption, and the red line the actual consumption), and (4) the total PV production. (Color figure online)

From the comparison of the figures, we can notice that when the players are taking care to consume the local PV production, they really adapt their consumption to this production. Even if the effect is very slight for the EV, we can see when we compare Figs. 3 and 4 that the EV decreases its consumption when PV generators stop producing. We can particularly notice this effect at the end of the day after 18:00, when PV generators stop producing. In scenario (b), the EV does not change at all its consumption to fit to the PV production. For the battery, the effect is more visible. In scenario (b), it prefers to charge when the electricity price is low and to discharge when the electricity price is high, and to keep a median SOC (here 50%). In scenario (a), it is charging during all the period of PV production, no matter if the price is higher. For the loads, when they do not pay attention to consume local production (scenario (b)), they adjust their consumption profile in order to decrease the price they pay for electricity. However, when they prefer to consume the local PV production (scenario (a)), then they adjust their consumption to the PV production, leading to an increase

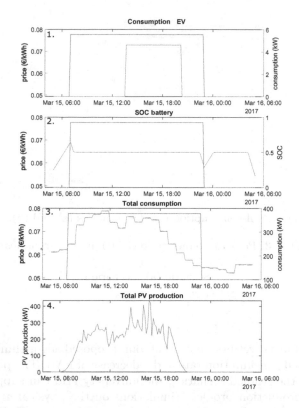

Fig. 4. Results for scenario (b), for: (1) the EV, (2) the battery, (3) the aggregated load (the green line shows the desired consumption, and the red line the actual consumption), and (4) the total PV production. (Color figure online)

of the self-consumption rate. In our case, the cost paid for electricity is then higher, due to the profile of the chosen cost function.

Figure 5 compares the self-consumption rate obtained for both scenarios. It confirms that when the players are more sensible to consumer the local PV production (scenario (a)), then the self-consumption rate increases (scenario (b)). Moreover, we calculate the peak to average ratio (PAR) in both scenarios (Table 3). Scenario (a) leads to a decrease of the PAR of about 13% compared to scenario (b). Indeed, when they favour the local PV production (scenario (a)), the players adapt their consumption so that it fits to the PV production. Thus, they require less energy from the distribution grid when PV generators are not producing anymore. Moreover, in this scenario, the battery stores energy when PV production is high and releases it at night. As a consequence, even if the global consumed energy is the same in both scenarios, in scenario (a), players manage to decrease the peak power seen from the distribution grid, resulting in a reduction of the PAR.

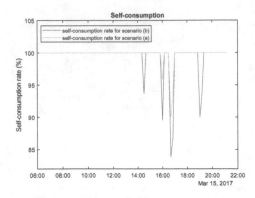

Fig. 5. Self-consumption rate for scenarios (a) and (b).

Table 3. Peak to average ratio (PAR) in both scenarios

	Scenario (a)	Scenario (b)
PAR	1.75	1.98

These preliminary results show that our proposed algorithm leads to an increase of the self-consumption rate and a decrease of PAR. The physical model ensures that in the studied scenarios, the university grid can support the consumption and production profiles. Simulations on the physical grid are necessary to guarantee that the algorithm provides feasible solutions. This is a very important point as the idea behind our work is to provide a concrete solution to improve energy sharing among a local energy community.

Moreover, another interesting perspective is to include a price function that reflects in real time the production and consumption on the local grid: when consumption is higher than local production, the price will increase. This would encourage the grid elements to preferentially consume the local production, even in case that they are only sensible to the electricity cost.

5   Perspectives and Conclusion

In this paper, we propose a concrete framework to improve energy sharing between producers and consumers among a local community energy, for example the grid of Lille Catholic University. In this way, we maximise the use of local photovoltaic production and thus the self-consumption rate.

Our approach combines three tools: game theory for distributed optimisation, a physical model of the grid to guarantee the stability of the grid, and a communication layer with blockchain. The combination of these tools is an innovative approach and constitutes a distributed method for better use of distributed renewable energy sources on local energy community. The approach with game theory enables each actor to specify its particular preferences and to act freely to reach these goals. Thus, our framework reflects the distributed nature of electric grids, where various actors are following very diverse goals.

The first results are promising and show an increase of self-consumption rate. However, we plan to continue this work, and specifically to focus on the following tasks. First, the development of the smart contract with the blockchain is a key point for a real distributed implementation. It will enable to concretely deploy the optimisation method on a peer-to-peer communication network. As we mentioned in Sect. 3, the smart contract will automatically trigger the optimisation algorithm and collect the results.

Second, the price function needs to reflect in real time the consumption and production inside the local grid. The creation of a small electricity market between the players is an interesting option to encourage loads to consume when the PV production is high. In this perspective, we expect interesting further results.

Moreover, some additional questions regarding the overall stability of the system should be answered, especially when we add a new player, for example when a new electric vehicle arrives at a charging station. The issue of the global efficiency of the system, in particular regarding the performances and the consumption of the blockchain.

References

1. Snapshot of Global PV Markets. Technical report, IEA PVPS (2019)
2. McKenna, E., Pless, J., Darby, S.: Solar photovoltaic self-consumption in the UK residential sector: new estimates from a smart grid demonstration project. Energy Policy **118**, 482–491 (2018). https://doi.org/10.1016/j.enpol.2018.04.006
3. Villar, C., Neves, D., Silva, C.: Solar PV self-consumption: an analysis of influencing indicators in the Portuguese context. Energy Strat. Rev. **18**, 224–234 (2017). https://doi.org/10.1016/j.esr.2017.10.001
4. Luthander, R., Widén, J., Nilsson, D., Palm, J.: Photovoltaic self-consumption in buildings: a review. Appl. Energy **142**, 80–94 (2015). https://doi.org/10.1016/j.apenergy.2014.12.028
5. Stephant, M., Hassam-Ouari, K., Abbes, D., Labrunie, A., Robyns, B.: A survey on energy management and blockchain for collective self-consumption. In: 2018 7th International Conference on Systems and Control (ICSC), pp. 237–243. IEEE (2018). https://doi.org/10.1109/ICoSC.2018.8587812
6. Saad, W., Han, Z., Poor, H.V., Basar, T.: Game-theoretic methods for the smart grid: an overview of microgrid systems, demand-side management, and smart grid communications. IEEE Signal Process. Mag. **29**(5), 86–105 (2012). https://doi.org/10.1109/MSP.2012.2186410
7. Dehghanpour, K., Nehrir, H.: Real-time multiobjective microgrid power management using distributed optimization in an agent-based bargaining framework. IEEE Trans. Smart Grid **9**(6), 6318–6327 (2018). https://doi.org/10.1109/TSG.2017.2708686
8. Nguyen, H.K., Song, J.B., Han, Z.: Distributed demand side management with energy storage in smart grid. IEEE Trans. Parallel Distrib. Syst. **26**(12), 3346–3357 (2015). https://doi.org/10.1109/TPDS.2014.2372781

9. Sikorski, J., Haughton, J., Kraft, M.: Blockchain technology in the chemical industry: machine-to-machine electricity market. Appl. Energy **195**, 234–246 (2017). https://doi.org/10.1016/j.apenergy.2017.03.039

10. Mengelkamp, E., Gärttner, J., Rock, K., Kessler, S., Orsini, L., Weinhardt, C.: Designing microgrid energy markets: a case study: the Brooklyn Microgrid. Appl. Energy **210**, 870–880 (2018). https://doi.org/10.1016/j.apenergy.2017.06.054

11. Kang, J., Yu, R., Huang, X., Maharjan, S., Zhang, Y., Hossain, E.: Enabling localized peer-to-peer electricity trading among plug-in hybrid electric vehicles using consortium blockchains. IEEE Trans. Ind. Inform. **13**(6), 3154–3164 (2017). https://doi.org/10.1109/TII.2017.2709784

12. Foti, M., Greasidis, D., Vavalis, M.: Viability analysis of a decentralized energy market based on blockchain. In: 2018 15th International Conference on the European Energy Market (EEM), pp. 1–5. IEEE (2018). https://doi.org/10.1109/EEM.2018.8469906

13. Münsing, E., Mather, J., Moura, S.: Blockchains for decentralized optimization of energy resources in microgrid networks. In: 2017 IEEE Conference on Control Technology and Applications (CCTA), pp. 2164–2171, August 2017. https://doi.org/10.1109/CCTA.2017.8062773

14. Molzahn, D.K., et al.: A survey of distributed optimization and control algorithms for electric power systems. IEEE Trans. Smart Grid **8**(6), 2941–2962 (2017). https://doi.org/10.1109/TSG.2017.2720471

15. Pilz, M., Al-Fagih, L.: Recent advances in local energy trading in the smart grid based on game-theoretic approaches. IEEE Trans. Smart Grid (2017). https://doi.org/10.1109/TSG.2017.2764275

16. Marler, R., Arora, J.: The weighted sum method for multi-objective optimization: new insights. Struct. Multidiscip. Optim. **41**(6), 853–862 (2010). https://doi.org/10.1007/s00158-009-0460-7

17. Yang, B., Johansson, M.: Distributed optimization and games: a tutorial overview. In: Bemporad, A., Heemels, M., Johansson, M. (eds.) Networked Control Systems. LNCIS, pp. 109–148. Springer, London (2010). https://doi.org/10.1007/978-0-85729-033-5_4

18. Rosen, J.: Existence and uniqueness of equilibrium points for concave N-person games. Econometrica **33**(3), 520–534 (1965). https://doi.org/10.2307/1911749

19. Macdonald, M., Liu-Thorrold, L., Julien, R.: The blockchain: a comparison of platforms and their uses beyond bitcoin. Working Paper, pp. 1–18 (2017)

20. Gonzalez-Longatt, F.M., Rueda, J.L. (eds.): PowerFactory Applications for Power System Analysis. Springer, Cham (2014). https://doi.org/10.1007/978-3-319-12958-7

Internet of Things; Monitoring; Network Communications

Development of an Internet of Things System for Smart Home HVAC Monitoring and Control

Aníbal A. Alves[1], Vitor Monteiro[2], J. G. Pinto[2], Joao L. Afonso[2], and Jose A. Afonso[1(✉)]

[1] CMEMS-UMinho Center, University of Minho, Guimarães, Portugal
jose.afonso@dei.uminho.pt
[2] ALGORITMI Research Centre, University of Minho, Guimarães, Portugal

Abstract. This paper presents the development and test of an Internet of Things (IoT) system applied to the monitoring and control of an HVAC (Heating, Ventilation and Air Conditioning) system that includes parameters such as temperature, humidity, air quality, human presence and smoke detection. For this purpose, a hybrid wireless network combining Bluetooth Low Energy (BLE) and IEEE 802.11/Wi-Fi was implemented inside a house. An online database for the synchronization of the HVAC data, which was developed using the Amazon Web Services (AWS) cloud platform, allows the user to access the data and control the system parameters through the Internet using an Android mobile app. A smart temperature control system was also developed in the BLE/Wi-Fi gateway to keep the room temperature inside a user-defined range. The functionalities and performance of the proposed system were both validated through experimental tests.

Keywords: Internet of Things · Smart home · Bluetooth Low Energy · Wireless sensor networks

1 Introduction

Over the last few decades, technological advances have enabled a large part of the world's population to have access to the Internet, and this access is increasingly being done through mobile devices, using either cellular data networks or Wi-Fi. This trend, coupled with the increasing incorporation of sensor devices in a variety of equipment, opens a wide range of opportunities for the growing market of Internet of Things (IoT) applications, in areas such as transportation, healthcare, agriculture, industrial automation, smart home, among others.

The IoT enables physical objects to interact with the surround environment without requiring human intervention, and to communicate with each other to share information and to coordinate decisions. The IoT allows connecting billions of objects through the Internet, so there is the need to define a layered architecture to handle the complexity associated to the different required tasks. In this sense, there has been an increasing number of proposed architectures, but there is not a consensual reference model yet. In

© ICST Institute for Computer Sciences, Social Informatics and Telecommunications Engineering 2020
Published by Springer Nature Switzerland AG 2020. All Rights Reserved
J. L. Afonso et al. (Eds.): SESC 2019, LNICST 315, pp. 197–208, 2020.
https://doi.org/10.1007/978-3-030-45694-8_15

[1], the authors present a five-layer model, where the first one, Object's layer, represents the physical sensors and actuators of the IoT that aim to collect and process information. The second layer, Object Abstraction, represents how the data is transferred from the physical objects. The third layer, Service Management, pairs a service with its requester, based on addresses and names. The fourth layer, Application, is responsible for providing high-quality smart services to meet customer's needs. Finally, the fifth layer, Business, defines the steps to build a business model based on the developed IoT system.

In order to maximize the lifetime of battery-operated sensor devices, it is desirable the use of low-power wireless sensor networks (WSN) technologies, such as Bluetooth Low Energy (BLE) [2] or IEEE 802.15.4/ZigBee [3]. WSNs enable new applications but require non-conventional paradigms for protocol design [4]. With characteristics such as low cost, low energy consumption [5], low latency and high reliability, as well a native hardware and software support provided by most current mobile devices, BLE takes a leading position for the implementation of IoT sensor devices over ZigBee in many areas of application [6]. However, since both BLE and ZigBee devices do not implement the TCP/IP (Transmission Control Protocol/Internet Protocol) protocol stack, they require the introduction of a gateway device into the system to allow communication with other IoT devices, such as an IoT server or a mobile client [7].

In order to store the data collected by the sensor devices, a database is required. The successful implementation of an IoT system requires service provision with ubiquity, reliability, high-performance, efficiency and scalability. A way to achieve all of these goals is merging the IoT and the cloud computing concepts, as suggested in [8].

Concerning related work, in [9], the authors presented a networking solution for connecting BLE devices with the IoT, enabling end-to-end IP connectivity to the BLE devices in an efficient manner, especially in the aspect that are most critical for IoT devices: energy consumption and memory footprint of the implementation. In [7], the authors proposed a smartphone-based IoT gateway implemented as a software service that provides universal and ubiquitous Internet access to BLE connected IoT devices This approach uses the smartphone both as an IPv6 router for less resource-constrained endpoints and as a BLE proxy, relaying profile data from the sensor device to the cloud.

The smart home IoT system presented in this paper uses BLE to collect heating, ventilation and air conditioning (HVAC) data from sensor devices and send the information to an implemented BLE/Wi-Fi gateway, which also communicates with other local devices, such as actuators. Regarding data storage, the developed system provides communication with a remote IoT server, in a cloud-based architecture, allowing the collected data to be accessible through the Internet. A mobile app (client) was also developed in order to allow access to the data for the user. The developed system is capable of a smart temperature control on a desired room inside a configurable temperature range.

The rest of this paper is organized as follows. Section 2 presents an overview of the developed system architecture and components. Section 3 describes the development of the home network components, namely the BLE nodes and the gateway. Sections 4 and 5 describe the development of the IoT cloud services and the IoT client (mobile app), respectively. Section 6 presents experimental results concerning functional and non-functional aspects of the developed IoT system. Finally, Sect. 7 presents the conclusions.

2   System Overview

The developed IoT system is constituted by several components that exchange data with each other, as shown in Fig. 1. Inside the smart home, the IoT devices communicate using a local hybrid BLE/Wi-Fi wireless network infrastructure, whose main components are the BLE sensor nodes, the BLE/Wi-Fi gateway, a wireless router (which provides connection to the Internet and acts as the local Wi-Fi access point) and actuator nodes. Besides the local components, the developed IoT system also includes an Android mobile app (client) and an AWS (Amazon Web Service) cloud server.

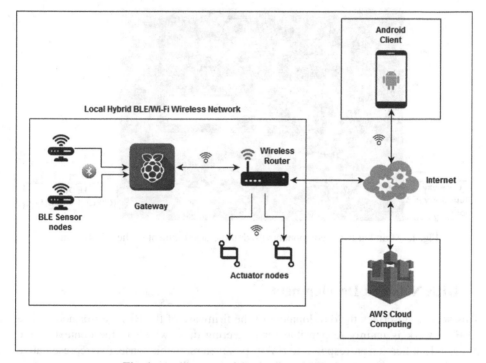

Fig. 1. Architecture of the developed IoT system.

The proposed architecture supports several sensor nodes and actuator nodes. Each BLE sensor node comprises two main components: a BLE device and a sensor, which may send data to the BLE device using an analog-to-digital converter (ADC) or a digital interface, such as UART (Universal Asynchronous Receiver-Transmitter), SPI (Serial Peripheral Interface) or I2C (Inter-Integrated Circuit). Likewise, each actuator node is composed by a wireless device (either Wi-Fi or BLE) attached to an actuator.

The HVAC system works under the control of the local gateway even in case of failure of the Internet connection. When the Internet connection is available, the HVAC data collected by the BLE devices (sensor nodes) is also forwarded through the gateway, the Wi-Fi wireless router and the Internet infrastructure, until it reaches the cloud server, for storage. The Android client allows the user to access the data stored in the cloud server and send commands to configure and control the smart home devices (e.g., to define the minimum and maximum temperature for a room).

The BLE devices used in the development and test of the system prototype were PSoC 4 BLE modules [10], from Cypress Semiconductor. Each BLE module was attached to a development board provided by the CY8CKIT-042-BLE-A kit, as shown in Fig. 2. The BLE/Wi-Fi gateway was implemented using a Raspberry Pi 3 Model B [11], whereas the HVAC sensors and actuators were emulated using personal computers (PCs), which also acted as the actuator nodes' Wi-Fi devices. The development of each component of the IoT system is described in the next sections.

Fig. 2. Main hardware components used in the development of the IoT system.

3   BLE Network Development

This section describes the development of the firmware of the BLE sensor nodes. The BLE network is mainly responsible for collecting data, which in the context of the proposed application corresponds to HVAC parameters. In this sense, five representative sensors were considered: smoke detection, temperature, humidity, air quality, and human presence detection. The data generated by these sensors was emulated using a PC-based Java application, which was developed using the IntelliJ IDEA IDE. The sensor data was transferred to the BLE modules using a serial data interface.

BLE devices have different roles at different layers of the Bluetooth protocol stack [12]. In this sense, the BLE modules were configured as slaves at the link layer, peripherals devices at the GAP (Generic Access Profile) layer and servers at the GATT (Generic Attribute Profile) layer, whereas the BLE/Wi-Fi gateway (Raspberry Pi) was configured as master, central device and client, respectively.

3.1   BLE Nodes Design

As referred before, the CY8CKIT-042-BLE-A development kit [10] was used for the implementation of the BLE slave/peripheral devices. Besides the PSoC 4 BLE module, this kit includes a development board (BLE pioneer), which allows programming and debugging the BLE module firmware through a PC. The C code for the BLE module microcontroller was developed using PSoC Creator 4.2 Integrated Development Environment (IDE). As referred before, all BLE modules act as peripheral devices, therefore, all of them include the same basic PSoC components.

In the PSoC Creator project environment, the main component included in the design diagram of the sensor nodes is called BLE. This component is used to configure the BLE protocol parameters, such as advertising packets, connection interval, and the BLE notifications. It was necessary to create a GATT service and its characteristics. This component allows the use of predefined services, for example, a heart rate monitor or a proximity sensor, with its own characteristics; however, for this system, it was necessary to create new characteristics for each sensor value to be sent over BLE. Each sensor is connected to its respective BLE sensor node and has its own service. Of the five HVAC sensor values, one (smoke detection) is sent to the central device using BLE notifications, while the other four (temperature, humidity, air quality, and presence detection) are read by the central device (gateway) each 20 s (configurable). In order to allow the connection between the peripheral and central devices to be made automatically, it was necessary to include the Universally Unique Identifier (UUID) of the service in the advertisement packet, which was achieved in the "GAP Settings" tab of the BLE component. Two characteristics were created on the BLE component of each of the five sensor nodes: one characteristic represents the corresponding HVAC sensor value, whereas the other characteristic stores the ID (identifier) of the room where the sensor node was placed.

The second main component included in the design was a serial data interface, to collect the data from the sensors. In this prototype, we used the UART component provided by the PSoC Creator. For this component, it was only necessary to configure the same UART parameters as the Java application that was used to generate the HVAC data, such as the baud rate, which was set to 9600 bps.

A function called CustomEventHandler was used to detect and handle all events associated with the BLE stack. These events can be triggered by the central device when it connects or disconnects to the peripheral device or when the peripheral device announces its presence to the central device. It is also responsible for managing writing requests, made by the central device, to characteristics that have writing permission. On the developed system, the only characteristic with write permission was the room ID, which is configurable from the mobile app.

3.2 Gateway Development

A Raspberry Pi 3 Model B was used to implement the BLE/Wi-Fi gateway and act as the central device for the BLE network. The development was made in Python and using the Raspbian operating system. An external library called Pexpect was installed to allow the BLE communication with the peripheral devices. This library can generate processes related to certain applications, controlling them and handle the response based on provided response patterns. On the developed gateway application software, it was used to automate the command "hcitool lescan" for monitoring BLE devices that are in an advertising state to central devices. JSON (JavaScript Object Notation) and Urllib2 libraries were also used, the former for converting data to JSON format and the latter for sending HTTP (HyperText Transfer Protocol) requests to store the collected data in the cloud. It was also necessary the installation of BlueZ, an official Linux Bluetooth protocol stack, to handle the communication with BLE devices.

The developed BLE/Wi-Fi gateway provides bidirectional communication between the sensor nodes, the cloud server database and the actuator nodes (which were implemented as mains powered Wi-Fi devices). For this purpose, the first task is to search and connect to the desired BLE sensor nodes. Then, the central device needs to subscribe to notifications from the smoke detector. After that, the central device application starts to read the sensor values from the peripheral devices periodically and send the data to the cloud database. Figure 3 shows a flowchart representing these tasks of the Raspberry Pi gateway application.

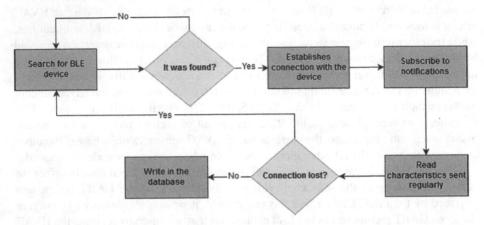

Fig. 3. Flowchart for the data collection and storage tasks of the Raspberry Pi application.

The Raspberry Pi application is also responsible for the smart control of the temperature, sending commands to turn on/off the actuator. Each time this application reads a temperature value and room ID from a BLE peripheral device, it checks if the temperature is inside the defined range for that room (stored in the gateway). If not, the application sends a command via Wi-Fi socket to the corresponding actuator, changing its state accordingly. This is possible because the gateway stores the IP addresses of the actuators.

4   Cloud Services Development

This section describes the IoT services developed for the proposed system using the AWS cloud services platform, namely the database structure defined and the implemented functions. Instead of the traditional server-based approach where the developer needs to handle the infrastructure management tasks, such as cluster provisioning, patching, operating system maintenance and capacity provisioning, a serverless solution, which shifts these operational responsibilities to the AWS, was used. This solution is based on three individual services provided by the AWS: The Amazon Relational Database

Service (RDS), the AWS Lambda, and the AWS API Gateway service. The choice of AWS over other cloud services providers was made based on an analysis of cost, performance and security [13].

4.1 RDS Database

RDS is a free relational database service for new accounts during the first year, offering 750 h per month. An alternative to this service is the Dynamo DB service, which similar to RDS, but implements non-relational databases. The first step in the development of the database structure was to identify the data to be collected and to be shown to the user, which includes: (i) User data, representing the information provided when the user registers on the mobile app; (ii) Building data, containing the building address, name and ID; (iii) HVAC data, containing temperature, humidity, air quality and presence detection data, a timestamp and the room ID; (iv) Smoke detection data, containing the room ID and a timestamp; (v) Configuration data, including the maximum and minimum temperature values for the smart temperature control and other parameters.

For the implementation of the database on the AWS console, it was necessary to create an RDS instance, as well as making other configurations [14]. After that, the MySQL Workbench software [15] was used to develop all the tables and fields necessary to store the data. Even though smoke detection belongs to the HVAC parameters data, a separate MySQL table was created because this data was sent using BLE notifications, so it might have a different timestamp from the remaining parameters. It was also necessary to create inbound and outbound rules and apply them to the created instance in order to ensure access control to the data by other applications.

4.2 AWS Lambda

The AWS Lambda is a service that allows running code without provisioning or managing servers. This service executes the code when needed and scales automatically from a few requests per day to thousands per second. The free year offers 1 million requests to the created functions per month. The code can be run for any type of application or backend service with zero administration. AWS Lambda can be used in response to events, such as changes to data in the Amazon Dynamo DB or RDS tables, to run code in response to HTTP requests using the Amazon API Gateway or simply to invoke code using API calls made using AWS SDKs (Software Development Kit).

For the proposed system, various functions were developed in NodeJS language. Each function is responsible for a functionality, as for example, getting the last HVAC parameters values from its correspondent table from the RDS database. The AWS console allows the development of the functions in two different ways: editing the code online or uploading zip files with the code and necessary packages inside. In this work, the second way was chosen. The AWS Lambda also allows testing the developed functions by providing a test event with a JSON body. All the data sent to and received from the AWS Lambda is in JSON format. Further configurations were necessary to give permissions to the functions created to access to the RDS database.

4.3 Amazon API Gateway

The Amazon API Gateway is a service that makes easy to create, publish, maintain, monitor and secure APIs at any scale. It can create REST (Representational State Transfer) and WebSocket APIs that allow applications to access data from backend services, such as AWS Lambda. In the proposed system, the API Gateway was used to connect the functions developed in the AWS Lambda to a REST API. When creating the REST API in the AWS console, it was necessary to create resources. In this system, a resource can represent the HVAC data or the buildings and is used to build the path used on the HTTP requests methods. Each resource has been assigned to all the necessary methods, according to the needs by the different applications, such as GET, POST, DELETE or PUT. For the type of data to be received, JSON, it was necessary to configure each method and defining a body template for the GET methods in order to identify the parameters received by the HTTP requests. After the creation of the API, it was necessary to make it publicly accessible by creating a test stage. The Postman [16] software was used to test the created API.

5 Mobile App Development

This section describes the implementation of the mobile app (IoT client). It was developed using the Android Studio IDE. This application communicates with the AWS database using the API Gateway service.

The Android app requires permissions to use the Internet. In order to accomplish that, it is necessary to add dependencies to the *AndroidManifest.xml* file generated by the IDE when the application is created. The *build.gradle* file was also modified to allow the use of some required classes and layouts. Every layout implemented follows the Android guidelines by using the *ConstraintLayout*, which allows the application to run on any device, regardless its size. One of the most important classes used was the *AsyncTask*. This class allows that short asynchronous operations to run in the background, and it is usually used to perform network operations that do not require the download of much data. In the proposed system, it is used to do HTTP requests to the REST API.

The application allows the users to register or login using the classic email password combination. For registration, the user only needs his email, name and password. After the login, the user is presented with a list of buildings that he/she has access and can eliminate or add new ones. A long click on a building allows the user to go to the building rooms and a list of rooms is presented to the user. The user can add new rooms by simply introducing the room name or delete those already created. When the user adds a new room, a table is automatically created that contains a default maximum and minimum temperature values for that room. Clicking on a room opens the information panel related to its HVAC parameter values. The user can see the most recent values collected or change the temperature interval and room ID.

6 Experimental Results

This section presents results based on experimental tests performed for the overall system, and involves the evaluation of both functional features (data collection and presentation) and non-functional features (communication delay and reliability).

6.1   Data Collection and Presentation

The gateway is responsible for receiving the HVAC data from the BLE sensor nodes, process and send it to the AWS database and/or the actuators and handle the smart temperature control process. The mobile app, on the other hand, is responsible for presenting the collected data to the user and allowing manual control of the system.

The application has a bottom navigation menu that makes easy to change between functionalities. The default choice of the bottom navigation menu is the HVAC screen (Fig. 4), which shows the timestamp of the collected data, the temperature, humidity and air quality reading, as well as the state of the heating (on or off). The second option (Detectors) shows the data regarding the smoke and presence detectors and their corresponding timestamps. The last option (Configurations) allows the user to check and change the desired maximum and minimum temperature values and change the ID of the room where a sensor is located.

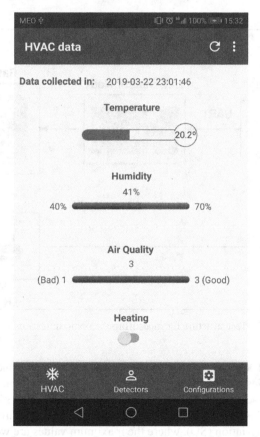

Fig. 4.   Example of values presented on the HVAC screen of the developed mobile app.

6.2 Communication Delay and Reliability

The communication delay, from the moment that the sensor data is generated until the control information is delivered to the respective actuator, is an important parameter, since it affects the performance of the system, namely the response time of the smart temperature control system. Therefore, a test setup was conceived and implemented in order to evaluate the performance associated to the temperature data sensing/actuation process, as shown in Fig. 5. The total delay is the sum of several partial delays in the path through different devices from the source to the destination, including data transmission times in the different data interfaces (UART, BLE and Wi-Fi), as well as medium access delays and processing delays. The measured total delay corresponds to the time elapsed since the data is sent by the source (start time) until it is received in the destination (end time). The same device (a PC running a Java application) was used as source and destination in order to provide a common clock, which is necessary for the calculation of the delay.

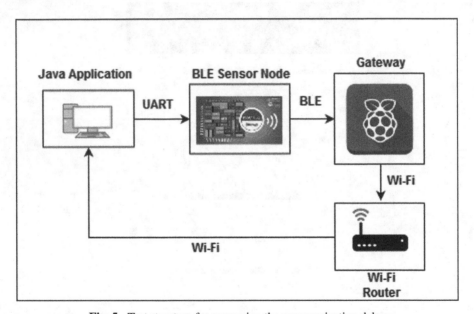

Fig. 5. Test structure for measuring the communication delay.

During the test, 1000 data packets were generated at the source and the same amount was received at the destination; therefore, the communication reliability was 100%. The test was replicated a second time, with similar results. Table 1 shows the main representative measures for the delay obtained in the two performed tests, minimum, maximum, mean and standard deviation (SD), where the maximum values are well below the typical HVAC deadline requirements. Figure 6 shows the distribution of the communication delay for the samples obtained during test 1, where it can be seen that 97% of the delay samples are in the range from 100 to 300 ms. These results are satisfactory, given the slow evolution of the HVAC parameters along the time.

Table 1. Main statistics concerning the measured communication delay.

Tests	Min. (ms)	Max. (ms)	Mean (ms)	SD (ms)
Test 1	110	563	194	57.6
Test 2	109	320	186	43.6

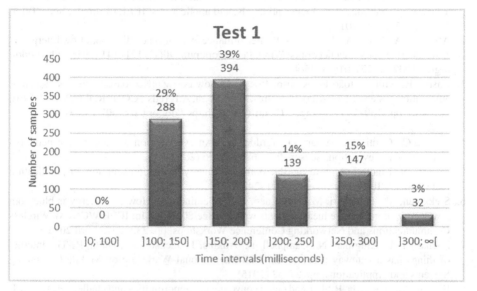

Fig. 6. Distribution of the communication delay for test 1.

7   Conclusions

This paper described the development of a smart IoT system that allows the user to monitor and control HVAC parameters in a smart home using a mobile app. The proposed system is composed by multiple data processing and communication components that work together to perform the desired functions. The BLE/Wi-Fi gateway plays a central role in this system, with relevance to both the data communication and the processing algorithms of the HVAC application, such as the smart temperature control algorithm. An online database was also developed using the AWS cloud platform, in a serverless approach, and a mobile app (IoT client) was developed for the Android mobile operating system.

The developed system was validated through experimental tests comprising the evaluation of its main functionalities, ranging from data collection at the BLE sensor nodes to the presentation at the mobile app, as well as the evaluation of its performance in the path between the sensors and actuators. The communication reliability was 100% and the obtained delay results are adequate, since the variation of the HVAC parameters along the time occurs in a much slower way.

Acknowledgments. This work is supported by FCT with the reference project UID/EEA/04436/2019.

References

1. Al-Fuqaha, A., Guizani, M., Mohammadi, M., Aledhari, M., Ayyash, M.: Internet of things: a survey on enabling technologies, protocols, and applications. IEEE Commun. Surv. Tutor. **17**(4), 2347–2376 (2015)
2. Afonso, J.A., Maio, A.J.F., Simoes, R.: Performance evaluation of Bluetooth Low Energy for high data rate body area networks. Wirel. Pers. Commun. **90**(1), 121–141 (2016). https://doi.org/10.1007/s11277-016-3335-4
3. Castro, P., Afonso, João L., Afonso, José A.: A low-cost ZigBee-based wireless industrial automation system. In: Garrido, P., Soares, F., Moreira, A.P. (eds.) CONTROLO 2016. LNEE, vol. 402, pp. 739–749. Springer, Cham (2017). https://doi.org/10.1007/978-3-319-43671-5_62
4. Buratti, C., Conti, A., Dardari, D., Verdone, R.: An overview on wireless sensor networks technology and evolution. Sensors **9**(9), 6869–6896 (2009)
5. Kamath, S., Lindh, J.: Measuring Bluetooth Low Energy power consumption. In: Application Note AN092, Texas Instruments, pp. 1–24 (2012)
6. Siekkinen, M., Hiienkari, M., Nurminen, J.K., Nieminen, J.: How low energy is bluetooth low energy? comparative measurements with ZigBee/802.15.4. In: IEEE WCNCW Wireless Communications and Networking Conference Workshops, pp. 232–237, April 2012
7. Zachariah, T., Klugman, N., Campbell, B., Adkins, J., Jackson, N., Dutta, P.: The internet of things has a gateway problem. In: 16th International Workshop on Mobile Computing Systems and Applications, pp. 27–32 (2015)
8. Biswas, A., Giaffreda, R.: IoT and cloud convergence: opportunities and challenges. In: IEEE World Forum on Internet of Things (WF-IoT), Seoul, South Korea (2014)
9. Nieminem, J., et al.: Networking solutions for connecting bluetooth low energy enabled machines to the internet of things. IEEE Netw. **28**(3), 83–90 (2014)
10. Cypress Semiconductor: CY8CKIT-042-BLE-A Bluetooth Low Energy 4.2 Compliant Pioneer Kit. https://www.cypress.com/documentation/development-kitsboards/cy8ckit-042-ble-bluetooth-low-energy-42-compliant-pioneer-kit
11. Raspberry Pi Foundation: Raspberry Pi 3 Model B. https://www.raspberrypi.org/products/raspberry-pi-3-model-b/
12. Bluetooth Special Interest Group: Specification of the Bluetooth System, Covered Core Package Version: 5.0, Kirkland, WA, USA, December 2014
13. Amazon: Amazon Web Services (AWS) - Cloud Computing Services. https://aws.amazon.com/pt/
14. Amazon: 10-Minute Tutorials with Amazon Web Services (AWS). https://aws.amazon.com/getting-started/tutorials/
15. Oracle Corporation: MySQL: MySQL Workbench. https://www.mysql.com/products/workbench/
16. Postman, Inc.: POSTMAN I API Development Environment. https://www.getpostman.com/

WaterAMI - Water Automated Metering Infrastructure Based on an Energy Aware Wireless Mesh Network Communication Protocol

Alexandra Vieira[1]([✉]) [iD], Carlos Patrão[2] [iD], Tiago Gonçalves[3], Paulo Monteiro[1], Sylvain Marcelino[3], Edmundo Filipe[3], João Damasceno[4], Hélio Pereira[5], Catarina Sousa[5], Paulo Oliveira[5], and João Carvalho[3]

[1] ApplianceARTS, Figueira da Foz, Portugal
{alexandravieira,pmonteiro}@appliancearts.com
[2] Institute of Systems and Robotics, University of Coimbra, Coimbra, Portugal
carlospatrao@isr.uc.pt
[3] CWJ-Power Electronics, Figueira da Foz, Portugal
{tiagogoncalves,smarcelino,efilipe,jcarvalho}@cwj.pt
[4] Águas da Figueira, Figueira da Foz, Portugal
joao.damasceno@aguasdafigueira.com
[5] Aquapor, Lisbon, Portugal
{heliopereira,catarinasousa,paulooliveira}@aquaporservicos.pt

Abstract. The WaterAMI is an Integrated Management of Efficiency System (IMES) of Water Distribution Networks (WDN) supported in an Automated Metering Infrastructure (AMI). It has a positive impact in energy consumption and in the water management, on one hand decreasing the water losses, on the other, by measuring and controlling water resources as well as water demand, supported in data science by predictive analytics.

The communications between devices of WaterAMI are realized through a Low Power Wide Area Network - All for Everyone - Energy Aware (LPWAN-AfE-EA), developed by CWJ Power Electronics. The AfE-EA protocol uses a mesh topology that grants the coverage of all the water infrastructure's devices, including devices placed in building's basements, normally not covered by other IoT communications protocols.

In order to maximize the operational performance of entire network, AfE-EA uses an efficient math algorithm that computes efficiently the Optimal Hop-Constrained Maximum Capacity Spanning Tree (OH-CMCST), which maximizes the routing path energy capacity and minimizes the number of hops of a battery-operated or energy constrained AMI's communications network, by taking in account the strengths of radio signal links and the State of Charge (SoC) of all batteries that power the smart sensors.

The WaterAMI is already installed and in full operation in several WDNs in Portugal. Where it solved constrains of previously installed similar systems.

This publication presents the main features of AfE-EA protocol, compares with other LPWANs and briefly describes AfE-EA implementation in the first application of WaterAMI in Portugal.

© ICST Institute for Computer Sciences, Social Informatics and Telecommunications Engineering 2020
Published by Springer Nature Switzerland AG 2020. All Rights Reserved
J. L. Afonso et al. (Eds.): SESC 2019, LNICST 315, pp. 209–220, 2020.
https://doi.org/10.1007/978-3-030-45694-8_16

Keywords: Water · Automated metering infrastructure · Communication
protocol · Energy aware · Mesh wireless network · Wireless sensors · Smart city

1 Introduction

Over the last 20 years, the Internet of Things (IoT) technologies have evolved significantly [1]. The IoT refers to the inter connection and exchange of data among devices/sensors [2]. The combination of different devices with wireless communication forms a network named Wireless Sensor Network (WSN). The WSN provides a promising infrastructure for numerous control and monitoring applications fields [3] namely, Agriculture [4], Industrial, Utilities [5], Security, Asset Tracking, Smart Metering, Smart Cities, Smart Buildings/Facilities and Smart Homes.

The IoT technologies aim to efficiently utilize the resources, improve the quality of living, and reduce the cost of management and administration of resources [6]. Once each application field has specific requirements, to implement a WSN is necessary to select the appropriated communication protocol. Currently, specific applications such as Smart Cities require technological solutions with long range, low data rate, low energy consumption, and cost-effectiveness [2]. In response to these requests the LPWAN technology has been created [7].

LPWAN technology provides several communication protocols namely, Long Range (LoRa) [8], SigFox, and Narrow-Band Internet of Things (NB-IoT) [2]. Despite their promise, these protocols are still in their infancy with a high number of challenges in terms of spectrum limitation, coexistence, mobility, scalability, coverage, security, and application-specific requirements such as data rates and real-time communication which make their adoption challenging [6]. So the selection of the communication protocol with more advantages for one application, takes into account the present requirements of each network layer, separately [7], and also the future needs of the network that can arise with a possible growth of infrastructure [6].

To address the issues of coverage of all devices, battery lifetime of each device and cost-effectiveness, an AfE-EA protocol developed by CWJ Power Electronics is presented in this paper. In addition, the AfE-EA protocol allows the creation of a network highway for all the Smart City's devices, by integrated devices from the different infrastructures (e.g. luminaries, valves, sensors and controllers), in a concept of multi-infrastructure operation and management. Also, the AfE-EA protocol can integrate devices from different communication protocols, by the use of adequate hardware/interconnectable gateways (NB-IoT, LoRa, etc.).

The WDN study, implemented in Figueira da Foz, Portugal, uses the LPWAN-AfE-EA technology in a real deployment scenario of CELBI's neighborhood Measuring & Control Station (M&CS). The AfE-EA, embedded in a smart water telemetry solution named WaterAMI, provides successful results for the M&CS.

The paper is organized as follows: Sect. 2 presents a brief review of technological options for IoT; Sect. 3 describes AfE-EA protocol; Sect. 4 describes the WaterAMI solution, namely based in the sensor device Wireless Water Meter Transceiver (WWMT), with embedded AfE-EA protocol; Sect. 5 details a study case with WaterAMIs. Finally, Sect. 6 presents the main conclusions of this publication.

2 Technological LPWAN Options for IoT

The exponential growth of the number of companies based in IoT connectivity technologies boost the development of different wireless communication technologies [9]. These technologies characterized by specific features are selected in function of applications' requirements. The key requirements for IoT networks are coverage, battery life, costs, scalability and performance flexibility. These requirements drive up to the emerge of a new wireless communication technology, the LPWAN, which is characterized by the ability of connecting a significant number of devices, covering big areas using just one base station or gateway, and lowering power consumption [5]. SigFox, LoRa, and NB-IoT are the three leading LPWAN technologies that compete for large-scale IoT deployment.

SigFox is the most mature and widespread IoT technology, already deployed in 31 countries [2]. It is defined by a high coverage and communication range [10]: up to 10 km in urbane zone and up to 40 km in rural zone. Its bidirectional communication is limited to 140×12 bytes (uplink) and 4×8 bytes (downlink) messages/day [2]. SigFox adopters need to leverage on a communication infrastructure provided and owned by SigFox, which limits the options for coverage improvement and network optimization [10]. Between the three leading LPWAN technologies, SigFox has the lowest end-device cost [11]. Like LoRa, SigFox uses unlicensed ISM bands (868 MHz in Europe, 915 MHz in North America, and 433 MHz in Asia) that have no additional costs. Both technologies have very high interference immunity [2].

LoRaWAN® is a bi-directionally communication protocol [12], like NB-IoT, constituted by a LoRa physical layer. It is a low-power long-range wireless protocol [13] which can reach ranges up to 5 km in urbane zone and up to 20 km in rural zone. In opposition to SigFox and NB-IoT, it has an unlimited number of messages/day. The payload length of LoRa (243 bytes) is higher than SigFox and lower than NB-IoT which has a payload length of 1600 bytes [2]. The network density of LoRa and SigFox affects its performance which drops exponentially as the number of end-devices grows. One significant advantage of the LoRaWAN® ecosystem is its flexibility [14], i.e., its adaptability to local/private network deployment. The LoRa technology is currently deployed in 42 countries.

Standardized by the 3rd Generation Partnership Project (3GPP), NB-IoT is a communication technology based on narrow band radio technology which is in development [2]. It uses licensed Long Term Evolution (LTE) frequency bands (e.g. 700 MHz, 800 MHz, and 900 MHz) [1] and is message-based, similar to SigFox and LoRa, but with a higher data rate [11] (i.e., NB-IoT up to 200 kbps, LoRa up to 50 kbps, and SigFox up to 100 bps). NB-IoT has the lowest coverage of the three LPWANs which indicates that it has a low capacity to penetrate deep indoor (e.g. basements). By contrast, NB-IoT has a high scalability [2] which allows the network growing over the time without disrupting existing services [5]. It allows connectivity of up to 100 thousand end-devices per cell compared to 50 thousand per cell for SigFox and LoRa [2]. NB-IoT has the higher Maximum Coupling Loss (MCL): NB-IoT 164 dB, LoRa 157 dB, and SigFox 153 dB [15]. Once MCL defines the range, NB-IoT has the lower range capacity, i.e., <1 km in urbane zone and <10 km in rural zones. Followed by LoRa, NB-IoT has the higher Quality of Service (QoS) [2]. However, it also has the higher end-device cost [11] which adds to the frequency spectrum use cost. Despite NB-IoT has low interference immunity, it has the higher network security [7]. From a global interoperability perspective, NB-IoT undoubtedly has the clearest advantage, being the output of extensive global standardization processes, followed by SigFox technology. The interoperability of LoRa is not guaranteed due to its highly customizable nature [5].

SigFox, LoRa, and NB-IoT, end-devices are in sleep mode most of the time when they are not in operation. The sleep mode reduces the amount of consumed energy and extends the battery lifetime of the devices. However the energy consumption of these protocols is still too high for the requirements of most of the online or quasi-online telemetry applications. The NB-IoT technology has the lower battery lifetime due to the additional energy consumption of the synchronous communication process and QoS handling [2]. In example, with a battery of 5 Wh, a MCL = 150 dB, and a medium payload of 50 bytes/2 h; the end-device lifetime of SigFox and LoRa is 13 years and of NB-IoT is 11 years [11]. Note that these values only take into account the energy consumption for communications, the other energy consumptions are neglected, namely the energy used by water transducers to perform measurements and data storage. However, NB-IoT offers the advantage of low latency. The higher values in latency performance are obtained by SigFox [2].

With the advent of IoT era, the number of connectivity links is growing exponentially causing emergence of the massive IoT networks which can connect tens of thousands of devices and covering hundreds of square kilometers. The LPWAN technologies mentioned above can be used in massive IoT applications, but their utilization would increase the cost and add some extent contradicts in their value proposition of being able to provide wider connectivity for less [5].

Based in meshed networks, a brand-new alternative is now available, the AfE-EA protocol, which is described in next chapter. The AfE-EA network connects a myriad of nodes in densely, sparse, and wider areas, with whole coverage of all the nodes, at same time. It allows the real cost-effectiveness of the IoT solutions, completely in accordance with the particular QoS requirements of the customers.

3   AfE-EA Protocol

AfE-EA is a LPWAN communication protocol developed by CWJ Power Electronics. The designation of the "All for Everyone", or shorter AfE, means that all the IoT nodes of an infrastructure ecosystem can communicate efficiently among them, through the formation of a meshed network, by providing a communications highway, which can be used by all different IoT devices of a smart infrastructure (smart city, smart building or smart home).

The meshed technology allows the connectivity of an ultra-high number of devices significantly higher than SigFox and LoRa [5]. Wireless meshed networks can cover wide geographical areas, using IoT technologies with high coverage since the backbone that connects the gateways can be selected in function of application's requirements. So, LPWAN-AfE-EA can simultaneously connects the devices of a massive IoT network, providing regional and national geographical reach through multi-hop between end-devices extending hundreds of kilometers from the gateway (i.e., high scalability), and overcomes the coverage constraints, e.g. related with hard geographical topology requirements, either in high urban density, or in low rural density.

The performance of AfE-EA protocol relays in Wireless M-Bus networks. However, unlike Wireless M-Bus Standard (EN 13757-5 Wireless M-Bus relaying) that only supports one hop relaying, AfE-EA supports an infinite number of hops which provides it with ultra-high coverage. In each hop, the communication can be realized bidirectional through different frequency bands, including the 169, 433, and 868 MHz and 2.4 GHz frequencies. To maximize the network coverage, according to the algorithm, every node of a LPWAN-AfE-EA network can be set as a router network role.

Other significant advantage of AfE-EA is the energy consumption which, in specific cases, is lower than in other communication protocols already described, due to the relative short transmission distances between nodes compared to star topologies [5]. Although a mesh network will require a higher number of hops, the AfE-EA algorithm minimizes the number of hops using a lower transmission power. The simple processor present in each one of the nodes, their energy efficiency and the fact that the algorithm takes into account the Sate of Charge (SoC) of each node, increases lifetime expectance of the network and justifies the nomenclature EA – Energy Aware, in the protocol designation. Depending on end-devices, its battery lifetime, when using AfE-EA protocol can be up to 15 years. The lifetime of the network is increased by: (1) the reduction of the power consumption which is obtain with the realization of coordinated short transmissions between nodes; and (2) the use of an efficient algorithm to compute an Optimal Hop-Constrained Maximum Capacity Spanning Tree (OH-CMCST) which maximizes the routing path energy capacity and minimizes the number of hops of a battery-operated or energy constrained AMI's communications networks. After each periodic computation of the OH-CMCSTs, performed by the Control Center (CC), the nodes follow the route that assures the lower possible communication latency to a gateway, maximizes the period of operation and assures the total coverage of the devices that compose the network. The need of computing a new OH-CMCST can arise when a communication link becomes less reliable; a new device is integrated on the network; a node is reaching the configured limit of available energy; or when there is the need to change data flow.

The computation of OH-CMCST from the data concentrators (DC) (or gateways) to all the others nodes, or from the nodes to the DC, is realized taking into account the State of Charge (SoC) and the average energy consumption of each node, i.e., the network role selected for each node minimizes the energy consumption to the lower possible value and maximizes the available stored energy. Note that all nodes from the extremities of the network tree, i.e., nodes without descendants, optionally, can be configured to a deep sleep mode and only wake up at defined periods. Being the hop-constrained spanning trees a NP-Hard problem, CWJ Power Electronics developed a mathematical algorithm which reduces the computational complexity, in polynomial time, of the OH-CMCST calculation. This algorithm allows the computation of thousands of nodes in a low cost/low capability processor or micro-controller (even to run dozens of thousands of nodes by a regular processor).

The QoS of AfE-EA is assured by its capacity of response to any outage, interruption, throughput and latency of network connectivity [5]. A link communication can fail unexpectedly due to multiple reasons, such as obstacles or tampering. Using alternative OH-CMCST of the multiple OH-CMCSTs calculated for each network, AfE-EA has the capability of self-optimizing and self-healing, with enhanced network security architecture (through the employment of standard approaches such as AES 128 bits encryption).

AfE-EA has a maximum payload length (i.e., 128 bytes/message) lower than LoRa, which was designed in accordance with the requirements of most of the field applications, and not by devices' constraints. However, it has a throughput than can excesses the NB-IoT results, e.g., at 2.4 GHz AfE-EA data rate is 250 kbps. At the same frequency, also has a very interesting latency result (i.e., 4 ms for each hop/2.4 GHz). Consequently, AfE-EA has an elevated QoS.

The diversity of Industry 4.0 or Digitalization project businesses require IoT technologies with flexible Level of Service Agreements (LSA), which in case of the AfE-EA, is a really big advantage due to the determinism of QoS. In opposition to SigFox and NB-IoT, or even, LoRa, AfE-EA network (as a private network meshed solution) can be well suited and adapted for specific, unique and local requirements of end-users namely, improvement of coverage in buildings' basements with hard radio coverage. The cost-effectiveness of the AfE-EA also is significantly better than NB-IoT, SigFox, or LoRa.

In addition, LPWAN-AfE-EA solution has decoupled the software layer from the hardware layer, and thus enables the protocol to benefit from the economies of large scale of any hardware platform from different manufacturers of radio modules, which solves the interoperability issues usually encounter in the rollout processes of new technologies.

Although meshed networks, like AfE-EA, are established in a quite different way of the common star configurations (P2MP) available on the market, a comparison needs to be performed. Figure 1 summarizes AfE-EA in terms of different IoT factors and compares them with SigFox, LoRa and NB-IoT. Thus, should be denoted that in the practical terms, although AfE-EA was specifically designed to overcome the LPWAN protocols, their features are not fairly comparable, due to the different nature of the communication principles, namely the restricted modes of operation based on limited/reduced up-links and down-links, the spray-and-pray transmissions, the costs of telecommunications fees, the hard paybacks of investments, etc.

The crescent demand of deployments in smart cities and smart buildings & facilities are based on monitoring and control the myriad of different services, supported by IoT devices namely, artificial lighting, urban solid waste, irrigation of green spaces, quality of air, car parking spots and traffic, people traffic, security, safety, water, electricity, and gas distribution. The high diversity of IoT devices available can be integrated into a whole AfE-EA communication network, which can consequently contributes to the creation of network communications highways for all smart city or smart building & facilities. These highways allow all different IoT devices be monitored and managed/controlled by a single Control Center (CC). They also allow the integration of new devices at any moment without adding new communication fees and, at the same time, making possible the return of investment in short-time, which depending on the use case, can be as low as one or two years.

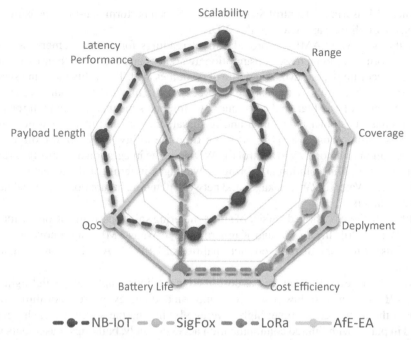

Fig. 1. Respective advantages of NB-IoT, SigFox, LoRa and AfE-EA in terms of IoT factors (adapted from [2])

4 WaterAMI

Water is vital for the existence of humans, animals and plants and consequently it is a basic requirement for numerous sectors. Although water covers over 70% of the Earth, only 1% is fresh water. The increase of the world population from 7 billion currently to over 10.5 billion by 2050, and the growing of the humans' life-styles of current and emergent societies are increasing the water demand.

The balance between water demand and availability has reached a critical level in many areas of Europe (water scarcity). In addition, more and more areas are adversely affected by changes in the hydrological cycle and precipitation patterns (droughts) [16]. The consideration of all these facts arise the importance of treat water as one of the most important resource available on Earth. So to identify and prevent the water leakages in residential and distribution networks [17], which in Europe are in average higher than 50% [18], it was introduced on the market the water telemetry solutions.

Aware of water importance, CWJ Power Electronics developed a smart metering solution: a water automated metering infrastructure, named WaterAMI (illustrated in Fig. 2) for real-time monitoring and control of WDNs, through an Integrated Management of Efficiency System (IMES).

WaterAMI allows the change of concept, from the conventionally called "tele-metering", to a new concept called "tele-measuring/control", which finally allows that the "designed" Measuring & Control Stations (M&CS) can perform real-time measurement and control of all the parameters of the WDN.

By the way, WaterAMI can provide direct readings for end-consumers, who can use this information to increase consumption awareness and can adapt their consuming behaviors accordingly, i.e., avoiding waste of resources [12]. The utility metering service operator can remotely obtain the readings, stored every 15 min (or other configured value) with a precision of one liter, and consequently eliminates the incorrect human readings that can create customer complaints and/or dissatisfaction, and increase water utility companies' exploration costs [19]. At same time the utility can use the bidirectional communication functionality to control the WDN, by the integration of controlled valves or other devices. This solution also brings advantages in terms of the detection of the Non-Revenue Water (NRW), leakages and network planning in function of the real needs of the consumers.

Although, there is a high diversity of smart metering solutions available on the market (e.g. WAVIoT [20], Itron [21], and Kamstrup [22]), WaterAMI is an innovative solution because it uses the disruptive functionalities of LPWAN-AfE-EA communication protocol.

AfE-EA has several advantages, as described in previous chapter, and it highlights the WaterAMI solution with: low power consumption and energy aware algorithms which increases the networks' lifetime; high coverage by having the ability to reach devices located in places with limited communication access namely, buildings' basements with high radio signal constraints, metal boxes or similar enclosures; bidirectional communication from the Control Center (CC), through the water Measuring & Control Stations (M&CS), to the end-point water utilization.

The proof of concept of AfE-EA protocol was performed in 2017 at "Águas da Figueira (AdF)" WSN, in Figueira da Foz, Portugal. The WaterAMI solution was implemented taking into account the custom requirements in places, with known radio communications issues, designated by the water utility's management entity. In these places other smart devices were previously tested, with different communication protocols that were not able to provide reasonable coverage, in accordance with expected level of QoS. The 1st place was a neighborhood area with 7 condo buildings that had about 100 water meters, installed inside metal boxes, at the buildings basements, with identified issues in radio frequency coverage. The Data Concentrator (DC) of WaterAMI solution, operating as Control Center (CC), was installed in the headquarters' water utility, and had the ability to compute the OH-CMCST trees with the links among all the 100 nodes, in about 7 ms, using a low-cost processor (ARM Cortex-A8, 1 GHz). Even with the identified radio coverage constrains, the meshed topology of the AfE-EA protocol allowed the successful coverage of all the devices, as intended. Other places with identified radio coverage issues were identified and successfully deployed with 100% coverage.

From the general knowledge, the use of batteries is a big issue of smart sensors, once the power of batteries is limited [23] and their replacement can be a difficult and expensive task. So CWJ Power Electronics is already developing an update version of WWMT which is powered by energy collected from the water circulation [24], i.e., powered by energy harvesting technology. While the next generation of WaterAMI is not

Fig. 2. The WaterAMI is composed by a Wireless Water Metering Transceiver (WWMT), powered by standard non-rechargeable/depletion batteries, prompt to be installed in conventional water meters (e.g. JANZ JV400). After, reading the data with an incremental encoder, the WWMT sends the data collected through AfE-EA communication protocol to DC.

available, the WWMT, illustrated in Fig. 2, is already commercialized with successful results, as proved in the case study described in next chapter.

5 Case Study

Water utilities Management Entities (ME) are currently requiring smart solutions to monitoring and control their WDNs. As above mentioned, since 2017, CWJ Power Electronics has deployed the WaterAMI solution at Figueira da Foz, Portugal, according to their custom requirements and in places with known radio communications issues, designated by the water utility "Águas da Figueira (AdF)".

At the moment of writing this article, Águas da Figueira (AdF) is in the process of smart meters' rollout, has already deployed more than 5000 Wireless Water Meter Transducers (WWMT), that send the data collected to the Control Center (CC), installed at the water utility's headquarters, through the AfE-EA communications network. Those first chosen places to rollout represent the different kinds of deployment densities, in urban, peri-urban, or rural areas, which are representative of the entire WDS.

However, for the purpose of this article, beyond the demonstration of efficiency of AfE-EA communication protocol, will be demonstrated the cost-effectiveness of the WaterAMI solution, by allowing the increment of water sales revenues, at same time, allowing the mitigation of the exploration costs (reducing water leakages, energy, labor, etc.).

Therefore, was chosen a representative neighborhood area of the AdF's WDS, designed as a Measuring & Control Station (M&CS), called CELBI's MC&S, which is an urban zone of the municipality with an area extension of 98 ha, where are in service 498 WWMT assembled over the conventional water meters. These smart devices form a meshed network of 3.68 km with 300 branches where each node communicates with other node using AfE-EA protocol. Figure 3 shows the real deployment scenario of CELBI's M&CS with the smart devices scattered along the area. The CC, installed in the headquarters' water utility, has the ability to compute the OH-CMCST trees with

Fig. 3. WaterAMI solution installed in CELBI's M&CS: each green point signs out one WWMT, i.e., a network node (Color figure online)

the links among all the 498 nodes, in about 19.3 ms, using a low-cost processor (ARM Cortex-A8, 1 GHz, 512 MB of RAM), which is suitable for real-time operation in terms of the QoS adopted by the agreed LSA.

The heart of the WaterAMI, the AfE-EA protocol, allows the communication of data from/to places where are deployed the smart devices. There are devices deployed inside metal boxes, at the buildings' basements, which normally causes deficient radio frequency coverage in competitors' solutions. Even with this constrains, the meshed topology of the AfE-EA protocol allows the successful coverage of all smart devices without the limitations as for example LoRa that would require need an additional gateway to insure the coverage of the end-devices implemented on basements.

With the WaterAMI solution, the utility can monitor directly all the water network of the study zone through the remote collection, in real time, of water consumption of final costumers, and calculate the Non-Revenue Water (NRW), which are the difference between the water injected in WDN and the accounted consumption. These loses are the product of leakages (in networks pipes and in house of final consumer), pipe bursts and unauthorized/unused water (i.e., water theft). When a NRW is detected the WaterAMI platform emits an alert alarm. With the identification of hits approximate location, the water utility can activate the necessary means, to for instance, send the technical team to inspect and repair the problem, or close/open existent electronic valves, or even send an alert message to the final consumer if a leakage is detected inside his house.

With this investment, at this neighborhood alone, the utility verified a reduction of water losses from 23% at the implementation moment, from the beginning of May 2019, when compared with the homolog month, in May of 2018, to 12% in June of 2019, which represents 354 m^3/month of water savings and about 9.511 €/year.

Taking into account these results, the utility will have the payback of the system (water meter + WWMT including AfE-EA protocol) in about 2.8 years, this has a lifetime of about 12 years. Or, if only in terms of the WWMT, the payback could be of 1.8 years, by having in consideration that the replacing of the water meter is enforced by legal and regulatory requirements.

6 Conclusion

This paper has described an energy-efficient communication protocol developed by CWJ Power Electronics. The wireless meshed network based in AfE-EA protocol allows the coverage of thousands, or even, dozens of thousands of devices, even the ones located in places with radio frequency coverage constrains or hidden by signal obstacles. Moreover, by using the OH-CMCST algorithm, it can maximize the network lifetime and minimize the number of hops, minimizing the latency.

Other advantage of this protocol is the possibility to be embedded in different IoT devices, using different frequency bands, that could be already deployed or have better hardware features for the specific application.

WaterAMI and his communication protocol was the one of other solutions tested at the WDN in Figueira da Foz, Portugal, but was the only that best fitted the service requirements of the water utility, providing the total coverage of the water meters. The results of this case study have demonstrated that in places where the previously used other IoT solutions based on different communication protocols have coverage and cost-effective limitations, the AfE-EA could successfully establish communications and provide data readings from all the water meters, at same time that provided short payback times.

By the way, was proved that the WaterAMI solution is a completely cost-effectiveness solution, once has very short payback periods, at same time that increment the sales revenues and reduce the exploration costs – WaterAMI is a double sense performance "driving force" for water utilities management entities.

Taking into account the positive results of the current case study, CWJ Power Electronics is now integrating the AfE-EA protocol in several public utilities, such like, outdoor lighting, water, sewage, car parking, irrigation and waste, into one whole integrated management of efficiency system, throughout Portugal country.

References

1. Chen, M., Miao, Y., Hao, Y., Hwang, K.: Narrow band Internet of Things. IEEE Access **5**, 20557–20577 (2017)
2. Mekki, K., Bajic, E., Chaxel, F., Meyer, F.: A comparative study of LPWAN technologies for large-scale IoT deployment. ICT Express **5**, 1–7 (2019)
3. Pule, M., Yahya, A., Chuma, J.: Wireless sensor networks: a survey on monitoring water quality. J. Appl. Res. Technol. **15**(6), 562–570 (2017)
4. Zeman, K., et al.: Wireless M-Bus in industrial IoT: technology overview and prototype implementation. In: European Wireless 2017 (2017)

5. Northstream – WIREPAS: Massive IoT: different technologies for different needs (2017). http://northstream.se/northstreamwp/wp-content/uploads/2017/06/Massive-IoT-different-technologies-for-different-needs.pdf. Accessed 02 July 2019
6. Ismail, D., Rahman, M., Saifullah, A.: Low-power wide-area networks: opportunities, challenges, and directions. In: Workshops ICDCN 2018: Workshops Co-located with the International Conference on Distributed Computing and Networks, Varanasi, India (2018)
7. Qin, Z., Li, F.Y., Li, G.Y., McCann, J.A., Ni, Q.: Low-power wide-area networks for sustainable IoT. IEEE Wirel. Commun. **26**(3), 140–145 (2019)
8. Ikpehai, A., et al.: Low-power wide area network technologies for Internet-of-Things: a comparative review. IEEE Internet Things J. **6**(2), 2225–2240 (2018)
9. Alam, M., Jan, M.A., Shu, L., He, X., Chen, Y.: Editorial: current and future trends in wireless communications protocols and technologies. Mobile Netw. Appl. **23**(3), 377–381 (2018). https://doi.org/10.1007/s11036-018-1026-y
10. Kamstrup.   https://www.kamstrup.com/en-en/water-solutions/water-meter-reading/communication-technologies. Accessed 14 June 2019
11. Tsavalos, N., Hashem, A.A.: Low Power Wide Area Network (LPWAN) Technologies for Industrial IoT Applications. SE-221 00 Lund, Sweden (2018)
12. Alvisi, S., et al.: Wireless middleware solutions for smart water metering. Sensors **19**(19), 1853 (2019)
13. SSTPL. https://www.sstpl.in/solution/metering/watermeter.php. Accessed 14 June 2019
14. Sinha, R.S., Wei, Y., Hwang, S.-H.: A survey on LPWA technology: LoRa and NB-IoT. ICT Express **3**, 14–21 (2017)
15. Altice Labs: IoT cellular networks, October 2017. https://www.alticelabs.com/content/WP-IoT-Cellular-Networks.pdf. Accessed 04 July 2019
16. Farah, E., Shahrour, I.: Smart Water for Leakage Detection: Feedback about the Use of Automated Meter Reading Technology (2017)
17. McKinsey Global Institute: Smart cities: digital solutions for a more livable future, June 2018. https://www.mckinsey.com/~/media/mckinsey/industries/capital%20projects%20and%20infrastructure/our%20insights/smart%20cities%20digital%20solutions%20for%20a%20more%20livable%20future/mgi-smart-cities-full-report.ashx. Accessed 04 July 2019
18. European Commission: Water Scarcity & Droughts – 2012 Policy Review – Building blocks Non-Paper (2012). https://ec.europa.eu/environment/water/quantity/pdf/non-paper.pdf. Accessed 04 July 2019
19. Crainic, M.S.: Overview of the current state of the art in the domain of domestic water meters Part II water meters for smart metering systems, pp. 63–83, April 2011
20. WAVIoT: Smart Water Metering. https://waviot.com/iot/solutions/smart-metering/smart-water-metering. Accessed 14 June 2019
21. Itron. https://www.itron.com/emea/solutions/who-we-serve/water. Accessed 14 June 2019
22. Kamstrup: MULTICAL® 21/flowIQ® 210x. https://www.kamstrup.com/en-en/water-solutions/smart-water-meters/multical-21. Accessed 14 June 2019
23. Tuna, G., Gungor, V.: Energy harvesting and battery technologies for powering wireless sensor networks. In: Industrial Wireless Sensor Networks (2016)
24. Alrowaijeh, J.S., Hajj, M.R.: Autonomous self-powered water meter. Appl. Phys. Lett. **113**(3), 033902 (2018)

A Versatile High Frequency Electricity Monitoring Framework for Our Future Connected Home

Benjamin Völker(✉), Marc Pfeifer, Philipp M. Scholl, and Bernd Becker

Chair for Computer Architecture, University of Freiburg,
Freiburg im Breisgau, Germany
{voelkerb,pfeiferm,pscholl,becker}@informatik.uni-freiburg.de

Abstract. In our homes a lot of devices are powered by electricity without us knowing the specific amount. As electricity production has a large, negative environmental impact, we should be more aware about how devices consume power and how we can adapt our daily routine to decrease our electricity requirements. Methods such as *Non-Intrusive Load Monitoring* (NILM) can provide the user with precise device level electricity data by measuring at a single point in a houses' electricity network. However, the time resolution of most off-the-shelf power meters is not sufficient for NILM or the meters are locked down for security reasons. Therefore, we have developed our own versatile energy metering framework which consists of a high frequency electricity metering device, a versatile backend for data processing and a webapp for data visualization. The developed hardware is capable of sampling up to 32 kHz, while the software framework allows to extract other power related metrics such as harmonic content. The system's application ranges from providing transparent electricity usage to the user up to generating load forecasts with fine granularity.

Keywords: Load monitoring · NILM · NIALM · Electricity feedback

1 Introduction

Electricity is omnipresent without us really thinking about it. We use it while we brew our morning coffee, while on our way to work, while at work and while spending free time with our family. In 2014, the yearly global average electricity consumption per capita was 3353 kWh [5] worldwide which is topped by an average person in the US at 12 305 kWh. This is equivalent to approximately 6.49 t of CO_2 per capita per year in the US according to [6]. Besides CO_2, electricity production is the largest contributor to global greenhouse gas emission with approximately 29% [1]. As a way to reduce our electricity consumption without giving up our morning coffee D [8] stated that an "appliance specific breakdown" should be provided instead of just the monthly whole house energy

© ICST Institute for Computer Sciences, Social Informatics and Telecommunications Engineering 2020
Published by Springer Nature Switzerland AG 2020. All Rights Reserved
J. L. Afonso et al. (Eds.): SESC 2019, LNICST 315, pp. 221–231, 2020.
https://doi.org/10.1007/978-3-030-45694-8_17

consumption. This would make end users more aware about their electricity consumption. If a device level electricity breakdown is provided, energy hungry devices e.g. the 30 year old freezer can be identified easily. Further, gamification aspects could be applied to our daily electricity consumption. As an example, a contextual positive energy feedback - possibly a simple reward - could be provided if the TV has been used less often during the last weak. Such feedback can be applied by integrated device level electricity data with standard human activity recognition systems.

However, as long as devices do not expose their electricity consumption, retrofittable solutions need to be applied. Device level metering can be added using off-the-shelf power measurement units like *Kill-A-Watt* [9]. This approach is known as intrusive load monitoring (ILM). It requires the user to attach measurement units to all or a subset of appliances across the residence. This is a laborious process and for devices directly connected to the mains like the stove impractical for non-electricians. Furthermore, if a large set of these measurement units is deployed, their total self-consumption might not be negligible. An alternative approach to ILM is Non-intrusive Load Monitoring (NILM). This approach uses a single measurement unit installed at the houses fuse box which measures the composite load of all appliances in the home. Disaggregating this composite load into the load of each individual appliance is challenging. Hence, disaggregation algorithms typically require to analyze different macroscopic as well as microscopic features in both time and frequency domain. Therefore, data of high sampling-rates is required. For example the algorithms used in [4] and [16] use power harmonics up to the 20th which requires a sampling-rate of at least 2 kHz according to the *Nyquist Theorem*.

Such data can not be provided by existing infrastructure in our homes, since typical smart meters - which may internally sample with such high frequencies - only provide the electricity data with a temporal resolution of <1 Hz. Furthermore, due to security concerns, interfacing with these smart meters is often restricted to the grid operator.

In this paper we discuss the requirements for a versatile, retrofittable electricity monitoring system. We further propose a hardware and software framework that meets these requirements. The resulting embedded system is comprised of a smart meter like device installed in the residences' fuse box and a software backend which gathers the sampled raw voltage and current measurements and distributes electricity information via network or unix domain sockets to arbitrary clients. An example client is a disaggregation module splitting the total electricity consumption into the individual devices consuming power. We have installed the system in the office kitchen of our chair to analyze its long term performance. It provides real time electricity feedback and is used to record datasets which can be used to evaluate load disaggregation algorithms.

2   Related Work

The authors of the The Reference Energy Disaggregation Data Set (REDD) [11] used a custom build recording interface to recorded the whole house electricity consumption of six different homes for several weeks. To measure the aggregated current and voltage signals at the mains, they used *NI-9239* analog to digital converters. To scale down the mains voltage onto the measurement range of the ADC, they used an 1:100 oscilloscope probe (*Pico TA041*). For current sensing, they used split core current transformers (*SCT-013*). The sampling rate was 16 kHz with an ADC resolution of 24 bit. A laptop was connected to log the raw data and to send low frequency versions to an external server.

The authors of the UK Domestic Appliance-Level Electricity dataset (UK-DALE) [10] recorded 655 days of data with a sampling rate of 16 kHz of a single home in the UK. They used an off-the-shelf USB sound card with a stereo line in interface connected to a PC. The voltage was transformed to line level using AC-AC transformer and a voltage divider while current is transformed using split core current transformer. However, only a single phase was recorded. Recording the whole house supply would require to use three sound cards (in Europe). The authors of [7] presented a hardware and software system to provide the device level electricity consumption for a building. Their hardware system is comprised of a dedicated power monitoring chip (ADE7880), a microcontroller to interface with the chip and an ethernet interface. Unfortunately, they do not provide any information about achievable sampling rates or the cost of the proposed system. The software consist of an applet that is able to identify on- and off-events of devices which have an active power consumption that is "significantly different of each other".

Kriechbaumer et al. [13] have developed a measurement system embedded into an off-the-shelf power strip. They used six hall effect sensors (*ACS712*) to measure the current consumption at each plug and one AC-AC converter to measure the overall plug's voltage. The analog output of these sensors is converted into the digital domain using seven 12 bit unipolar ADCs (*MCP3201*). A combination of a microcontroller and a single board PC handles the digital data acquisition. Therewith, they can measure up to six different devices with an adjustable sampling frequency of up to 50 kHz. Their setup allows a "mobile" data collection of all devices with power plugs. But they cannot measure devices directly connected to the mains like the lighting or the stove. More recently, the same authors developed a measurement systems which can be installed at a residences fuse box to measure the aggregated power consumption. They used hall effect current transformers (*HAL 50-S*) for current sensing and 6 V AC-AC transformers for voltage sensing. Using a 16 bit ADC (*AD7656A*) and an FPGA, they are capable of sampling raw current and voltage waveforms up to 250 kHz. However, they do not reveal any information about the costs of their system. Since the used components (Latte Panda, 3x Hall Effect Sensors, Lattice FPGA, ADC, etc.) already cost 400 €, a relatively large system price (≈500 €) is assumed.

Kriechbaumer et al. have proposed a set of requirements for an electricity data acquisition hardware (DAQ) which is summarized in Table 1. We have added the requirement "**R11**: safe external interfaces" since we are dealing with high voltages, we have to make sure that interfacing with the system is safe.

Table 1. Requirements for electricity data acquisition hardware, adapted from [13]

R1 high sampling rates	**R6** synchronized world clock
R2 long term recordings	**R7** precise time-stamping
R3 common file format	**R8** high resolution and accuracy
R4 data compression	**R9** persistent data storage
R5 low price (per appliance)	**R10** resources for data processing
	R11 safe external interfaces

Our contribution is three fold:

1. We provide a versatile framework comprised of both hardware and software to provide high frequency electricity data in near real-time. The time delay between data recording and provision is determined by the transmission channel alone. This transmission can be performed over a wired or wireless channel. The data can be further distributed to other client modules using unix domain (IPC) or network socket connections.
2. The provided raw measurements are of high horizontal (up to 32 kHz) and vertical (24 bit) resolution.
3. Instead of being restricting to a specific task, the framework can adapt to the users need and either serve as just a recording interface for long term electricity datasets (see **R2**), provide real-time electricity data to further data analytic modules or directly display historic and real-time consumption to the end user.

3   Hardware Setup

The measurement system is a self build prototype board encapsulated in a DIN housing to allow a rail mount inside a houses' fuse box. The voltages of all three main legs are measured using voltage dividers with a ratio of ≈1:1000. The currents are measured using split core burden-less current transformers (*YHDC SCT-013*) with a ratio of 1:2000. Such electromagnetic current transformers are inexpensive solutions to measure high currents without changing the electrical wiring. Compared to other contact-less current sensing techniques, they also show a high linearity at a high measurement range. The used split core variants are also fairly easy to install. The induced smaller current is transformed into a voltage using two $7.87\,\Omega$ burden resistors per channel. The analog signals are fed into a dedicated electricity monitoring chip (*ADE9000* [2]). The *ADE9000* has a seven input ADC with a sampling rate of up to 32 kHz (see **R1**), a resolution of 24 bit, and a very high signal to noise ratio of 96 dB which meets requirement **R8**. This allows to measure up to 3 voltage and 4 current channels covering the three phase input of typical homes in Europe (L_1, L_2, L_3 and N). As noted, the *ADE9000* is dedicated for electricity monitoring and, therefore, has additional internal hardware to calculate electricity related metrics such as active, reactive and apparent power, phase shift etc. These measures and the raw voltage and current samples can be retrieved via a galvanically isolated SPI interface (see **R11**) as shown in Fig. 1. The main controller inside the measurement system is a WiFi and Bluetooth enabled microcontroller (*ESP32*). Since this microcontroller is very powerful with its 240 MHz dual core processor, it can simply relay the sampled data e.g. over a TCP connection or execute/incorporate several algorithms for energy analysis (see **R10**).

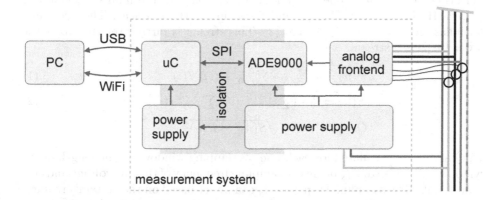

Fig. 1. Overview of the measurement system.

In addition it can also serve as a lightweight web-server in order to provide a simple user feedback without the requirement of any external server. If we take a closer look at the systems' typical environment such as a shielded fuse box located in the basement, we expect WiFi connection to be poor. Therefore, we added the ability to connect an external antenna over a *SMA* connector. A *USB-serial* interface (*FTDI-FT2232H*) allows to change the systems firmware or to gather the electricity data over a reliable wired channel instead of WiFi.

Measuring the voltage directly using voltage divider has a very high accuracy (see **R8**) compared to indirect methods but leads to safety requirements. We focused on meeting these requirements not only to meet **R11** but to meet standards according to IEC 61010-1, IEC 60950, DIN EN 60664-1 (clearance distances) and IEC 61000-4-5.

The price of the measurement system is roughly 150 € depending on the production volume, making it an affordable solution to retrofit smart metering to an existing home (see **R5**).

4   Software Backend

The software backend is split into multiple individual modules. These modules communicate over TCP sockets. This allows to distribute or centralize all calculations.

The main module that interfaces directly with the measurement system is the *Data Collector* module (see Fig. 2). It is connected to it over a TCP or USB serial connection. The measurement system can be configured using the data collector to only provide raw voltage and current signals, active ($P(n)$), reactive ($Q(n)$) and apparent ($S(n)$) power or the signals harmonics. However, to simplify the data collection process and to restrict data throughput, the standard configuration of the measurement system is to provide raw voltage and current waveforms, since other measures can be directly calculated from it but not vice versa. The calculation of active, reactive and apparent power is therefore performed at the data collector module on the basis of the mains frequency f_l (e.g. 50 Hz in Asia and Europe and 60 Hz in North America). The according formulas are shown in (1), (2) and (3). This stream is further referred to as the lower frequency stream.

$$P(n) = \frac{1}{N} \cdot \sum_{i=0}^{N-1} U(i) \cdot I(i) \tag{1}$$

$$S(n) = \frac{1}{N} \cdot \left(\sum_{i=0}^{N-1} U(i) \cdot \sum_{i=0}^{N-1} I(i) \right) \tag{2}$$

$$Q(n) = \sqrt{S(n)^2 - P(n)^2} \tag{3}$$

P, Q and S are calculated for each non-overlapping window n. The length of the window is $N = \frac{f_s}{f_l}$ with f_s being the sampling frequency of the raw voltage and current signals. The sampling frequency f_s can be set based on the system's requirement up to 32 kHz. To keep the amount of data reasonable while still allowing to retrieve information about higher frequency harmonics, a sampling rate of 8 kHz is typically chosen. This value is also based on the findings of [3] that, "there may be little additional benefit between 15–40 kHz because of the noise in that range in real buildings".

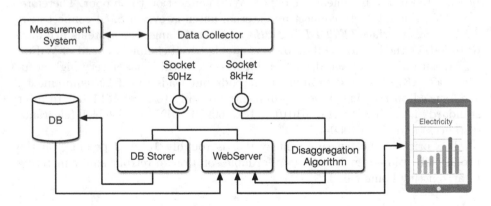

Fig. 2. Overview of the proposed system.

Other modules can subscribe for specific data streams i.e. the calculated power signals or the raw voltage and current signals.

One client type is the *DB Storer* module. It subscribes to the stream which outputs the calculate active, reactive and apparent power (at frequency f_L) and stores it into a *NoSQL* database. Since NoSQL does not require a fixed predefined data layout, it allows to change storage schemes later on.

Another type of client is the *Disaggregation* module. Its main purpose is to disaggregate the composite load into the load of each individual appliance connected. As a typical disaggregation algorithm also analyzes higher harmonic features such as frequency components in the signal up to 4 kHz (e.g. [16]), it requires input data of higher frequency. Therefore, the module 'subscribes' to the raw voltage and current stream. The disaggregation result can further be subscribed by other modules such as a web-server. The web-server is a another client module. It connects to the lower frequency stream for a real-time electricity feedback and also to the database for historic electricity data. The data is transported via web-sockets to the client. The client can be an arbitrary browser running on a PC or mobile device.

5   Software Frontend

The frontend is an interactive web application. Therewith, the user has the flexibility to use any tablet, phone or PC to interface with the system. An overview of the web application is shown in Fig. 3. A dashboard like modular layout allows to display just the information the user wants to be shown. We have seen that mounting a tablet displaying the current real-time electricity consumption e.g. at a house's kitchen makes the user aware of sudden changes of the power consumption. The user can than relate these changes directly to their actions (e.g. turning on the stove).

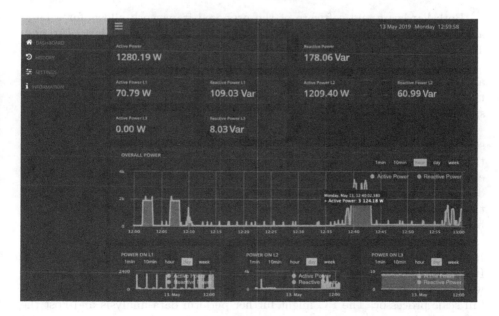

Fig. 3. Software frontend. Website showing the real time power consumption of our chair's office kitchen.

6 Flexibility

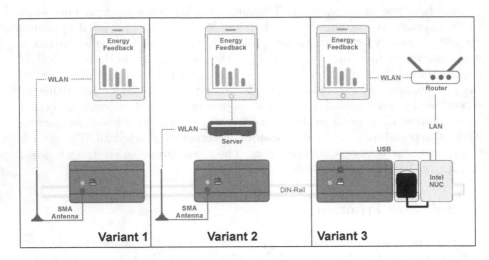

Fig. 4. Overview of different variants of the hardware setup. All variants involve the measurement system (ms) in green and a tablet. Variant 1: The ms opens a WiFi access point and performs lightweight data processing. Variant 2: An external server performs data processing and hosting a website for the tablet. Variant 3: An embedded PC is installed inside the fuse box for further data processing like electricity disaggregation; it is connected to the ms over USB and can further host the web server. (Color figure online)

Both hardware and software of the proposed framework allows for a large amount of user flexibility. Figure 4 shows the setup of different hardware variants. The basic and mandatory setup is variant 1.

Variant 1 is comprised of the measurement system explained in Sect. 3 and a tablet for visual feedback. A dedicated tablet app will connect over TCP to the measurement system and configures it to stream the data at the required sampling-rate. This data is then shown and processed in the tablet application.

Variant 2 adds an external server inside or outside the local network. This server is connected over TCP to the measurement system. It handles the additional data processing e.g. a disaggregation algorithm and hosts a web server as explained in Sect. 4. Therewith, instead of a dedicated tablet app, a web-app is displayed on the tablet. The web application is explained in Sect. 5. This further allows to exchange the tablet with any other device equipped with a web browser.

Variant 3 requires the most hardware but also shows the highest versatility. Instead of an external server, an embedded PC is installed inside the fuse box. It is connected over a USB serial connection to the measurement system. Therewith, the data is acquired over a robust wired connection and processed on a full scale processor. The PC might further perform data analysis and host the web application.

The modular structure of the overall framework allows to use it for generating real time electricity feedback using the web application, record long term electricity datasets by storing the raw data to file or to test and compare different NILM algorithms in situ with a live system by simply interfacing with the raw data socket.

As NILM algorithms develop, they might require smaller sampling rates in the future without performance loss or different electricity related features such as the harmonic content. The proposed hardware is be able to adapt and supply just the features the algorithm requires, so that resampling or data conversion is outsourced to the measurement system itself which might even reduce the energy consumption of overall system itself.

7   Generating Datasets

Since the majority of existing NILM systems rely on supervised learning methods, one of the main remaining challenges is to obtain training data. We, therefore, added the ability to hook up a recording module onto the raw data streams. This recording module can store the raw voltage and current streams into file. We choose to store these streams as wavpack encoded floating point values inside a matroska multimedia container, as this allows to store multiple streams (e.g. the consumption of each main leg) in a single file meeting requirement **R3**. The chosen container format further allows to apply different audio encoders to the raw data. We have chosen wavpack since it features lossless compression with a high compression rate as stated in requirement **R4**. A discussion of different audio encoders is presented in [12] and [14]. The container format allows to store subtitle streams as well. Subtitles can be used to store ground truth labels together with the data in a single file. One remaining challenge is to generate these ground truth labels (e.g. ON-phases of a particular device) which has to be done manually after the recording. One attempt to automate this process is proposed in [15] by using additional intrusive sensors directly connected to the monitored appliances. If data with ground truth has been generated, it can later on be used to train supervised NILM algorithms.

We further used Variant 3 of the system and successfully recorded over one month of aggregated raw voltage and current waveforms sampled at 8 kHz. This field test shows that requirement **R2** is met. Data has been stored to disc at regular time intervals of 20 min (see **R9**) resulting in approximately 420 GB of overall data. Figure 5 shows the electricity consumption of our chair's office kitchen for one day. Timestamping was performed using the recording PC since it features an accurate world clock (see **R6, R7**).

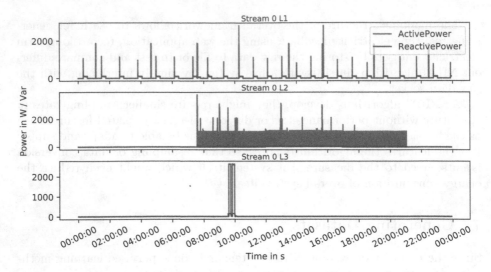

Fig. 5. One day electricity consumption of our chair's office kitchen. L_1 shows spikes of the refrigerator and heating cycles of the water therm. L_2 shows the coffee machine, the kettle and lighting and L_3 the consumption of the dishwasher which has been turned on at around 9 am.

8   Conclusions and Future Work

We have proposed a hardware and software framework to get the hands on real-time electricity data. The developed smart meter hardware allows to sample high resolution electricity data (raw voltage and current wave-forms) up to 32 kHz. This allows to further analyse high frequency components in the electricity signal. We discussed three hardware-setup variants which allow for different flexibility levels. Furthermore, we have introduced a software backend which can provide and store different electricity related metrics such as active and reactive power at various sampling-rate. We used a modular backend structure with socket communication between the modules to implement a publish and subscribe model. Different backend modules can subscribe to any data streams for further data processing. Moreover, we implemented a web server which hosts an interactive web application. The web app shows the real time electricity consumption as well as historic data.

As mentioned, generating ground truth data for better datasets remains challenging. Therefore, we are planning to instrument our chair's office kitchen with an RFID based access system to log the time when a specific device is used and the person who uses it. We hope that this will improve the quality of the generated datasets which might be also used for e.g. human activity recognition. According to the application rule *VDE-AR-N 4101* for German fuse boxes, a *RJ45* connector has to be installed in new meter cabinets allowing to e.g. connect new smart meters. Therewith, we plan to develop an updated version of our measurement system which will feature an Ethernet connector for a reliable wired connection and a desktop class processor to be able to centralize all calculations without loosing the flexibility to distribute them.

References

1. United States Environmental Protection Agency: Sources of greenhouse gas emissions (2014). https://www.epa.gov/ghgemissions/sources-greenhouse-gas-emissions. Accessed 24 Jan 2018
2. Analog Devices: High Performance, Multiphase Energy, and Power Quality Monitoring IC, April 2017. Rev. A
3. Armel, K.C., Gupta, A., Shrimali, G., Albert, A.: Is disaggregation the holy grail of energy efficiency? The case of electricity. Energy Policy **52**, 213–234 (2013)
4. Bouhouras, A.S., Chatzisavvas, K.C., Panagiotou, E., Poulakis, N., Parisses, C., Christoforidis, G.C.: Load signatures development via harmonic current vectors. In: 2017 52nd International Universities Power Engineering Conference (UPEC), pp. 1–6. IEEE (2017)
5. World Energy Council: Electricity use per household (2014). https://wec-indicators.enerdata.net/household-electricity-use.html. Accessed 24 Jan 2018
6. Emse, H.: Co2 calculator (2019). http://www.klimaneutral-handeln.de/php/kompens-berechnen.php#rechner. Accessed 23 Oct 2019
7. Felgueiras, M.C., Cruz, N., Martins, F., Martins, R.: Buildings sustainability-the non-intrusive load-identification system contribution. J. Clean Energy Technol. **4**(5), 367–370 (2016)
8. Fischer, C.: Feedback on household electricity consumption: a tool for saving energy? Energ. Effi. **1**(1), 79–104 (2008)
9. P3 International: Kill-a-watt (2017). http://www.p3international.com/products/p4400.html. Accessed 24 Jan 2019
10. Kelly, J., Knottenbelt, W.: The UK-DALE dataset, domestic appliance-level electricity demand and whole-house demand from five UK homes. Sci. Data **2**, 150007 (2015)
11. Kolter, J.Z., Johnson, M.J.: REDD: a public data set for energy disaggregation research. In: Workshop on Data Mining Applications in Sustainability (SIGKDD), San Diego, CA, vol. 25, pp. 59–62 (2011)
12. Kriechbaumer, T., Jorde, D., Jacobsen, H.A.: Waveform signal entropy and compression study of whole-building energy datasets. In: Proceedings of the Tenth ACM International Conference on Future Energy Systems, e-Energy 2019, pp. 58–67. ACM (2019)
13. Kriechbaumer, T., Ul Haq, A., Kahl, M., Jacobsen, H.A.: Medal: a cost-effective high-frequency energy data acquisition system for electrical appliances. In: Proceedings of the Eighth International Conference on Future Energy Systems, e-Energy 2017, pp. 216–221. ACM (2017)
14. Scholl, P.M., Völker, B., Becker, B., Laerhoven, K.V.: A multi-media exchange format for time-series dataset curation. In: Kawaguchi, N., Nishio, N., Roggen, D., Inoue, S., Pirttikangas, S., Van Laerhoven, K. (eds.) Human Activity Sensing. SSAE, pp. 111–119. Springer, Cham (2019). https://doi.org/10.1007/978-3-030-13001-5_8
15. Völker, B., Scholl, P.M., Becker, B.: Semi-automatic generation and labeling of training data for non-intrusive load monitoring. In: Proceedings of the Tenth International Conference on Future Energy Systems, e-Energy 2019. ACM (2019)
16. Völker, B., Scholls, P.M., Schubert, T., Becker, B.: Towards the fusion of intrusive and non-intrusive load monitoring: a hybrid approach. In: Proceedings of the Ninth International Conference on Future Energy Systems, e-Energy 2018, pp. 436–438. ACM (2018)

Construction and Validation of a Low-Cost System for Indoor Air Quality Measurements in Livestock Facilities

Leonardo Delgado[1]($\boxtimes$), Manuel Feliciano[2], Laercio Frare[3], Leonardo Furst[1], Paulo Leitão[4], and Getúlio Igrejas[4]

[1] Instituto Politécnico de Bragança, Campus de Santa Apolónia, 5300-253 Bragança, Portugal
leonardo12delgado@gmail.com
[2] Centro de Investigação de Montanha (CIMO), Instituto Politécnico de Bragança, Campus de Santa Apolónia, 5300-253 Bragança, Portugal
[3] Department of Biological and Environmental Sciences (DAAMB), Universidade Tecnológica Federal do Paraná, Campus Medianeira, Medianeira, PR 85884000, Brazil
[4] Research Centre in Digitalization and Intelligent Robotics (CeDRI), Instituto Politécnico de Bragança, Campus de Santa Apolónia, 5300-253 Bragança, Portugal

Abstract. In recent years, there has been an increase in demand for food of animal origin. The number of intensive production systems such as pig and poultry farming has been increasing more and more and exerting great impacts on the environment, due to a large amount of particulate material and gaseous pollutants that are generated within these facilities. Thus, low-cost devices emerge as a cheap alternative that provides farmers with information on indoor air quality in its facilities. However, it is important that these devices make precise and accurate measurements, providing reliable concentration readings. Therefore, the objective of this study is the construction and validation of a low-cost system capable of measuring, storing and sending, via the mobile network, the concentrations of hydrogen sulfide, ammonia, carbon dioxide, $PM_{2.5}$, PM_{10}, temperature, and relative humidity. Preliminary inter-comparison tests showed that the built system had a reliable behavior in relation to all variables, even though the CO_2 sensor was the one with the highest determination coefficient. The built device is able to provide continuous monitoring of atmospheric pollutants concentrations, at low cost and with simple handling.

Keywords: Livestock · Sensors · Indoor air quality

1 Introduction

In spite of the large adaptation of the intensive production, many livestock buildings such as those adopted successfully in monogastric species (e.g., pigs and poultries) are concentrated in a single point [1]. Between 1961 and 2017, there was a worldwide increase in pig production from 400 million to almost 1 billion heads per year, while poultry production rose from 3.9 to 22.8 billion annually [2].

J. L. Afonso et al. (Eds.): SESC 2019, LNICST 315, pp. 232–245, 2020.
https://doi.org/10.1007/978-3-030-45694-8_18

These intensive production systems have increasingly impacted the environment, with the emission of greenhouse gases (GHG's) [3], as well as contributing to the contamination of the outdoor and indoor air, due to the emission of pollutants as ammonia (NH_3) [4], particulate matter less than 10 μm ($PM_{2.5}$, PM_{10}) [5], hydrogen sulfide (H_2S) [6] and carbon dioxide (CO_2) [7].

Long-term exposures to these substances within these livestock facilities can cause respiratory complications in agricultural workers as well as in the animals living there, which can result in severe diseases [8]. Many studies report the importance of the use of indoor air quality (IAQ) measurement and control devices, in order to determine the concentrations of pollutants and to develop mitigation measures and technologies [9].

Despite the importance of monitoring indoor levels of those pollutants, the conventional solutions (e.g., gas analyzers, dust monitors) can often reach acquisition costs, routine calibration and maintenance exceeding tens of thousands of euros, requiring also large spaces for their installation as well as skilled labor, which dissuades facilities managers to perform regular monitoring [10, 11].

In this context, the use of low-cost devices can bring with them innovative contributions, such as the integration of these systems into a wide network of sensors and computational technologies, and, therefore, facilitating the detection of pollutants present in the indoor air of livestock facilities [10, 12]. One of the great advantages of low-cost gas sensors is the wide variety of options available on the market, being catalytic, thermal, electrochemical, optical, infrared, semiconductors and surface acoustic wave type sensors, and its different performance characteristics, such as sensitivity, selectivity, detection limit, response time, among others aspects [13].

An important feature that must be considered when constructing indoor air pollutant monitoring systems with low-cost sensors is the cross-sensitivity between interfering gases and the gas of interest. As shown in the literature [14], the development of many gas detection systems is limited because the sensors are susceptible to undergo interferences from other gases. Therefore, because they are low-cost devices, inadequate values of pollutants can be measured, deceiving system users and limiting their use in higher precision applications. In such cases it is necessary to validate the sensors, performing calibrations in the laboratory and in the facilities, using statistical procedures to guarantee product quality [15].

Therefore, the objective of this work is the construction and validation of a system composed of a network of low-cost integrated sensors for pig and poultry facilities capable of remotely registering, storing and sending data to a server of the concentrations of pollutants obtained over time.

2 Device Architecture

For the construction and development of the low-cost monitoring system, semiconductor, electrochemical and optical sensors were integrated to detect the gases of interest and to measure the temperature and relative humidity of the indoor air of the livestock facilities. Along with the sensors, the system integrates modules for visualization, storage, and data transmission over GSM/GPRS network to a data server.

All the sensors used, with the exception of the NH_3 sensor, are digital. This means that the interface between the processing board and the sensors is easier to make, since they have a pre-calibration and do not require analog to digital conversion procedures. For the NH$_3$ sensor the Arduino internal Analog to Digital Converter (ADC) was used to obtain the digital value of the ammonia concentration.

An Arduino Mega 2560 board was used for processing and converting the data with perceptible responses to the user. It is possible to have an overview of the system in Fig. 1. The modules and sensors used will be detailed below.

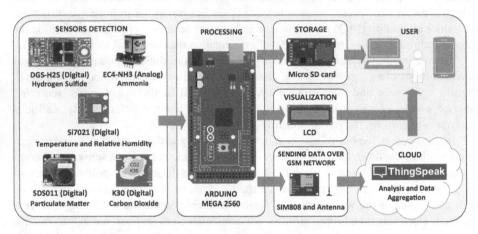

Fig. 1. Overview of the prototype architecture.

2.1 Modules and Sensors Used

All gas sensors chosen were based on the concentration ranges reported in different studies, performed by other authors, conducted in pig and poultry facilities. It is possible to observe in Table 1 the limits found in the indoor air of these facilities and the limit of operation of the chosen sensors.

Hydrogen sulfide sensor DGS-H$_2$S is an electrochemical sensor from Spec Sensors, with a measurement range of 0 to 10 ppm and a resolution of 10 ppb. The lifetime of the sensor depends on the operating conditions and can vary from 5 to 10 years. It is a sensor little affected by cross-sensitivity caused by other gases.

Ammonia sensor EC4-NH$_3$-100 is an electrochemical sensor from Pewatron. It has a measuring range of 100 ppm and a resolution of 0.1 ppm, with a life expectancy of 24 months. As a great benefit, it does not show cross-sensitivity to other gases. To facilitate the connection of the sensor to the system, an Easyboard was used, in which the sensor is connected. This module offers a stable voltage, digital results, and temperature measurement which the user can select as the measurement channel.

Carbon dioxide sensor K30 is an optical sensor of CO$_2$ meter, has an operating range of 0 to 10,000 ppm, with a resolution of 30 ppm. It is a sensor that comes with an integrated algorithm capable of self-correcting over a period of time. The principle of operation of this device is Non-dispersive Infrared (NDIR), therefore it does not present cross-sensitivity since only the ideal wavelength to absorb the molecules of CO$_2$ is deviated (band 4.28 μm) [23].

Table 1. Concentration range of pollutants in pig and poultry housing found in the literature.

Air pollutant and environmental parameters	Sensor (Operation range)	Range of indoor air pollutant at pig housing	Range of indoor air pollutant at poultry housing	Unit
Hydrogen Sulfide	DGS-H_2S (0–10,000)	15–6,180 [16]	30–2,240 [16]	ppb
Ammonia	EC4-NH_3-100 (0–100)	2–87 [16, 17]	1–50 [16, 18]	ppm
Carbon Dioxide	K30 (0–10,000)	1,000–5,000 [16]	500–3,000 [16, 18]	ppm
$PM_{2.5}$	SDS011 (0–1,000)	15.2–415 [17, 19]	81–380 [18]	$\mu g \cdot m^{-3}$
PM_{10}		116–1,746 [17, 19]	135–5,003 [18, 20]	
Temperature	Si7021-A20 (−40–125)	18.1–29.4 [21, 22]	16.2–29.1 [22]	°C
Relative humidity	Si7021-A20 (0–100)	41.0–84.0 [21, 22]	41.2–92.9 [22]	%

SDS011 particulate sensor, also an optical sensor and manufactured by Nova Fitness Co. Ltd., has detection range from 0–1,000 $\mu g \cdot m^{-3}$ and a resolution of 0.3 $\mu g \cdot m^{-3}$. It detects both $PM_{2.5}$ and PM_{10} and the lifetime of this sensor is 8,000 h. In the lower region of the sensor, there is a coupled fan that assists in the passage of the particles.

Temperature (T) and relative humidity (RH) Si7021-A20 sensor, is a semiconductor sensor from Sparkfun, operates with a measuring range of 0 to 100% for RH and 3% resolution, and from −40 °C to 125 °C with a resolution of 0.4 °C. This device comes with factory calibration data stored in non-volatile memory, so it is not necessary to recalibrate or make changes to its operating code.

In conjunction with the sensors, three modules have been installed: a liquid crystal display for local visualization of the detected gases, particulate matter, temperature and relative humidity values; a micro SD card module that communicates through a file system to record all measured values locally (operates as backup system); and a GPRS/GSM Quad-band SIM808 module that allows sending data to a remote server (ThingSpeak), via mobile network using a SIM card, and that can operate in the frequency bands 850/900/1,800/1,900 MHz which allows its use worldwide.

2.2 Cross-Sensitivity

As the most relevant devices in this study, the EC4-NH_3-100 ammonia sensor and DGS-H_2S hydrogen sulfide sensor were chosen because of little or no typical response to other gases that may be present at the site of study. According to manufacturers of the sensors Spec Sensors [24] and Pewatron [25], concentrations of some pollutants on the H_2S and NH_3 sensors were applied with the purpose of verifying the reading for each gaseous substance that may interfere with the reading of the gas of interest. The measurements observed for both sensors in the presence of other compounds, is shown in Table 2.

Table 2. DGS-H_2S and EC4-NH_3-100 cross-sensitivity.

Compounds (molecular formula)	Applied concentration H_2S [24] sensor (ppm)	Typical response H_2S sensor [24] (ppm H_2S)	Applied concentration NH_3 [25] sensor (ppm)	Typical response NH_3 [25] sensor (ppm NH_3)
Hydrogen Sulfide (H_2S)	10	10	50	0
Chlorine (Cl_2)	10	−2.2	1	0
Nitrogen Dioxide (NO_2)	10	−2	–	–
Sulfur Dioxide (SO_2)	20	1.7	–	–
Nitric Oxide (NO)	50	1.2	–	–
Carbon Monoxide (CO)	400	1.1	100	0
Carbon Dioxide (CO_2)	–	–	5,000	0
Ozone (O_3)	5	−0.9	–	–
Methane (CH_4)	500	0.1	–	–
Ammonia (NH_3)	100	0.1	100	100
N-Heptane (C_7H_{16})	500	<0.5	–	–
Hydrogen (H_2)	–	–	100	0
Isopropanol (C_3H_5OH)	–	–	1,000	0

3   Validation of the Low-Cost Monitoring System

For a preliminary validation of the prototype, the equipment was submitted to a controlled environment in which it was possible to have greater control of the gases generated by the manure. The variables controlled in the test were ammonia, carbon dioxide, temperature and relative humidity.

Manure was placed inside a smaller box that contained holes and, in turn, this box was placed inside a larger box along with the built prototype (collecting data from 1 in 1 min) and with other commercially available equipment used as 'reference' instruments – the multi-gas analyzer Gasera One and the DirectSense® IQ-610 probe.

The multi-gas analyzer Gasera One was coupled to the box through a hose, by using a ¼″ Teflon tubing. After the gas is drawn by the pump into the instrument, concentrations are measured by means of acoustic detection, based on the cantilever-enhanced photoacoustic. Concentrations are obtained and readings are shown to the user through a display [26]. Gasera was programmed to collect data in 3 min periods and to measure the concentration of substances of interest, such as NH_3.

The DirectSense® IQ-610 probe was placed inside the box and it operates through the Non-dispersive Infrared principle. This probe is connected to the PDA Socket® SoMo 650-DX.

Despite not having been performed the analysis in a livestock facility, these environments are very dynamic due to the animals it contains, therefore, many factors influence the variation of the concentrations of pollutants, such as the flow of ventilation, the movements, breaths and digestive processes of these animals. Thus, it was chosen sampling periods of 1 min. All the experiment built can be visualized in Fig. 2.

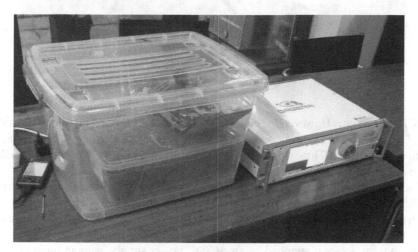

Fig. 2. Controlled environment built for data validation.

All data obtained from the 'reference' equipment and prototype were worked on the Microsoft Excel 2016 spreadsheet. This way, it is possible to make comparisons of the sensitivity of low-cost sensors by comparing them with the detection of 'reference' equipment as a function of time. Arithmetic averages were also performed every 10 min, and thus, the best range was chosen to determine the equation of the line and the coefficient of determination R^2, and therefore to use this correction in the algorithm of the low-cost system developed.

4   Results and Discussion

The indoor air quality monitoring system for pig and poultry housing was built to meet two needs: low-cost sensors and modules and minimal interference with reactive gases that can be found in these facilities. Figure 3 shows the constructed prototype.

Thus, the values detected by the sensors are processed by the Arduino Mega board and stored on the 4 Gb micro SD card in a period of 1 min in the CSV format to facilitate the editing of the data in spreadsheets. The obtained concentrations can be viewed on

Fig. 3. IAQ system built for pig and poultry facilities.

the LCD in real time. However, the collected data is also sent over a mobile data network using General Packet Radio Service (GPRS) technology to a cloud. These values are sent to the Internet of Things (IoT) platform, called ThingSpeak. Therefore, the values can be aggregated, viewed, analyzed and downloaded by the user.

The operating conditions of the prototype are based on the conditions under which the installed sensors and modules can operate. Therefore, the system operates well between temperatures of 0 to 40 °C, a relative humidity of 15 to 90% and atmospheric pressure between 86 and 110 kPa.

The system power is supplied by an AC/DC power supply, with an input of 100 to 240 V AC 50/60 Hz and an output that is 9 V – 2 A. The typical measured average current consumed by the board with all sensors and modules is 710 mA, with consumption peaks of 2.25 A. The peaks are associated with the high-power consumption at startup of the SIM808 module.

The total cost for the purchase of the components and production of the prototype was €467.80. However, the cost could reach €371.38 if the cheaper sellers are selected. The maintenance of the system is based on the lifetime of the sensors. In the case of large-scale production, the circuit used in the prototype must be completely redesigned to become a single printed circuit board (PCB). Therefore, as soon as the microcontroller is integrated into the board, the rest of the components are easily incorporated and the production cost is further minimized, while remaining a well-finished and professional job.

Often the 'reference' equipment is characterized by a high price, due to its innovative technology employed and robustness. Typically, a 'reference' equipment used to analyze indoor pollutants can cost from €5,000 to €30,000 or more.

In some cases, it can be built using low cost sensors integrated into a PCB and sold at a high price (€5,000), but there is still an interfering pollutant. In other cases, there may be a patented technology that differentiates the gas and particle analyzer from other products on the market, plus great reliability, support, and removal of interfering pollutants, which will characterize the equipment at an even higher price ($>€30,000$).

Thus, the prototype built in this study is characterized as low-cost because the set of sensors and components used is 10 to 60 times cheaper than the 'reference' equipment.

The time spent learning on system construction and on code developing were 44 days, as shown in Table 3. The sensors chosen comply with Directive 2015/863/EU of the European Parliament and of the Council of the European Union [26], also known as RoHS 3, which deals with the restriction of the use of certain dangerous substances, such as lead, mercury, cadmium, etc., for the manufacture of electrical and electronic components.

Table 3. Expenses of the built system and time used for construction.

Components and sensors	Acquired price ($€$)	Lowest price available ($€$)	Time spent (days)
DGS-H_2S	63.55	63.55	4
K30	74.70	74.70	3
EC4-NH_3-100	90.00	90.00	6
SDS011	43.20	13.89	3
Si7021	9.95	1.22	2
SIM808 module	34.42	22.87	15
Arduino Mega 2560 + LCD and micro SD card modules	51.45	7.65	8
Other components[a]	100.53	97.50	3
Total	467.80	371.38	44

[a]Wire jumper, resistors, capacitors, BOB-12009, Easyboard adapter.

4.1 Data Validation

The process of validating data when designing a device is very important because it allows to verify the accuracy of the equipment. From the validation, it is also possible to carry out the calibration. In this way, the system built can delivery precise and reliable readings to the meat producers.

The two tests performed on the K30 CO_2 sensor, Fig. 4, even at different times of 8 h and 4 h 30 min, show us behavior similar to Graywolf, used as the 'reference' equipment. It is also verified in Fig. 4(a), that greater intensification occurred in the anaerobic digestion, due to the greater light exposure between 3 h and 5 h and near 7 h, as a consequence there was a higher CO_2 production, causing the sensor reaches its 10,000 ppm threshold during the test. However, in Fig. 4(b), due to less light exposure, smaller amounts of CO_2 were produced, peaking at 9,528 ppm with the 'reference' equipment.

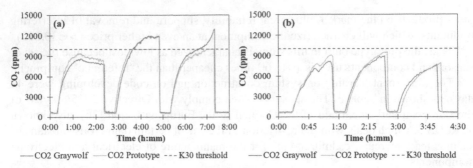

Fig. 4. Behavior of the K30 sensor and IQ-610 Graywolf equipment during (a) 8 h and (b) 4 h 30 min.

Based on the Graywolf and Prototype concentrations, it was possible to find the line equation, which will be used for correcting the prototype sensor reading, so that the detected values are closer to the equipment used as 'reference'. As shown in the Fig. 5(a) and (b) the coefficient of determination R^2 reached values higher than 0.998 in both cases. Even tested in different time periods, the line equation resembles in both experiments. The selected time range for performing the arithmetic mean in Fig. 5(a) was 0 to 2 h 15 min and in Fig. 5(b) from 0 to 1 h 20 min. However, the best linear fit was in the second test, with in R^2 of 0.9985.

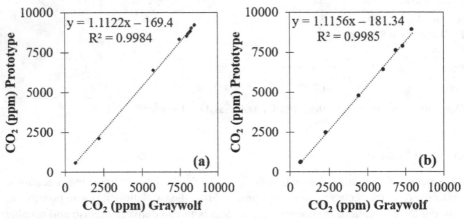

Fig. 5. Linear equation and coefficient of determination R^2 performed in (a) first test and (b) second test of the CO_2 sensor and Graywolf.

During the first 8 h assay, the Si7021 air temperature sensor proved to be promising well, because the temperature ranged from 22 to 27 °C, while the Graywolf temperature ranged from 22 °C to 27 °C, Fig. 6(a). On contrary, for the relative humidity, there were a large deviation between both sensors, with the low-cost sensor ranging from 38 to 60%

and the 'reference' equipment ranged from 29 to 49%, Fig. 6(b). It is possible to verify in the first test that the Si7021 sensor presents coarse signals because the *int* data type was used to determine the T and RH variables, so the detected values are represented in their entire format.

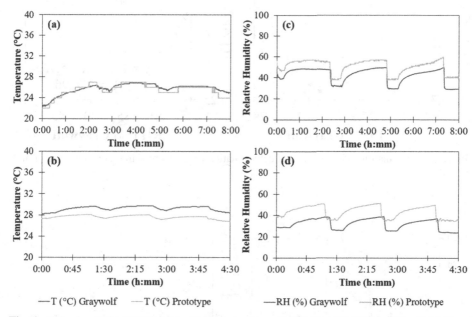

Fig. 6. Behavior of the Si7021 and reference equipment to (a) T and (b) HR in 8 h and (c) T and (d) RH in 4 h 30 min.

For the second 4 h 30 min test, the *int* data type was changed to *float*, improving the representation precision of the Si7021 obtained measurements. The detected temperature of the prototype varied from 27 °C to 28 °C, and that of the reference equipment from 28 to 30 °C, with a variation of 2 °C, this variation can happen due to the error of the sensor itself, not being significant (Fig. 6(c)). With regard to the relative humidity it ranged from 35% to 51% in the prototype, and from 24 to 39% in IQ-610 Graywolf (Fig. 6(d)).

From the second test, the linear equation was generated in order to adjust the temperature and relative humidity of the prototype Si7021 sensor, causing the adjusted values to approximate the values detected by the Graywolf equipment. Good coefficient of linear determination values were also generated, for T ($R^2 = 0.9692$, Fig. 7(a)) and for RH ($R^2 = 0.9296$, Fig. 7(b)). The range that best fit the data pairs X and Y in the linear regression for T was between 3 h and 4 h 30 min and for HR between 2 h 50 min and 3 h 50 min.

It is worth mentioning that the analysis only mirrors the values found for T between 23 to 29 °C and HR between 31 to 49%. Therefore, it will be necessary to subject the system built to regimes with large amplitudes of relative humidity and temperature to obtain an improved linear regression.

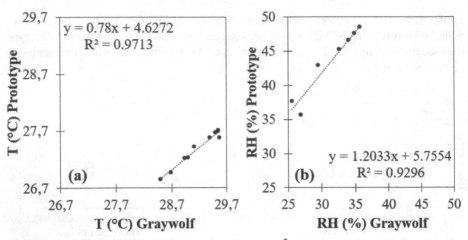

Fig. 7. Linear equation and coefficient of determination R^2 performed in second test to (a) T and (b) RH.

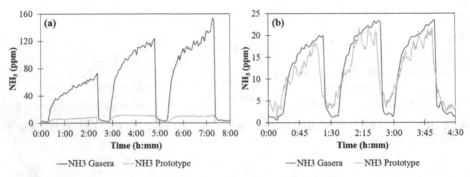

Fig. 8. Behavior of the EC4-NH$_3$-100 sensor relative to the reference equipment for the (a) first test and (b) second test.

Concerning the NH$_3$, the EC4-NH$_3$-100 sensor, during the 8 h test, showed maximum peaks of 12 ppm and minimum values close to zero, while the readings Gasera One reached much higher values, ranging from 2 to 154 ppm, Fig. 8(a). Theses higher values were expected as the test being carried out in the daytime period, with a great amount of sun light, causing a greater release of ammonia during the acidogenesis phase of a very intensified anaerobic digestion process [27, 28].

In the second test, the NH$_3$ sensor gain was adjusted to improved detection. Thus, according to Fig. 8(b), a promising improving in the detection of ammonia was observed, even with small abrupt variations. Because the second test was performed in an area of low light exposure, the low-cost sensor detection range was 1 to 21 ppm and the Gasera One varied from 1 to 23 ppm.

Linear regression was also used to find the equation that best fit the values acquired by the low-cost sensor. It is possible to observe an improvement in the coefficient of determination. In the first experiment $R^2 = 0.9573$, (Fig. 9(a)) and in the second $R^2 = 0.9805$, (Fig. 9(b)), demonstrating a better performance of the EC4-NH$_3$-100 sensor.

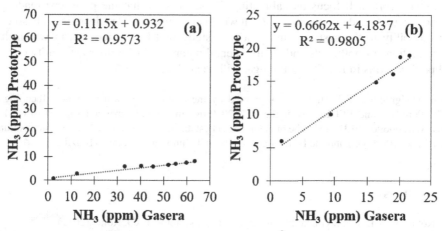

Fig. 9. Linear equation and coefficient of determination R^2 performed in (a) first test and (b) second test of the NH$_3$ sensor and Gasera.

The SDS011 particulate sensor has not yet been validated due to the construction of a suitable environment to perform a reliable inter-comparison experiment.

The hydrogen sulfide sensor DGS-H$_2$S will also be validated in a very near future by performing a multipoint calibration against a standard bottle of H$_2$S.

No tests were performed on livestock facilities because the equipment was only in the construction, validation, calibration phase. Subsequently, the prototyping phase will be carried out and then tests will be carried out on pig and poultry farms.

5 Conclusion

With the scientific and technological evolution, new possibilities have arisen to build more compact and low-cost gas detection systems, which consequently improve the management of the internal air quality of livestock installations. These devices provide the farmer with more efficient control of the concentrations of gaseous and particulate contaminants that are formed and released within these facilities, enabling the development of mitigating solutions to reduce environmental and health impacts.

The monitoring system built is capable of detecting particulate matter (PM$_{2.5}$ and PM$_{10}$), and gaseous pollutants such as hydrogen sulfide, ammonia, carbon dioxide, in addition to measuring environmental parameters such as temperature and relative humidity.

Through the process of data validation, it was possible to visualize a great similarity between prototype and 'reference' equipment readings, as shown by the coefficient of determination of each sensor. The carbon dioxide sensor is the one that presents the best coefficient of determination $R^2 = 0.9985$, the other sensors presented accurate results. From the line equation, corrections will be made to the algorithm in all sensors. The objective is to approximate the detected values of the built equipment to the values of the reference equipment.

Future work will focus on calibrating the sensors so that the prototype readings provide accurate and precise responses. It will also be encapsulated, bringing robustness and durability to the system. Finally, a case study will be carried out, in which the concentrations of pollutants and environmental parameters of indoor air quality of pig and poultry farms in Brazil and Portugal will be analyzed.

Acknowledgments. This study was supported by the Fundação para a Ciência e Tecnologia (FCT, Portugal) and FEDER under the PT2020 Program through financial support to CIMO (UID/AGR/00690/2013) and by the bilateral project established between the Polytechnic Institute of Bragança (Portugal) and the Federal University of Technology – Paraná (Brazil).

References

1. Robinson, T.P., et al.: Global livestock production systems. FAO, Rome (2011)
2. Food and Agriculture Organization of the United Nations Statistics Database. http://www.fao.org/faostat/en/#home. Accessed 07 Feb 2019
3. Arrieta, E.M., González, A.D.: Energy and carbon footprints of chicken and pork from intensive production systems in Argentina. Sci. Total Environ. **673**, 20–28 (2019)
4. Leip, A., et al.: Impacts of European livestock production: nitrogen, sulphur, phosphorus and greenhouse gas emissions, land-use, water eutrophication and biodiversity. Environ. Res. Lett. **10**(11), 1–13 (2015)
5. Cambra-López, M., Aarnink, A.J., Zhao, Y., Calvet, S., Torres, A.G.: Airborne particulate matter from livestock production systems: a review of an air pollution problem. Environ. Pollut. **158**(1), 1–17 (2010)
6. Zheng, S., Jin, X., Chen, M., Shi, Q., Zhang, H., Xu, S.: Hydrogen sulfide exposure induces jejunum injury via CYP450s/ROS pathway in broilers. Chemosphere **214**, 25–34 (2019)
7. Ecim-Djuric, O., Topisirovic, G.: Energy efficiency optimization of combined ventilation systems in livestock buildings. Energy Build. **42**(8), 1165–1171 (2010)
8. Banhazi, T., Aland, A., Hartung, J.: Air Quality and Livestock Farming. Taylor & Francis Group, London (2018)
9. Ni, J., Heber, A.J., Darr, M.J., Lim, T.T., Diehl, C.A., Bogan, B.W.: Air quality monitoring and on-site computer system for livestock and poultry environment studies. Trans. ASABE **52**(3), 937–947 (2009)
10. Bamodu, O., Osebor, F., Xia, L., Cheshmehzangi, A., Tang, L.: Indoor environment monitoring based on humidity conditions using a low-cost sensor network. Energy Procedia **145**, 464–471 (2018)
11. Ropkins, K., Colvile, R.N.: Critical Review of Air Quality Monitoring Technologies for Urban Traffic Management and Control (UTMC) Systems. Urban Traffic Management & Control (UK) (2000)
12. Ni, J., Heber, A.J., Darr, M.J., Lim, T.T., Diehl, C.A., Bogan, B.W.: Air quality monitoring and data acquisition for livestock and poultry environment studies. In: Iowa State University Digital Repository (eds.) Livestock Environment VIII - Proceedings of the 8th International Symposium, pp. 1021–1028 (2008)

13. Yunusa, Z., Hamidon, M.N., Kaiser, A., Awang, Z.: Gas sensors: a review. Sens. Transducers **168**(4), 61–75 (2014)
14. Manap, H., Muda, R., O'Keeffe, S., Lewis, E.: Ammonia sensing and cross sensitivity evaluation with atmosphere gases using optical fiber sensor. Procedia Chem. **1**(1), 959–962 (2009)
15. Rai, A.C., et al.: End-user perspective of low-cost sensors for outdoor air pollution monitoring. Sci. Total Environ. **607–608**, 691–705 (2017)
16. Heyden, C.V., Demeyer, P., Volcke, E.I.: Mitigating emissions from pig and poultry housing facilities through air scrubbers and biofilters: state-of-the-art and perspectives. Biosys. Eng. **134**, 74–93 (2015)
17. Shen, D., et al.: Distribution and physicochemical properties of particulate matter in swine confinement barns. Environ. Pollut. **250**, 746–753 (2019)
18. Winkel, A., Mosquera, J., Aarnink, A.J., Koerkamp, P.W., Ogink, N.W.: Evaluation of oil spraying systems and air ionisation systems for abatement of particulate matter emission in commercial poultry houses. Biosys. Eng. **150**, 104–122 (2016)
19. Ransbeeck, N.V., Langenhove, H.V., Demeyer, P.: Indoor concentrations and emissions factors of particulate matter, ammonia and greenhouse gases for pig fattening facilities. Biosys. Eng. **116**(4), 518–528 (2013)
20. Melse, R.W., Hol, J.M.: Measures to reduce fine dust emission from poultry houses: biofiltration of exhaust air of a manure drying system at a barn for laying hens. Report No. 498. Livestock Research, Wageningen University & Research, Netherlands (2012). (in Dutch)
21. Chmielowiec-Korzeniowska, A.: The concentration of volatile organic compound (VOCs) in pig farm air. Ann. Agric. Environ. Med. **16**, 249–256 (2009)
22. Cambra-López, M., Winkel, A., Mosquera, J., Ogink, N.W., Aarnink, A.J.: Comparison between light scattering and gravimetric samplers for PM10 mass concentration in poultry and pig houses. Atmos. Environ. **111**, 20–27 (2015)
23. Kwon, J., Ahn, G., Kim, G., Kim, J., Kim, H.: A study on NDIR-based CO_2 sensor to apply remote air quality monitoring system. In: 2009 ICCAS-SICE, Fukuoka, Japan, pp. 1683–1687 (2009)
24. SPEC Sensors. https://www.spec-sensors.com/wp-content/uploads/2017/01/DGS-H2S-968-036.pdf. Accessed 15 Feb 2019
25. Pewatron.   https://www.pewatron.com/fileadmin/products/datasheets/188/EC4-NH3-1_1620-21570-0019-E-0217.pdf. Accessed 15 Feb 2019
26. European Parliament and of the Council of the European Union, Directive 2015/863/EU - List of substances subject to restriction. Official Journal of the European Communities, Brussels, 31 March 2015
27. Cheng, J.: Biomass to Renewable Energy Processes. CRC Press, Taylor & Francis Group, Boca Raton (2018)
28. Horan, N.J., Yaser, A.Z., Wid, N. (eds.): Anaerobic Digestion Processes: Applications and Effluent Treatment, 1st edn. Springer, Singapore (2018). https://doi.org/10.1007/978-981-10-8129-3

Acoustic Simultaneous Localization and Mapping Using a Sensor-Rich Smartphone

Xi Yu Song[1(✉)], Mei Wang[2], Hong-Bing Qiu[1], and Xueming Wei[1]

[1] Ministry of Education Key Laboratory of Cognitive Radio and Information Processing, Guilin University of Electronic Technology, Guangxi Zhuang Autonomous Region, Guilin 541004, China
{songxiyu,qiuhb}@guet.edu.cn, 31696712@qq.com
[2] College of Information Science and Engineering, Guilin University of Technology, Guilin 541004, China

Abstract. The problem of simultaneous localization and mapping (SLAM) has been extensively studied by using a variety of specialized sensors. In this paper, we show that the SLAM could be realized using a sensor-rich smartphone. We assume that an indoor pedestrian always carries a sounding smartphone and the pedestrian moves autonomously inside a room. At every step, the loudspeaker of the smartphone produces a chirp pulse (frequency band is in the upper of human hearing area), the microphone of this smartphone registers the echoes, and the inertial sensors record the accelerometer and gyroscope readings, then the position of the moving pedestrian and the geometry map of the room are done simultaneously. However, when in a rectangular room of regular shape, reconstructing the room geometry at each sound source position is quite redundant. To avoid this redundancy and improve the sound source localization performance, we address SLAM by Matrix Analysis-based geometry estimation, and then this information is applied to the real-time positioning requirements taking the advantage of multi-source information fusion concept. Finally, we show the effectiveness of the proposed SLAM method by experiments with real measured acoustic events, the result fully demonstrates that the proposed SLAM method could be easily implemented using the smartphone carried by the pedestrian.

Keywords: Room geometry reconstruction · Smartphone-based self-positioning · Simultaneous localization and mapping

1 Introduction

The goal of simultaneous localization and mapping (SLAM) is to reconstruct both the trajectory of the moving target and the map of the environment. Studies on SLAM are presented a lot for example in wifi [1], ranging [2], visual [3] and their fusion [4, 5]. However, SLAM solution based on echoes are minimal [6]. Three problems in this field have recently received considerable attention [7]: the first one is room geometry reconstruction, the second one is self-localization of the moving target, and the third one is the simultaneous localization and mapping.

© ICST Institute for Computer Sciences, Social Informatics and Telecommunications Engineering 2020
Published by Springer Nature Switzerland AG 2020. All Rights Reserved
J. L. Afonso et al. (Eds.): SESC 2019, LNICST 315, pp. 246–253, 2020.
https://doi.org/10.1007/978-3-030-45694-8_19

Room geometry reconstruction is a popular and useful topic in acoustic SLAM. Many estimation works of the room geometry, or the reflective surfaces, have been proposed. However, to easily distinguish the echo orders used in room geometry reconstruction, most of these works rely on microphone arrays, which is high cost and not easy to carry with [8, 9]. Inspired by works introduced in [10–12], which show that room geometry reconstruction can be achieved by one single microphone and only one sound source, we realize that the room geometry reconstruction work could also be conducted using a sensor-rich smartphone, which could be regarded as a setup with colocated source and receiver since the distance between them (source and receiver in a smartphone) is very close.

With the reconstruction results, one can enhance source localization performance, i.e., contraction positioning range from the room level [13] to the sub-meter level [14]. In this work, we proposed a method of combining infrastructure-free indoor acoustic self-positioning with pedestrian dead reckoning (PDR) self-positioning, which verifies the rationality of PDR results through the acoustic constraint between a sound source and its image sources.

The solution for the acoustic SLAM seems to always jointly localizing target in an unknown room and estimating the room geometry from echoes. It should be necessary for a robot in the rooms of complex construction, irregular shape and severe non-line of sight situation. However, when in a rectangular room of regular shape, reconstructing the room geometry at each sound source position is quite redundant. How to avoid this redundancy and improve the sound source localization performance is what we aim to. Instead of estimating the room geometry on every single step of the moving target, we address SLAM by Matrix Analysis-based geometry estimation, and then room geometry information is applied to the real-time positioning requirements. Moreover, the multi-source information fusion concept is applied to simpler the single channel acoustic SLAM problem. Finally, we show that those acoustic SLAM problems can be solved by taking advantage of a sensor-rich smartphone.

2 Theory

We define a room to be a K-faced rectangular room, the pedestrian holding a smartphone in this room is modeled as a sound source (the loudspeaker of the user smartphone), for ease of explanation, pedestrian and sound source are hereafter equivalently used in this paper. We worked in two-dimensional (2D) space, ignoring the floor and the ceiling, given $K = 4$. Image source model proposed by Allen and Berkley [15] is adopted to model room acoustics, as shown in Fig. 1.

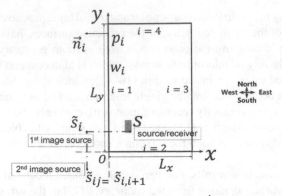

Fig. 1. Illustration of the image source model for 1st and 2nd -order images. One corner of the room denoted by O is taken as the original point. Sound source denoted by S is placed at an unknown initial position, wall index i is marked in anti-clockwise order. $p_i, i = 1, \ldots, K$, is an arbitrary point on wall w_i. n_i is the outward pointing normal vector of wall w_i. $\tilde{s}_i$ is the 1st -order image source of S corresponding to wall w_i. $\tilde{s}_{ij}$ is the 1st -order image source of $\tilde{s}_i$ corresponding to the $(i + 1)$ st wall. $[L_x, L_y]$ is the unknown room size, i.e., the required room geometry information.

2.1 Matrix Analysis-Based Room Geometry Reconstruction

When the loudspeaker S of the smartphone chirps in an indoor environment, the smartphone microphone M records both the direct path of the sound and its reflections from the walls. We set up the link between the 1st and 2nd -order images as described in [10] and use the same notation:

$$Q = A^2 E + E A^2 - 2 A N^T N A. \tag{1}$$

Where $N \overset{\text{def}}{=} [n_1, \ldots, n_K]$ denotes the normal matrix, and is easy to be determined by the geometry directions, $A = diag(a_1, \ldots, a_K)$, $a_i = \|\tilde{s}_i\|$. It is well known all the early reflections should be within 0.05 s after the source stops sounding, to simplify the processing of the 1st and 2nd -order echo measurements for A and Q, we adopt the generalized cross correlation (GCC) given by the phase transform (PHAT) in the time domain [16] to separate arrivals that were close in time.

We assume that the pedestrian sounds at the beginning point, $R(\tau)_{s,r}$ represents the GCC-PHAT, the subscript s and r represents the emitting and receiving signals, respectively. To reduce the number of measurements, the first $M = 0.2 f_s$ peaks of $R(\tau)_{s,r}$ are chosen to form the peak combination cells $\mathcal{C}_{1st}$ and $\mathcal{C}_{2st}$, where f_s is the sample frequency:

$$\mathcal{C}_{1st} = C_M^K, \quad \mathcal{C}_{2st} = C_M^{K(K-1)/2}. \tag{2}$$

Each cell element in C_{1st} is used to compose A, and each cell element in C_{2st} is used to compose Q with a form of $Q = \left(\|\tilde{s}_{ij}\|^2 \right)$, which means Q has the 2nd-order delays as its elements. Match the A and Q using Eq. (1), and hold the A if this equation succeeds. Thus, we have A and Q as:

$$A \leftarrow diag[\left\| c * \left(\frac{C_{1st}(m)}{f_s} \right) \right\|, \quad m = 1, \ldots, M. \tag{3}$$

$$Q \leftarrow \left(\|C_{2st}(m)\|^2 \right), \quad m = 1, \ldots, M. \tag{4}$$

Where c is the sound speed. Once the A is confirmed, the required room geometry information $[L_x, L_y]$ and the position of the initial position $S(x, y)$ of S could be obtained:

$$L_x = (\|\tilde{s}_1\| + \|\tilde{s}_3\|)/2, \, L_y = (\|\tilde{s}_2\| + \|\tilde{s}_4\|)/2. \tag{5}$$

$$S(x, y) = S(\|\tilde{s}_1\|/2, \|\tilde{s}_2\|/2). \tag{6}$$

2.2 Self-localization of the Moving Target

Even though the reconstruction could generate the every position estimation of the moving pedestrian, the matching process of A and Q from C_{1st} and C_{2st} is very time-consuming. Therefore, we only carry out such analysis at the very beginning of the moving pedestrian self- localization, then the results of one-time geometry estimation and the initial position of sound source will be used as the known priori for moving pedestrian self-localization. Actually, these results are the necessary condition of our prior work (about moving pedestrian self-localization) introduced in [14]. Here, we give a brief review of the moving pedestrian self-localization process. According to pedestrian dead reckoning (PDR) model, the position of S at time $t + 1$ could be inferred by the position of S at time t with the step length L_{tra} and the heading angular θ as

$$S_{t+1}(x) = S_t(x) + L_{tra}cos \, \theta. \tag{7}$$

$$S_{t+1}(y) = S_t(y) + L_{tra}sin \, \theta. \tag{8}$$

Where $S_t(x)$ and $S_t(y)$ are the $x - axis$ and $y - axis$ position of S at time t, when $t = 0$, it means S is on the initial position $S(x, y)$. Thus, with the isosceles trapezoid model (ITM) introduced in [6], the 1st -order echo measurements can be concluded as

$$\begin{cases} r_{m_{t+1,i}} = r_{m_{t,1}} \pm 2L_{tra}cos\theta, i = 1, 3, S_{t+1}(x) > S_t(x) \\ r_{m_{t+1,i}} = r_{m_{t,1}} \pm 2L_{tra}sin\theta, i = 2, 4, S_{t+1}(y) > S_t(y) \\ r_{m_{t+1,i}} = r_{m_{t,1}} \mp 2L_{tra}cos\theta, i = 1, 3, S_{t+1}(x) < S_t(x) \\ r_{m_{t+1,i}} = r_{m_{t,1}} \mp 2L_{tra}sin\theta, i = 2, 4, S_{t+1}(y) < S_t(y) \end{cases} \tag{9}$$

Where $r_{m_{t,i}}$ is the distance between S and its 1st -order image source for the ith wall at time t. Here, $i = 1$ refers specifically to the west wall, thus $r_{m_{t,1}} = 2S_t(x)$. $r_{m_{t+1,i}}$ is the distance between S and its 1st -order image source for the ith wall at time $t + 1$.

However, the widely used PDR method only provides a relative position estimate, with its accuracy degrading over time due to accumulative error. Thus, the adaptive step length algorithm presented by Shin et al. [17] and a heading correction method similar to the one presented by Deng et al. [18] are adopted to alleviate acumulative error impact. Furthermore, our proposed Sound Pressure Level Constraint with the help of room geometry information $[L_x, L_y]$ can verify the rationality of PDR results. Finally, pedestrian position value $\bar{S}_t$ is computed by the Levenberg–Marquardt algorithm-based weighted nonlinear least squares [19]:

$$\bar{S}_t = arg\min_{S_t} \varepsilon(S_t) \tag{10}$$

$$\varepsilon(S_t) = \left(d\left(r_{m_{t,k}}\right) - d\left(r_{e_{t,k}}\right)\right)^T * D^{-1} * \left(d\left(r_{m_{t,k}}\right) - d\left(r_{e_{t,k}}\right)\right) \tag{11}$$

where $(\cdot)^T$ is the transpose operation, $(\cdot)^{-1}$ is the inverse operation, and D is the noise covariance matrix. $D = \sigma^2 I_{K-1}$, where σ^2 is the noise covariance and I is the identity matrix. We refer readers to [14] for more details about $r_{e_{t,k}}$ and $r_{m_{t,k}}$.

3   Experiments

To verify the proposed approach, a field test was carried out on the cloister on Level 5 of the Library building, Jinji Campus, GUET, Guilin, Guangxi Zhuang Autonomous Region, China. The geometry of the cloister consists of labs, offices and classrooms, as shown in Fig. 2. The four sides of the library cloister are doors, glass windows, and walls; the ceiling is mainly glass and with steel stent supports; and the floor is covered with ordinary tile. The whole cloister is a rectangular ring. The cloister size was $[L_x, L_y]_{real} = [19, 35]$. The beginning point was set at $S(x, y) = [1.5, 9]$.

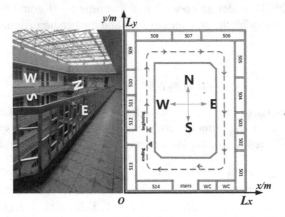

Fig. 2. Illustration of the fifth corridor of the Jinji Campus Library in GUET. GUET: Guilin University of Electronic Technology. The dashed lines are the reference walking lines. A small green triangle dot denotes the beginning point and a red one denotes the ending point. The dominant directions are denoted as E: East, S: South, W: West, N: North. (Color figure online)

To evaluate the performance of our approach when actual obstacles are present, especially in indoor situations, where pedestrians walk, all testing data collection took place during different days covering different times of the day. During the collection, students and staffs walked around normally as usual.

The data collection tool used in this experiment was a Huawei Rongyao 7 smartphone installed with a chirp application developed by our team and already authorized by China National Intellectual Property Administration, which was used to emit and store the chirp sound signal. The chirp sample frequency was set as $f_s = 44.1$ kHz, the duration was $T = 0.006$ s, the lower frequency was $f_0 = 16$ kHz, the upper frequency was $f_1 = 22$ kHz, and the emitting interval was 0.3 s. The PDR sample frequency was set as $f_{pdr} = 20$ Hz.

With the Matrix Analysis-based Room Geometry Reconstruction method, we get the self-localization trajectory of the moving target as shown in red dot line in Fig. 3. The data in Table 1 shows the differences between the true value and the estimated value, and confirms the performance of the proposed method.

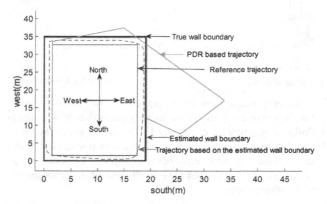

Fig. 3. Performance illustration of the proposed acoustic SLAM.

Table 1. Comparison of reconstruction results.

Parameters	True value	Estimated value	Errors
Room geometry information $[L_x, L_y]$ (m)	[19, 35]	[19.2, 34.7]	[0.2, 0.3]
Position of beginning point $S(x, y)$ (m)	[1.5, 9]	[1.2, 9]	[0.3, 0]

From the results shown in Fig. 3, we can infer the following conclusions:

① The output of the PDR trajectory (the green line) is continuous and has a similar shape to the reference trajectory (the blue line), but as time increased and the number of pedestrian steps increased, accumulative errors occurred in the accelerometer and gyroscope, resulting in positioning failure.

② Although the horizontal error of room reconstruction is 0.2 m and the vertical error is 0.3 m, the estimated wall boundary (the red line) is very close to the true one (the black line); If you simply use the indoor map application, this effect can already meet the application needs.

③ When this estimated room geometry information $\left[L_x, L_y\right]_{estd}$ is applied in source positioning, the tracking trajectory (the red dot line) is always consistent with the trend of the reference trajectory.

④ Despite there is difference between the estimated wall boundary and the true wall boundary, the positioning trajectory (the red dot line) under the estimated wall boundary is still within the effective range of the true wall boundary. Moreover, error distribution depicted in Fig. 4 shows that the source positioning accuracy belongs to the decimeter level, which can meet the application needs of indoor SLAM robots and service robots.

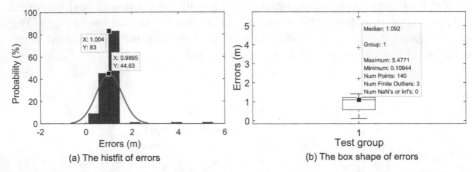

(a) The histfit of errors   (b) The box shape of errors

Fig. 4. Analysis of the proposed system errors. (a) is histfit of positioning errors, it shows the error probability distribution of every step of the moving pedestrian. 83% of the positioning error is around 1.0 m. Positioning errors far exceeding 1.0 m correspond to the three outliers in (b). They are related to the last two turns of the estimated trajectory (the red dot line) shown in Fig. 2. The cause of the outliers is the cumulative error of the smartphone's low cost gyroscope. However, the mean error of as low as 1.092 m verifies the effectiveness of the proposed smartphone based acoustic SLAM. (Color figure online)

4 Conclusions

In this paper, by taking advantage of the multi-source information extracted from the smartphone carried with a moving indoor pedestrian, we show the ways to solve the three significant SLAM problems and verify that the acoustic SLAM could be realized using a sensor-rich smartphone. Instead of redundantly reconstructing the room geometry at each sound source position in a rectangular room of regular shape, we consider about how to improve the sound source localization performance with the priori of room geometry. The proposed smartphone based acoustic SLAM shows us the validity of multi-source information fusion in single channel acoustic SLAM.

Acknowledgments. This work was supported by the Ministry of Education Key Laboratory of Cognitive Radio and Information Processing, the Wireless Broadband and Signal Processing Guangxi Key Laboratory.

Funding. This work was funded by the National Natural Science Foundation of China (Grant No. 61771151), by the GUET Excellent Graduate Thesis Program (Grant No. 16YJPYBS02), by the Guangxi Natural Science Foundation (Grant No. 2019GXNSFBA245103), and by the Guangxi Key Laboratory of Wireless Communication and Signal Processing Program (GXKL06180109).

References

1. Lawrence, N.D., Ferris, B., Fox, D.: WiFi-SLAM using gaussian process latent variable models. In: International Joint Conference on Artificial Intelligence. Morgan Kaufmann Publishers Inc. (2007)
2. Djugash, J., Singh, S., Kantor, G., et al.: Range-only SLAM for robots operating cooperatively with sensor networks. In: IEEE International Conference on Robotics & Automation. IEEE (2006)
3. Zhou, H., Zou, D., Pei, L., et al.: StructSLAM: visual SLAM with building structure lines. IEEE Trans. Veh. Technol. **64**(4), 1364–1375 (2015)
4. Djugash, J., Singh, S.: Motion-aided network SLAM with range. Int. J. Robot. Res. **31**, 604–625 (2012)
5. Deibler, T., Thielecke, J.: Fusing odometry and sparse UWB radar measurements for indoor slam. In: Workshop on Sensor Data Fusion: Trends. IEEE (2014)
6. Krekovic, M., Dokmanic, I., Vetterli, M.: EchoSLAM: simultaneous localization and mapping with acoustic echoes. In: IEEE International Conference on Acoustics. IEEE (2016)
7. Dokmanic, I., Daudet, L., Vetterli, M.: From acoustic room reconstruction to SLAM. In: IEEE International Conference on Acoustics. IEEE (2016)
8. Dokmanić, I.: Acoustic echoes reveal room shape. Proc. Nat. Acad. Sci. U.S.A. **110**(30), 12186–12191 (2013)
9. Tervo, S., Korhonen, T.: Estimation of reflective surfaces from continuous signals. In: IEEE International Conference on Acoustics Speech & Signal Processing. IEEE (2010)
10. Dokmanić, I., Lu, Y.M., Vetterli, M.: Can one hear the shape of a room: the 2-D polygonal case. In: IEEE International Conference on Acoustics, Speech, and Signal Processing (ICASSP). IEEE (2011)
11. Krekovíc, M., Dokmanić, I., Vetterli, M.: EchoSLAM: simultaneous localization and mapping with acoustic echoes. In: IEEE International Conference on Acoustics (2016)
12. Moore, A.H., Brookes, M., Naylor, P.A.: Room geometry estimation from a single channel acoustic impulse response. In: Signal Processing Conference. IEEE (2014)
13. Peters, N., Lei, H., Friedland, G.: Name that room: room identification using acoustic features in a recording. In: ACM International Conference on Multimedia (2012)
14. Song, X., Wang, M., Qiu, H., Luo, L.: Indoor pedestrian self-positioning based on image acoustic source impulse using a sensor-rich smartphone. Sensors **18**, 4143 (2018)
15. Allen, J.B., Berkley, D.A.: Image method for efficiently simulating small-room acoustics. J. Acoust. Soc. Am. **65**(S1), 943–950 (1998)
16. Knapp, C., Carter, G.: The generalized correlation method for estimation of time delay. IEEE Trans. Acoust. Speech Signal Process. **24**(4), 320–327 (2003)
17. Shin, S.H., Chan, G.P.: Adaptive step length estimation algorithm using optimal parameters and movement status awareness. Med. Eng. Phys. **33**, 1064–1071 (2011)
18. Deng, Z., Cao, Y., Wang, P., Wang, B.: An Improved heuristic drift elimination method for indoor pedestrian positioning. Sensors **2018**, 18 (1874)
19. Mensing, C., Plass, S.: Positioning algorithms for cellular networks using TDOA. In: Proceedings of the IEEE International Conference on Acoustics Speech and Signal Processing Proceedings, Toulouse, France, 14–19 May 2006

Power Quality; Power Electronics

Advanced Load-Shift System: An Experimental Validation of the ac-dc Converter as Shunt Active Power Filter

Ana M. C. Rodrigues$^{(\boxtimes)}$, Vítor Monteiro, Tiago J. C. Sousa, Tiago Alves,
J. G. Pinto, and João L. Afonso

ALGORITMI Research Centre, University of Minho, Guimarães, Portugal
{arodrigues,vmonteiro}@dei.uminho.pt

Abstract. This paper presents a load-shift system with advanced functionalities to interface the power grid (PG). When compared with the conventional approach, an advanced load-shift system (aLSS) permits the compensation of power quality (PQ) problems for the grid-side, namely problems related to current harmonics, current imbalance, and power factor. The proposed aLSS is composed by a bidirectional ac-dc converter to interface the PG and by a bidirectional dc-dc converter to interface an energy storage system (ESS). Since the main innovation is related with the PG interface, the focus of this work is on the analysis of the ac-dc converter, which is based on a three-phase four-leg converter. A theoretical study and the details concerning the control algorithm are presented and discussed along the paper. A laboratory prototype of the proposed aLSS was developed and the details of implementation are described in the paper. Experimental results obtained with the developed prototype prove that the aLSS contributes for the technology progress in this area, validating a new concept of operation concerning the PQ on the PG side.

Keywords: Current control · Three-phase ac-dc converter · Power quality · Advanced load-shift system · *p-q* theory

1 Introduction

Nowadays, due to the climate change and global warming, there is a growing use of renewable energy sources. However, most of them have as main disadvantage the intermittence in the production of electric energy [1, 2]. In this context, the concept of demand side management (DSM) using load-shifting systems comes up. This concept began to be studied some decades ago and consists in storing energy in periods of less demand and, posteriorly, use the stored energy in periods of higher demand [1]. The DSM is an important concept in smart grids and smart homes, since it allows the production and storage of energy in the same installation, allowing to take advantage of the energy price difference throughout the day, contributing for establishing a dynamic model of energy

J. L. Afonso et al. (Eds.): SESC 2019, LNICST 315, pp. 257–268, 2020.
https://doi.org/10.1007/978-3-030-45694-8_20

management [3]. Therefore, from the consumer perspective, an advanced load-shift system (aLSS) allows to reduce energy costs, since the consumption from the power grid (PG) is minimized. Furthermore, it enables to reduce the contracted power to a lower grade by reducing the requirements of the power from the grid [4, 5]. Nevertheless, despite the benefits of the introduction of an aLSS, the initial investment is high [6, 7]. As aforementioned, from the PG point of view, the aLSS is seen as a system capable of consuming or producing power [5]. Therefore, it is extremely important an operation with high levels of power quality (PQ), i.e., with sinusoidal currents and high power factor (in three-phase systems, also with balanced currents), as demonstrated in [8–10] and [11]. Nevertheless, when it is not necessary to exchange power with the PG, the LSS is inactive, representing an opportunity to add new functionalities to the power converters. Moreover, such functionalities can be added also during the operation as LSS (i.e., when exchanging power with the PG). Therefore, this paper focuses on the experimental validation of the ac-dc converter of the LSS as a shunt active power filter (SAPF), which is the key differentiating factor when compared with the conventional approaches. With this functionality for the LSS, besides exchanging active power with the grid, the aLSS also allows to reduce the PQ degradation (as harmonic distortion of the current, current imbalance, and low power factor) [12–14]. In this way, the ac-dc converter of the LSS operates with the key characteristics of a SAPF [15–18]. It is important to note that the PQ problems must be solved, since, in the long term, they can cause malfunctions in sensitive equipment, causing a reduction in their life time and high monetary costs to the consumer. In the literature can be found several publications that present the three-phase four-leg voltage source converters for interface of renewable energy source with the PG and for SAPF applications [19–21].

This paper is organized as follows: Sect. 2 presents the proposed aLSS; Sect. 3 presents the proposed control algorithm; Sect. 4 presents the experimental validation; Sect. 5 presents the conclusions.

2 Proposed advanced Load-Shift System (aLSS)

Figure 1 shows the structure of the proposed aLSS, which is composed by a bidirectional ac-dc converter to interface the PG with the dc-link, and by a bidirectional dc-dc converter to interface between the dc-link and the batteries, used as energy storage system (ESS). As mentioned in the introduction, the focus of this paper is the ac-dc converter, which is responsible for controlling the power consumption from the grid (active rectifier operation) or for controlling the power injection (inverter operation), in both cases with sinusoidal and balanced currents in the PG side. Regardless of whether the ac-dc converter is supplying power or not to the dc-dc converter, or injecting power into the PG, the ac-dc converter can be used to compensate current harmonics, current imbalance, neutral currents and for correcting the power factor of the electrical installation.

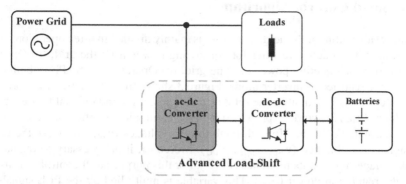

Fig. 1. Proposed structure for the advanced Load Shift System (aLSS).

The topology of the three-phase ac-dc converter used in the aLSS is presented in Fig. 2. As shown, the topology uses a three-phase four-leg voltage source ac-dc converter (in a total of eight switching devices, IGBTs in this case), and a dc-link formed by a capacitor (in fact, in the experimental validation, a set of capacitors were used in series). In the connection of the ac-dc converter with the PG, inductive coupling filters are used. Depending on the switching states assumed by the IGBTs, the converter can produce three voltage levels ($-v_{DC}$, 0, and $+v_{DC}$).

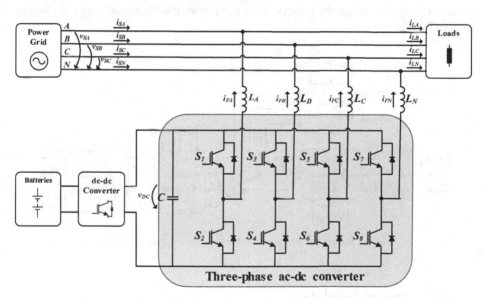

Fig. 2. Topology of the three-phase ac-dc converter used in the aLSS.

3 Proposed Control Algorithm

The control algorithm of the ac-dc converter is mainly divided in three operation modes: (a) Operation as an active rectifier for consuming power from the grid; (b) Operation as an inverter for injecting power into the grid; (c) Operation as SAPF in both cases, i.e., in active rectifier or inverter mode. Figure 3 shows the schematic of the proposed control algorithm. To calculate the reference currents, it is fundamental to use a phase-locked loop (PLL) to avoid the propagation of the harmonic distortion of the PG voltage into the currents [22]. Therefore, through the PG voltages (v_{SA}, v_{SB}, v_{SC}), the unitary PLL signals are obtained (v_{pllA}, v_{pllB}, v_{pllC}). Moreover, it is necessary to regulate the dc-link voltage (v_{DC}) to its reference (v_{DC}^*). For this purpose a PI controller is used to obtain the regulation power (p_{reg}). This variable is multiplied by the PLL signals and the reference currents are obtained (i_{regA}^*, i_{regB}^*, i_{regC}^*). When the ac-dc converter operates as SAPF, it is fundamental to calculate the compensation currents. For that, through the p-q theory, using as input parameters the load currents (i_{LA}, i_{LB}, i_{LC}) and the fundamental component of the PG voltages (v_{pllA}, v_{pllB}, v_{pllC}), are calculated the compensation currents (i_{CA}^*, i_{CB}^*, i_{CC}^*). Then, the reference currents (i_A^*, i_B^*, i_C^*, i_N^*) are obtained by summing the regulation currents with the compensation currents. The neutral reference current (i_N^*) is obtained by the sum of the reference currents (i_A^*, i_B^*, i_C^*). In order to control the currents (i_{FA}, i_{FB}, i_{FC}) according to the references (i_{FA}^*, i_{FB}^*, i_{FC}^*), a predictive current control is used. The output of the current control results in four reference voltages (v_{CA}^*, v_{CB}^*, v_{CC}^*, v_{CN}^*) that are compared with a triangular carrier to obtain the pulse-width modulation (PWM) signals to be applied to the IGBTs.

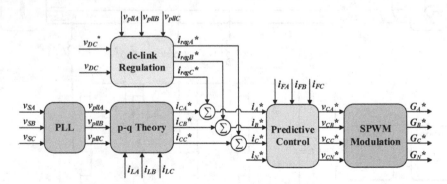

Fig. 3. Schematic of the control algorithm used in the aLSS.

4 Experimental Validation

This section presents the developed prototype and the main experimental results obtained to validate the proposed control strategy applied to the ac-dc converter of the aLSS when operating as: (a) Active rectifier; (b) Inverter; (c) SAPF.

4.1 Developed Prototype

In this item, the developed prototype of the three-phase ac-dc converter of the aLSS is described in detail, which is divided in two parts: (a) Power stage circuit (including both the ac-dc and dc-dc converters); (b) Control system (based on a single platform for all the aLSS).

The developed power stage is formed by the ac-dc converter and by four inductive coupling filters for connecting the converter in parallel with the PG. The ac-dc converter is formed mainly by four IGBT modules (model SKM100GB176D from Semikron) with four gate protection boards, and by four IGBT gate drivers (model SKHI 22AH4R from Semikron) for actuating the IGBTs with a fixed switching frequency of 20 kHz and a configured deadtime of 3.3 μs. The dc-link is composed by three capacitors (model B43456-A5568-M from EPCOS) connected in series, forming a total capacitance of 1867 μF and a maximum voltage of 1350 V.

Figure 4 shows a block diagram of the developed control system divided into the signal acquisition circuits, the signal conditioning circuits, the signal processing circuits, and actuation circuits. Initially, the variables of the system are acquired, with a sampling frequency of 40 kHz, by voltage sensors (LV 25-P from LEM) and current sensors (LA 100-P from LEM). The acquired signals from the sensors are adapted to digital signals for being read by the digital signal processor (DSP) TMS320F28335 from Texas Instruments. This conversion is performed through an external analog-to-digital converter circuit mounted in a signal conditioning board which also integrates an error detection circuit. Therefore, after implementing the control algorithms in the DSP, the PWM output signals are sent to the IGBT gate drivers through a command circuit for adapting the PWM signals to the 3.3 V TTL to 15 V CMOS logic required by the gate drivers.

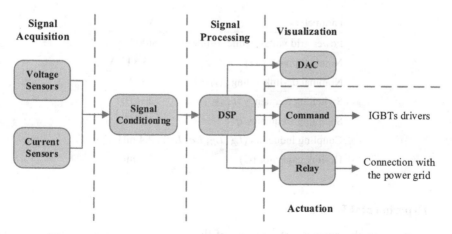

Fig. 4. Block diagram of the control system structure used in the aLSS.

Figure 5 shows the developed prototype of the aLSS integrated in the workbench used in the experimental setup, and Table 1 presents a summary of the main nominal characteristics of the ac-dc converter.

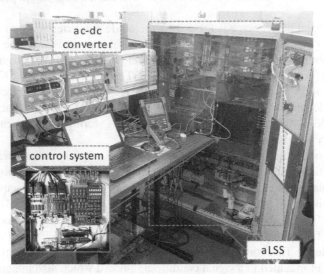

Fig. 5. Developed prototype of the aLSS integrated in the workbench.

Table 1. Nominal characteristics of the ac-dc converter.

Parameter	Value
Power grid voltage (line-to-line)	400 V
Nominal power (S_3)	13.8 kVA
Nominal dc-link voltage (v_{DC})	800 V
Switching frequency (f_{sw})	20 kHz
Sampling frequency (f_s)	40 kHz
Coupling inductors (L_A, L_B, L_C, L_N)	2.4 mH
Dc-link capacitor (C)	1.8 mF

4.2 Experimental Results

This item shows the experimental results of the three-phase four-leg ac-dc converter operating in the three main modes: (a) Operation as an active rectifier for consuming power from PG; (b) Operation as an inverter for injecting power to the PG; (c) Operation as SAPF in both cases, i.e., in active rectifier or inverter mode. It is important to note that, for safety reasons, during the experimental validation the ac-dc converter was connected to the PG through a variable three-phase autotransformer followed by a 20:3 transformer, thus the line-to-line voltage of the PG is 100 V.

Operation as Active Rectifier
In this operation mode, a resistive load of 26 Ω was connected in parallel with dc-link and the dc-link voltage was regulated to 200 V. Figure 6 shows the stages of the dc-link voltage regulation. In stage (1), the ac-dc converter is not connected to the PG, thus the dc-link voltage is 0 V. In stage (2), the ac-dc converter is connected to the PG by pre-charge resistors. During this stage, the dc-link is charged to the peak voltage of the line-to-line PG voltage (147 V). Thereafter, in stage (3), the ac-dc converter is connected directly to the PG, and in stage (4) begins the dc-link voltage regulation to the reference average voltage (200 V). When the dc-link voltage stabilizes, the resistive load is connected to the dc-link and, as it can be seen, the dc-link voltage is set at 200 V (stage (5)).

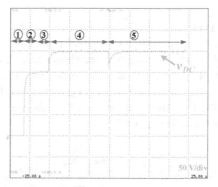

Fig. 6. Experimental results of the ac-dc converter operating as active rectifier during the dc-link voltage regulation: (1) ac-dc converter turned-off; (2) Pre-charge of the dc-link voltage; (3) Direct connection of the ac-dc converter to the PG; (4) dc-link voltage regulation to the defined reference; (5) Load connection.

Figure 7(a) presents, for phase A, the PG voltage (v_{SA}) and the grid current (i_{SA}) during stage (5). As can be seen, the PG current is sinusoidal and in phase with the PG voltage. On the other hand, it is possible to observe that the PG current (i_{SA}) follows its reference current ($i_{SA}{}^*$). Figure 7(b) shows the harmonic spectrum of the PG currents (i_{SA}, i_{SB}, i_{SC}), with a total harmonic distortion (THD%) of 1.4%.

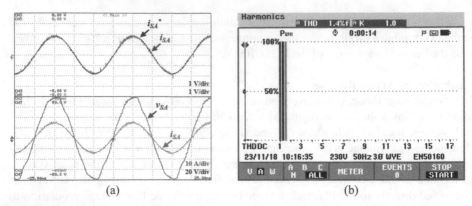

(a)   (b)

Fig. 7. Experimental results of the ac-dc converter operating as active rectifier: (a) Reference current ($i_{SA}{}^*$), voltage (v_{SA}) and current (i_{SA}) in phase A of the PG; (b) Harmonic spectrum of the PG currents.

Operation as Inverter

For the operation mode as inverter, the dc-link was powered by a power supply of 300 V and it was defined for the PG currents a sinusoidal reference current with RMS value of 5 A. The results of this experimental test are shown in Fig. 8. As it can be seen in Fig. 8(a), the PG currents (i_{SA}, i_{SB}, i_{SC}) are sinusoidal with a peak value of 7 A and in phase opposition with the PG voltages (v_{SA}, v_{SB}, v_{SC}), meaning that the ac-dc converter is injecting energy into the PG. Moreover, as Fig. 8(b) shows, the produced currents in the PG (i_{SA}, i_{SB}, i_{SC}) present a THD% of 2.6%.

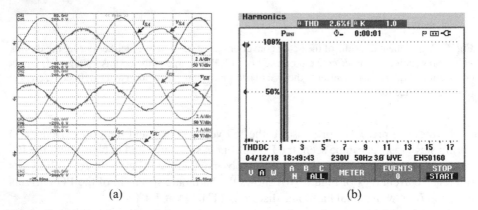

(a)   (b)

Fig. 8. Experimental results of the ac-dc converter operating as inverter: (a) PG voltages (v_{SA}, v_{SB}, v_{SC}) and currents (i_{SA}, i_{SB}, i_{SC}); (b) Harmonic spectrum of the PG currents.

Operation as SAPF

In the operation mode as SAPF, the dc-link voltage was regulated to 400 V and some loads were connected to the PG. As can be seen in Fig. 9(a), the currents consumed by the loads (i_{LA}, i_{LB}, i_{LC}, i_{LN}) contain a high harmonic component with a THD$_\%$ of 76.8% (Fig. 9(b)) and a low power factor. Moreover, the load currents are imbalanced, leading to a high neutral current.

In other to compensate the PQ problems caused by the loads connected to the PG, the SAPF produces the compensation currents (i_{FA}, i_{FB}, i_{FC}, i_{FN}) presented in Fig. 10. Figure 11 shows the PG voltages (v_{SA}, v_{SB}, v_{SC}) and currents (i_{SA}, i_{SB}, i_{SC}, i_{SN}) after the compensation, where it can be seen that the currents are approximately sinusoidal, balanced and in phase with the correspondent voltages. On the other hand, through the harmonic spectrum analysis of the PG currents, it can be observed that the THD$_\%$ is reduced from 76.4% to 6.4% (Fig. 11(b)).

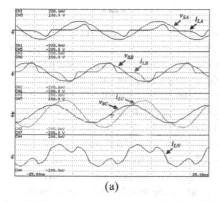 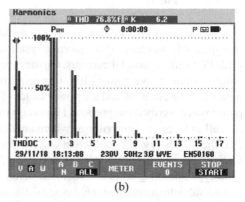

(a)   (b)

Fig. 9. Experimental results of the ac-dc converter operating as SAPF before compensation: (a) PG voltages (v_{SA}, v_{SB}, v_{SC}) and load currents (i_{LA}, i_{LB}, i_{LC}, i_{LN}); (b) Harmonic spectrum of the load currents.

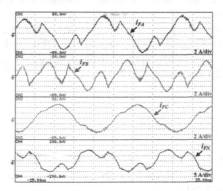

Fig. 10. Experimental results of the ac-dc converter operating as SAPF: Compensation currents (i_{FA}, i_{FB}, i_{FC}, i_{FN}).

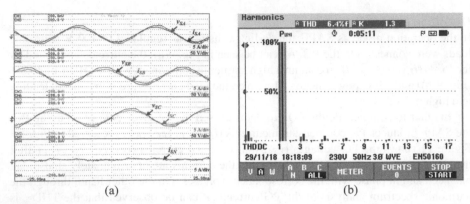

Fig. 11. Experimental results of the ac-dc converter operating as SAPF after compensation: (a) PG voltages (v_{SA}, v_{SB}, v_{SC}) and currents ($i_{SA}, i_{SB}, i_{SC}, i_{SN}$); (b) Harmonic spectrum of the PG currents.

5   Conclusions

This paper presents an ac-dc converter of an advanced Load-Shift System (aLSS), which is responsible for charging the storage system (batteries) or injecting energy in the power grid (PG) with sinusoidal currents. On the other hand, when the load-shift system is operating as shunt active power filter, it is responsible for compensating the harmonics and balance of the currents, and the power factor of the electrical installation. Throughout this paper was described the proposed topology of the three-phase four-leg ac-dc converter, as well as its control algorithms, where are detailed the synchronization system with the PG, the p-q theory, the predictive current control and the sinusoidal pulse width modulation. An experimental validation was performed in order to validate the developed prototype operating as active rectifier, inverter and SAPF. The presented experimental results validate the implemented control algorithms, showing that for the operation mode as active rectifier, the absorbed currents in the PG are sinusoidal and balanced with unitary power factor. When the ac-dc converter operates as inverter the produced currents in PG are sinusoidal in phase opposition with correspondent voltages. In the operation as SAPF, the PG currents are approximately sinusoidal with a low total harmonic distortion.

Acknowledgment. This work has been supported by FCT – Fundação para a Ciência e Tecnologia with-in the Project Scope: UID/CEC/00319/2019. This work has been supported by the FCT Project QUALITY4POWER PTDC/EEI-EEE/28813/2017, and by the FCT Project newERA4GRIDs PTDC/EEI-EEE/30283/2017.

References

1. Ho, W.S., Hashim, H., Lim, J.S., Klemeš, J.J.: Combined design and load shifting for distributed energy system. Clean Technol. Environ. Policy **15**(3), 433–444 (2013). https://doi.org/10.1007/s10098-013-0617-3

2. Reddy, K.S., Kumar, M., Mallick, T.K., Sharon, H., Lokeswaran, S.: A review of Integration, Control, Communication and Metering (ICCM) of renewable energy based smart grid. Renew. Sustain. Energy Rev. **38**, 180–192 (2014). https://doi.org/10.1016/j.rser.2014.05.049. ISBN 1364-0321, ISSN 13640321

3. Gungor, V.C., et al.: Smart grid and smart homes: key players and pilot projects. IEEE Ind. Electron. Mag. **6**(4), 18–34 (2012). ISSN 1932-4529

4. ERSE - Entidade Reguladora dos Serviços Energéticos. Regulamento de Relações Comerciais do setor elétrico (2017)

5. Dusonchet, L., Ippolito, M.G., Telaretti, E., Zizzo, G., Graditi, G.: An optimal operating strategy for combined RES-based generators and electric storage systems for load shifting applications. In: International Conference on Power Engineering, Energy and Electrical Drives, vol. 5, pp. 552–557 (2013). https://doi.org/10.1109/PowerEng.2013.6635668. ISBN 9781467363921, ISSN 21555516

6. Leonardo-Energy: Electric load management in industry, January 2009. ISBN 2950787886

7. Capiau, T., Van Daele, L.: Application note - load management of industrial systems, p. 30 (2016)

8. Han, B.-M.: Grid-tied power converter for battery energy storage composed of 2-stage DC-DC converter. J. Electr. Eng. Technol. **8**(6), 1400–1408 (2013). https://doi.org/10.5370/JEET.2013.8.6.1400. ISBN 9781479913039, ISSN 19750102

9. Pinto, J.G., et al.: Power electronics converters for an electric vehicle fast charging station with storage capability. In: Afonso, J.L., Monteiro, V., Pinto, J.G. (eds.) GreeNets 2018. LNICST, vol. 269, pp. 119–130. Springer, Cham (2019). https://doi.org/10.1007/978-3-030-12950-7_10. 10.2174/9781608052851112010 1, ISBN 9781608052851

10. Monteiro, V., Pinto, J.G., Afonso, J.L.: Experimental validation of a three-port integrated topology to interface electric vehicles and renewables with the electrical grid. IEEE Trans. Ind. Inform. **14**(6), 2364–2374 (2018). https://doi.org/10.1109/TII.2018.2818174. ISSN 15513203

11. Pinto, J.G., Monteiro, V., Goncalves, H., Exposto, B.: Bidirectional battery charger with grid-to-vehicle, vehicle-to-grid and vehicle-to-home technologies. In: 39th Annual Conference of the IEEE Industrial Electronics Society, Vienna, pp. 5932–5937 (2013). ISBN 9781479902231

12. Subjak, J.S., McQuilkin, J.S.: Harmonics – causes, effects, measurements, and analysis: an update. IEEE Trans. Ind. Appl. **26**(6), 1034–1042 (1990)

13. Afonso, J.L., Martins, J.S.: Qualidade da energia eléctrica. Rev. o Electr. pp. 66–71 (2005). ISSN 0874-9019

14. Cividino, L.: Power factor, harmonic distortion; causes effects and considerations. In: 14th International Telecommunications Energy Conference, pp. 1–7 (1992)

15. Halpin, S.M.: Power Quality Tutorial, November 2008

16. Afonso, J.L., Pinto, J.G., Gonçalves, H.: Active power conditioners to mitigate power quality problems in industrial facilities (2013). https://doi.org/10.5772/53189

17. Martins, J.S., Couto, C., Afonso, J.L.: Qualidade de energia eléctrica. 3º Congr. Luso-Moçambicano Eng. – CLME 2003 Eng. e Inovação para o Desenvolv., pp. 219–231 (2003)

18. Neves, P., Gonçalves, D., Pinto, J.G., Alves, R., Afonso, J.L.: Single-phase shunt active filter interfacing renewable energy sources with the power grid. In: IEEE Conference, November, pp. 3264–3269 (2009). ISBN 9781424446490

19. De Kooning, J., Meersman, B., Vandoorn, T., Renders, B., Vandevelde, L.: Comparison of three-phase four-wire converters for distributed generation. In: 2010 45th International Universities Power Engineering Conference (UPEC), pp. 1–6 (2010). ISBN 9780956557025

20. Pinto, J.G., Pregitzer, R., Monteiro, L.F.C., Afonso, J.L.: 3-phase 4-wire shunt active power filter with renewable energy interface key words. In: ICREPQ 2007- International Conference on Renewable Energies and Power Quality, no. 1, pp. 28–30 (2007). ISBN 9788461147076
21. Pregitzer, R., Costa, J., Martins, J., Afonso, J.: Filtro activo paralelo com interface entre fontes de energia renovável e a rede eléctrica. In: Conferência Int. sobre Energias Renov., pp. 89–94 (2006). ISBN 9789728822071
22. Barbosa Rolim, L.G., Rodrigues da Costa, D., Aredes, M.: Analysis and software implementation of a robust synchronizing PLL circuit based on the pq theory. IEEE Trans. Ind. Electron. 53(6), 1919–1926 (2006). https://doi.org/10.1109/TIE.2006.885483. ISSN 0278-0046

A Novel Single-Phase Shunt Active Power Filter Based on a Current-Source Converter with Reduced Dc-Link

Catia F. Oliveira, Luis A. M. Barros, Joao L. Afonso, J. G. Pinto, Bruno Exposto, and Vitor Monteiro$^{(\boxtimes)}$

ALGORITMI Research Centre, University of Minho, Braga, Portugal
{c.oliveira,vmonteiro}@dei.uminho.pt

Abstract. Nowadays, the majority of electronic equipment behave as nonlinear loads, introducing Power Quality (PQ) problems into the Power Grid (PG), namely, current harmonics and low power factor. These PQ problems contribute to the reduction of the efficiency of the transmission and distribution PG, as well as induce the malfunctioning of sensitive loads connected to the PG. Therefore, the development of equipment able to mitigate these PQ problems is extremely important. In this context, this paper presents a novel single-phase Shunt Active Power Filter (SAPF) based on a current-source converter, where the key differencing factor, when compared with the conventional approach, is the reduced dc-link. As the proposed topology requires a reduced dc-link, it represents a relevant advantage, since a typical current-source converter needs an inductor with a high inductance in dc-link, which results in higher losses, costs and component sizing. The proposed SAPF with reduced dc-link is introduced in detail along the paper and a comprehensive comparison with the conventional SAPF is established based on computer simulations. Besides, an experimental validation was carried-out with a developed laboratory prototype, validating the main advantages of the proposed SAPF with reduced dc-link.

Keywords: Current harmonics · Current source converter · Shunt active power filter · Power quality

1 Introduction

The shunt active power filter (SAPF) is used for power factor correction, for current harmonics elimination and, in case of three-phase systems, for current unbalances compensation [1–3]. In addition, as presented in [4] and [5], to mitigate the power quality (PQ) problems, the SAPF can also be used for interfacing renewable energy sources with the power grid (PG). Moreover, as presented in [6], in [7] and in [8], the functionalities of SAPF can be incorporated in electric vehicle battery chargers, representing a relevant contribution for the future smart grids, where the electric vehicle can be seen as a dynamic controllable load in the PG.

© ICST Institute for Computer Sciences, Social Informatics and Telecommunications Engineering 2020
Published by Springer Nature Switzerland AG 2020. All Rights Reserved
J. L. Afonso et al. (Eds.): SESC 2019, LNICST 315, pp. 269–280, 2020.
https://doi.org/10.1007/978-3-030-45694-8_21

Concerning the structure of the SAPF, depending on the dc-link constitution, it can be classified as a voltage-source or as a current-source [9]. A comparison between both structures for simple applications of SAPF is presented in [10] and for applications of electric mobility is presented in [11]. Since the focus of this paper is the current-source, a more detailed explanation is provided for this structure.

The current-source SAPF is composed by a coupling CL filter with the power grid and by an inductor in the dc-link. The dc-ac power converter is composed by semiconductors totally controlled such as MOSFETs, IGBTs or RB-IGBTs. These devices, in comparison with GTOs and BJTs, can operate with higher switching frequencies, requiring smaller output passive filters, translating into a more compact and cheaper solution. In addition, the input impedance is higher, which results in low power consumption [12]. However, when using IGBTs, it is needed to connect them in series with diodes, in order to ensure reverse-blocking, thus it is avoided that the current flows by the antiparallel-diodes of IGBTs. However, an alternative to this method consists in replace the IGBTs with the diodes in series by RB-IGBTs, which the use of diodes becomes unnecessary [13, 14]. The current-source SAPF needs an inductor in dc-link with a huge value of inductance, which is necessary to reduce the ripple of the current for an acceptable value in dc-link.

The aim of this paper is to present a topology that allows the reduction of the inductance value of the inductor in dc-link. Moreover, the operation losses are reduced as well as the dimensions and the costs of the component are diminished. On the other hand, an inductor with reduced inductance value in dc-link allows a faster current control and thus, the average value of current can be minimized. In this context, the main contributions of this paper are: (a) A novel topology for a SAPF based on a current-source power converter with reduced dc-link; (b) A SAPF constituted by RB-IGBTs in the main inverter; (c) An experimental validation of the proposed SAPF.

2   SAPF with Reduced Dc-Link: Proposed Topology

As described in the introduction, the main contribution of this paper is the reduced dc-link of the SAPF. For this purpose, it is adopted a topology of a current-source inverter with a modified dc-link. This topology consists of a hybrid energy storage, composed by one inductor, one capacitor, two diodes and two IGBTs [15]. The conventional topology of a single-phase current-source SAPF based on RB-IGBTs is presented in Fig. 1, while the proposed single-phase current-source SAPF with reduced dc-link is presented in Fig. 2. As shown, the main differentiating factor of the proposed topology is the dc-link, however, also the coupling filter with the power grid is different from the conventional solution of CL filter [16]. Concerning the reduced dc-link, it is shown the dc-dc power converter in series with the single-phase current-source SAPF.

3   Proposed Control Algorithm

Concerning the simulation of the dc-dc converter, the first step consists in calculate the loads active power. By multiplying the load current by the fundamental component of the load voltage obtained through EPLL [17] algorithm it is obtained the instantaneous power, p. Subsequently, using a sliding average algorithm, it is possible to obtain the

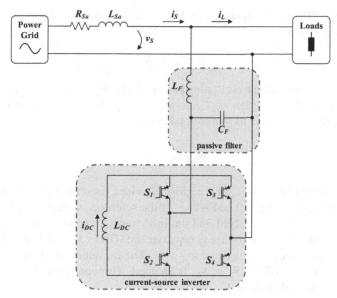

Fig. 1. Electrical schematic of the conventional single-phase SAPF based on a current-source inverter.

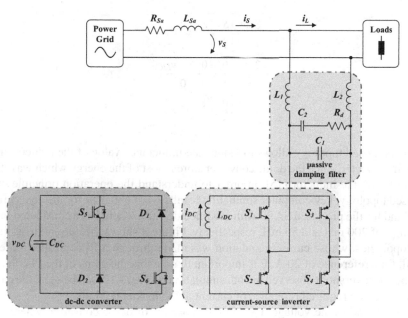

Fig. 2. Electrical schematic of the proposed topology of the single-phase SAPF based on a current-source inverter with reduced dc-link.

average value, $\bar{p}$. Then, the calculation of the oscillating component of the instantaneous power is determined by (1).

$$\tilde{p} = p - \bar{p} \tag{1}$$

After the calculation of the oscillating power, $\tilde{p}$, it is possible to obtain the reference voltage for the dc-dc converter, $v_{out}{}^*$, dividing $\tilde{p}$ by the current value measured in inductor of dc-link, i_{DC}, such as represented in (2).

$$v_{out}^* = \frac{\tilde{p}}{i_{DC}} \tag{2}$$

The modulation of the converter is performed with a fixed frequency of 40 kHz, with three switching states: $+v_{DC}$, 0 and $-v_{DC}$. If the reference voltage, $v_{out}{}^*$, is positive, both IGBTs S_5 and S_6 are enabled and the instantaneous voltage, v_{out}, is equal to $+ v_{DC}$, whereas if the reference voltage is negative, the IGBTs S_5 and S_6 are disabled and the instantaneous voltage v_{out} is equal to $-v_{DC}$. The instantaneous voltage value, v_{out}, is zero when only one IGBT, S_5 or S_6, is enabled. The operation states of the dc-dc converter are presented in Table 1.

Table 1. Operation states of the dc-dc converter.

State	S_5	S_6	v_{out}
1	1	1	$+v_{DC}$
2	0	0	$-v_{DC}$
3	1	0	0
4	0	1	0

The proposed topology allows to reduce the inductance value of the inductor in dc-link of the inverter, since the dc-dc converter stores most of the energy which was stored exclusively by the inductor [15]. In order to understand the operation principle of the proposed topology, key computer simulation results were obtained for the conventional SAPF and for the proposed SAPF with modified dc-link, where were considered inductors, L_{DC}, of 200 mH and 50 mH, respectively. Figure 3 shows the current in dc-link in both topologies, whose current regulation was made through a PI controller presented in [18], for a reference of 20 A. It is important to note that the gains of the PI controller influence the overshoot observed in both simulation results. As it can be seen, the current stabilizes for the required reference of current at the instant 0.25 ms.

Figure 4 shows the voltage, v_{DC}, in the capacitor of dc-dc converter, where it can be observed that since the instant 0.2 s, the dc-dc power converter is activated and the capacitor, C_{DC}, starts storing energy with a maximum voltage of, approximately, 400 V. As part of the energy is stored in the capacitor, the inductor of the inverter does not need a huge inductance value, representing the key advantage of the proposed topology.

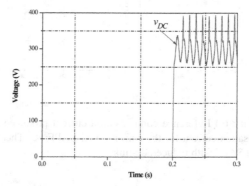

(a)   (b)

Fig. 3. Simulation results of dc-link current, i_{DC}, regulation: (a) Conventional SAPF; (b) SAPF with reduced dc-link.

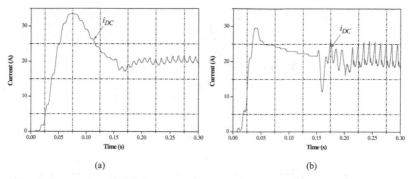

Fig. 4. Simulation result of the dc-link regulation of the proposed dc-dc power converter SAPF with reduced dc-link.

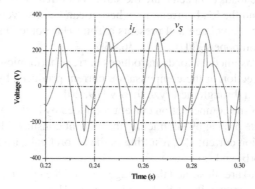

Fig. 5. Simulation results of the power grid voltage, v_S, and the load current, i_L, in both topologies.

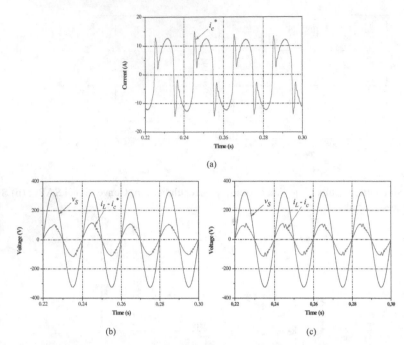

Fig. 6. Simulation results: (a) Reference compensation current produced by the Fryze theory, (b) Theoretical compensation current for the conventional SAPF; (c) Theoretical compensation current for the proposed SAPF with reduced dc-link.

Considering both topologies, simulation results were also obtained to analyze the compensation of PQ problems. Therefore, at the time 0.22 s the loads are connected in both simulations. The loads connected are the same for both topologies. Figure 5 shows the PG voltage, v_S, and the load current, i_L, where it can be observed that the current is delayed in relation to the voltage and presents a Total Harmonic Distortion in relation to the fundamental component, THD$_{\%f}$, of 36.45%.

As the current consumed by loads introduces current harmonics in the power grid, it is necessary the injection of the compensation current produced by the SAPF, which in this case is obtained through the Fryze theory [19, 20].

Figure 6(a) shows the compensation current produced by both SAPFs. The behavior of Fryze theory can be proven by subtracting the current consumed by loads, i_L, by the reference compensation current, i_c^*, resulting in the theoretical current in the source, as it is showed in Fig. 6(b) and (c).

Finally, in Fig. 7(a) are illustrated the voltage, v_S, and the current, i_S, in the grid after compensation for the conventional SAPF, where the THD$_{\%f}$ of current is reduced to 4.25%. On the other hand, as shown in Fig. 7(b), with the proposed SAPF with reduced dc-link, the source current, i_S, is almost sinusoidal, presenting a THD$_{\%f}$ of 7.78%.

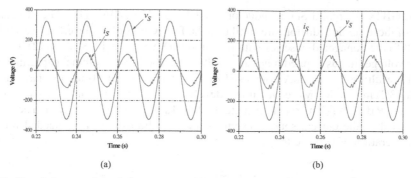

Fig. 7. Simulation results of the power grid voltage, v_S, and power grid current, i_S, after compensation: (a) Conventional SAPF; (b) Proposed SAPF with reduced dc-link.

4 Evaluation and Comparison

With the help of the computer simulations it is possible to compare the two topologies in more detail. In Table 2 are presented the inductance values used in both simulations, the THD$_{\%f}$ and the power factor (PF). As can be observed, the inductance of the inductor in dc-link used in the SAPF with reduced dc-link is four times lower in comparison with the inductor that composes the dc-link of the conventional SAPF. On the other hand, in both simulations, it is obtained a unitary PF. However, the THD$_{\%f}$ is somewhat higher than that obtained in conventional SAPF. Analyzing the simulation results, it can be concluded that the proposed topology has more advantages, once it was proved that it is possible to reduce the inductance value of the inductor in dc-link of the current-source inverter.

Table 2. Comparison between the conventional SAPF and the proposed SAPF with reduced dc-link.

Parameters	Conventional SAPF	SAPF with reduced dc link
Inductance (mH)	200	50
THD$_{\%f}$	4.25	7.78
PF	0.99	0.99

Once validated the principle of operation of the proposed topology, a prototype of the dc-dc converter and the single-phase current-source inverter was developed (Fig. 8). Thereafter, are presented the main experimental results obtained for the proposed SAPF with reduced dc-link. The current-source inverter is composed by two legs with two RB-IGBTs (Fuji Electric, model FGW85N60RB) in each leg. In each RB-IGBT is connected a protection circuit against overvoltage. Besides that, in order to ensure the protection of the inverter, are connected varistors in parallel with the RB-IGBTs and with the dc-link, whose actuation voltage is of 510 V. On the other hand, the dc-dc converter consists of two IGBTs (Fairchild Semiconductor, model FGA25N120ANTD). The protection circuit of these semiconductors are similar to the RB-IGBTs of the inverter. In each leg, the IGBTs are connected in series with one diode (IXYS, model DSEP 29-12). For the dc-link voltage, it was defined a nominal voltage of 400 V and nominal capacitance of 100 μF, resulting in a dc-link composed by five capacitors of 20 μF (Vishay, model MKP1848C) in parallel. Moreover, it was developed three driver boards, two of them to actuate the RB-IGBTs and one to actuate the IGBTs of the dc-dc converter. The driver boards used to the current-source inverter generates the overlap-time needed for the correct operation of the inverter.

Fig. 8. Final prototype of the dc-dc converter and the single-phase current-source inverter fixed to heatsink.

Figure 9 shows the PG voltage, v_S, and the signal generated by the EPLL, v_{PLL}. It should be noted that the transient verified, shows that the output signal of the EPLL, v_{PLL}, rapidly reaches the synchronism with the PG voltage. Despite the PG voltage being distorted, the output signal of the EPLL, v_{PLL}, is sinusoidal and in phase with the power grid fundamental voltage, as intended.

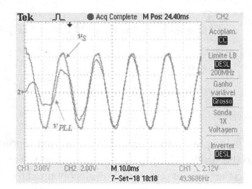

Fig. 9. Experimental results of the proposed SAPF with reduced dc-link: Synchronism of the EPLL, v_{PLL}, with the power grid voltage, v_S.

To ensure the correct operation of the single-phase current-source inverter, it is necessary to establish an overlap-time between the two command signals. It is important to mention that only one superior semiconductor, S_1 or S_3, and inferior semiconductor, S_2 or S_4, are connected, except during the overlap-time. Therefore, when one of the superior semiconductors is open, the other superior semiconductor starts conducting, the same happens with the inferior semiconductors. In Fig. 10, it can be observed the overlap-time with duration of 1 μs between the two command signals.

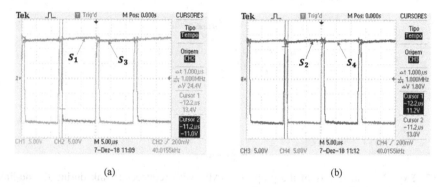

(a)   (b)

Fig. 10. Experimental results of the proposed SAPF with reduced dc-link concerning the overlap-time between the gate signals of the semiconductors: (a) S_1 and S_3; (b) S_2 and S_4.

In order to verify the effectiveness of the Fryze theory, it is calculated the theoretical current in the power grid side, subtracting the measured current in load, i_L, from the compensation current, $i_c{}^*$. Therefore, the theoretical current in the grid side can be demonstrated through the MATH functionality available in oscilloscope, *Tektronix* TPS 2024, which allows the calculation previously described. Figure 11 shows the theoretical current in source, $(i_L - i_c{}^*)$, the load current, i_L, the compensation current, $i_c{}^*$, and the signal generated by EPLL, v_{PLL}.

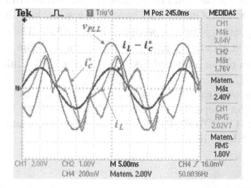

Fig. 11. Experimental results of the proposed SAPF with reduced dc-link concerning the Fryze theory: Load current, i_L; Compensation current, $i_c{}^*$; Theoretical current in the grid side, $(i_L - i_c{}^*)$; Signal generated by the EPLL, v_{PLL}.

After that, it was performed the regulation of the current in dc-link of the inverter, applying the PI controller. The performance of the PI control technique is validated for a reference current of 2 A. Figure 12 illustrates the behavior of the current in dc-link, i_{DC}, where it can be observed that the measured current in dc-link, i_{DC}, after the initial transient, follows perfectly the reference current, i^*. For this reason, it can be concluded that the control technique has a good performance.

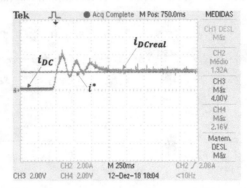

Fig. 12. Experimental results of the proposed SAPF with reduced dc-link during the dc-link current regulation: Reference current, i^*; Dc-link current, i_{DC}.

5   Conclusions

This paper proposes a novel current-source shunt active power filter (SAPF), aiming to reduce the inductance value, to minimize the costs, the losses and the dimensions of the system. Throughout the paper are described in detail the simulations realized, where it was proved the possibility of reducing the value of inductance for a considerably low value. Moreover, this paper presents the operation principle of the dc-dc converter that has a crucial role in the proposed topology. Due to the hybrid energy storage strategy, part of the energy is stored by the capacitor of the dc-dc converter, and thus, it is not necessary a huge inductor in the dc-link. On the other hand, it is approached the power theory used for obtaining the compensation current produced by the SAPF. The developed prototype is presented and describe in detail. Finally, are presented the main experimental results, validating the operation of the proposed SAPF with reduced dc-link.

Acknowledgment. This work has been supported by FCT – Fundação para a Ciência e Tecnologia with-in the Project Scope: UID/CEC/00319/2019. This work has been supported by the FCT Project QUALITY4POWER PTDC/EEI-EEE/28813/2017, and by the FCT Project newERA4GRIDs PTDC/EEI-EEE/30283/2017.

References

1. Rashid, M.H.: Power Electronics Handbook. Academic Press, Cambridge (2001). ISBN 0125816502

2. Chaudhari, K.R., Trivedi, T.A.: Analysis on control strategy of shunt active power filter for three-phase three-wire system. In: Transmission & Distribution Conference and Exposition – Latin America, IEEE PES, pp. 1–6 (2014)
3. Pinto, J.G., Gonçalves, H., Afonso, J.L.: Condicionadores Ativos de Potência para Mitigação de Problemas de Qualidade de Energia Elétrica em Instalações Industriais. Rev. Robótica 90, 56–58 (2013)
4. Neves, P., Gonçalves, D., Pinto, J.G., Alves, R., Afonso, J.L.: Single-phase shunt active filter interfacing renewable energy sources with the power grid. In: IEEE Conference, pp. 3264–3269 (2009). https://doi.org/10.1109/iecon.2009.5415208
5. Pinto, J.G., Pregitzer, R., Monteiro, L.F.C., Afonso, J.L.: 3-phase 4-wire shunt active power filter with renewable energy interface key words (1), 28–30 (2007). https://doi.org/10.24084/repqj05.350
6. Monteiro, V., Pinto, J.G., Afonso, J.L.: Improved vehicle-for-grid (iV4G) mode: novel operation mode for EVs battery chargers in smart grids. Int. J. Electr. Power Energy Syst. 110, 579–587 (2019)
7. Rodrigues, M.C.B.P., Souza, I., Ferreira, A.A., Barbosa, P.G., Braga, H.A.C.: Integrated bidirectional single-phase vehicle-to-grid interface with active power filter capability. In: COBEP Power Electronics Conference (COBEP), pp. 993–1000, October 2013
8. Rauchfu, L., Foulquier, J., Werner, R.: Charging station as an active filter for harmonics compensation of smart grid. In: IEEE ICHQP International Conference on Harmonics and Quality of Power, pp. 181–184, May 2014
9. Singh, B., Al-haddad, K., Chandra, A.: A review of active filters for power quality improvement. 46(5), 960–971 (1999). https://doi.org/10.1109/41.793345
10. Pinto, J.G., Exposto, B., Monteiro, V., Monteiro, L.F.C., Afonso, J.L.: Comparison of current-source and voltage-source shunt active power filters for harmonic compensation and reactive power control. In: IEEE IECON 38th Annual Conference of the IEEE Industrial Electronics Society, Montreal, Canada, pp. 5143–5148, October 2012
11. Monteiro, V., Pinto, J.G., Exposto, B., Afonso, J.L.: Comprehensive comparison of a current-source and a voltage-source converter for three-phase EV fast battery chargers. In: CPE International Conference on Compatibility and Power Electronics, Lisboa, Portugal, pp. 173–178, June 2015
12. Jang, S.R., Ryoo, H.J., Goussev, G., Rim, G.H.: Comparative study of MOSFET and IGBT for high repetitive pulsed power modulators. IEEE Trans. Plasma Sci. 40(10, PART 1), 2561–2568 (2012). https://doi.org/10.1109/tps.2012.2186592
13. Salo, M., Pettersson, S.: Current-source active power filter with an optimal DC current control. In: 37th IEEE Power Electronics Specialists Conference 2006, PESC 2006, pp. 1–4 (2006). https://doi.org/10.1109/pesc.2006.1711975
14. Routimo, M., Salo, M., Tuusa, H.: Comparison of voltage-source and current-source shunt active power filters. IEEE Trans. Power Electron. 22(2), 636–643 (2007). https://doi.org/10.1109/TPEL.2006.890005
15. Pettersson, S., Salo, M., Tuusa, H.: Optimal DC current control for four-wire current source active power filter. In: 2008 Twenty-Third Annual IEEE Applied Power Electronics Conference and Exposition, pp. 1163–1168 (2008). https://doi.org/10.1109/apec.2008.4522869
16. Hensgens, N., Silva, M., Oliver, J.A., Cobos, J.A., Skibin, S., Ecklebe, A.: Optimal design of AC EMI filters with damping networks and effect on the system power factor. In: 2012 IEEE Energy Conversion Congress and Exposition, ECCE 2012, vol. 7, no. 2, pp. 637–644 (2012). https://doi.org/10.1109/ecce.2012.6342761
17. Karimi-Ghartemani, M., Iravani, M.R.: A method for synchronization of power electronic converters in polluted and variable-frequency environments. IEEE Trans. Power Syst. 19(3), 1263–1270 (2004). https://doi.org/10.1109/TPWRS.2004.831280

18. Caceres, G.A.V., Lizarazo, J.C.G., Villalobos, M.A.M., Suarez, J.F.P.: Active power filters: a comparative analysis of current control techniques. In: 2010 IEEE ANDESCON, pp. 1–6 (2010). https://doi.org/10.1109/andescon.2010.5631646
19. Staudt, V.: Fryze - Buchholz - Depenbrock: a time-domain power theory, pp. 1–12 (2008). https://doi.org/10.1109/isncc.2008.4627481
20. Czarnecki, L.S.: Budeanu and Fryze: two frameworks for interpreting power properties of circuits with nonsinusoidal voltages and currents. Electr. Eng. **80**, 359–367 (1997). https://doi.org/10.1007/bf01232925. No. Teoria de Potência

Three-Phase Smart Energy Meter
for Grid-Connected PV Installations

Manel Hlaili[1], Amira Haddouk[1], Khaoula Khlifi[1], Mechergui Hfaiedh[1],
Vítor Monteiro[2(✉)], and João L. Afonso[2]

[1] Research Laboratory: LISIER, Ecole Nationale Supérieure des Ingénieurs de Tunis,
University of Tunis, Tunis, Tunisia
hlaili_manel@yahoo.fr
[2] ALGORITMI Research Centre, University of Minho, Guimarães, Portugal
vmonteiro@dei.uminho.pt

Abstract. High levels of solar energy are a good orientation for the development
of grid-connected power converters used in the interface of photovoltaic (PV)
installations with the power grid. In this case, in order to define control strategies
and the respective tariffs, the injected power into the grid must be accounted using
an energy meter. Therefore, in this paper, the implementation of a three-phase
smart energy meter for PV installations is presented, ensuring the registration
of the electrical energy supplied to the grid. This three-phase energy meter consists of Hall-effect sensors, used to adapt the high voltages and currents with the
analog circuits of the signal conditioning, which is connected to a DSP. The developed energy meter ensures data acquisition and processing and, based on that, the
energy calculation and standardization in real time. As presented along the paper,
a detailed metrology analysis was developed to identify the smart meter metrological characteristics. Through the experimental validations, it was possible to
validate the main features of the developed smart energy meter for grid-connected
PV installations.

Keywords: Photovoltaic · Energy meter · DSP · Metrological analysis

1 Introduction

Solar photovoltaic (PV) installations can make significant contributions towards to solve
some of the most energy problems that we are facing, nowadays, around the world. Power
demand is continuously increasing; however, the electricity utilities are unable to meet
this rapidly increasing demand. Solar PV systems, which are used to convert sunlight
into electricity, are increasing, are pollution free, and are a renewable energy source.
The power is produced by directly transforming a free and unlimited energy source into
electricity. However, in order to benefit from a PV installation, variables as the cost of
installation and the system efficiency are extremely relevant. Typically, the electricity
generated from a solar PV installation is injected into the grid, after conditioning to suit
all the conditions of the grid integration [1]. The power produced by the PV system can

© ICST Institute for Computer Sciences, Social Informatics and Telecommunications Engineering 2020
Published by Springer Nature Switzerland AG 2020. All Rights Reserved
J. L. Afonso et al. (Eds.): SESC 2019, LNICST 315, pp. 281–290, 2020.
https://doi.org/10.1007/978-3-030-45694-8_22

be consumed by the user, where the PV system is installed, or can be injected into the grid, similar to a nuclear power plant or a hydroelectric power plant, but with a lower value of injected power [2].

A system of double counting (purchase-sale) makes it possible to resell the power produced in extra, as well as to consume the available power in the grid when there is no Sun. The unit is entirely automated and managed by a controlled power electronics converter. Thus, the context of this type of managed installation is based on the intermittent power production associated with the non-controllable profile consumption, which is difficult to anticipate. In fact, it is the independent factor (the energy from the sun depends of the weather conditions) which restricts the power consumption from the PV. The energy produced by PV modules is directly consumed by the pay loads and the possible production overflow is injected into the grid. Indeed, the energy context and the gas emissions regulations for greenhouse effects, as well as the fossil energy resources reduction, compel us to support renewable energy installations, such as PV systems [3].

This article deals with the necessity of an energy meter to be installed into a solar PV system connected to the grid. From the physics point of view, the power produced by the solar PV system is consumed in priority by local loads (in this case a silo) and only the surplus power is injected into the grid. Thus, a three-phase smart energy meter has been designed for such purpose, which is a subject that has recently attracted a pertinent attention with many advantages and projects around the world due to the technical feasibility in several countries.

2 Proposed Solution Used for the Energy Meter

Figure 1 shows a block diagram of the solar PV system interfaced with the power grid, where the block diagram of "system connection to the grid" represents the contactors and switch breakers. The strategy used to measure the total active power is following described.

The voltage and current signals of each phase of the grid are used as input for a multiplier, model AD734, which is followed by a digital low-pass filter. Using the voltage and current signals, as well as the output voltage of each multiplier, it is calculated, respectively, the voltage and current RMS values and the power. The total power is:

$$P_t = P_1 + P_2 + P_3 \qquad (1)$$

According to Fig. 2, the power feed by each phase can be calculated as following described. At the Hall-effect sensors (voltage and current) output we have:

$$v_{1v}(t) = k_V . V_{1M} . \cos(\omega t) \qquad (2)$$

$$v_{1I}(t) = k_I . I_{1M} . \cos(\omega t - \phi) \qquad (3)$$

It is important to note that at the output of each sensor (voltage and current) is obtained a voltage signal proportional to the measured voltage or current at the input side.

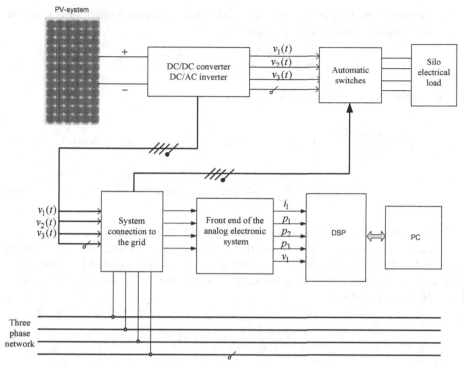

Fig. 1. Block diagram of the solar PV system: connection to the grid with the energy meter.

Therefore, the output voltages $v_{1V}(t)$ and $v_{1I}(t)$, relative to each phase of the grid, are applied to the AD734 multiplier, which gives at its output their product, according to:

$$v_{xy} = \frac{k_I.k_V.k_{xy}.V_{1M}I_{1M}.\cos(\phi)}{2} + \frac{k_I.k_V.k_{xy}.V_{1M}I_{1M}.\cos(2\omega t - \phi)}{2} \tag{4}$$

or

$$v_{xy} = k_p[P_0 + p_{ac}(t)] \tag{5}$$

where:

$$k_p = \frac{k_V k_I k_{xy}}{2};$$

P_0: represent the active power;
$p_{ac}(t)$ represent the alternative power component.

If $v(t)$ and $i(t)$ are not sinusoidal, we have:

$$v(t) = \sum_{n=1}^{\infty} V_n \cos(n\omega t - \phi_n) \text{ and } i(t) = \sum_{n=1}^{\infty} I_n \cos(n\omega t - \phi_n)$$

To extract the average power, we use an RC filter which performers an integration function. Using the trigonometric transform as:

$$\cos \alpha \times \cos \beta = \frac{1}{2} \cos(\alpha - \beta) + \frac{1}{2} \cos(\alpha + \beta) \tag{6}$$

then the average power consumed by the load is:

$$P = \frac{1}{T} \sum_{n=1}^{\infty} \frac{V_n I_n}{2} \int_0^T (\cos(\phi_{nv} - \phi_{ni}) + \cos(2n\omega t - \phi_{nv} - \phi_{ni}))dt \tag{7}$$

$$p = \sum_{n=1}^{\infty} \frac{V_n I_n}{2} \cos(\phi_{nv} - \phi_{ni}) \tag{8}$$

The power exchange is performed when $v(t)$ and $i(t)$ are with the same frequency (fundamental component). To increase the acquisition system accuracy, we acquired the signal at the multiplier (AD734) output, and then we use a digital low-pass filter, instead of an analogue filter. The system acquires a number M of samples during a time $T_m = M.T_s$, so the power is:

$$P = \frac{1}{k_p} \frac{1}{M} \sum_{i=1}^{M} v_{xy}(i) \tag{9}$$

Knowing the values of active power, voltage and current, for each phase of the grid, it is calculated the apparent power, defined by:

$$S = V.I \tag{10}$$

and the phase angle, defined by:

$$\varphi = \cos^{-1}\left(\frac{P}{S}\right). \tag{11}$$

To determine the energy, the power is summed with an integral time of 1 s, such as:

$$W(j) = \sum_{i=1}^{\infty} P_{0i} \times t_i \tag{12}$$

The conversion to kWh is given by:

$$W(kWh) = W(j) \times \frac{1}{10^3 \times 3600} \tag{13}$$

The current and voltage acquisition are performed as following described. Since the output voltage sensor presents a sinusoidal signal, a DC component is added in order to acquire these variables by the digital controller:

$$v_{v-acq}(t) = V_{dc} + v_v(t) \tag{14}$$

To extract $v_v(t)$, it's necessary first to read sampled data from the ADC and store it in a location in the Static Random Access Memory (SRAM), where it cannot be overwritten by new data. The first task to perform on the data is then to remove any DC offset. This is carried out calculating the mean value as:

$$\bar{v}_{acq} = \frac{1}{N} \sum_{n=1}^{N} v_{acq}(n) \tag{15}$$

$$V_{v-acq-RMS} = \frac{1}{N} \sqrt{\sum_{n=1}^{N} v_{acq}^2(n)} \tag{16}$$

Then, the RMS value is given by:

$$V_{v-RMS} = \sqrt{V_{v-acq-RMS}^2 - \bar{v}_{acq}^2} \tag{17}$$

The RMS grid voltage and current are:

$$V_{RMS} = \frac{1}{k_V} V_{V-RMS} \tag{18}$$

$$I_{RMS} = \frac{1}{k_I} V_{I-RMS} \tag{19}$$

The electric energy measurement and management was performed via a DSP. This last is used, also, for the solar PV system management feeding a wheat silo. It has excellent performance in terms of speed and digital analogue acquisition means, so we have exploit it to conceive a smart energy meter, which has several interesting metrological futures. Figure 2 shows the electronic part of the energy meter. The control algorithm used to determine the energy is shown in Fig. 3.

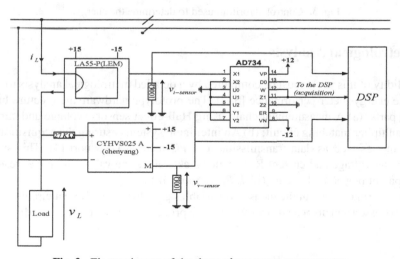

Fig. 2. Electronic part of the three-phase smart energy meter.

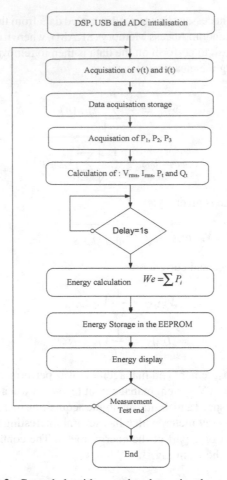

Fig. 3. Control algorithm used to determine the energy.

3 Metrological Analysis

The validity of this study must be completed by a detailed metrological analysis to illustrate the energy meter performance [5–7]. The prototype hardware architecture brings up two parts: (a) A measurement chain using Hall-effect sensors (voltage and current) and a multiplier matching circuit; (b) An intelligent system ensuring the acquisition and processing, as well as data transmission to a PC using a USB port [4]. This system delivers the voltage and current RMS values, as well as the values of active, reactive, and apparent power, and energy (U, I, P, Q, S and W).

The information about the measured variables goes through different circuits before being processed and displayed. The signal to be processed, by the DSP, is first digitalised as:

$$V_{xy-acq} = k_p . P = \frac{V_{ref}}{2^n} N_x \qquad (20)$$

From (18) we calculate the power P:

$$P = \frac{q}{k_p} N_x \tag{21}$$

where:

$q = \frac{V_{ref}}{2^n}$: is the quantum (or analogue resolution of the ADC);
n: the number of bits;
Nx: the decimal conversion number.

Knowing k_p and acquiring v_{xy}, v_V, and v_I, so the power load the voltage and current RMS values and the energy consumed are determined during a time Δt.

To estimate the precision measurements, the schematic diagram presented in Fig. 4 is used.

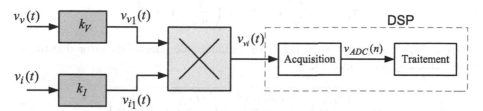

Fig. 4. Schematic diagram for acquiring the variables using the DSP.

The analogue to digital converter (ADC) performs the signal samples at the multiplier output. The ADC introduces a noise due to the quantization that can be represented by the following modelling. Figure 5 shows the ADC modelled schematic diagram.

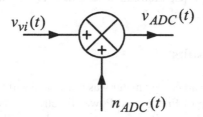

Fig. 5. ADC modelled schematic diagram.

$$v_{ADC}(t) = v_{vi}(t) + n_{ADC}(t) \tag{22}$$

Then:

$$v_{ADC}(t) = \frac{1}{2} k_V k_I k_{xy} V_{M_1} I_{M_1} (\cos(\varphi_v - \varphi_i) + \cos(2\omega t + \varphi_v + \varphi_i))$$
$$+ n_{mult}(t) + n_{ADC}(t) \tag{23}$$

The estimated power average value is determined by dividing Eq. (22) with the term $k_V k_I k_{xy}$, which gives:

$$P = \frac{2}{k_V k_I k_{xy}} \frac{1}{M} \sum_{i=1}^{M} v_{ADC}(iT_e)$$
(24)

For the aquisition an ADC of 12 bits and a reference DC voltage of 3.3 V is used. So its quantum (q) is equal to:

$$q = \frac{V_{réf}}{2^{12}} = \frac{3.3}{4096} = 0.810 \, [mV]$$
(25)

The parameters involved in Eq. (25) are independent. Then we use the error propagation method:

$$\sigma p = \sqrt{\left(\frac{\partial p}{\partial q}\right)^2 (\sigma q)^2 + \left(\frac{\partial p}{\partial k_p}\right)^2 (\sigma k_p)^2}$$
(26)

From Eq. (27), which gives the error variance, the uncertainty error due to the measurement system is evaluated:

$$\frac{\sigma_p}{p} = \sqrt{\left(\frac{\sigma q}{q}\right)^2 + \left(\frac{\sigma k_V}{k_V}\right)^2 + \left(\frac{\sigma k_I}{k_I}\right)^2 + \left(\frac{\sigma k_{xy}}{k_{xy}}\right)^2}$$
(27)

$$\frac{\sigma_p}{p}(\%) = \sqrt{\sum \left(\frac{\sigma x_i}{x_i}\right)^2} \times 100$$
(28)

Sensors with an accuracy of 0.1% and a multiplier with an accuracy of 0.2% are selected. After all calculations and using an auto calibration system for each data acquisition operation, the error propagation can be less than 0.4% for a voltage range of 230 V per phase and a current range of 20 A.

4 Experimental Results

To validate the theory, a smart energy meter was developed and tested in the Power Electronics Laboratory (Group of Energy and Power Electronics, GEPE) at the University of Minho, Portugal. All the acquisitions are processed by a DSP and then transferred to a PC via USB. In terms of implementation, the Hall-effect sensors ensure galvanic isolation and measurement accuracy, and the smart energy meter offers a versatile voltage and current connections from 50 V to 400 V AC up to 100 A. The experiment results are presented in following graphs. Figure 6 shows the workbench of the energy meter.

Fig. 6. Workbench of the energy meter.

5   Conclusion

In this paper, a smart energy meter is presented, this last allows to measure, in real time, the power injected into the power grid from a solar photovoltaic (PV) installation. The developed system has the flexibility and the ability to be changed in order to be adapted for various electrical environments. Indeed, the proposed method consists in using analog multipliers and the extraction of the power information is performed by a sliding average digital filter. This method is easier to implement and requires lower computation resources. For the energy meter design, a metrological evaluation has been developed and treated. The designed energy meter can serve any other application in residential or industrial sectors.

Acknowledgments. This work has been supported by FCT – Fundação para a Ciência e Tecnologia within the Project Scope: UID/CEC/00319/2019. This work is financed by the ERDF – European Regional Development Fund through the Operational Programme for Competitiveness and Internationalisation – COMPETE 2020 Programme, and by National Funds through the Portuguese funding agency, FCT – Fundação para a Ciência e a Tecnologia, within project SAICTPAC/0004/2015 – POCI – 01–0145–FEDER–016434.

References

1. Spertino, F., Graditi, G.: Power conditioning units in grid-connected photovoltaic systems: a comparison with different technologies and wide range of power ratings. Sol. Energy **108**, 219–229 (2014)
2. Manel, H.: Development and control of power electronics for a photovoltaic power generation system for on-grid off-grid operation, thesis: Electrical Engineering, Tunis, High National School of Engineers of Tunis, January 2017
3. Iwata, H., Okada, K.: Greenhouse gas emissions and the role of the Kyoto Protocol, Graduate School of Global Environmental Studies, Kyoto University, Japan, April 2010

4. Bhaskar, S., Sreenivasulu, S., Polaiah, B.: Intelligent system for single phase energy meter billing and action taking using wireless network. Int. J. Adv. Inf. Commun. Technol. **1**, 446–451 (2014)
5. Ganurkar, S., Gour, P.: Prepaid energy meter for billing system using microcontroller and recharge card. Int. J. Core Eng. Manag. **1**, 12–18 (2014)
6. Khlifi, K., Haddouk, A., Ayari, A., Hfaiedh, M.: Measurement of active power, electrical energy, and TRMS voltage and current using the dual slope conversion technique. Turk. J. Electr. Eng. Comput. Sci. **26**, 1081–1092 (2018)
7. Ahlem, A., Hfaiedh, M., Amira, H., Manel, H.: Developing a novel method: calculating the deformation factor to control energy consumption. In: 3rd International Conference on Green Energy and Environmental Engineering (GEEE) - Proceedings of Engineering & Technology (PET), pp. 68–75 (2016)

Towards Green Data Centers

Safae Bourhnane[1]([⊠]), Mohamed Riduan Abid[2], Rachid Lghoul[2], Khalid Zine-Dine[3], Najib Elkamoun[1], and Driss Benhaddou[4]

[1] Faculty of Sciences, LAROSERI Laboratory, Chouaib Doukkali University, El Jadida, Morocco
s.bourhnane@aui.ma, elkamoun.n@ucd.ac.ma
[2] School of Science and Engineering, Al Akhawayn University, Ifrane, Morocco
{r.abid,r.lghoul}@aui.ma
[3] School of Sciences, Mohamed V University, Rabat, Morocco
zinedinekhalid@fsr.ac.ma
[4] College of Technology, University of Houston, Houston, USA
dbenhaddou@uh.edu

Abstract. Green Computing has been the trend among computer scientists for its eco-friendliness. It serves as a great solution to be integrated with Smart Grids (SG). Data stemming from SGs falls under the realm of Big Data as it is voluminous, various, and has a great velocity. Hence, these data need processing and storage. For this, High-Performance Computing, through clustering a set of computers, proves necessary. Nowadays, with the hardware advances that the world is witnessing, the Raspberry Pi (RP) creates a number of opportunities to deploy cost-effective and energy-efficient clusters, which respect the concepts of Green Computing. In this paper, we are presenting the work done within a USAID sponsored project which aims at developing a SG testbed at Al Akhawayn University in Ifrane, Morocco. We are presenting the deployment of a 5-node cluster based on RPs. The cluster has Hadoop installed and runs the TestDFSIO and Terasort benchmarks for the performance analysis in addition to an energy efficiency analysis.

Keywords: Big Data · Hadoop · Raspberry Pi · HPC · Smart Grids · Green Computing · Cost-effectiveness · Energy-efficiency

1 Introduction

Nowadays, Green Computing constitutes a fashion among IT practitioners and companies. The main motivation behind this shift is the realization that energy consumption is significantly increasing which has a direct impact on the environment. Furthermore, a significant amount of the energy consumed worldwide goes to the manufacturing, storage, operation, and cooling of data centers. This is mainly due to the increasing compute power required by different applications in different fields, and by diverse companies and institutions [1].

© ICST Institute for Computer Sciences, Social Informatics and Telecommunications Engineering 2020
Published by Springer Nature Switzerland AG 2020. All Rights Reserved
J. L. Afonso et al. (Eds.): SESC 2019, LNICST 315, pp. 291–307, 2020.
https://doi.org/10.1007/978-3-030-45694-8_23

Green Computing is a perfect solution for Smart Grids (SG) as it respects the energy efficiency as one of its main building blocks.

SG have been introduced to accommodate for the increasing demand of energy all over the world. The "Grid" refers to the traditional electrical system that is responsible for bringing energy from power plants to end users. The term "Smart" refers to a set of features added to the traditional grid that makes is intelligent. Actually, the smartness of the SG resides in the two-way communication system that allows electricity to flow in both directions: from the power plant to the end-user and the other way around.

The SG has a set of meters, instruments, and equipment that are connected to each other and to the grid. The communication between all the components is done via a specific and well-chosen protocol [2].

Since all the components are connected, we can infer that SGs generate huge amount of data that has all the aspects of Big Data. It goes without saying that Big Data requires two major operations: processing and storage. Bringing up processing, High-Performance Computing (HPC) is the first thing that comes to one's mind. HPC is usually provided through two main venues: supercomputers, and clusters of commodity computers. The solution of supercomputers is no longer adopted because of the high cost of purchase, maintenance, and staff. Companies nowadays are opting for solutions that involve clustering computers to achieve the high performance.

HPC is mostly used in solving advanced and more complicated problems in addition to performing research activities [3]. Now, with the advent of hardware, the Raspberry Pi provides new opportunities to deploy energy-efficient and cost-effective clusters.

Clusters of Raspberry Pi have been trending in the last decade and have been the center of interest of many researchers and practitioners in the field. However, the community did not provide a closer look at the performance of these clusters, nor at their energy efficiency.

In this paper, we are testing the performance of a 5-node Raspberry Pi cluster running Hadoop. For this, we used two main benchmarks: Hadoop TestDFSIO and Terasort. The results obtained have been compared to the ones of a study that was previously carried on using the same benchmarks on a cluster of commodity computers. In addition to that, we are measuring the energy consumption of the cluster when running the Terasort on the biggest dataset of our experiment.

The rest of the paper is organized as follows: Sect. 2 presents the work previously done in using Raspberry Pis to run HPC jobs. In Sect. 3, we present the background of the work done in this paper. Then, in Sect. 4, we describe the experimental setup in addition to the technologies used. The next section presents the results and analysis of the experiments. The last section discusses the conclusions and the future work.

2   Related Work

Raspberry Pi clusters have been the trend of cluster computing for the last years. A significant amount of work has been carried out using Raspberry Pis as a cost-effective and energy-efficient alternative. This section presents different attempts to deploy Raspberry Pi clusters.

Helmer et al. in [4] are describing their work done in deploying a Raspberry Pi cluster that consists of 300 nodes. They are presenting the first steps consisting of setting up and configuring the hardware along with the system software, in addition to the maintenance and the monitoring of the system. Furthermore, they discuss some of the limitations that would hinder the deployment of their cluster. These reside in the low processor speed that does not go beyond 700 MHz, and the card performance that is relatively slow which is explained by the actual design of the flash memory. However, they did not present any benchmarks to test the performance of their cluster.

Iridis-pi is another low-cost cluster that is meant for demonstration [5]. The cluster consists of 64 Raspberry Pis Model B, each having a 700 MHz ARM1176JZF-S RISC processor, and 256 MB of RAM. The cluster is hosted on a Lego chassis. The interconnection between the nodes is done via commodity Ethernet cables. The system has a total of 16 GB of RAM and 1 TB of flash storage capacity. For the numerical compute power assessment, the well-known LINPACK benchmark was used for the single-node performance, and High-Performance LINPACK (HPL) benchmark was used to measure the throughput of the entire cluster. Concerning the benchmarking results, the single-node execution showed a computational performance peak of around 65000 kflops. Also, large problem sizes in HPL benchmark showed a good scalability when increasing the number of nodes, however, the scalability was not significant when it came to small problems because of the network overhead.

A very famous use of Raspberry Pis in data processing is what is known as the Glasgow Raspberry Pi Cluster [6]. In their paper, the authors present the "PiCloud" as a set of clusters of Raspberry Pi devices that emulate the entire stack of the cloud. The cluster contains 56 Model B Raspberry Pi devices that are interconnected using a multi-root tree topology. Each one of the Raspberry Pis uses 16 GB SD card which could support up to 3 co-located concurrent virtualized hosts realized through Linux Containers. Therefore, the virtualization component of the Cloud is provided through the containers and not through virtual machines. The deployment of this cloud is still not mature according to the authors, they are still investigating the adaptation of the *libvirt* framework that allows for an easier and more secure management of the virtual resources. Plus, they have a plan of implementing sophisticated live migration with their PiCloud.

Nick Schot has presented a study about the feasibility of Raspberry Pi based data centers for Big Data applications in [6]. The paper is taking a closer look at the benefits and potentials of using Raspberry Pi in a micro data center with Big Data applications as its main purpose. The author presented an analysis of the performance, the scalability, energy consumption, and ease of management. For this, Hadoop framework was used. As results, the cluster showed a moderate performance with the bottleneck being the SD card and more specifically the random write speed which turned out to be extremely low (1.26 MB/s). Regarding the power consumption, the experimentations revealed that Raspberry Pi requires very little power even when operating under load. One Raspberry Pi consumes about 2 W and remains relatively cool at about 55 °C.

This paper extends the work previously done by assessing the performance using the TestDFSIO and the Terasort benchmarks. We measure the running time for both benchmarks and the energy consumed while running the Terasort benchmark.

3 Background

3.1 Raspberry Pi

Raspberry Pi was first introduced to allow for easier access to computing education in underdeveloped countries. It was first launched in 2012 within the open source ecosystem. The very first board had a single-core, 700 MHz CPU, and no more than 256 MB RAM, while the latest model has a quad-core, 1.4 GHz CPU, and 1 GB of RAM [7].

The very popular use of Raspberry Pi over the world reside in learning programming and building hardware projects, home automation, and industrial applications.

Raspberry Pi is a computer that runs Raspbian Linux operating system, which is open source with a set of open source software running on top of it. From hardware perspectives, it provides a set of General-Purpose Input/output (GPIO) that allow the interaction with the external world through sensors for example. The GPIOs also allow to control electric components through actuators and hence explore the Internet of Things (IoT).

3.2 Hadoop

Understanding Hadoop requires the understanding of the Big Data and its issues related to the traditional processing system.

The Relational Database Management Systems used to focus on structured, semi-structured, and unstructured data. This did not solve the following problems:

- Storage of the colossal amount of data.
- Storage of heterogeneous data.
- Access and processing speed.

Hadoop emerged to solve these problems through bringing a framework that allows for a distributed storage of data for later parallel processing.

Hadoop has two main components: The first one being HDFS (Hadoop Distributed File System), is the component responsible for the distributed storage of the data under different formats. The second component is YARN (Yet Another Resource Negotiator). It takes care of the resource management in Hadoop and allows for jobs allocation.

HDFS can be seen as an abstraction. It is represented as a single unit that is meant to store Big Data stemming from different sources. However, the storage is actually done across multiple nodes in a distributed manner that follows the master-slave architecture.

YARN takes care of all the processing activities by allocating resources and ensuring the scheduling of the tasks. It has two major components: ResourceManager and NodeManager. The ResourceManager is the master node that receives processing requests and then passes parts of them to the NodeManagers. Every Datanode has a NodeManager that is installed and that does the actual processing [8].

3.3 Green Computing

Green Computing refers to the practice of efficient and eco-friendly computing. Many companies have realized that going green would help a lot in maintaining good public relations and significantly reducing the cost. Hence, Green Computing has been the trend among companies and industries. However, going Green is not straightforward.

According to [9], ICT industry was responsible for 3% of the world energy consumption in 2012. This is supposed to increase by 20% a year.

Green Computing has five core green technologies: Green Data Centers, Virtualization, Cloud Computing, Power Optimization, and Grid Computing.

In addition to that, it has the following benefits:

- Reducing energy consumption of computing resources while performing heavy operations.
- Saving energy in idle states.
- Reducing computing wastes.

3.4 MiGrid Research Project

This section of the paper presents the work done in implementing a SG at Al Akhawayn University in Ifrane as a testbed within a USAID sponsored project. This project aims at developing a holistic testbed platform that integrates smart buildings, renewable energy production, and storage.

The general architecture of the SG is depicted in the figure below (Fig. 1) [10].

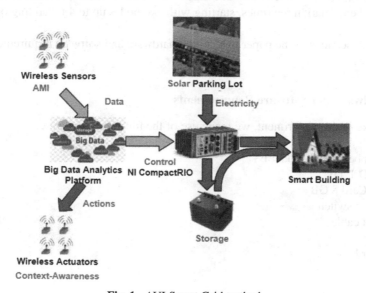

Fig. 1. AUI Smart Grid testbed

The architecture consists of the following elements:

1. Wireless Sensor Network: It is supposed to sense data in the environment where it is deployed. We based our technology choices and architecture on the thesis in [11].

2. Big Data Analytics Platform: It is meant to store and process the big data coming from the wireless sensor network [12]. This platform consists of a cluster of Raspberry Pis, which is implemented and tested performance wise.
3. Wireless Actuator Network: A set of wirelessly connected actuators that take care of translating the signals received into actions.
4. NI CompactRIO Controller: It is the main controlling unit of the system that decides on whether to inject the energy produced to the grid or to store it in batteries.
5. Solar Parking Lot: It is the main renewable energy source.
6. Storage Device: It consists of Hydrogen batteries that are meant to store the excess of energy produced by the solar station for later usage.

In this paper, we are tackling the Big Data Analytics Platform part through building an HPC cluster using Raspberry Pis and assessing its performance. This cluster is deployed in our testbed and hence needs to respect two main constraints: cost-effectiveness and energy-efficiency.

4 Experimental Setup

In order to test the performance of our Raspberry Pi cluster, we ran a set of experiments using two main Hadoop benchmarks: Terasort and TestDFSIO.

Our cluster contains five nodes: one master, and four workers. For each dataset size, we ran the benchmark three times, starting with two nodes up to 4 by adding one node at a time.

The next sections of the paper present the hardware and software requirements and architectures.

4.1 Hardware and Software Requirements

For the sake of this experiment, we made use of the following hardware.

- 5 x Raspberry Pi 3 Model B+
- 5 x HDD 1 TB
- 5 x SD Card 8 GB
- An 8-port switch
- Ethernet cables
- Monitor
- Keyboard
- Mouse

The specifications of the Raspberry Pi used are described in Table 1 below:

Table 1. Raspberry Pi specifications

Spec	Raspberry Pi 3 B+
CPU type/speed	ARM Cortex-A53 1.4 GHz
RAM size	1 GB SRAM
Integrated Wife	2.4 GHz and 5 GHz
Ethernet speed	300 Mbps
PoE	Yes
Bluetooth	4.2
Cores	4

Initially, we used SD cards of 8 GB. We assumed that more space will be required to store all the data stemming from the SG. Thus, we extended the storage to 1 TB using external HDDs.

Regarding the software requirements, the main piece of software used in this experiment is Hadoop version 2.7.

The hardware architecture opted for is depicted in Fig. 2.

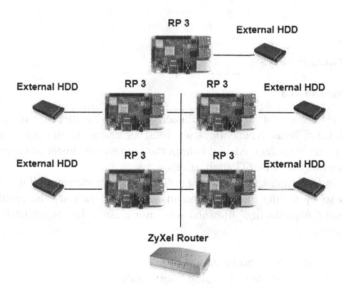

Fig. 2. Hardware architecture

The choice of RPs stems from the nature of the research project and aligns with the energy efficiency concept introduced by the SG. Thus, we are targeting a green processing unit that costs less than the traditional one, and eventually consumes less energy all without being less performant.

Each one of the physical nodes shown above is running Hadoop according to the following software architecture and based on whether the node is a master or a slave. The software architecture is shown in Fig. 3.

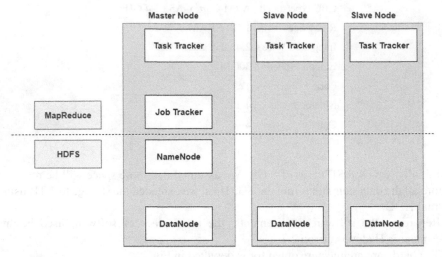

Fig. 3. Software architecture

5   Results and Analysis

5.1   Benchmarks Used

To assess the performance of our Hadoop cluster, we used two main benchmarks: Terasort and TestDFSIO. The Terasort benchmark was used because we sorting is one of the main operations done on SG's data. Also, it is important to test the cluster I/O speed wise as this feature is widely used by SG applications.

The Terasort Benchmark is used to test both Hadoop components: HDFS et MapReduce. It does so by sorting different amounts of data to measure the capabilities of distributing and "mapreducing" files and jobs in a cluster. The benchmark has three main components.

- Teragen: It generates the random data to be sorted.
- Terasort: Sorts the generated data using MapReduce.
- TeraValidate: It is used to validate the output of the Terasort component.

The second benchmark used is TestDFSIO. It is basically a "read" and "write" test for HDFS. It is mainly used as stress test for HDFS to discover the bottlenecks and have an idea about how fast the cluster is in terms of I/O.

The dataset used for the Terasort benchmark and that is given by the Teragen function has the following format: (10 bytes key) (10 bytes row_id) (78 bytes filler). The key consists of random characters (e.g. '~'), the row_id identifies the row by an integer, and the filler consists of characters from A to Z.

5.2   Results

Performance Results

The performance results were obtained through running the Terasort benchmark on the cluster using four different dataset sizes: 100 Mb, 1 GB, 10 GB, and 30 GB.

We tested the cluster using 2, 3, and 4 nodes and we compare the results with the ones obtained in [13]. Each test was performed three times and then the mean time was calculated. The results of running the Terasort are shown in Fig. 4 below.

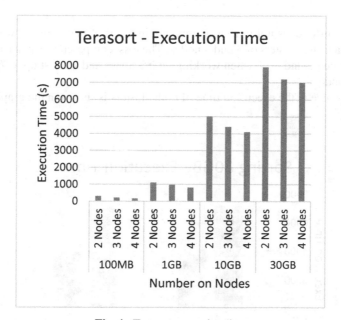

Fig. 4. Terasort execution time

As we can notice from the graph above, scaling up in the cluster helped gaining performance wise as the execution time goes from 299 s to 159 s to sort 100 MB of data, and from 7905 s to 7001 s when sorting 30 GB of data.

To be able to assess the results obtained, we compared them with the results of another cluster of commodity hardware and that runs the same benchmark. This cluster is using the Dell OptiPlex 755 computer with the specification shown in the Table 2 below.

Table 2. Dell OptiPlex 755 features

Characteristic	Value
RAM total memory	975 MB
Disk space	160 GB
Number of processors	2
Processor model	Intel® Core™2 Duo CPU E4500 @ 2.20 GHz
CPU architecture	I386/i686
CPU op-mode(s)	32-bit, 64-bit
Linux Kernel	Distributor ID: Ubuntu Description: Ubuntu 12.04.3 LTS Release: 12.04 Codename: precise

The RPi cluster does not introduce any gain in terms of performance when sorting 30 GB of data using clusters of 3 and 4 nodes. The loss, compared to the normal cluster, was found to be around 20% when working with 3 nodes and we lost up to 75% with a cluster of 4 nodes.

The difference in the execution time of both clusters is shown in the graph of Fig. 5 below.

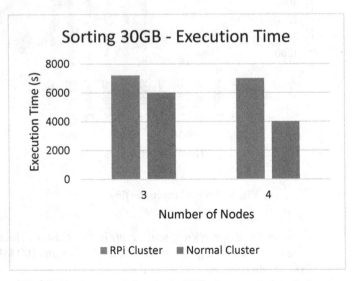

Fig. 5. Terasort execution time of RPi cluster and normal cluster

Stress Testing Results

For the stress testing of the cluster, we used the TestDFSIO benchmark. We start by writing different sizes of files, mainly 100 MB, 1 GB, 10 GB, and 100 GB. Then we read the same files. At each read/write operation we measure the execution time. The results of the write operation are shown in Fig. 6 below.

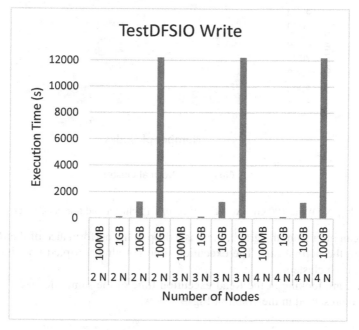

Fig. 6. TestDFSIO write execution time

As shown in the graph above, there is a slight gain in the performance as the execution time decreases when adding nodes to the cluster. The increase of the performance is noticed when dealing with bigger file sizes. However, we cannot really notice the execution time of writing 100 MB as it is very low. It is shown separately in Fig. 7.

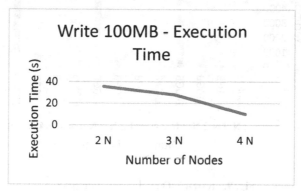

Fig. 7. Write 100 MB - execution time

We are comparing the results obtained with the ones of the commodity cluster described previously. The results of the comparison are shown in Fig. 8.

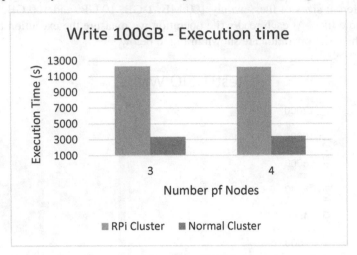

Fig. 8. Write 100 GB execution time of RPi cluster and normal cluster

As we can infer from the graph, there is a drop in the performance of the RP cluster compared to the normal one. The execution time got almost tripled up when writing 100 GB for both clusters.

Next, we are looking at the Read execution time of the same file size. The results obtained are presented in the graph of Fig. 9 below.

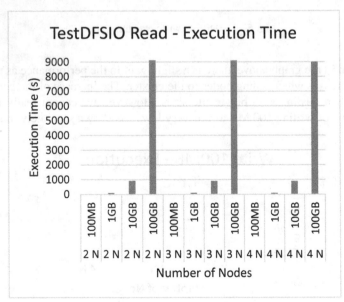

Fig. 9. TestDFSIO read - execution time

The execution time of reading 100 MB is very low compared to the other datasets. We are presenting it separately in the graph of Fig. 10 below.

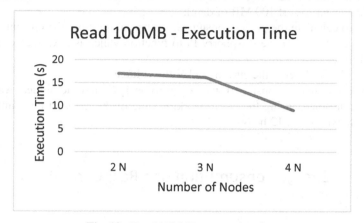

Fig. 10. Read 100 MB - execution time

The comparison between the two clusters is described in Fig. 11 below. As we can notice, we lost a lot in terms of performance as the reading on 100 GB of data using the Raspberry Pi cluster takes almost triple the time compared to the normal cluster. Also, we can notice that scaling up in the cluster does not help gaining performance wise.

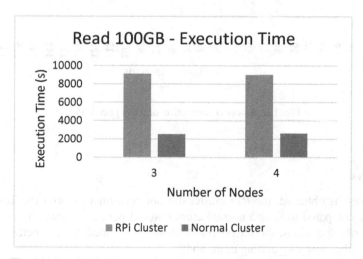

Fig. 11. Read 100 GB execution time of RPi cluster and normal cluster

Energy Consumption

For the energy consumption analysis, we measured the current needed by one Raspberry Pi while performing the Terasort benchmark with 100 MB of data in a 5-node cluster.

We noticed that the current varies between a maximum value of 0.10 A when the Raspberry Pi is performing jobs, and a minimum of 0.04 A when it is in an idle state. The current was measured using a multimeter each second for 159 s (which is the time taken by the cluster to sort 100 MB of data).

In order to calculate the power consumed, we had to multiply the current obtained by the voltage needed for the Raspberry Pi to function which is 5 V, according to the following formula:

Pc = I * V, with I being the current and V the voltage.

The minimum power consumed was found to be 1 W, and the highest was 10 W. The power consumed during the entire working time of the Terasort benchmark with 100 MB is shown in Fig. 12 below.

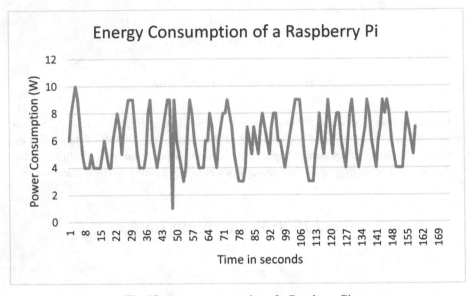

Fig. 12. Power consumption of a Raspberry Pi

5.3 Analysis

From the results obtained, the RPi cluster did not perform well with the TestDFSIO benchmark compared to how a normal cluster would perform. However, and in both read and write operations, the Raspberry Pi cluster performed slightly better when we scaled up in the cluster by adding more nodes.

In the next figures (Figs. 13 and 14), we are looking at the throughput of both read and write operations.

Based on the results of the commodity hardware (CH) cluster described previously in this paper regarding the TestDFSIO benchmark, we can notice that the Raspberry Pi is relatively slow compared to a normal computer. The comparison of the throughput of both cluster (with 3 nodes) and with the same dataset sizes is shown in Fig. 15.

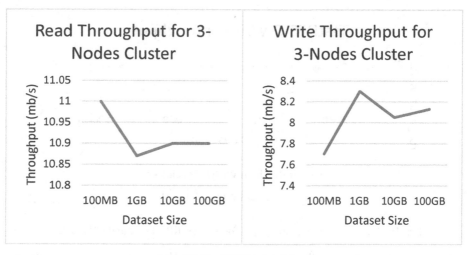

Fig. 13. TestDFSIO throughput

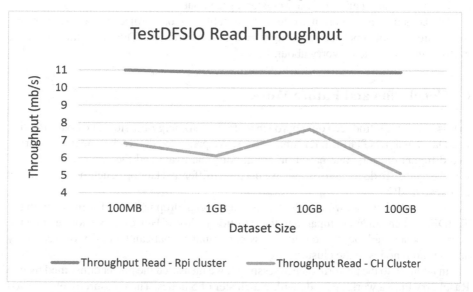

Fig. 14. TestDFSIO read throughput for 3 nodes RPi cluster and CH cluster

Concerning the Terasort benchmark, the Raspberry Pi cluster did not perform better than the traditional cluster, however, the drop in the performance is not as significant as the one with the TestDFSIO benchmark.

The Terasort took longer time to be completed. This is mainly due to the low computing power of the Raspberry Pis. The relatively low performance of the Terasort may be overcome by adding more nodes to the cluster.

By looking at the power consumption of the Raspberry Pi in a working mode, we can notice that the consumption is low which leaves room to add more nodes to the cluster

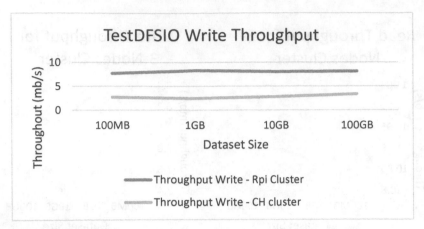

Fig. 15. TestDFSIO write throughput for 3 nodes RPi cluster and CH cluster

without being worried about the energy consumption. Hence, this respects the concept of Green Computing and make our cluster a green one.

We consider this solution to be very suitable for our project since the platform in question is not supposed to perform real-time operations. This does not make the performance an issue to worry about.

6   Conclusion and Future Work

In this paper, we introduced our approach to deploy an energy-efficient and cost-effective Big Data Analytics Platform for Smart Grids. We presented the work done in comparing two different clusters: one based on commodity hardware and the other one based on Raspberry Pis. To do the assessment, we used two different Hadoop benchmarks: Terasort and TestDFSIO.

The results have shown that there was a significant drop in the performance with the TestDFSIO benchmark compared to the traditional cluster. However, we noticed that the Terasort benchmark delivered a little less performance that can be easily overcome by adding more nodes to the cluster.

In addition to the performance assessment, we measured the power consumed by one Raspberry Pi in a working mode within a cluster of 5 nodes. The measurements showed that a Raspberry Pi does not consume a significant amount of power. This means that the cluster can be scaled up without worrying about the power consumed.

Based on the results of this experiment, both performance and energy consumption wise, we can say that our cluster is a green one. Hence, the big data analytics platform conceived for the SG testbed is well suited for the general concept.

As future work, we intend to measure the energy consumption of one machine in a traditional cluster, so that we can compare the energy consumed under the same workload. In addition to that, we will be testing the Raspberry Pi cluster with real data that we will be gathering from our real-world testbed.

Acknowledgment. This work is sponsored by US-NAS/USAID under the PEER Cycle 5 project grant# 5-398, entitled "Towards Smart Microgrid: Renewable Energy Integration into Smart Buildings".

References

1. Ray, I.: Green Computing. Chandigarh Science Congress (CHASCON) (2012). https://doi.org/10.13140/2.1.1546.0164
2. Yacout, D.: An Introduction to Smart Grid. Institutes of Graduates Studies and Research, Alexandria (2013)
3. Techopedia: High-Performance Computing (HPC). Technopedia. https://www.techopedia.com/definition/4595/high-performance-computing-hpc. Accessed 31 May 2019
4. Abrahamsson, P., et al.: Affordable and energy-efficient cloud computing clusters: the Bolzano Raspberry Pi cloud cluster experiment. In: IEEE International Conference on Cloud Computing Technology and Science, pp. 170–175 (2013). https://doi.org/10.1109/cloudcom.2013.121
5. Cox, S.J., Cox, J.T., Boardman, R.P., Johnston, S.J., Scott, M., O'Brien, N.S.: Iridis-pi: a low-cost, compact demonstration cluster. Cluster Comput. **17**(2), 349–358 (2013). https://doi.org/10.1007/s10586-013-0282-7
6. Tso, P., et al.: The Glasgow Raspberry Pi cloud: a scale model for cloud computing infrastructures. In: Distributed Computing Systems Workshops (ICDCSW). IEEE (2013). https://doi.org/10.1109/icdcsw.2013.25
7. OpenSource: What is Raspberry Pi?. https://opensource.com/resources/raspberry-pi. Accessed 29 Mar 2019
8. Sinha, S.: What is Hadoop? Introduction to Big Data & Hadoop, 22 May 2019. https://www.edureka.co/blog/what-is-hadoop/. Accessed 01 June 2019
9. Jindal, G., Gupta, M.: Green computing "Future of Computers". Int. J. Emerg. Res. Manag. Technol., 14–18 (2012)
10. Abid, M.R., Lghoul, R., Benhaddou, D.: ICT for renewable energy integration into smart buildings: IoT and big data approach. In: IEEE AFRICON (2017). https://doi.org/10.1109/afrcon.2017.8095594
11. Abid, M.R.: Link Quality Characterization in IEEE 802.11s Wireless Mesh Networks. Auburn University, Auburn (2010)
12. Achahbar, O., et al.: Approaches for high-performance big data processing: applications and challenges. In: Big Data: Algorithms, Analytics, and Applications (2015). https://doi.org/10.1201/b18050
13. Achahbar, O., Abid, M.R.: The impact of virtualization on high performance computing clustering in the cloud. Int. J. Distrib. Syst. Technol. **6**, 65–81 (2015)

Author Index

Abbes, Dhaker 180
Abid, Mohamed Riduan 291
Afonso, João L.   3, 18, 33, 47, 58, 73, 88, 127, 197, 257, 269, 281
Afonso, Jose A.   3, 127, 197
Alves, Aníbal A.   197
Alves, Tiago 257
Antunes, Carlos Henggeler   110

Barros, Luis A. M.   18, 269
Becker, Bernd 221
Benhaddou, Driss 291
Bourhnane, Safae 291
Bunagan, Juan Miguel P.   165

Carvalho, João 209

Damasceno, João 209
Delgado, Leonardo 232

Elkamoun, Najib 291
Eloja, Philip Joshua P.   98
Exposto, Bruno 269

Feio, Miguel C.   127
Feliciano, Manuel 232
Ferreira, Joao C.   3
Ferreira, João Carlos 73
Ferreira, Paula 140
Filipe, Edmundo 209
Frare, Laercio 232
Furst, Leonardo 232

Gonçalves, Tiago 209
Gonzales, Ryan Christopher T.   165

Haddouk, Amira 88, 281
Hassam-Ouari, Kahina 180
Hfaiedh, Mechergui 281
Hlaili, Manel 281

Igrejas, Getúlio 232

Jorda, Niko Avel F.   98

Khlifi, Khaoula 88, 281

Labrunie, Antoine 180
Leitão, Paulo 232
Lghoul, Rachid 291

Machado, Luís 47, 58
Magalhães, Pedro L.   110
Marcelino, Sylvain 209   •
Martins, António P.   18, 33
Mataloto, Bruno 73
Mechergui, Hfaiedh 88
Monteiro, Paulo 209
Monteiro, Vítor   3, 47, 58, 73, 88, 127, 197, 257, 269, 281
Morais, Vítor A.   33

Oliveira, Catia F.   269
Oliveira, Paulo 209

Patrão, Carlos 209
Pedrasa, Michael Angelo A.   98, 165
Pedrosa, Delfim 47, 58
Pereira, Elizabete 140
Pereira, Hélio 209
Peremans, Herbert 150
Pfeifer, Marc 221
Pinto, J. G.   18, 47, 197, 257, 269

Qiu, Hong-Bing 246

Robyns, Benoît 180
Rodrigues, Ana M. C.   257

Salgado, Jose A.   127
Santos, Diogo 73
Saviuc, Iolanda 150

Scholl, Philipp M.   221
Silva, Luis M.   127
Song, Xi Yu   246
Sousa, Catarina   209
Sousa, Tiago J. C.   3, 47, 58, 257
Stephant, Matthieu   180

Tanta, Mohamed   18

Van Passel, Steven   150
Vieira, Alexandra   209
Völker, Benjamin   221

Wang, Mei   246
Wei, Xueming   246

Zine-Dine, Khalid   291

Printed in the United States
By Bookmasters